HISTORY

OF

OLIVER CROMWELL

AND THE

ENGLISH COMMONWEALTH.

HISTORY

OF

OLIVER CROMWELL

AND THE

ENGLISH COMMONWEALTH,

FROM THE EXECUTION OF CHARLES THE FIRST TO THE DEATH OF CROMWELL:

BY M. GUIZOT,

TRANSLATED BY ANDREW R. SCOBLE.

IN TWO VOLUMES.

VOL. I.

ADVERTISEMENT.

THE history of the English Revolution, its origin and consequences, extends over a period of sixty-three years—from the accession of Charles I., in 1625, to the fall of James II., in 1688; and is naturally divided, by the great events which it includes, into four periods. The first of these comprehends the reign of Charles I., his conflict with the Long Parliament, his defeat and death; the second contains the history of the Commonwealth, under the Long Parliament and Cromwell; the third is marked by the Restoration of the Monarchy, after the brief Protectorate of Richard Cromwell; and the fourth comprises the reigns of Charles II. and James II., and the final fall of the royal race of Stuart.

Each of these four periods will form the subject of a special work by M. Guizot. The first of these has already appeared; the second is now published; and the other two are in progress. Together, the four works will constitute a complete picture of the most important epoch in our history.

With regard to the present Volumes, I need say nothing, except so far as my own share in them is concerned. I have endeavored to make as literal a translation as was compatible with our English idiom; and, in all cases, I have carefully verified the references, and given the *ipsissima verba* of the authorities quoted by M. Guizot. The historical documents which form the Appendix to each Volume, are, for the most part, now printed for the first time, and are derived from the Archives of Simancas, the Archives of the French Foreign Office, and various collections of manuscripts in the public libaries of Paris.

ANDREW R. SCOBLE.

LINCOLN'S INN,
FEBRUARY, 1854.

CONTENTS

OF THE FIRST VOLUME.

BOOK I.

BOOK II.

BOOK III.

BOOK IV.

HISTORY

OF

OLIVER CROMWELL

AND

THE ENGLISH COMMONWEALTH.

BOOK I.

ORGANIZATION OF THE REPUBLICAN GOVERNMENT—FORMATION OF THE COUNCIL OF STATE—RESISTANCE OF THE COUNTRY—TRIAL AND CONDEMNATION OF FIVE ROYALIST LEADERS: LORDS HAMILTON, HOLLAND, CAPELL, AND NORWICH, AND SIR JOHN OWEN—EXECUTION OF HAMILTON, HOLLAND, AND CAPELL—PUBLICATION OF THE "EIKON BASILIKE"—ROYALIST AND REPUBLICAN POLEMICS: MILTON AND SALMASIUS—OUTBREAK AND INSURRECTION OF THE LEVELLERS—JOHN LILBURNE—DEFEAT OF THE LEVELLERS—TRIAL AND ACQUITTAL OF LILBURNE—TYRANNY OF THE PARLIAMENT—INCREASING GREATNESS OF CROMWELL.

IN a previous work, I have related the downfall of an ancient monarchy, and the violent death of a king who was worthy of respect, although he governed his people badly and unjustly. I have now to relate the vain efforts of a revolutionary assembly to found a republic; and to describe the ever-tottering, but strong and glorious government of a revolutionary despot, whose bold and prudent genius commands our admiration, although he attacked and destroyed, first legal order, and then liberty, in his native land. The men whom God chooses as the instruments of his great designs, are full of contradiction and of mystery; in them are mingled and combined, in undiscoverable proportions, capabilities and failings, virtues and vices, enlightenment and error, grandeur and weakness; and after having filled the age in which they lived with the splendor of their actions and the magnitude of their destiny, they remain personally obscure in the midst of their glory, alternately cursed and worshipped by the world which does not know them.

At the opening of the Long Parliament, on the 3d of November, 1640, the House of Commons consisted of five hundred and six members. In 1649, after the execution of the King, when it abolished kingship and proclaimed the Commonwealth, there scarcely remained a hundred who took part in its sittings and acts. During the month of February, the House divided ten times; and at the most numerous division, only seventy-seven members were present to record their votes.[1]

Thus mutilated and reduced to the condition of a victorious coterie, this assembly set to work, with an ardor full at once of strong faith and deep anxiety, to organize the republican government. On the 7th of February, 1649, the same day on which it abolished kingship by an express decree, it voted the creation of a Council of State, "to be henceforth the executive power;" and five members, Scott, Ludlow, Lisle, Holland, and Robinson, chosen from among the staunchest republicans, were ordered "to present to the House instructions to be given to the Council of Estates; and likewise the names of such persons as they conceive fit to be of that Council."[2]

[1] Old Parliamentary History, vol. ix. p. 12; Journals of the House of Commons, vol. vi. pp. 128, 130, 132, 140, 141, 143, 147.

[2] Commons' Journals, vol. vi. p. 133. I may here mention that, at this

Six days after, on the 13th of February, Scott presented his report to the House. All the practical functions of the Government were vested in the Council of State. It received power to dispose of the national forces and revenues; to direct the police; to repress all rebellion; to arrest, interrogate, and imprison all who should resist its orders; to conduct the relations of the State with foreign powers; to administer the colonies; and to watch over the interests of commerce: being thus invested with almost absolute power, under the control and in obedience to the instructions of Parliament—the sole depositary of the national sovereignty.[1]

On the two following days, the House proceeded to appoint the forty-one Councillors of State, voting specially on each name. Five ex-peers of the realm,[2] the three chief judges,[3] the three leaders of the army, Fairfax, Cromwell, and Skippon, and thirty country gentlemen and citizens, nearly all of whom were members of the House, were elected. The nomination of the five peers met with objections; the democrats wished to exclude them, as well as the House of Lords itself, from all participation in the government of the Commonwealth; but the more prudent politicians, on the contrary, gave an eager welcome to these noblemen, who were still powerful by their wealth and name, and whom fanaticism or meanness had connected with the party which had destroyed

period, England had not yet adopted the reformed Gregorian Calendar, and that her chronology was ten days behind that of the Continent. The 7th of February in England, in the seventeenth century, would therefore correspond with the 17th of February on the Continent. For convenience of reference to the English authorities which I quote, I have adopted the English date in speaking of English events.

1 Commons' Journals, vol. vi. pp. 138, 139.

2 The Earls of Denbigh, Mulgrave, Pembroke, and Salisbury, and Lord Grey of Wark.

3 Henry Rolle, Chief Justice of the Upper Bench; Oliver St. John, Chief Justice of the Common Bench; and John Wylde, Chief Baron of the Exchequer.

their order. The entire list proposed by the Commissioners of the Parliament was adopted, with the exception of two names, Ireton and Harrison, who were probably thought too devotedly attached to Cromwell, and for whom two republicans were substituted, conspicuous for their uncompromising distrust of the army and its leaders. They were all appointed for a year.[1]

When they met for the first time, on the 17th of February, 1649, they were required to sign an engagement, expressing approbation of all that had been done in the King's trial, in the overthrow of kingship, and in the abolition of the House of Lords. Only fourteen Councillors of State were present at this meeting; thirteen signed the proposed declaration without hesitation, and a fresh meeting was convoked for the next day but one; thirty-four members then attended, and on the same day Cromwell gave a report to Parliament of what had occurred. Six other Councillors of State, making nineteen in all, had signed the engagement; but twenty-two persisted in refusing it. They stated that they were resolved, in future, faithfully to serve the government of the House of Commons, as it was the supreme power, the only one which remained in existence, and therefore necessary to the liberties and safety of the people; but, from various motives, and in terms more or less distinct, they refused to give their sanction to all the past. The House in great excitement, proceeded at once to deliberate on this report, forbidding all the members present to leave the hall without express permission; but political good sense acted as a check upon passion; to originate dissensions among the republicans, in the first days of the Commonwealth, would, it was felt, be madness; the regicides knew that, if left alone, they would not be strong enough to maintain their position;

[1] Commons' Journals, vol. vi. pp. 140—143; Ludlow's Memoirs, p. 123; Godwin's History of the Commonwealth, vol. iii. p. 12.

and the House merely ordained that the Councillors of State whom it had appointed should all meet to confer together on what had best be done under the circumstances, and should afterwards communicate their decision to Parliament. The matter was arranged without further difficulty; the pledge of fidelity which the dissidents offered for the future was accepted, and they took their seats beside the regicides in the republican Council of State.[1]

This compromise was to a very great extent the work, on the one hand of Cromwell, and on the other, of Sir Harry Vane, the most eminent, the most sincere, the most able, and the most chimerical of the non-military republicans. He was an ardent revolutionist, and he detested revolutionary violence. When, on the 6th of November, 1648, the army expelled the entire Presbyterian party from the House of Commons, Vane boldly denounced that act, and ceased to take part in the sittings of the mutilated House. He protested still more strongly against the trial of the King, and ever since that period, he had resided at his country-seat at Raby, completely unconnected with public affairs. But the Commonwealth was the object at once of his faith and of his aspirations; as soon as it appeared, he belonged to it, heart and soul. Cromwell, who cared little for the embarrassments which might at a future time be occasioned him by the allies of whom he had present need, immediately used every effort to induce Vane once more to give the republican government the support of his talents, his devotedness, and his influence. Vane resisted at first, but in a way which showed he soon would yield. He it was, who, setting aside the past, suggested the oath of fidelity for the future; and Cromwell, quite sure that this would be enough to secure Vane to the

[1] Commons' Journals, vol. vi. pp. 139, 146; Whitelocke's Memorials, p. 382; Cromwelliana, p. 52; Godwin's History of the Commonwealth, vol. iii. pp. 28—31.

service of the Council of State and to the Parliament, was one of the most eager to express his entire approval of the suggestion.[1]

Cromwell was right, for no sooner had they taken their seats than this same Vane, and that same majority of the Council of State who had refused to take any share in the responsibility of the regicides, elected[2] as their president, John Bradshaw, the President of the High Court which had condemned Charles I.; and three days after, Vane, with several of his colleagues, proceeded to "a small house in Holborn, which opens backwards into Lincoln's Inn Fields," to offer the post of Latin Secretary to the Council to a kinsman of Bradshaw's, who had recently maintained, in an eloquent pamphlet, "that it is lawful to call to account a tyrant, or wicked king, and after due conviction, to depose, and put him to death!"[3] That man was Milton.

At the same time that it was engaged in the constitution of the Council of State, the House turned its attention also to the courts of law; an urgent question, for the day for the opening of their quarterly sessions was at hand, and no one for a moment admitted the possibility of interrupting the course of justice. Of the twelve principal judges, ten had been appointed by the Parliament itself since the outbreak of the civil war; and yet, on the 8th of February, 1649, six of them refused to give any oath of fidelity to the Commonwealth, and the other six would only consent to continue the discharge of their functions on condition that, by a formal declaration of the House, the ancient laws of the country

[1] Forster's Statesmen of the Commonwealth, vol. iii. pp. 125—127; Godwin's History of the Commonwealth, vol. iii. p. 31.

[2] On the 10th of March, 1649.

[3] Todd's Life of Milton, pp. 63, 70; Carlyle, Cromwell's Letters and Speeches, vol. ii. p. 16; Godwin's History of the Commonwealth, vol. iii. p. 36.

should be maintained, and that the judges should continue to take them as the rule of their decisions. These demands were complied with, and the six judges who had tendered their resignation were not replaced until the following summer.[1]

The Earl of Warwick, the Lord High Admiral, lived on intimate terms with Cromwell; but he was a decided Presbyterian, who inspired the republicans with no confidence, and who himself preferred his own ease to their service. His office was taken from him on the 20th of February, 1649; the powers of the Admiralty were vested in the Council of State, which delegated them to a committee of three members, of whom Vane was the chief; and the command of the fleet passed into the hands of three officers, Edward Popham, Richard Dean, and Robert Blake—the last a literate and warlike Puritan, who had already given proof of his great qualities as a soldier, and who was destined to augment at sea the power and glory of the Commonwealth, which he served with austere and unflinching devotedness.[2]

The House had revised and arranged every department of the administration; the legislation and diplomacy of the country, the courts of justice, the police, the finances, the army and the fleet, were all in its hands. To appear as disinterested as it was active, it permitted those members who had separated from the conquering party, at the moment of its definitive rupture with the King, to resume their seats in its midst; but it required from them at the same time such a disavowal of their former votes that very few could persuade themselves to take advantage of this concession. To

[1] Commons' Journals, vol. vi. pp. 134—136; Whitelocke's Memorials, pp. 378—380; Clarendon's History of the Rebellion, vol. vi. p. 247.

[2] Commons' Journals, vol. vi. pp. 147, 149, 150; Godwin's History of the Commonwealth, vol. iii. p. 35; Hepworth Dixon's Life of Blake, pp. 114—122.

fill up the vacancies thus created, it authorized some new elections, but in very small numbers—seven only in the space of six months—for it distrusted the electors; and it even directed the formation of a committee for the purpose of framing a new electoral law, to regulate the assembling of a new Parliament. But these were mere demonstrations, not *bonâ fide* and effectual resolutions. Henry Martyn told the House, "That he thought they might find the best advice from the Scripture: for when Moses was found upon the river, and brought to Pharaoh's daughter, she took care that the mother might be found out, to whose care he might be committed to be nursed; which succeeded very happily." Applying this, he continued: "Our Commonwealth is yet an infant of a weak growth, and a very tender constitution: and therefore my opinion is, that nobody can be so fit to nurse it as the mother who brought it forth; and that we should not think of putting it under any other hands, until it hath obtained more years and vigor."[1]

Henry Martyn did not say enough: not only was the Commonwealth unable to exist without the care of the Parliament which had given it birth, but when that all-powerful Parliament wished to impart full vigor to the Commonwealth, it found itself too weak to accomplish that work, and could only fluctuate between precipitation and postponement, hesitation and violence. The acts voted on the 7th of February, for abolishing the kingly office and taking away the House of Peers, were not definitively adopted until the 17th and 19th of March; and when the House ordained their official proclamation in the City of London, the Lord Mayor, Reynoldson, positively refused to proclaim them. When summoned to the bar, ten days afterwards, he alleged the

[1] Commons' Journals, vol. vi. pp. 129, 130, 133, 136, 210; Godwin's History of the Commonwealth, vol. iii. pp. 33—35; Forster's Statesmen of the Commonwealth, vol. iii. p. 324; Ludlow's Memoirs, p. 134.

scruples of his conscience in justification of his conduct. The House condemned him to pay a fine of two thousand pounds, and to be imprisoned for two months; and ordered the election of another Lord Mayor. Alderman Thomas Andrews, one of the King's judges, was elected; but though the House did not think it wise to require of him immediately that official proclamation of the Commonwealth which his predecessor had refused to make, it gave intimation of more rigorous intentions with regard to the City. "They believe they may make sure of the metropolis," wrote the President de Bellièvre, the French ambassador in England, to M. Servien, "either by causing the election of other magistrates who are devoted to their service, or by absolutely suppressing the form of government which has hitherto been observed, and establishing one of the officers of the army as Governor of the city—as it is believed they intend to do. But, according to all appearance, although it may be their intention to do this at some time or other, they will be contented for the present with establishing their authority therein, without any display of violence." On the 10th of May following, more than a month after the election of the new Lord Mayor, and more than three months after the death of Charles I., the authority of the House was not established in the city, for the Commonwealth had not yet been proclaimed there. Inquiry was made into the cause of this delay, and twenty days after, on the 30th of May, the proclamation at length took place, in the absence of several of the aldermen, who declined to take any part in the ceremonial, and amid the strongest manifestations of popular disapprobation. "It was desired," wrote M. de Croullé, the secretary of the President de Bellièvre, to Cardinal Mazarin, "that this act should be effected in the ordinary form of a simple publication, without the mayor and aldermen being supported by any soldiers, in order to show that no violent means had been resorted to;

but a quantity of people having assembled around them with hootings and insults, compelled them to send for some troops, who first drove away all the bystanders, and thus they finished their publication."[1]

The aldermen who had absented themselves were called to the bar of the House, and they unhesitatingly confessed the motives of their absence. Sir Thomas Soames, who was also a member of the House, stated: "That it was against several oaths which he had taken as an alderman of London, and against his judgment and conscience." Alderman Chambers said: "That his heart did not go along with the work, in that business." They were both deprived of their municipal functions, and declared incapable of holding any public office. Sir Thomas Soames was even expelled from the House. But when it became necessary to replace them, it was found very difficult to obtain persons willing to be their successors, and seven successive refusals attested the ill-will of the citizens. A dinner offered to the House, by that faction in the city which was devoted to its cause, was a poor compensation for these checks; and in order to put the municipal body in a position to discharge its functions, it was found necessary to give to forty, and even, in certain cases, to ten of its members, the right to act in its name.[2]

The same obstacles and the same resistance were met with everywhere. The Parliament ordained the destruction, in all public places, of the King's arms, and all other emblems of royalty; and this order, though renewed four times,[3] was so

[1] Commons' Journals, vol. vi. pp. 133, 166, 168, 177, 179, 206, 221; Whitelocke's Memorials, pp. 393, 394; Leicester's Journal, p. 73; Letters of the President de Bellièvre to M. Servien (12th April, 1649), and of M. de Croullé to Cardinal Mazarin (14th June, 1649), in the Archives des Affaires Etrangères de France.

[2] Commons' Journals, vol. vii. pp. 221, 222; Whitelocke's Memorials, pp. 384, 404, 405; Godwin, vol. iii. p. 97.

[3] On the 15th of February and 9th of August, 1649, the 9th of April, 1650,

imperfectly obeyed that, two years after the establishment of the Commonwealth, Parliament was obliged to make the parochial authorities responsible for its execution, and to authorize them to pay the expenses out of the parish rates. A simple oath of fidelity to the Commonwealth was required of all the beneficed clergy, of the members of the Universities of Oxford and Cambridge, of all public functionaries, sheriffs, justices of peace, and others; and refusals arrived by thousands, publicly sanctioned by the gravest authorities, among others, by the Assembly of the Presbyterian Clergy in London, which met in May, 1650.[1] It was only in the month of January, 1650, a year after the death of the King, that they ventured to change the names of those vessels in the fleet which were suggestive of departed royalty.[2] In the spring of that same year, a new frigate was launched at London, in presence of the whole Council of State. It was proposed that it should be named *The Commonwealth of England*, "but it was thought," wrote M. de Croullé to Cardinal Mazarin, "that if the vessel were to perish, as all vessels are liable to do, it would be a bad omen;"[3] and so that hazardous satisfaction was dispensed with.

Nothing is more irritating to power, and especially to a conquering power, than the consciousness of its weakness; and when it experiences this feeling, it immediately seeks some opportunity of manifesting its strength, by way either of diversion or of revenge. The republican Government of England, thus hampered in its progress, had in its hands some of the most eminent of the Royalist leaders: the Duke of

and the 5th of February, 1651; Commons' Journals, vol. vi. pp. 142, 276, 394, 531.

[1] Commons' Journals, vol. vi. pp. 306, 427; Neal's History of the Puritans, vol. iv. pp. 8, 10; Reliquiæ Baxterianæ, book i. p. 64.

[2] Commons' Journals, vol. vi. p. 340.

[3] M. de Croullé to Cardinal Mazarin (2 May, 1650); Archives des Affaires Etrangères de France.

Hamilton, the Earl of Holland, the Earl of Norwich, Lord Capell, and Sir John Owen—valiant survivors of the last struggles of the civil war, who had fallen, at different times, into the power of the Parliament, and had been its prisoners for many months. At one moment they almost believed themselves in safety. In November, 1648, the two Houses voted that the Duke of Hamilton should pay a fine of one hundred thousand pounds sterling, and that the other four should be banished from the country.[1] But before this vote had been carried into execution, the Presbyterians, by whose influence it had been passed, were expelled from the House of Commons, and the Independents, left sole masters of the field, formally revoked it, and detained the five leaders in prison, announcing, at the same time, their intention to bring them to trial.[2] Regardless of his perilous position, when, a few days after, a more important trial, that of the King, commenced, Lord Capell, with the enthusiasm of a high-minded gentleman, and of a valiant soldier, wrote from his cell in the Tower, on the 15th of January, 1649, to Cromwell, to represent to him the enormity of such a crime, and to conjure him to save the King. "I frankly give you leave to think," he said in this remarkable letter, "nor do I value the inconvenience it could draw along with it, that there is not that honest expedient in the world to serve him by, that I would not hazard myself in to employ for him; nor do I know what earthly felicity it is could be so welcome to me as to advance a step beyond any other in my duty towards him. But my present condition refuseth me the ability of anything else but that of invocating the favor of God for him, and making my addresses to you, whom I take to be the figure that gives the denomination to the sequence of a great many ciphers that follow you." He then set forth at great length, and in terms

[1] Commons' Journals, vol. vi. p. 72.

[2] On the 13th of December, 1648; Commons' Journals, vol. vi. p. 96.

sometimes of reproach and sometimes of flattery, all the motives of religion, justice, policy, duty, honor, interest, pride, and personal ambition, which might combine to influence Cromwell's decision; and he concluded with these words: "Sir, my conclusion shall be very plain, because you may thereby be the better assured of my sincerity in all the rest. The ancient constitutions and present laws of this kingdom are my inheritance and birthright; if any shall think to impose upon me that which is worse than death, which is the profane and dastardly parting from these laws, I will choose the lesser evil, which is death. I have also a right in kingship, the protector of those laws: this is also, by a necessity and conjunction with that other, dearer to me than life. And lastly, in this King is my present right, and also obligations of inestimable favors received from him. I would to God my life could be a sacrifice to preserve his! Could you make it an expedient to serve that end, truly I would pay you more thanks for it than you will allow yourself from all your other merits from those you have most obliged, and die your most affectionate friend, CAPELL."[1]

Cromwell returned no answer to this letter, but he did not forget it. He possessed that pitiless sagacity which, while it enabled him to recognize the value of an enemy, only convinced him of the necessity of putting him out of the way. On the 1st of February, the House resolved on erecting a new High Court of Justice, to consist of sixty members, of whom fifteen should form a quorum. Bradshaw was appointed President of this Court. It was commissioned to "hear, try, and adjudge divers delinquents," among whom the Duke of Hamilton, the Earls of Holland and Norwich, Lord Capell, and Sir John Owen were specially named; and orders were

[1] Lady Theresa Lewis's Lives from the Clarendon Gallery, vol. ii. pp. 102, 264.

given that their trial should immediately be proceeded with.[1]

On the following day, the 2d of February, as soon as night had fallen, Lord Capell, whom one of his friends had provided with a cord, let himself down from his room in the Tower into the ditch below. He had been informed as to what part of the ditch he would find it most easy to traverse; but he either mistook the place to which he had been directed, or the water and mud were deeper than his informant had expected, for he sank into the mire to his chin, and was on the point of giving up his attempt and shouting for assistance. His tall stature and undaunted courage, however, saved him; he succeeded in reaching the other side, where his friends were expecting him. He was conducted by them to the Temple, where he remained concealed for two days. The Government, enraged at his escape, used the utmost diligence for his discovery. One of his most faithful friends thought that he would be unable to remain in safety in a place of so much resort as the Temple, and that he would find a surer asylum in a small house in Lambeth Marsh. That same evening Lord Capell, accompanied by his friend alone, went out for the purpose of taking the first boat they should find at the Temple Stairs. It was so late that only one remained. They entered it, and told the boatman to row them to the other side of the river. Lord Capell was carefully disguised; but whether his companion inadvertently called him *My Lord*, as was generally reported, or whether some other circumstance awakened his suspicions, the boatman determined to follow his two passengers on landing; and having watched them into the house, went at once to an officer, and asked him "what he would give him to bring him to the place where the Lord Capell lay?" The

[1] Commons' Journals, vol. vi. p. 128.

officer promised him ten pounds; the boatman fulfilled his promise; Lord Capell was seized, and the next day returned a prisoner to the Tower.[1]

On the 9th of February, the Court began its sittings; fifty of the Commissioners appointed to form it were present. The five prisoners were brought to the bar, as different in attitude and language as in condition and character. The Duke of Hamilton was a great nobleman, a court politician, sincerely attached to the king, whom he had always desired to serve, but still more anxious to maintain his influence and popularity in Scotland, his native land, where he was careful to keep on good terms with all parties, and cared little to aggravate the difficulties or dangers of his master, if he could diminish or delay those which threatened himself. Lord Holland was a frivolous and reckless courtier, fond of money and pleasure, and characterized by very little faith, ability, or morality; he had curried and obtained favor, first with the Duke of Buckingham, then with Queen Henrietta Maria, then with the King himself, and finally with the Parliament, passing, as his necessities or fears dictated, from one party to another; decried by all who knew him; maintaining relations of a suspicious nature with the Court of France; and regarded with jealous enmity by Cromwell, either because of some slighting language he had used concerning him, or, as it is said, on some lady's account. The Earl of Norwich was a jovial and good-natured Cavalier, anxious to do his duty to the King and to serve his friends, and inspiring his enemies with neither fear nor resentment. Sir John Owen was a simple Welsh gentleman, honest and courageous, without any thought of ambition or personal advantage, an obscure martyr of the cause he had embraced,

[1] Lady Theresa Lewis's Lives from the Clarendon Gallery, vol. ii. pp. 105—107; Clarendon's History of the Rebellion, vol. vi. pp. 258—260; Whitelocke's Memorials, p. 377.

and utterly unconscious that there was any merit in his devotedness. Lord Capell came last, as noble in heart as in race, the worthy descendant of a grandfather who had been celebrated in his county for his eminent virtues and olden hospitality. "He kept a bountiful house," said his grandson of him, "and showed forth his faith by his works; extending his charity in such abundant manner to the poor, that he was bread to the hungry, drink to the thirsty, eyes to the blind, and legs to the lame, and might be justly styled a great almoner to the King of kings."[1] Lord Capell had worthily represented in Parliament, at court, and in the camp, the solid virtues of his family; and Charles I. had had experience, as the necessities of the time required, both of his independence and his loyalty. These five men, thus thrown together in misfortune, formed, by their union, an almost complete and faithful type of the royalist party, in its noblest as well as in its least honorable elements; and that entire party seemed represented and arraigned in their persons, before the Court which began to sit in Westminster Hall, a few days after the dissolution of that which had tried and judged the king.[2]

Hamilton maintained a severe countenance, and asked for time to send to Scotland for certain papers which he required. The Court granted him an insufficient delay, and when he prayed for more time, he was told, "that it was for prisoners to prepare their proofs against the trial, he having been in prison so long." After his condemnation, he was urgently solicited to make certain revelations about the past. Cromwell even sent messengers to offer him not only his life, but the restitution of his former fortune if he would do so; but he indignantly refused, saying, that "if he had as many

[1] Lady Theresa Lewis's Lives from the Clarendon Gallery, vol. i. p. 252.

[2] State Trials, vol. iv. col. 1155; Clarendon's History of the Rebellion, vol. vi. pp. 252—266.

lives as hairs on his head, he would lay them all down rather than redeem them by so base a means."[1] The effect of supreme and irrevocable misfortune is to elevate those souls which it does not deprive of all virtue.

The Earls of Holland and Norwich merely attempted to diminish the gravity of the charges brought against them, and to produce a favorable impression on the minds of their judges by the modesty of their demeanor.[2]

Lord Capell was not only dignified; he was haughty and undaunted. Without paying any attention to the Court, he gazed severely on the audience, as if to reproach them with the complicity of their presence. He maintained that by the terms of the capitulation of Colchester, and the explanations of the Lord General Fairfax himself, his life had been secured to him. "I am a prisoner of war," he said: "I had a fair quarter given me, and all the gowns in the world have nothing to do with me." In any case, he demanded to be tried by his peers: "Though king and lords be laid aside, yet the fundamental laws of the land are still in force." He called the attention of the Court to "Magna Charta and the Petition of Right; he desired to see his jury, and that they might see him, and said he believed that a precedent could not be given of a subject tried for his life, but either by Bill in Parliament, or by a jury." In reply, President Bradshaw told him "that he was tried before such judges as the Parliament thought fit to assign him; and who had judged a better man than himself."[3]

[1] State Trials, vol. iv. cols. 1156, 1187, 1188, 1191, 1211; Whitelocke's Memorials, p. 381.

[2] State Trials, vol. iv. cols. 1195—1250; Whitelocke's Memorials, pp. 381, 385, 386.

[3] State Trials, vol. iv. cols. 1209—1214; Whitelocke, pp. 380, 381, 383; Lady Theresa Lewis's Lives from the Clarendon Gallery, vol. ii. pp. 108—115; Clarendon's History of the Rebellion, vol. vi. pp. 253—255.

When the Attorney-General concluded by demanding that he should be hanged, drawn, and quartered, Lord Capell "seemed to startle;" but speedily recovering himself, he told the Court "that however he was dealt with here, he hoped for a better resurrection hereafter."[1]

They were all five condemned to be beheaded. When the president had pronounced this sentence, Sir John Owen made a low bow to the Court, and gave them humble thanks. On being asked by one of the bystanders what he meant, he said aloud, "it was a very great honor to a poor gentleman of Wales to lose his head with such noble lords," and added, with an oath, "that he was afraid they would have hanged him."[2]

The High Court, however, was irresolute; and either from a desire to act with clemency, or with a view to shift the responsibility of such rigorous proceedings, after having condemned the prisoners, it referred the execution of their sentence to the sovereign decision of Parliament.[3]

On the next day, the 7th of March, the Earl of Warwick, the brother of Lord Holland, with Lady Holland, Lady Capell, and several other relatives and friends of the prisoners, presented themselves at the door of the House of Commons, and requested permission to intercede personally for the lives of those against whom the High Court of Justice had pronounced sentence of death. They were admitted, and presented their petitions. But, after some hours' debate, the House resolved "not to proceed any further upon these petitions, but to leave them to the justice of the Court that sentenced them." The republican leaders would have preferred, without interfering further in this melancholy affair, to profit by the severity of the judges whom they had ap-

[1] Whitelocke, p. 381.

[2] Clarendon's History of the Rebellion, vol. vi. pp. 255, 256.

[3] State Trials, vol. iv. col. 1188; Whitelocke, p. 386.

pointed; but the Court was resolved not to allow the whole weight to rest upon its shoulders; it granted the condemned a respite of two days, that they might again appeal to Parliament.[1]

Thus compelled to decide, the republican leaders consulted only their animosities and their fears. The Duke of Hamilton, as an individual and as a Scotchman, inspired no interest; his petition was unhesitatingly rejected. Lord Holland had many friends; his brother and his wife were there to plead his cause; he was naturally of an obliging and kindly disposition; in his passage through all parties he had in all formed connections and rendered services: but Cromwell and Ireton detested and despised him; his petition was rejected by a majority of one vote. With regard to the Earl of Norwich, the votes were equally divided; but Lenthall, the Speaker of the House, said, "that he had received many obligations from him; and that once, when he had been like to have incurred the King's displeasure, by some misinformation, which would have been very penal to him, Lord Norwich had by his credit preserved him, and removed the prejudice that was against him; and therefore he was obliged in gratitude to give his vote for the saving him." Lord Norwich was saved, as Lord Holland had just been condemned, by a majority of one vote. No one was there to defend Sir John Owen; but Colonel Hutchinson said to Ireton, who was sitting next to him: "It grieves me much to see that, while all are laboring to save the lords, a gentleman, that stands in the same condemnation, should not find one friend to ask his life; and so am I moved with compassion that, if you will second me, I am resolved to speak for him, who, I perceive, is a stranger and friendless." Ireton promised to do so: Hutchinson obtained the poor Welsh knight's petition, which had

[1] Commons' Journals, vol. vi. p. 158; State Trials, vol. iv. col. 1216.

been left in the hands of the clerk of the House, delivered it, spoke for him so nobly, and was so effectually seconded by Ireton, that Sir John Owen's life was saved by a majority of five votes.[1]

Lord Capell now remained—the object, on the part of his family and friends, of the most passionate solicitude and the most active efforts; every means was tried to save him; money was offered, and even given, to persons who promised the support of their influence. A long debate took place on his petition; some spoke in his favor, extolling his virtues, and saying "that he had never deceived them, or pretended to be of their party, but always resolutely declared himself for the King." Cromwell then rose, and in the opening of his speech, manifested more esteem and kindness for Lord Capell than any previous speaker had done; "but my affection for the public," he continued, "so much weighs down my private friendship that I cannot but tell you, that the question now is, whether you will preserve the most bitter and the most implacable enemy you have? I know the Lord Capell very well, and I know that he would be the last man in England that would forsake the royal cause. He has great courage, industry, and generosity; he has many friends who would always adhere to him; and as long as he lived, what condition soever he was in, he would be a thorn in your sides. And, therefore, for the good of the Commonwealth, I shall give my vote against the petition;" and it was rejected, by what majority we cannot accurately ascertain.[2]

The execution was fixed for the following day, the 9th of March, 1649. During the night, Lord Capell requested his

[1] Commons' Journals, vol. vi. pp. 159, 160; Whitelocke, p. 386; Memoir of Colonel Hutchinson, pp. 339, 340; Ludlow's Memoirs, p. 123; Clarendon's History of the Rebellion, vol. vi. p. 258.

[2] Lady Theresa Lewis's Lives from the Clarendon Gallery, vol. ii. p. 120; Clarendon's History of the Rebellion, vol. vi. p. 260.

friend, Dr. Morley, who had visited him in his prison, to administer to him the sacrament. "I desire to receive it," he said, "from a minister of the King's party, and according to the liturgy of the Church of England. * * * * I think I cannot accuse myself of any great known sin, committed against the light of my conscience, but one only—and that is, the giving my vote in Parliament for the death of my Lord of Strafford; which I did against my conscience, not out of any malice to the person of the man, but out of a base fear, and carried away with the violence of a prevailing faction; for which I have been and am heartily sorry, and have often with tears begged and, I hope, obtained pardon of Almighty God. If you think it necessary or fit, I will confess this great and scandalous sin of mine, together with the cause of it, openly upon the scaffold, to God's glory, and my own shame." Dr. Morley encouraged him in this virtuous intention. The next morning, Lord Capell's family visited him—his wife, his eldest son, two of his uncles, and his nephew, all together, for they were not permitted to see him separately. He kept them with him an hour, lovingly but sadly endeavoring to sustain their courage, and to address to them his last counsels. "I would not," he said to his son, "I would not have you neglect any honorable and just occasion to serve your King and country with the hazard of your life and fortune; yet I would have you to engage yourself (as I, thanks be to God for it! have done) neither out of desire of revenge, nor hope of reward, but out of a conscience of your duty only. The best legacy I can leave you is my prayers for you, and a verse of David's Psalms, which I command you, upon my blessing, to make a part of your daily prayers, as I have always made it a part of mine, viz., 'Teach me thy way, O Lord, and lead me in a plain path.' For I have always loved plainness and clearness both in my words and actions, and abhorred all doubling and dissimulation, and so I would have you to do also." When the moment of parting arrived, Lady Capell's strength failed her, and she was carried away in a fainting fit. "Well, doctor," said Lord Capell, as soon as he was left alone with his friend Morley, "the hardest thing that I had to do here in this world is now past, the parting with this poor woman. I believe I shall be called upon presently to go to the place where I am to take my leave of all the rest of the world, and, I thank my God, I find myself very well disposed to it, and prepared for it. I am in good hope that, when I come to die, I shall have nothing else to do but to die only." Yet he wrote twice to his wife, during the short interval between their separation and the scaffold. "Let me live long here in thy dear memory. I beseech thee, sorrow not unsoberly, unusually. God be unto thee better than an husband, and to my children better than a father. I am sure He is able to be so: I am confident He is graciously pleased to be so."[1]

The Duke of Hamilton was brought first to the scaffold, which had been erected on an open space before Westminster Hall. He died with dignified courage, after having addressed the bystanders in simple and quiet language, modestly justifying his life, and professing his steady attachment to the dead king whom he had served, and to the absent king whose return he hoped for, although he would not witness it. As he spoke, the rays of the sun fell full on his face; he was advised to change his position; "No," he said, "I hope to see a brighter sun than that very speedily." On the previous evening, Lord Holland had manifested considerable anguish and weakness; he was ill in body and uneasy in mind; but at the last moment, supported by two Presbyterian ministers, who had accompanied him to the scaffold, he exhibited becoming firmness. Lord Capell ap-

[1] State Trials, vol. iv. cols. 1230, 1231; Lady Theresa Lewis's Lives from the Clarendon Gallery, vol. ii. pp. 137—145.

peared last, and alone, on the scaffold. "Sir," said the officer who commanded the execution, "is your chaplain here?" "No," he replied, "I have taken leave of him;" and perceiving that some of his servants were weeping, he said, "Restrain yourselves, gentlemen, restrain yourselves." Then, turning to the officer, he asked, "Did the Lords speak with their hats off, or no?" "With their hats off," replied Colonel Beecher. Lord Capell then took off his hat, and spoke briefly and firmly, showing equal frankness and decision as a royalist and as a Christian. He did as he had promised Dr. Morley; he accused himself of his vote against Lord Strafford. "I do here profess to you," he said, "that I did give my vote to that bill against the Earl of Strafford. Truly this I may say, I had not the least part nor degree of malice in doing of it. But I must confess again, to God's glory, and the accusation of mine own frailty, and the frailty of my nature, that truly it was unworthy cowardice not to resist so great a torrent as carried that business at that time."[1] People and soldiers, friends and strangers, all beheld him die with mingled feelings of admiration and respect.

It is one of the first duties of history to render full justice to those virtuous and courageous martyrs, whose deaths act so powerfully on the feelings of nations, and give fresh vitality in the hearts of men to those causes which have suffered defeat on the field of battle. With the exception of the republican party, the whole nation was inspired with indignation and sorrow by the death of Lord Capell. The war was at an end; the blood of the King had been shed, in expiation, it was affirmed, of all the bloodshed which he had occasioned. Why, then, more victims? Why these severities inflicted, on prisoners made in a war which had terminated, by judges whom the laws did not recognize, and whose

[1] State Trials, vol. iv. cols. 1188—1194, 1220—1235; Lady Theresa Lewis's Lives from the Clarendon Gallery, vol. ii. pp. 145—153.

authority could be defended only by scholastic subtleties? The Parliament itself felt that it could not persevere in such a course. It had still to decide the fate of several royalist leaders, both ecclesiastical, civil, and military. Against fifteen of them it decreed perpetual banishment, and the confiscation of all their property; it ordered that five should be proceeded against by court-martial for armed insurrection; it determined that two others, the Marquis of Winchester and the Bishop of Norwich, should be detained in prison as long as might be deemed necessary; and it voted that two only, Sir John Stowel and Judge David Jenkins, should be brought to trial for their lives, not before any extraordinary tribunal, but before the regular courts of assize. But even this vote was not carried into effect; for they both remained in prison, Jenkins until the year 1656, and Sir John Stowel until the Restoration. The Parliament became anxious to avoid publicity; it forbade the publication of the debates and acts of the High Court which had condemned Lord Capell; pamphlets were seized, journalists were gained over; and a committee was appointed to prepare measures for repressing abuses of the liberty of the press.[1] Silent acts of severity were substituted for public prosecutions and the scaffold.

But the Parliament had not the sole disposal of publicity and fame. A few days after the death of the king appeared the "Eikon Basilikè, or Portraiture of his Sacred Majesty in his Solitudes and Sufferings," which was said to be the work of Charles I. himself, and which, under the form of pious meditations, revealed to England the reflections, feelings, impressions, hopes, and griefs—indeed, the whole soul of the King, during the course of his trials. Aware, even before the execution of Charles, that this book was being

[1] Commons' Journals, vol. vi. pp. 164, 165, 276, 298; Godwin's History of the Commonwealth, vol. iii. pp. 43, 44, 343—348.

printed, the republican leaders, foreseeing the injury it could not fail to do them, made every effort to prevent its publication.[1] They did not succeed, however; the work got rapidly into circulation; forty-seven editions of it were printed, and more than forty-eight thousand copies distributed in England during the course of the year; and it was immediately translated and read with avidity in France, and throughout all Europe. The effect which it everywhere produced was prodigious; attachment for the memory of the King became passion, and respect, worship; his enemies were regarded as the murderers of a saint. It is to the "Eikon Basilikè" that Charles I. is principally indebted for the name of the Royal Martyr.

The work was not by him; external testimony and internal evidence both combine to remove all doubt on the matter. Dr. Gauden, Bishop, first of Exeter, and afterwards of Worcester, under the reign of Charles II., was its real author; but the manuscript had probably been perused and approved, perhaps even corrected, by Charles himself, during his residence in the Isle of Wight. In any case, it was the real expression and true portraiture of his position, character, and mind, as they had been formed by misfortune: it is remarkable for an elevation of thought which is at once natural and strained; a constant mingling of blind royal pride and sincere Christian humility; heart-impulses struggling against habits of obstinate self-consciousness; true piety in the midst of misguided conduct; invincible, though somewhat inert, devotion to his faith, his honor, and his rank; and as all these sentiments are expressed in monotonous language, which, though often emphatic, is always grave, tranquil, and even unctuous with serenity and sadness, it is not surprising that such a work should have profoundly

[1] March 16, 1649; Commons' Journals, vol. vi. p. 166.

affected all royalist hearts, and easily persuaded them that it was the King himself who addressed them.[1]

The Parliament felt that it could not remain silent in presence of so powerful a public emotion, and it directed Milton to answer the Eikon. That sublime and austere genius, who in his youth had determined, in opposition to paternal authority, to devote himself entirely to poetry and literature, was animated by an ardent passion for liberty: not for that real and true liberty which results from respect for all rights and for the rights of all, but for an ideal and absolute liberty, both religious, political, and domestic; and his mighty mind revelled, on this subject, in noble ideas, lofty sentiments, grand images, and eloquent words, without his troubling himself to inquire whether, in the world around him, positive facts and his own personal actions corresponded with his principles and hopes. He was able to serve, and he did in fact serve, the tyranny, first of an assembly, and afterwards of a single man, so long as, in the intellectual order of things, he could profess and defend liberty. He was a glorious and melancholy instance of the blinding effect which imagination, abstract reasoning, and eloquent language can produce on a great, but passionately dreamy intellect, and a stern but noble heart.

Milton quickly wrote and published his Eikonoklastes, a lengthy and cold, although violent, refutation of the Eikon Basilikè. Milton did not understand Charles I. and his feelings, nor could he appreciate the sentiments with which the King inspired the royalist party: he reproduced against him, with the utmost puritan and republican animosity, all the threadbare statements, all the true or false accusations, which, during ten years, had been current throughout England, without taking into consideration the new ideas and im-

[1] A separate treatise on the authenticity of the Eikon Basilikè, will be found in my *Etudes Biographiques sur la Révolution d'Angleterre.*

pressions which recent events had originated in men's hearts, and without adorning this retrospective diatribe by any vigor or elegance of language. It produced only a very slight effect in England; but on the Continent, and in France especially, it excited the liveliest resentment; and at the request of Charles II., the celebrated Protestant scholar, Saumaise, better known by his Latinized name of Salmasius, then an honorary professor at the University of Leyden, undertook to refute it. To express his indignation, Salmasius had not waited to be retained by Charles, and paid for his services: eight days after the execution of the King, he had, in a sudden and spontaneous letter, passionately denounced his enemies and judges.[1] The "Royal Defence for Charles I., addressed to Charles II.," produced a great sensation, more even from the name of its author than for the merit of the work itself. It was a scholarly, clever, and occasionally eloquent, but immoderate and untasteful panegyric of monarchy in general, an enthusiastic apology for Charles I., and a violently-abusive attack of the English republicans and their defender. When the work of Salmasius reached London, the Government took it into consideration; and at a sitting of the Council of State, at which it is said, Milton was present, it was decided that he should reply to it. He did so without delay, and with far more talent and success than he had exhibited and obtained when attacking Charles I. himself. His first and second "Defence of the People of England, in answer to Salmasius's Defence of the King," are models of passionate discussion, both of a general and of a personal character; the Commonwealth is defended in them, in its principles as well as in its actions, with unshrinking firmness; and Milton brings himself before his readers, alluding to his personal history, his manner of

[1] This letter is dated February 17, 1649; Carte's Ormonde Letters, vol. i. pp. 255—258.

life, and the blindness he had contracted by his application to this very work, with an eloquence by turns noble and touching; diffusing everywhere, even over false ideas and blameworthy actions, that splendor of thought and language which attracts and charms, though it may not convince, and sometimes even may irritate. The success of these republican replies was great, on the Continent as well as in England; Queen Christina of Sweden expressed her admiration of them to Salmasius himself; and the States-General of Holland thought it advisable to suppress the Royal Defence of the Leyden professor. Indignant at this treatment, he fell ill and died, leaving an "Answer of Claude Saumaise to John Milton," which was published after his death. Other writers, both royalists and republicans, French and English, entered the arena; Milton joined once more in the controversy, from personal irritation rather than from political necessity; and this great discussion, which had begun with apologies for a despotic King and a revolutionary Parliament, ended obscurely in a coarse and vulgar quarrel between literary men, who insulted one another with persevering acrimony.[1] When it at length terminated, the republican government had long ceased to take any interest in it; more pressing cares and more dangerous enemies had absorbed its attention.

On the 20th of January, 1649, the very day on which the King appeared for the first time before the High Court which had been appointed to try him, the Lord General Fairfax and the General Council of Officers of the army, had presented their plan of republican government to Parliament, under the title of "An Agreement of the People of England, and the places therewith incorporated, for a secure and present peace, upon grounds of common right, freedom, and safety." This plan, prepared, it is said, by Ireton, consisted

[1] Todd's Life of Milton, pp. 123—136; Mitford's Life of Milton, pp. 77—95; Milton's Prose Works, vols. iv. and vi. (London, 1851).

of ten articles, the essential dispositions of which were as follow:—

1. That the present Parliament dissolve on the 30th of April, 1649.

2. That the Representative (they rejected the word Parliament) of the whole nation consist of 400 persons.

3. That the people choose themselves a Representative once in two years, and that the Representative continue its session during six months: That the electors and members of the Representative be natives or denizens of England, assessed towards the relief of the poor, not servants to and receiving wages from any particular person, aged twenty-one years and upwards, and housekeepers dwelling within the division for which the election is: That none shall be electors for seven years, or eligible for fourteen years, who have sided with the King against the Parliament during the late wars, or who shall offer or support any forcible opposition to the present agreement: That no member of the Council of State, nor any officer of any salaried forces in army or garrison, nor any treasurer or receiver of public money, shall, while such, be elected to be a Representative; and in case any lawyer be chosen into any Representative, or Council of State, he shall be incapable of practice as a lawyer during that trust.

4. That 150 members at least be always present in each sitting of the Representative at the passing of any law, or doing any act, whereby the people are to be bound; but that sixty may make a House for debates or resolutions that are preparatory thereunto.

5. That each Representative shall, within twenty days after their first meeting, appoint a Council of State for the managing of public affairs, until the tenth day after the meeting of the next Representative.

6. That in each interval betwixt biennial Representatives,

the Council of State, in case of imminent danger or extreme necessity, may summon a Representative to be forthwith chosen, and to meet for a session of not above eighty days.

7. That no member of any Representative be made either receiver, treasurer, or other officer, during that employment, saving to be a member of the Council of State.

8. That the Representative have the supreme trust, in order to the preservation and government of the whole; and that their power extend to the erecting and abolishing of courts of justice and public offices, and to the enacting, altering, repealing, and declaring of laws, and the highest and final judgment concerning all natural and civil things; but not concerning things spiritual or evangelical.—Certain limitations to this sovereign power were here indicated for the safeguard of civil liberties, the financial engagements of the State, and the disabilities which lay on the royalist party.

9. That the Christian religion be held forth and recommended as the public profession in this nation, which we desire may, by the grace of God, be reformed to the greatest purity in doctrine, worship, and discipline, according to the word of God; the instructing of the people thereunto in a public way, so it be not compulsive, as also the maintaining of able teachers for that end, is allowed to be provided for by our Representatives; the maintenance of which teachers may be out of the public treasury, and we desire not by tithes: That Popery or Prelacy be not held forth as the public way or profession in this nation: That to the public profession so held forth none be compelled by penalties or otherwise, but only may be endeavored to be won by sound doctrine and the example of a good conversation: That all such who profess faith in God by Jesus Christ have equal liberty and protection, so as they abuse not this liberty to

the civil injury of others, or to actual disturbance of the public peace.

10. That whosoever shall, by force of arms, resist the orders of the Representative (except in case where such Representative shall evidently render up or take away the foundations of common right, liberty, and safety, contained in this agreement), shall lose the benefit and protection of the laws, and shall be punishable with death, as an enemy and traitor to the nation.[1]

These were the views of the politic republicans, of the moderate men, both military and civil, who had already managed or closely watched the affairs of the nation; but they were far from satisfying the ideas and passions of all the party that had made war against the King, and overthrown monarchical rule. No sooner was it installed than the republican government found itself face to face with an ardent democratic and mystical opposition; and a man presented himself who, with indomitable courage and devotedness, became, not the leader, for no one was leader in that camp, but the interpreter, defender, and popular martyr, of all the disaffected. That man was John Lilburne.

Nor was this a new part for him to play; during the reign of Charles I., he had already braved sufferings and won popularity. Even against the Republican Parliament, he had recently, on the occasion of the King's trial, commenced a violent opposition, denouncing the appointment of a High Court, and demanding that the King should be judged in conformity to the laws of the country, and by an independent jury. Not that he was possessed by the spirit of demagogic cynicism, and desired to humiliate fallen royalty, but he was animated by a strict respect for the common law, and for the legal safeguards which it secures to every

[1] Old Parliamentary History, vol. xviii. pp. 516—536.

Englishman. He attacked, with even more vehemence, the High Court which was erected to try Lord Capell and his companions, and he even offered them his services for their defence, so anxious was he to find opportunities for gratifying his love of disputation. In the city, where his youth had been passed, and in the army, where he had served with distinction, he had old connections and numerous friends—citizens and apprentices, officers and soldiers, mystical sectaries and fanatics—all passionately attached, as he was, to the most ultra-democratic ideas and opinions, all equally argumentative and disputatious, never making the slightest allowance for the conditions of social order, or the necessities of the ruling power, but always ready to criticize and attack the government whenever it ran counter to the instincts of their conscience, or the fantasies of their mind, or the recently-acquired habits of their revolutionary independence, or the pretensions of their pride. Lilburne used every means to promote the fermentation of all these humors; he was particularly anxious to resuscitate among the inferior ranks of the army, the practice of holding meetings and preparing petitions—in fact, all the apparatus of agitators delegated by their regiments, of which Cromwell and the Independents had made such effectual use to intimidate the Parliament. At a council of officers held at Whitehall, on the 22d of February, 1649, it was resolved to take severe measures against these intrigues; and Fairfax issued general orders to the army, forbidding all meetings and deliberations as contrary to discipline, but recognizing the right of the soldiers to petition, provided they first informed their officers of their intention to do so.[1] Lilburne immediately published a pamphlet,[2] under the title of "England's New

[1] Whitelocke's Memorials, p. 383.

[2] On the 22d of February, 1649. See Guizot's Etudes Biographiques, pp. 172, 173.

Chains Discovered," in which he violently attacked this abuse of power on the part of men who, not long before, had so often authorized and stimulated their subordinates to indulge in all the excesses of liberty. At the same time five soldiers signed and presented to Fairfax a petition to complain of the obstacles thus placed in the way of their right of petition; "Be pleased to consider," they wrote, "that we are English soldiers, engaged for the freedom of England, and not outlandish mercenaries, to butcher the people for pay, to serve the pernicious ends of ambition and will in any person under Heaven."[1]

Fairfax immediately referred this petition to the council of war, which condemned the five soldiers to ride with their faces towards their horses' tails in front of their respective regiments, to have their swords broken over their heads, and to be cashiered. This sentence was carried into execution at once, on the very day that the High Court of Justice condemned Lord Capell to death. A few days after, Lilburne published a new pamphlet, entitled "The Hunting of the Foxes from Newmarket and Triploe Heath to Whitehall by Five small Beagles, or the Grandie-Deceivers Unmasked;" a narrative at once burlesque and tragical of the petition and punishment of the five soldiers; and a burning invective against the commander who had inflicted such chastisement upon them. "Was there ever," says Lilburne in his introduction, "a generation of men so apostate, so false, and so perjured as these? Did ever men pretend an higher degree of holiness, religion and zeal to God and their country than these? They preach, they fast, they pray, they have nothing more fre-

[1] Old Parliamentary History, vol. ix. p. 49; Commons' Journals, vol. vi. p. 151; Whitelocke, pp. 383—385; The Hunting of the Foxes from Newmarket and Triploe Heath to Whitehall by Five small Beagles, p. 17; Godwin's History of the Commonwealth, vol. iii. pp. 45—59; Guizot's Etudes Biographiques sur la Révolution d'Angleterre, pp. 149—173.

quent than the sentences of sacred Scripture, the name of God and of Christ, in their mouths. You shall scarce speak to Cromwell about anything but he will lay his hand on his breast, elevate his eyes, and call God to record; he will weep, howl, and repent, even while he doth smite you under the first rib. * * It is evident to the whole world that the now present interest of the officers is directly contrary to the interest of the soldiers; if you will uphold the interest of the one, the other must down; and as well may you let them bore holes through your ears, and be their slaves for ever, for your better distinction from freemen. For what are you now? Your mouths are stopped, you may be abused and enslaved, but you may not complain, you may not petition for redress. They are your lords, and you are their conquered vassals. There must be no standing against the officers; if they say the crow is white, so must the soldier; he must not lisp a syllable against their treacheries and abuses, their false musters, and cheating the soldiery of their pay; that soldier that is so presumptuous as to dare to article against an officer must be cashiered."[1]

And at the same time that he thus denounced the officers to the soldiers, Lilburne addressed to the Parliament the second part of his "England's New Chains Discovered;" another invective, equally furious and severe, in which he denounced to the civil power the leaders of the army, who were laboring, and had ever labored, to possess themselves of the mastery. "If your honorable House," he said, "should fail in performing that supreme trust which is really and essentially resident in your integrity, yet we shall not doubt but that what we have here presented and published will open the eyes and raise the hearts of so conscionable a number of the soldiery and people in all places, and make them so sensible

[1] Hunting of the Foxes, pp. 12, 13.

of the bondage and danger threatened, as that these men, this faction of officers, shall never be able to go through with their wicked intentions."[1]

The Parliament and the General Council of officers were equally irritated by these publications, and combined, against their new enemies, the weapons both of revolutionary violence and of constituted authority. Petitions arrived from several counties, expressing censure of the nascent opposition, and promising devoted adherence to the Parliament. Various congregations of sectaries, Anabaptists and others, sent to declare that it was against their wish that Lilburne's pamphlet, "England's New Chains Discovered," had been read in some of their meetings, and to express their entire disapprobation of it. Several regiments, at the suggestion of their officers, formally protested against the rising rebellion. The General Council of the army addressed to the House, on the 28th of March, 1649, a "humble petition," in which, after demanding the redress of certain administrative abuses which were injurious to the soldiers, they bore witness to the good understanding which subsisted between the Parliament and the army; and the House attached so much importance to this proceeding that it returned official thanks to the petitioners. "This day," said the Speaker to them, in the name of the House, "will be a day of much discontent to all the common enemies of you and us; but to all good men, that have engaged to carry on the good of the kingdom with us, it will be a great rejoicing and satisfaction, by this your modest and discreet petition. And, as in yourselves, it shows your moderation, so all those whose mouths are open to malice and detraction, will see that both the army and Parliament are unanimous in promoting the public good. The

[1] Lilburne, England's New Chains Discovered, part ii. p. 16; Old Parliamentary History, vol. xix. p. 51; Whitelocke, pp. 385, 390; Godwin's History of the Commonwealth, vol. iii. p. 60; Heath's Chronicle, p. 430.

things contained in your petition they consider as matter of great concernment, and intend to take them into immediate consideration; and as you have showed yourselves forward and faithful in former services, they have commanded me to return you the heartiest thanks I can for these your discreet and serious representations." And to sustain, by the energy of its own resolutions, these public manifestations on the part of its adherents, the House voted that Lilburne's pamphlet contained "much false, scandalous, and reproachful matter, highly seditious, and destructive to the present Government;" that its authors and distributors were guilty of high treason, and should be proceeded against as traitors; and that the Council of State should be enjoined to carry these resolutions into effect. The Council of State, on its part, directed Milton to prepare an answer to Lilburne's book; and on the following day, Lilburne himself, and his three principal associates, William Walwyn, Thomas Prince, and Richard Overton, were arrested and imprisoned in the Tower.[1]

Evidently, the majority of the republican party, both in the army, and throughout the country generally, with greater good sense than consistency, disavowed factious opponents, and wished to support its leaders and the Parliament. But extreme factions are never conscious of their weakness, for their feverish excitement makes them believe themselves strong, and hope is always found associated with the courage which leads men to brave martyrdom. From his confinement in the Tower, Lilburne published, under the title of "A Picture of the Council of State," a full narrative of his own arrest and that of his companions, with details of their examination, defence, and imprisonment; a remarkable exhibi-

[1] Commons' Journals, vol. vi. pp. 153, 168, 174, 177; Whitelocke's Memorials, p. 393; Godwin's History of the Commonwealth, vol. iii. pp. 60, 343.

tion of dignified pride and puerile bravado, of outspoken honesty and absurd vanity. Apostrophizing Cromwell and Ireton, he says: "Let them do their worst, I for my part bid defiance to them, assuredly knowing they can do no more to me than the devil did to Job. They have an army at command, but if every hair on the head of each officer or soldier were a legion of men, I would fear them no more than so many straws, for the Lord Jehovah is my rock and defence, under the assured shelter of whose wings I am safe and secure, and therefore will I sing and be merry. * * Courteous reader and dear countrymen, excuse, I beseech thee, my boasting and glorying, for I am necessitated to it, my adversaries' base and lying calumniations putting me upon it, and Paul and Samuel did it before me. And so I am thine, if thou art for the just freedoms and liberties of the land of thy nativity, John Lilburne, that never yet changed his principles from better to worse, nor could ever be threatened out of them, nor courted from them, that never feared the rich or mighty, nor ever despised the poor or needy, but always hath continued, and hopes by God's goodness to continue, *semper idem*."[1]

Lilburne did not limit his opposition to pamphlets, or to invectives against a few eminent men; he had in his mind certain moral and political ideas, very imperfectly systematized, but very popular among the lower classes, and which he ardently hoped to render triumphant. Already, on the 26th of February preceding, he had committed them to writing, and presented them, in the form of an address, to the House; as he was eager to oppose his own plan of government to that presented by the republican leaders, and to bring his Commonwealth into competition with theirs. The House had received his address as the propositions of an

[1] Lilburne's Picture of the Council of State, pp. 22, 23.

enemy are generally received, and had not honored it with any answer. Wounded at once in his self-love and in his polical faith, Lilburne published, while in prison, and in concert with his companions in captivity, a new "Agreement of the People of England," which contained a summary of their views with regard to social organization, and would, as they fondly hoped, bring into contempt that other Agreement which, three months before, the Council of Officers had submitted to Parliament. Composed of thirty articles, Lilburne's Constitution was not so different as he imagined from that for which he aspired to substitute it; it was unlike it, however, in several particulars, some of its arrangements being more just and liberal, and others more futile and impracticable. On the one hand, Lilburne gave far greater extent to the rights and liberties of individuals, and especially to liberty of conscience; on the other, he paid far less attention to the means of government, and instituted, against abuses of authority, many of those pretended guarantees which disorganize both society and government; for instance, he deprived the members of the existing legislative assembly of the right of being elected to sit in the succeeding Parliament. The republic of the General Council of officers could not have existed for any length of time—that of Lilburne could not even have begun to exist.[1]

At the very moment when he brought it forward, it received, from an originally obscure incident, a name which was fatal to its success. A band of thirty men appeared in Surrey, and announced that they would shortly number four thousand. Everard and Winstanley, the former of whom had once been a soldier, were their leaders. They began to dig the ground, and deposit in it seeds and roots, calling to

[1] Commons' Journals, vol. vi. p. 151; Whitelocke, p. 384; Lilburne's Agreement of the Free People of England.

them the people of the neighborhood, promising food and clothing to all who should join them, and threatening to pull down the palings of the adjacent parks. At the request of the county magistrates, Fairfax sent two troops of horse to arrest them. The leaders appeared before him with their hats on their heads, and on being asked why they did not remove them in the general's presence, replied, "Because he is only our fellow-creature." Everard defended their conduct, and asserted their rights. "We are," he said, "of the race of the Jews; all the liberties of the people were lost by the coming in of William the Conqueror, and ever since, the people of God have lived under tyranny and oppression worse than that of our forefathers under the Egyptians. But now the time of deliverance is at hand, and God will bring his people out of this slavery, and restore them to their freedom in enjoying the fruits and benefits of the earth. There has lately appeared to me a vision, which bade me, 'Arise and dig and plough the earth, and receive the fruits thereof, to distribute to the poor and needy, and to feed the hungry, and clothe the naked.' We intend not to meddle with any man's property, nor to break down any pales or enclosures, but only to meddle with what is common and untilled, and to make it fruitful for the use of man. But the time will suddenly be when all men shall willingly come in and give up their lands and estates, and submit to this community. We will not defend ourselves by arms, but will submit unto authority, and wait till the promised opportunity be offered, which we conceive is at hand."[1]

These men called themselves the Diggers, but the public named them the Levellers; and the name was immediately applied to all the small groups, either in the army or in the

[1] Whitelocke, pp. 396, 397; Godwin's History of the Commonwealth, vol. iii. p. 82; Cromwell's Letters and Speeches, vol. ii. pp. 29, 30.

country, who, influenced by political or religious ideas of a variously anarchical nature, desired another republic than that which was attempting to govern England, and gave it their most strenuous opposition. In vain did Lilburne and his friends protest against this name; in vain did they add to their scheme of constitution an article formally declaring that "no estates should be levelled, nor all things held in common."[1] The cognomen had a natural origin; scattered but striking facts and speeches served from time to time to confirm its applicability; it continued to be used as the designation of the whole party; and the republicans in possession of power, both in Parliament and in the army, had the good fortune that their revolutionary enemies were called the Levellers.

The struggle daily bordered more closely upon war; the slightest incident, whether serious or frivolous, might have kindled it. By the external relations which he maintained, and by the letters which he wrote, Lilburne, even while in prison, continued to foment an increasingly-dangerous agitation, both in the city and in the army. On the 11th of April, 1649,[2] the Parliament resolved to bring him and his three companions to trial; a committee of councillors of state and chief judges, presided over by Bradshaw, was appointed to consult as to the form of procedure most suitable under the circumstances; and six barristers were retained to plead against the prisoners at the trial. Such formidable preparations excited the most passionate emotions among the partizans of Lilburne; the House was inundated with petitions on his behalf, including one signed by ten thousand citizens of London and its vicinity, and another presented by thousands of women, who thronged the approaches to Westminster Hall from day to day. To the first of these petitions,

[1] Whitelocke, pp. 399, 400.

[2] Commons' Journals, vol. vi. p. 183.

the House replied with severity, that the four prisoners would be tried according to the laws, and that it expected all persons in England to acquiesce in the judgment of Parliament. To the second petition, no answer was returned. The women persisted. "There was a design," they said, "to fetch Lilburne and his fellow-prisoners out of the Tower at midnight to Whitehall, and there murder them. The House, by declaring the abettors of Lilburne's book traitors, have laid a snare for people, as hardly any discourse can be touching the affairs of the present time, but falls within the compass of that book: so that all liberty of discourse is thereby utterly taken away, than which there can be no greater slavery." In answer, the House bade the women, "Go home and wash their dishes;" to which some replied: "They had neither dishes nor meat left."[1]

In the midst of this excitement, eight regiments, four of infantry and four of cavalry, were appointed by lot to proceed to Ireland, where the civil war had recommenced. The soldiers, who felt little inclination for such an expedition, murmured violently; it was a difficult and an unpleasing service, in a despised and detested country; and they were to be sent thither without having had justice done them, before either their arrears had been paid or their rights recognized, before the government of the country had been firmly established, or the liberties of England definitely secured. A printed paper was immediately circulated through the barracks and in the streets, calling on the soldiers to claim their rights, and in the meanwhile, not to stir. A squadron of Colonel Whalley's regiment of cavalry, which had not been appointed by lot for service in Ireland, received orders to leave London; the men demanded previous satis-

[1] Commons' Journals, vol. vi. pp. 178, 189, 196; Whitelocke, pp. 393, 396—398. Clement Walker's History of Independency, part ii. p. 106; Godwin's History of the Commonwealth, vol. iii. p. 103.

faction of their claims, seized upon their standard, and formally refused to obey orders. Fairfax and Cromwell hastened to the spot, quelled the mutiny, sent off the regiment on its march, and selected fifteen of the mutineers to be tried by court-martial. Five of them were condemned to death. Lilburne immediately wrote to the Lord General, to protest against the "exercise of martial law, against any whomsoever, in time of peace," and to remind him that the violation of this principle "was one of the chiefest articles for which the Earl of Strafford lost his head." The republican general, however, did not hesitate. "You must make an end of this party," said Cromwell, in the Council of State, at the time of Lilburne's arrest, "or it will make an end of you, and you will be held the most foolish and ridiculous persons in the world, to have been overcome by so contemptible a sort of enemies." Cromwell understood both how to flatter and how to strike: without a moment's delay, four of the five condemned mutineers were pardoned, and the fifth, Robert Lockyer, was immediately shot in St. Paul's Churchyard. He was a brave young soldier, a pious sectary, an enthusiastic republican, greatly beloved by his comrades; his death produced upon them and their friends among the people, a profound impression of grief and anger; his corpse was watched, wept, and prayed over; and two days after, a procession as solemn as it was popular, conveyed it to the new churchyard in Westminster. A hundred horsemen, five or six abreast, went before the corpse; "the coffin was then brought, with six trumpets sounding a soldier's knell; then the trooper's horse came, clothed all over in mourning, and led by a footman. The corpse was adorned with bundles of rosemary, one half stained in blood; and the sword of the deceased along with them. Some thousands followed in rank and file; all had sea-green and black ribbon tied on their hats, and to their breasts; and the women brought up the rear." At the churchyard, a vast multitude of the better class of citizens, who had not thought fit to march through the city, awaited the arrival of the procession. It was the general opinion that such a funeral was a great affront to the leaders of the Parliament and army.[1]

Six days after this, news reached London, that insurrections had broken out at Banbury and Salisbury, in the regiments of Colonels Reynolds, Scroop, and Ireton; the soldiers had driven away their officers, with the exception of a few who had sided with them: and one of these, Captain Thompson, had published, under the title of "England's Standard Advanced," a manifesto demanding the abolition of the Council of State and of the High Court of Justice, the election of a new Parliament, the adoption of Lilburne's plan of government, and the immediate liberation of Lilburne and his fellow-prisoners; and declaring that "if a hair of their heads should perish, they will, God enabling them, avenge it seventy times seven fold upon the tyrants." Simultaneously with this news, information was received that, at Oxford and Gloucester, in the regiments of Colonels Harrison, Ingoldsby, and Horton, the excitement was extreme; and that most of the soldiers in those corps were already in correspondence with the insurgents, and were quite disposed to march and join them.[2]

It redounds greatly to the credit of the republican leaders, both parliamentary and military, that, at this critical moment, they exaggerated neither the evil nor the danger, but met it with prompt and firm, though moderate measures. They proceeded without fear or irritation, with faith in their right

[1] Whitelocke's Memorials, pp. 397—399; Clement Walker's History of Independency, part ii. pp. 161—164; Cromwelliana, pp. 55, 56; Carlyle's Letters and Speeches of Cromwell, vol. ii. pp. 31, 32.

[2] Clement Walker's History of Independency, part ii. pp. 168—173; Godwin's History of the Commonwealth, vol. iii. p. 71.

and in their power, acting as a government against rebels, and not as a faction against rivals. The Parliament voted that every attempt to overthrow, by action or writing, the established government of the Commonwealth, the authority of the House of Commons, or of the Council of State, or to excite any sedition in the army, should be considered an act of high treason; it enjoined its committee to terminate without delay the law against abuses of the liberty of the press; it took measures for strengthening the internal police of the city of London; and it ordained that Lilburne and his companions in the Tower should be separated from one another, and that all visits, all communications from without, should be forbidden them. This done, it remained calm, and left the generals to act as they thought best.[1]

Fairfax and Cromwell, on their part, were anxious first of all to make sure of the troops which they had with them, for the mutiny had spread in every direction; they accordingly reviewed, in Hyde Park, the two regiments which they commanded in person, and which bore their names. Cromwell spoke a good deal, sometimes to the troops generally, and sometimes to individual soldiers. What could they do better, he said, than adhere faithfully to the Parliament? It had punished delinquents; it had got a good navy afloat which would effectually protect commerce; it had guaranteed the exact payment of all that remained due to the army; it had passed resolutions for bringing its own session to a speedy termination, and for the assembling of future Parliaments; and as to martial law, whoever could not stand it was not fit to be a soldier, and his best plan would be to lay down his arms; he should have his ticket and get his arrears, just as those would who remained faithful to their standard. One trooper only made some objections, in a

[1] Commons' Journals, vol. vi. pp. 205, 207—209; Whitelocke's Memorials, p. 401; Old Parliamentary History, vol. xix. p. 122.

very unbecoming tone. Cromwell had him arrested; but immediately after, at the request of his comrades, who answered for his future good behavior, he pardoned him, and allowed him to resume his place in the ranks. Some of the men wore the sea-green badges of the Levellers, but they tore them from their hats. Both regiments manifested the utmost ardor; and, when the review was over, the two generals, full of confidence, set their troops at once in movement.[1]

Five days after, having marched nearly fifty miles in one single day, they came up, at Burford in Oxfordshire, with the insurgents, who were already somewhat dispirited by a check which they had received at Banbury, where Captain Thompson had begun the insurrection. Surprised and defeated by the vigorous attack of his colonel, Thompson's troop had been dispersed, and he himself had found safety in flight; a messenger, sent to the insurgents by Fairfax, had moreover lulled them into false security, and they imagined that negotiations would be opened with them. Cromwell entered Burford suddenly, in the middle of the night, with two thousand men, whilst Reynolds posted himself with a strong party at the other extremity of the town, to cut off the retreat of the rebels. They defended themselves for a few moments, "firing some shots out of windows;" but soon losing all hope, destitute of leaders, and scantily supplied with ammunition, about four hundred of them surrendered, and the others succeeded in making their escape. Fairfax immediately assembled a court-martial, which decided that the mutineers should be decimated. On the following day, in Burford churchyard, Cornet Thompson, brother to the chief leader of the insurrection, was brought out and shot first. All those who were to suffer the same punishment were on the leads of the church, witnessing the execution of

[1] Cromwelliana, p. 56; Cromwell's Letters and Speeches, vol. ii. pp. 32, 33.

their comrades, and awaiting their own turn. After Cornet Thompson came a corporal, and then a third, who all died with indomitable firmness, expressing sorrow for nothing they had done, and themselves giving the signal to fire. Cornet Dean was the fourth to be shot, a brave old soldier, whom the General knew well; he expressed penitence; Fairfax pardoned him, and no others were shot. Cromwell went into the church, called down the rest of the condemned mutineers, rebuked and admonished them, and reproached them for having so wickedly imperilled the good cause—the cause of God and of the country. "They wept," says a newspaper of the period; "they retired to Devizes for a time, were then restored to their regiments, and marched cheerfully for Ireland."[1]

Some bands were still roving about in Oxfordshire and Northamptonshire: Captain Thompson rallied them, and kept them together for a few days; but being vigorously attacked by Colonel Butler, he was soon left alone, and fled to a wood. Butler's soldiers pursued him thither; Thompson issued from his retreat, fell upon his assailants, killed or wounded three of them, was wounded himself, fell back again into the wood, and again desperately charged his pursuers, declaring he would never yield alive: whereupon, "a corporal, with seven bullets in his carbine," shot him dead.[2] With him ended the first and only serious insurrection of the Levellers.

At this success, the Parliament manifested an excess of joy which, for the first time, revealed its fears. The Speaker received orders to address the formal thanks of the House to Fairfax, Cromwell, and all their officers. Cromwell alone was present when the vote was passed, and to him the Speaker

[1] Cromwelliana, pp. 56, 57; Cromwell's Letters and Speeches, vol. ii. pp. 33—35; Whitelocke, p. 402; Heath's Brief Chronicle, pp. 431, 432.

[2] Whitelocke's Memorials, p. 403.

addressed himself. Three members were appointed to pay the same compliment to Fairfax. A day was named for a solemn general thanksgiving; two celebrated preachers among the Independents, John Owen and Thomas Goodwin, were requested to prepare sermons for the occasion; and when the day arrived, after having attended the religious services, the whole House went into the city, to a public dinner of congratulation, to which the Lord Mayor and Common Council had invited them. All the officers then in London, above the rank of lieutenant, were present at this dinner. When the members arrived at Grocers' Hall, the Lord Mayor presented to the Speaker, who immediately returned it to him, the sword which was borne before him—an honor which had never been paid to any but the King; and at the banquet, the Speaker occupied the royal seat. Just as the guests were about to sit down, the Earl of Pembroke, then simply a member of the House of Commons, but who, in reward for his baseness, and out of respect for his former dignity, had been placed next to the Lord General, called to Whitelocke to take that seat as senior Commissioner of the Great Seal. Whitelocke declined the honor. "What!" said the Earl, in a loud voice, so as to be heard by all the guests, "do you think that I will sit down before you? I have given place heretofore to Bishop Williams, to my Lord Coventry, and my Lord Littleton; and you have the same place that they had; and as much honor belongs to the place under a commonwealth as under a king; and you are a gentleman as well born and bred as any of them; therefore I will not sit down before you." Whitelocke yielded, with humble but satisfied vanity; and Lord Pembroke received the praises, and with them the contempt, of all the assembly.[1]

[1] Whitelocke, p. 406; Cromwelliana, p. 59; Letter of M. de Croullé to Cardinal Mazarin, (June 21, 1649,) in the Archives des Affaires Etrangères de France. See Appendix I.

At the conclusion of the banquet, the Lord Mayor, on the part of the city, presented to Fairfax a basin and ewer of beaten gold, worth one thousand pounds, and to Cromwell plate worth five hundred pounds; and the House, delighted at this flattering reception in a place where they had recently found it so difficult to obtain the proclamation of the Commonwealth, returned official thanks to the Lord Mayor, and appointed a special committee "to consider of some mark of favor and respect" whereby the Parliament might express its satisfaction with the city. Five weeks after, the House passed an act for settling the new park of Richmond on the Mayor and commonalty, and citizens of London, and their successors forever;[1] thus offering the spoils of the King for the pleasures of the city.

The leaders, however, fell into no illusion with regard to the dangers which still threatened them; they were too close observers of the people and the army to believe that the hopes they had just crushed were really extinct; they had been firm and calm during the struggle; they were prudent and moderate after the victory. They made it their endeavor to satisfy the legitimate or popular demands of the malcontents, or, at least, to awaken hopes that those demands would eventually be complied with. Measures were taken to secure the regular payment of the troops, to save the people from any abuse of military billets, to assist wounded soldiers and their families, to procure some relief for prisoners for debt, and to supply the poor of London with work.[2] Committees were appointed to report on the best means for improving the debased coinage, and for rendering the civil procedure of the law courts more expeditious and less onerous.[3] A general am-

[1] Whitelocke, pp. 406, 411; Leicester's Journal, p. 73; Commons' Journals, vol. vi. pp. 227, 263.

[2] Commons' Journals, vol. vi. pp. 155, 202, 208.

[3] Ibid. pp. 154, 211, 224, 240, 244.

nesty was also proposed;[1] and the question of the term and system to be adopted for the election of a new Parliament was frequently brought forward.[2] Laws were passed, on the one hand, for abolishing the constraints anciently imposed on the faith and worship of various denominations of Christians, and on the other hand, for repressing licentiousness of manners; for the opposition demanded at once more liberty and greater severity.[3] Nor were they content with general measures and legislative promises; they were anxious to show kindly dispositions towards the men who were most deeply compromised. Several leading men in the Parliament and army had conferences with the principal Levellers, with a view to endeavor to come to some agreement with them as to the reforms to be accomplished, and the means to be adopted for carrying on the government.[4] This spirit of conciliation extended as far even as to Lilburne himself. By placing him and his companions in solitary confinement, they had been deprived of the liberty of conversation generally allowed to prisoners; this was now restored to them.[5] One of the confidants of the dominant party, and even of Cromwell himself, the Rev. Hugh Peters, went, apparently of his own accord, and from a pure feeling of affectionate interest, to visit Lilburne in the Tower, to endeavor to mollify him by suggesting to him prospects of accommodation and liberty. The prosecution which had been commenced against him was postponed; his eldest son fell ill, paternal anxiety triumphed over political stubbornness, and Lilburne wrote to Henry Martyn, who had continued to regard him with friendly feelings, to request permission to leave the Tower

1 Ibid. p. 195; Whitelocke, p. 398.
2 Commons' Journal, vol. vi. pp. 199, 207, 210.
3 Commons' Journals, vol. vi. pp. 245, 295, 359, 410, 474.
4 Whitelocke's Memorials, p. 424.
5 Commons' Journals, vol. vi. pp. 208, 210.

and visit his wife and children. Permission was granted him, and this indulgence was afterwards almost habitually extended both to himself and to his companions.[1] The republican Parliament really felt a strong desire to make a sincere peace with the democratic and fanatical opposition which it had vanquished, and to induce them to return into the ranks of the party which, with all its forces united, was scarcely strong enough to maintain itself and govern the country, even by violence.

But there is nothing more indomitable than a narrow, subtle, and vain mind, joined to a brave and honest heart. Lilburne would, perhaps, though detesting them, have treated with enemies whom he believed as sincere in their convictions as himself; but he despised his conquerors as ambitious, interested, and abandoned hypocrites. Even their favors were, in his eyes, only concessions of their weakness, or artifices of their perfidy. He treated Hugh Peters, when he paid him a visit in the Tower, with coarse bluntness, and repelled his insinuations as assaults or snares. Peters reproached him with having, by his attacks, caused the misfortunes of the late rebellion, and laid bare the wounds of the Commonwealth. "If the sun shining upon the dunghill," answered Lilburne, "make it stink, whether is the fault in the sun or the dunghill?"[2] And in the space of three months, four new pamphlets bore witness to his indefatigable hostility. One of these pamphlets, addressed "to his honored friend, Cornelius Holland, Councillor of State," was a public challenge to political discussion. "Let your House," wrote Lilburne, "choose two men, I will choose two more, and they shall have power finally to decide the business betwixt us; and I will be content they shall appoint

[1] Commons' Journals, vol. vi. pp. 264, 292.

[2] A Discourse betwixt Lieut.-Colonel John Lilburne, close prisoner in the Tower of London, and Mr. Hugh Peters, upon May 25, 1649, p. 3.

Cromwell, Ireton, Bradshaw, and all the orators or pleaders they had against the King and the beheaded lords, or as many of them as they please, to plead against me, and I will have none but myself, singly, to plead my own cause against them all, provided the debate may be public, and that I may have free liberty to speak for myself; and if I cannot maintain mine own innocency and integrity, I will lose and forfeit all I have, yea, and my life to boot: but if you return me not an effectual answer to my present proposition within the next five days, I shall hold myself at liberty to do the best I can for my own preservation, by anatomizing what I know, either privately or publicly, of you or the rest of your associates."[1] And in two pamphlets, in fact, one directed by name against Cromwell and Ireton,[2] and the other containing a seditious provocation, addressed by ten city apprentices to the soldiers of the army in general, and of Fairfax's regiment in particular,[3] Lilburne took ample advantage of the right which he had thus reserved to himself.

These provocations were not altogether ineffectual. A new sedition broke out at Oxford, in Colonel Ingoldsby's regiment: the soldiers arrested and imprisoned their officers, including their colonel himself, who had been sent down in all haste by the Parliament to repress the mutiny. They chose a council of agitators from their own ranks, fortified themselves in the buildings of New College, and from that stronghold renewed all the demands of the Levellers. They expected, they said, a reinforcement of six thousand men from Northamptonshire, and as many more from the western counties, and from Kent; and, indeed, in many places, and

[1] John Lilburne to his honored friend Mr. Cornelius Holland, p. 5.

[2] An Impeachment of High Treason against Oliver Cromwell and Henry Ireton, by John Lilburne. London, August 10, 1649.

[3] An Outcry of the Young Men and Apprentices of London, August 29, 1649.

among several regiments, their example had its effect. Cornet Dean, whom Fairfax had recently pardoned in Burford churchyard, reappeared at the head of a band. But the ill success of the first insurrection, and the clement firmness of the generals, had left a profound impression, both on the army and the people, the movement succeeded neither in gaining ground nor in prolonging its existence. The officers who had been imprisoned at Oxford, quietly resumed their authority, first over the very sentinels who were guarding them, and next over the soldiers who were scattered through the streets. Ere long the entire regiment made submission to its colonel, and ten days after it had first broken out, the rebellion was entirely quelled.[1]

But a new and most important fact then became known for the first time. When Hugh Peters paid Lilburne a visit in the Tower: "Tell your masters, from me," said the prisoner to him, "that if it were possible for me now to choose, I had rather choose to live seven years under old King Charles's government, (notwithstanding their beheading him as a tyrant for it,) than live one year under the present government that now rule; nay, let me tell you, if they go on with that tyranny they are in, they will make Prince Charles have friends enough, not only to cry him up, but also really to fight for him, and to bring him into his father's throne."[2] Two months after, in his "Outcry of the Apprentices to the Soldiers," Lilburne reminded the army that "the apprentices ran in to their assistance, to uphold and maintain the fundamental constitution of this Commonwealth, viz., the interest and right of the people in their Parliaments, not engaging in the least against the person of the King, as king, or with any thoughts or pretence of destroying, but

[1] Commons' Journals, vol. vi. p. 293; Whitelocke's Memorials, pp. 424, 428.

[2] A Discourse between John Lilburne and Hugh Peters, p. 8.

regulating, kingship."[1] These sentiments, and this language had borne their fruit: the Levellers had entered into communication with the Cavaliers; and at the very moment when the Oxford mutiny broke out, a letter was intercepted from a Cavalier prisoner in the Tower, to Lord Cottington, one of the intimate advisers of Charles II., in France, which ran thus:—

"All our hopes depend on his Majesty's seeming compliance with Lilburne and the Levelling party, whose discontents increase daily. As touching the state of affairs here, his Majesty's friends have no possibility of embodying, unless the Levellers lead the way, which will be, I hope, suddenly put in execution. To that purpose, I desire some assistance may be given me, for without supplies of money, little can be expected, those I converse withal being either extremely needy or covetous."[2]

The Parliament could not fail to turn such facts to its advantage; and it used them as its principal argument in a long declaration, which it published against the Levellers, to justify the more rigorous measures which it proposed to adopt against them, and to strengthen the allegiance of its own partisans.[3] Accordingly, combining action with words, it ordained that Lilburne's trial should at once be proceeded with; and appointed an extraordinary commission of forty members to preside over the sentence, though the right of pronouncing upon the facts charged against the prisoner was left to the jury.[4]

The relatives and friends of Lilburne—his wife, who loved him tenderly, and shared his courage; and his brother, Colonel Robert Lilburne, an officer greatly respected by both

[1] The Outcry of the Young Men of London, p. 4.

[2] Old Parliamentary History, vol. xix. p. 193. [3] Ibid. pp. 177—200.

[4] Commons' Journals, vol. vi. p. 293.

the generals and the army—made every effort to save him from this trial. He even manifested some desire to avoid it himself, and offered to emigrate to the West Indies; but he published at the same time a pamphlet, to explain the motives of his departure, and keenly to debate the conditions on which he would consent to leave his native land.[1] No answer was returned to his proposition. Yielding to the entreaties of his wife, he then consented to request a delay. But to this application also he received no reply; the republican government had resolved to make a last effort against this insupportable enemy, and thought they were now sure to rid themselves of him.

The trial began at Guildhall, on the 24th of October, 1649. Lilburne displayed all the resources of his mind, and all the vigorous energy of his character, in making head against the learned and subtle magistrates who were his judges—some of them servile adherents of the government, and anxious to trammel his defence; the others honest and upright men, desirous to protect the prisoner in his just rights, but piqued and irritated at every instant by his abrupt sallies, and by the bitterness of his sarcasms or the violence of his invectives against the power whose representatives they were. The trial had lasted two days, and was approaching its termination, when Lilburne, turning suddenly towards the jury, thus addressed them:—

"Gentlemen of the Jury—You are my sole judges, the keepers of my life, at whose hands the Lord will require my blood. And therefore I desire you to know your power, and consider your duty, both to God, to me, to your own selves, and to your country; and the gracious assisting spirit and presence of the Lord God Omnipotent, the governor of heaven and earth, and all things therein contained, go along with

[1] This pamphlet is entitled "The Innocent Man's Second Proffer."

you, give counsel and direct you to do that which is just, and for His glory!"

"Amen! amen!" cried all the spectators with one voice. The judges looked at each other with some uneasiness, and requested Major-General Skippon to send for three more companies of foot-soldiers. The Attorney-General Prideaux, and the Lord Chief Justice Keble, who presided in the court, renewed their endeavors to convince the jury that both justice and necessity required the condemnation of the prisoner. After they had deliberated three quarters of an hour, the clerk of the court addressed the jury:—

"Gentlemen of the jury, are you agreed of your verdict?"

"Yes."

"Look upon the prisoner; is he guilty of the treasons charged upon him, or any of them, or not guilty?"

"Not guilty of all of them."

"Nor of all the treasons, or any of them that are laid to his charge?"

"Not of all, nor of any one of them."

At these words Guildhall resounded "with such a loud and unanimous shout as is believed was never heard before." It lasted for half an hour, during which the judges remained motionless on their seats, exposed to this wild outburst of popular satisfaction. The prisoner stood calmly at the bar, and it was observed that he appeared rather less haughty and animated than before. When the tumult had in some degree subsided, the clerk resumed:—

"Gentlemen of the jury, hearken to your verdict; the Court has heard it. You say that John Lilburne is not guilty of all the treasons laid unto his charge, nor of any one of them; and so you say all?"

"Yes, we do so."[1]

[1] State Trials, vol. iv. cols. 1270—1470.

Lilburne was taken back to the Tower, followed by the acclamations of the multitude; and during the whole of the night, bonfires were lighted in the streets. The government made an attempt to detain him still in prison; but in about a fortnight the discontent of the people, and the efforts of some prudent or friendly members of the House of Commons—among others, of Ludlow and Henry Martyn—obtained his liberation.

The Parliament was greatly irritated by this defeat, which was far more offensive to its self-love than dangerous to its power; for though Lilburne escaped from its hands, it retained its victory over the Levellers, who thenceforward gave up all attempts to rouse the country and army to rebellion, and remained satisfied with conspiring in secret. But this very victory was a futile one; the republican government derived no increase of strength from its triumph; its enemies, the King, the Cavaliers, and the anarchists, all fell beneath its blows, and yet it found itself compelled to continue, and even to aggravate, the severity of its proceedings towards them. To the ancient statutes regarding treason, it added new clauses of a more menacing character, for they provided that words should be considered equivalent to overt acts, and punished capitally.[1] Though the office of licenser of the press was abolished, a law was passed enacting the most tyrannical prohibitions and inquisitions in reference to obnoxious publications; not only did it impose very heavy penalties on the authors, printers, vendors, and distributors of seditious writings, but even the purchasers were bound, within twenty-four hours, to surrender their purchase to the nearest magistrate. It forbade all printing, except in the four cities of London, Oxford, Cambridge, and York. The publication of journals or collections of news, and the trade in books, both at home

[1] This bill was proposed on the 1st, and adopted on the 14th of May, 1649. Commons' Journals, vol. vi. pp. 199, 209.

and abroad, were placed entirely under the control of the government. All hawkers and public singers were suppressed, and whenever any one was found exercising either of these callings, he was seized, and taken to a house of correction to be whipped as a common rogue; and a fine was inflicted on every magistrate who neglected to fulfil this provision of the law.[1] The publication of the proceedings and debates before the High Courts of justice was stringently prohibited. In contravention of the laws and traditions of the country, the House of Commons, in several instances, constituted itself a court of justice, and condemned offenders, whom it could not hope to reach in any other way, to severe penalties, to exile, to heavy fines, and even to the pillory.[2] It enacted that no Cavaliers, Catholics, military adventurers, or other suspected persons, should be allowed to reside in London. When it found itself unable to bring any legal action against enemies of whom it stood in dread, it detained them arbitrarily in prison. At the moment when Lilburne, acquitted by the jury, took his departure from the Tower, a Presbyterian royalist, named Clement Walker, who had been expelled from Parliament in 1648 with the rest of his party, published his "Anarchia Anglicana," a passionate and partial history, but full of important facts and curious anecdotes relative to the republican party and its leaders. Walker took Lilburne's place in the Tower, and remained there untried until his death, which took place in 1651.[3] During that year, the Council of State transferred to different towns five of the most distinguished among the old Presbyterian leaders—Sir William Waller, Sir William Lewis, Sir John Clotworthy, Major-General

[1] This bill was proposed on the 9th of August, and adopted on the 20th of September, 1649. Commons' Journals, vol. vi. pp. 276, 298.

[2] Commons' Journals, vol. vi. pp. 354—356, 591; vol. vii. pp. 71—73, 75, 78, 79; Whitelocke, p. 340.

[3] Godwin's History of the Commonwealth, vol. iii. p. 347.

Browne, and Commissary-General Copley; and this order reveals the fact, that they had been confined in Windsor Castle ever since the establishment of the Commonwealth.[1]

All these severities did not succeed in inspiring the country, or even the republicans themselves, with faith in the strength and security of the Commonwealth. They were in full possession of power; they had deprived of all political activity both the high aristocracy and the radical democracy of their time—both the Royalists and the Levellers. Their internal anxieties already tormented them far more than all their enemies could have done. Conquerors and masters, they beheld arising in their midst a conqueror and a master with whom they knew not how to dispense, and against whom they were incapable of defending themselves. The new-born Commonwealth already felt that Cromwell dominated over it; at every crisis of peril or alarm it had recourse to him, and when the crisis was passed, it grew terrified at the credit and renown which he had acquired by saving it; and Cromwell, on his side, whilst lavish in his demonstrations of the most humble devotedness to the Commonwealth, gave continual expression to the aspirations of his ambition and his pride. Henry Martyn, who lived on terms of great familiarity with him, ventured one day, in the House, obstinately to thwart him in some of his wishes in regard to the army. Cromwell drew his dagger abruptly, and clapping it on the seat by him, expressed great anger against "Harry and his levelling crew." On another occasion, in a more gay and friendly mood, he called Martyn "Sir Harry;" upon which the republican arose, and bowing profoundly, said: "I humbly thank your Majesty! I always thought when you were king that I should be knighted."[2]

1 Ibid. p. 250; Order Book of Council, March 11, 1651.

2 Forster's Statesmen of the Commonwealth, vol. iii. p. 328; Mercurius Pragmaticus, Feb. 27 to March 5; Cromwelliana, p. 53.

The first year of the Commonwealth had not reached its term, and yet already pamphlets were seized at Coventry, entitled, "The character of King Cromwell;"[1] and on the 14th of June, 1651, M. de Croullé wrote to Cardinal Mazarin: "According to the belief of many persons, Cromwell is carrying his ideas beyond what would be warranted by the most reckless ambition."[2] The republican leaders met with no resistance in the government; but they stood alone, forced continually to extend the limits of their power, in the midst of irreconcilable enemies, whilst Cromwell grew in greatness beside them, to work their ruin by acting as their servant.

A desolating scourge, civil war, occurred to defer the outburst of these elements of discord, and to restore for a time to the Commonwealth that feverish unity and energy which were the sole conditions of its existence.

[1] Whitelocke's Memorials, p. 434.

[2] Archives des Affaires Etrangères de France.

BOOK II.

STATE OF PARTIES IN SCOTLAND AND IRELAND—CHARLES II. IS PROCLAIMED KING—SCOTTISH COMMISSIONERS AT THE HAGUE—WAR IN IRELAND—CROMWELL ASSUMES THE COMMAND—HIS CRUELTY AND SUCCESSES—MONTROSE'S EXPEDITION IN SCOTLAND—HIS DEFEAT, ARREST, CONDEMNATION, AND EXECUTION—CHARLES II. LANDS IN SCOTLAND—CROMWELL RETURNS FROM IRELAND, AND TAKES THE COMMAND OF THE WAR IN SCOTLAND—HIS DANGEROUS POSITION—BATTLE OF DUNBAR—CHARLES II. ENTERS ENGLAND—CROMWELL FOLLOWS HIM—BATTLE OF WORCESTER—FLIGHT AND ADVENTURES OF CHARLES II.—HE RETURNS TO FRANCE—CROMWELL RETURNS TO LONDON—TRIUMPHANT SUCCESS OF THE COMMONWEALTH.

Of the three kingdoms which had owned the sway of Charles I., England was the only one which contained a republican party sufficiently strong to obtain a temporary victory, and sufficiently bold to attempt to govern its conquest. From very different causes, Scotland and Ireland both remained thoroughly royalist, but with dispositions and under conditions which rendered them incapable of efficiently supporting the King, with whom they neither could nor would dispense. In neither of these two kingdoms, the royalists properly so called, were dominant: in Scotland the Presbyterians were the masters, and in Ireland the Catholics;—masters unequally tyrannical on account of the diversity of their positions, but equally malignant and blind, equally led by their religious passions to overstep their political designs, and unable either to estimate the rights and power of their adversaries, or to measure their own pretensions by their own real strength. Both were divided: in Scotland the violent Presbyterians predominated both in the Parliament and in the Church; but they had to contend with an opposition consisting of the moderate Presbyterians, who, in 1648, had made war against the English Parliament on behalf of Charles I., and who still reckoned numerous adherents, both among the aristocracy and in the army. In Ireland, a large portion of the Catholic aristocracy, from loyalty or from prudence, frankly supported, in concert with the majority of the Irish Protestants, the cause of the Protestant king; but they were trammelled, at every step, by the passions, suspicions, and exactions, as natural as they were ill-advised, of the Catholic population who marched beneath their banners. And in both kingdoms, around the dominant party thus internally disunited, other parties were in agitation, attached to contrary principles, inferior in numbers and influence, but active, brave, and persevering. In Scotland, on the one hand, were the pure royalists, who were so either from adherence to the Anglican faith, or from devotion to the principle of monarchy; and on the other, the independent sectaries, who were in communication with the English republicans and their Parliament. In Ireland, on the one hand, were the intractable Catholics, who were hostile to every Protestant government, whether monarchical or republican, and who opposed them both by turns, as their own temporary interest suggested; on the other, a small number of Protestant and republican English who had settled in Ireland, and a rather large number of timid Irish Catholics, who ranged themselves under the banner of the Parliament, because they believed in its strength, and for the sole purpose of delivering themselves from the perils of a conflict which could not possibly result in any victory to their own most cherished cause.

The rivalries of their leaders aggravated the dissensions of these parties. In Scotland, at the head of the fanatical

Presbyterians, stood the Marquis of Argyle, a prudent, persevering, and crafty man, fond of power and fearful of danger, a royalist more from tradition than from taste, more faithful to his dependents than to his masters, chiefly anxious to maintain his influence and secure his personal safety, and skilful in gaining for himself, in the party to which he was opposed, allies against his rivals. The execution of the Duke of Hamilton in London, had deprived the moderate Presbyterians of their old leader, who was ill replaced by his brother, Lord Lanark, who inherited his title and not his credit, and by Lord Lauderdale, a servile courtier with an independent mind, passionately malignant although profoundly indifferent, and thoroughly corrupt, notwithstanding his fanaticism. Montrose seemed born to charm and to command the pure royalists, as he was by far the most brilliant, the most alluring, the boldest, the most devoted, and the most presumptuous of them all. And from the ranks of the Edinburgh bar sprang up, for the small party of Scottish republican sectaries, a leader whom the English Parliament might have envied them;—Archibald Johnstone, Lord Warristoun, ardent, inventive, prompt, indefatigable, learned, and eloquent, with all the subtlety of a knave, and all the sincerity of a martyr. Ireland numbered among her leaders fewer men of eminence, whose names have survived the age in which they lived. More respected than he was feared or followed, the Marquis of Ormonde, Viceroy of Ireland for Charles II., as he had been for Charles I., presided over the efforts and discords of the royalist party in that country, with inexhaustible though often ineffective devotedness; and among the independent Irish who attached themselves exclusively to neither Parliament nor King, Owen Roe O'Neil is the only one who, by his successful audacity and his continual defections, has obtained any name in history. But a host of secondary leaders, important then though unknown now, were at work either among the people, or near the Viceroy, ardently pursuing, sometimes against their enemies, and sometimes against their rivals, their own advancement, or the deliverance of their faith and fatherland.

After the death of Charles I., the royalist feeling triumphed, at the outset, over these diversities and discords. At Edinburgh, on the 5th of February, and in Ireland, wherever Ormonde was the master, Charles II. was proclaimed king. The Parliament of Scotland had a new grievance against the English Parliament: the Commissioners who had been sent by it to London, first to advise, and then to protest, against the judgment of Charles I., had been brutally arrested at the moment when they were preparing to return to their country,[1] and conducted under escort to the Scottish frontier, in order to prevent any publication or communication with the people on their parts.[2] The conscience and the self-respect of the Scots were alike offended. Their Parliament decided that Commissioners should immediately be sent to the new King to invite him to return among them. Ormonde urged him at the same time to come to Ireland, where he would find three-fourths of the nation devoted to his cause; and the most formidable of the Irish chieftains, Owen Roe O'Neil himself, who had refused to treat with Ormonde, conveyed to Charles, by a private messenger, the strongest assurances of his fidelity.[3]

All these envoys arrived almost simultaneously at the Hague, where Charles was residing, under the protection of the Stadtholder, the Prince of Orange, his brother-in-law, and

[1] Commons' Journals, vol. vi. p. 452; Whitelocke, pp. 384, 385, 388.

[2] Parliamentary History, vol. xix. pp. 16—36, 40—48; Commons' Journals, vol. vi. pp. 131—135, 145.

[3] Whitelocke, pp. 381—383, 389, 392; Laing's History of Scotland, vol. iii. p. 436, Clarendon's History of the Rebellion, vol. vi. pp. 269—272, 282—283, 304—306: Carte's Ormonde Letters, vol. i. pp. 213, 231.

treated with considerate though reserved respect by the States-General of Holland. He was there surrounded by his wisest counsellors, those men whose advice the King his father, with the experience of misfortune, had expressly recommended him to follow—Lord Cottington, Sir John Colepepper, and particularly Sir Edward Hyde, the last passionately attached to monarchy and the Anglican Church, but a serious and able man, who remained faithful in exile, as on his native soil, to the religion, the laws, and the manners of his country. They had strongly urged Charles neither to establish himself in France, where they regarded the policy of Mazarin with great suspicion, nor to join his mother, the Queen-dowager, who resided partly at St. Germains, and partly at Paris, still little loved by the true English whom she loved little, and surrounded by Catholic priests and those frivolous and reckless courtiers, who, under the late King, had exercised, sometimes on the King's conduct, and always on the royal cause, so fatal an influence.

The perplexity of Charles was great: the Commissioners of the Parliament and Kirk of Scotland offered him very rigorous conditions: they required that he should separate from all his old friends, and especially from Montrose (who was detested by all the Presbyterians), that he should proceed almost alone to Scotland, that he should place himself entirely in the hands of the dominant party, that he should sign their Covenant of 1638, and, in short, that he should become, whether sincerely or hypocritically, a Presbyterian with them and like them. Although opposed to the fanatical Presbyterians, and while deploring their exactions, the moderate men, Lord Hamilton and Lord Lauderdale, advised Charles to resign himself to these conditions; and they insisted as strongly as any that he should absolutely give up Montrose, refusing to have any communication with him themselves, and insolently leaving the King's cabinet when he entered it.

Montrose, in his turn, exhorted Charles to repel all these pretensions, which would reduce him to servitude under the pretext of restoring him to his throne, and to rely, for his restoration to his kingdom, only on the sword; offering to be the first to draw it, and to lead the van, in order to open the way for him. Charles found the advice of Montrose the most to his taste, though he did not altogether believe in its soundness; but the Prince of Orange, backed by the letters of the Queen-mother, and by the general opinion of Holland, strongly urged him not to adopt it, but on the contrary to accept the propositions of the Scottish Commissioners—being unable to conceive that he should persist in refusing a kingdom which thus sought his acceptance, for the sake of supporting the Anglican Church and the bishops, who had already cost the King his father his crown and his life.[1]

It was suggested to Charles, who as yet had neither said nor done anything since the death of his father, that, on proceeding to Scotland, he should address a declaration to the English people, to explain to them his views and feelings, to revive the courage of his adherents, and to prevent any false interpretations to which his conduct might give rise. Hyde, who, in the council, had strongly opposed this step, was appointed to draw up the manifesto; but when he submitted the draft to his colleagues, notwithstanding the extreme pains he had taken to weigh every word of it, so many discordant objections were raised against it, and the impossibility of giving verbal satisfaction to the royalists of England without alienating those of Scotland and Ireland became so evident that, by common consent, it was resolved to persevere in that silence which had at first been maintained by instinct.[2]

[1] Carte's Ormonde Letters, vol. i. p. 238; Clarendon's History of the Rebellion, vol. vi. p. 306.

[2] Clarendon's History of the Rebellion, vol. vi. pp. 318—323.

Difficulties soon wearied Charles: the prospect of the unpleasantnesses and compromising falsehoods which awaited him in Scotland was regarded by him with repugnance; he started objections to the Scottish Commissioners, and gave them an evasive answer, which was equivalent, for the moment, to a refusal. At the same time he gave Montrose a secret commission, with the title of Lieutenant-Governor and Commander-in-chief of all the royal forces in Scotland, authorizing him to levy men and money in Europe, wheresoever he could obtain them, and to attempt a royalist expedition in his own country, at all risks. Then, announcing his resolution to proceed to Ireland, where nothing was required of him but his presence, Charles actually embarked and sent off, in two small ships, a portion of his suite and baggage: but alleging the propriety, before leaving the Continent, of going to France to pay a farewell visit to the Queen his mother, he indefinitely postponed his own departure.[1]

In reality, and although, as far as the number and loyalty of his partisans were concerned, his chief hope was in Ireland, he was by no means eager to repair thither, and thus to show himself to the Protestants of England and Scotland, surrounded by a Catholic people and army as his primary supporters. But precisely for these reasons, Ireland, immediately after the death of the King, became the object of serious attention and vigorous action on the part of the republican Parliament. In that country most of all, it expected to witness the outbreak of a royalist war, and there also it preferred to meet it. War against Ireland had always excited passionate enthusiasm in England, in almost all parties. This hostility of race, religion, and politics had been used against Charles I. with unfailing success; and from it

[1] Carte's Ormonde Letters, vol. i. pp. 263, 345; Clarendon's History of the Rebellion, vol. vi. pp. 285, 306—309; Wishart's Memoirs of Montrose, pp. 338—360.

the republicans hoped to derive the same advantages against his son. As soon as it became known in London that he had been proclaimed king in Ireland, and that Ormonde rallied almost the whole nation beneath his standard, it was resolved that he should be attacked there. At the same time that they abolished kingship and suppressed the House of Lords, the Commons voted 120,000*l.* a month for the support of an army of forty-four thousand men, a large portion of whom were to be employed in Ireland; and the Council of State received orders to confer with the General-in-chief and his principal officers "concerning the modelling of the forces that were to go into Ireland."[1]

Five days after, Scott stated to the House, in the united names of the Council of State and the Council of War, that the first measure to be taken for organizing the army and modelling the war in Ireland, was the appointment of a general to command the forces in that country. The House referred this appointment to the Council of State. It was thought that Lambert would be nominated, and most of Cromwell's friends had seemed to indicate him as the proper person to be selected. But some, with greater clearsightedness or quicker comprehension, unexpectedly proposed Cromwell himself, who was not present at the meeting. Being immediately informed of this, he appeared surprised and irresolute, and requested the Council of the army to name two officers of each regiment to join with him in a religious meeting for the purpose of invoking the Divine guidance in so important a matter. The result of this meeting was that he accepted the command, and the House confirmed his appointment. He signified his acceptance with great diffidence, and many expressions of "his own unworthiness, and disa-

[1] Commons' Journals, vol. vi. pp. 157, 159, 163, 170, 172, 182, 186, 188, 208; Whitelocke, pp. 385, 386, 391, 392.

bility to support so great a charge, and of the entire resignation of himself to their commands, and absolute dependence upon God's providence and blessing, from whom he had received many instances of His favor;" and he desired the House "that no more time might be lost in the preparations which were to be made for so great a work: for he did confess that kingdom to be reduced to so great straits, that he was willing to engage his own person in this expedition, for the difficulties which appeared in it; and more out of hope, with the hazard of his life, to give some obstruction to the successor which the rebels (for so he called the Marquis of Ormonde and the Irish royalists) were at present exalted with, that so the Commonwealth might still retain some footing in that kingdom, till they might be able to send fresh supplies, than out of any expectation that, with the strength he carried, he should be able, in any signal degree, to prevail over them."[1]

The House complied with his wishes, and in the pains which it took to insure the success of the war, we may recognize at every step the provident solicitude and the practical good sense of the leader whom it had appointed to the command. To console Fairfax for his inactivity, he was invested with the title of Generalissimo of all the Forces of the Parliament, both in England and Ireland; Cromwell was neither vain nor captious, and no one ever made greater concessions to the self-love of his rivals, especially when he was laboring to supplant them. He obtained as his major-general his son-in-law, Ireton, whose capacity, energy, and friendship he had fully tried. The regiments selected for his expedition formed a body of twelve thousand men; they were paid their arrears, were well provided with arms and ammunition, and

[1] Whitelocke, pp. 390, 391; Clarendon's History of the Rebellion, vol. vi. pp. 348, 349.

measures, on which Cromwell strenuously insisted, were taken to secure their regular recruitment. The accounts of the officers were settled, and they received considerable sums in advance of their pay. Other officers, who had abandoned Lord Inchiquin when he declared for the royal cause, returned to the service of the Parliament, and were treated with the same favor. Ample provision was made for the commissariat of the army. A number of vessels were placed at the general's disposal, and ordered to cruise off the coast of Ireland. A loan of 150,000*l.*, specially devoted to the necessities of this war, was opened in the City, and Cromwell himself superintended its negotiation. The Committee of Sequestrations was directed to press the payment of the sums due from those royalists who had been admitted to compound for their property, and these payments also had Ireland for their destination. Cromwell's prudence extended even beyond his special and warlike mission: a vigilant patron of his friends, he recommended those of them who had business to arrange with the Parliament to present their petitions immediately, and he insisted that justice should be done them before his departure. He obtained full justice for himself with regard to the liquidation of his arrears, for the settlement of his pay, which was considerable, and for the various supplementary grants which he needed. Finally, his commission secured to him the civil as well as the military command in Ireland, and its duration was fixed for three years.[1]

Having thus made sure of his material forces, Cromwell's next care was to provide means of moral action. The Commonwealth had few friends in Ireland: it was necessary,

[1] Commons' Journals, vol. vi. pp. 183, 184, 226, 232, 235, 240, 243, 248, 253, 254, 267, 270, 281, 288, 300, 301, 321, 328, 331; Whitelocke's Memorials, pp. 399, 401, 404, 409, 410, 412, 415, 421, 423, 426, 430.

therefore, to gain fresh adherents, or at least to thin the ranks of the enemy. Cromwell learned that one of the most influential and able men in Ireland, Lord Broghill—who, after having served by turns the King and the Parliament, had retired to his estates—had just arrived in London with the intention of crossing over to Holland to offer his services to Charles II. He sent one of his officers to say that he would wait on him, as he was anxious to have some conversation with him. Lord Broghill was astonished, and imagined that there must be some mistake, as he had not the honor of knowing the General. But a few minutes after, Cromwell arrived at his house, and, having first expressed the greatest kindness and esteem for him, proceeded to inform him that his designs were perfectly known, and that instead of proceeding to Spa for the benefit of his health, as his passport purported, he was going immediately to Charles Stuart, for purposes hostile to the Government. Broghill denied any such intention. Cromwell upon this assured him that he had good proof of what he said, and that he could show him his own letters to the purpose: "they have already been examined by the Council of State," he added, "who have made an order for your being committed to the Tower; but I have obtained a delay in executing the order, till I should previously have conferred with you." Lord Broghill admitted everything, thanked Cromwell for his kindness, and requested his advice. "I have obtained permission from the Council," answered Cromwell, "to offer you a command in the Irish war; you shall have the authority of a general officer, no oaths shall be imposed upon you, and you shall only be required to serve against the Irish Catholics." Broghill manifested some reluctance, and desired some time to consider the proposal. But Cromwell replied that that was impossible, as, the moment he left him with the offer unaccepted, he would instantly find himself a state prisoner.[1] They parted good friends, and three months afterwards they were both in Ireland serving the Parliament together.

About the same time there arrived in London some men well known for their Catholic fervor—Sir Kenelm Digby, Sir John Winter, and the Abbé Montague, who had already been frequently occupied in the affairs of Ireland, and who had always placed the cause of the Church far above that of the King. They were led to hope full liberty for their faith and worship in Ireland, provided that the Catholics of that country would disavow the temporal pretensions of the Pope, and raise ten thousand men for the service of the Commonwealth. Conferences took place through the medium of the Spanish ambassador: and to afford some test of the disposition of the Catholics, a learned priest, named Thomas White, in a pamphlet entitled, "The Grounds of Obedience and Government," maintained that the people might be released from their oath of allegiance by the evil conduct of their governor, and that, when he was once deposed, the common good might require them to submit rather than to attempt his restoration. On the Continent Charles II. and his counsellors grew alarmed, and warned Ormonde to be on his guard. And they had good reason to do so, for while this civil negotiation was being carried on in secret in London, Monk, at the suggestion of Cromwell, had concluded a suspension of hostilities with the great Catholic chief, O'Neil, in Ireland: which suspension covered the engagement of O'Neil to lend his assistance underhand to the operations of the army and generals of the Parliament. Cromwell had too unprejudiced a mind to underrate the strength of the Catholics in Ireland; and with equal unscrupulous-

[1] Carte's Ormonde Letters, vol. i. p. 249; Godwin's History of the Commonwealth, vol. iii. pp. 153—155; Cromwell's Letters and Speeches, vol. ii. p. 95.

ness, but greater secrecy than Charles II. had employed, he prepared to conciliate them, if the Protestant Parliament and public would permit him to do so, or to compromise and divide them, if he were forbidden to make use of them.[1]

He also attempted to renew some friendly relations with the Presbyterians themselves, his most recent and most ardent opponents—abstaining from all religious hostility to them, and giving them to understand that, in his opinion, their ecclesiastical system was the one which the State must eventually adopt and maintain. Before his departure for Ireland, he was anxious to make friends there, and to conciliate, or at least to pacify the enemies whom he left behind him in England.

He still delayed his departure, however. Was he merely desirous to wait until his troops had arrived, and were in readiness in Ireland, before he appeared there himself; or did he meditate some secret design? The Parliament began to feel some anxiety, for it was chiefly to get rid of Cromwell, and to find employment for the army, that it had so vigorously undertaken the Irish war, and made so many sacrifices for its effectual maintenance. The foreign ministers resident in London strongly doubted Cromwell's intention to go at all. "People continue to say," wrote M. de Croullé to Cardinal Mazarin, "that Cromwell will start at the end of this month, at latest. The opinion which I have to the contrary, is so conformable to that of many intelligent persons, that I cannot retract it, and until I am convinced by the news of his journey into that country, I shall persevere in that opinion. It can hardly be possible that Cromwell, who, according to the belief of many, carries his ideas beyond even the suggestions of the most undisciplined ambition, can resolve to abandon this kingdom to the mercy of

[1] Carte's Ormonde Letters, vol. i. pp. 216–222.

the plots which may be formed in his absence, and which his presence can prevent from being so much as undertaken."[1]

But, in the beginning of June, Ormonde entered the field, and, notwithstanding the dissensions of his party, and the wretched organization of his army, his successes were so rapid, that at the end of the month, Londonderry and Dublin were the only towns in Ireland which remained faithful to the Parliament. Cromwell took his resolution. On the 10th of July, a large number of his friends met at Whitehall; three ministers invoked the Divine blessing on his arms; and Cromwell himself, after two of his officers, Goffe and Harrison, had spoken, commented on several texts of Scripture which were appropriate to his undertaking. On the same day, at five o'clock in the evening, he set out for Bristol, "in that state and equipage," says a newspaper of the time, "as the like hath hardly been seen; himself in a coach, with six gallant Flanders mares, whitish-gray; divers coaches accompanying him, and very many great officers of the army; his lifeguard consisting of eighty gallant men, the meanest whereof a commander or esquire, in stately habit, with trumpets sounding. Of his lifeguard, many are colonels, and, believe me, it's such a guard as is hardly to be paralleled in the world. And now, have at you, my lord of Ormonde! you will have men of gallantry to encounter, whom to overcome will be honor sufficient, and to be beaten by them will be no great blemish to your reputation. If you say, 'Cæsar or nothing!' they say, 'A Republic or nothing!'"[2]

On reaching Bristol, and from motives which it is impossible to ascertain, Cromwell remained there nearly a month,

[1] Letter of the 14th June, 1649; Archives des Affaires Etrangères de France.

[2] Cromwelliana, p. 62; Whitelocke, p. 413.

going and coming between the different ports along the coast, superintending the embarkation of his troops, and receiving numerous visitors. The people thronged from the surrounding country to see him. His wife and several members of his family came to pass a few days with him. He seemed still to hesitate, and to quit the soil of England with great doubtfulness and effort.[1]

News, however, arrived from Ireland, which put an end to his lingerings. Before marching upon Dublin, Ormonde had written to the governor, Colonel Michael Jones, who had, until then, been regarded as a moderate Presbyterian, urging him "to leave that pretended Parliament, who had murdered their King, and would introduce anarchy," and promising him great rewards, if he would return to the royal cause. Jones answered, "that he understood not how his lordship came to that power; that the Parliament of England would never have consented to such a peace as his lordship had made with the rebels, without any provision for the Protestant religion; that he knew not how that could be established by an army of Papists; and that he had rather suffer in his trust, than purchase to himself the ignominy of perfidy by any advantage offered to him." Ormonde encamped before Dublin, hoping to reduce the place, as its garrison was weak, and he had adherents among the inhabitants. But, at the end of July, Cromwell's vanguard, assisted by a favorable wind, entered the port of Dublin, in spite of Ormonde's endeavors to prevent it. The garrison, thus strengthened, revictualled, and inspirited, demanded some bold action of its commander; and, on the 2d of August, Jones made so unexpected, so vigorous, and so successful a sortie against the camp of the besiegers, at the village of Rathmines, that, notwithstanding the desperate efforts of the superior officers

[1] Carlyle, Cromwell's Letters and Speeches, vol. ii. p. 37.

and of Ormonde himself, the whole of the royal army was thrown into disorder, put to rout with considerable loss, and obliged to raise the siege.[1]

Whatever may have been the cause of his delay in quitting England, it did not suit Cromwell's purpose that another should have the honor of subjugating Ireland. On the day following the arrival of this news, he set out; and as soon as he had embarked, while still in the port of Milford Haven, careful to show himself one of the foremost to celebrate the victory of Colonel Jones, he wrote to his friend, Richard Mayor, whose daughter had just been married to his eldest son Richard: "The Marquis of Ormonde besieged Dublin with nineteen thousand men or thereabouts; seven thousand Scots and three thousand more were coming to join him in that work. Jones issued out of Dublin with four thousand foot and twelve hundred horse; hath routed this whole army; killed about four thousand upon the place; taken 2,517 prisoners, above three hundred of them officers, some of great quality.[2] This is an astonishing mercy; so great and seasonable that indeed we are like them that dreamed. What can we say? The Lord fill our souls with thankfulness, that our mouths may be full of his praise—and our lives too; and grant we may never forget his goodness to us. These things seem to strengthen our faith and love, against more difficult times. Sir, pray for me, that I may walk worthy of the Lord in all that he hath called me unto!"

And this outburst of patriotic piety concludes by this trait of paternal solicitude: "I have committed my son to you; pray give him advice. I envy him not his contents; but I fear he should be swallowed up in them. I would have him

[1] Whitelocke, pp. 391, 419, 420; Commons' Journals, vol. vi. pp. 175, 278; Clarendon's History of the Rebellion, vol. vi. pp. 340—345.

[2] These round numbers are all greatly exaggerated. See Carte's Ormonde Letters, vol. ii. pp. 403, 407—411.

mind and understand business, read a little history, study the mathematics and cosmography; these are good, with subordination to the things of God. Better than idleness or mere outward worldly contents. These fit for public services, for which a man is born."[1]

Cromwell always manifested the greatest interest in his children, their temporal affairs as well as their moral tendencies; and in this, as in everything that concerned him, he brought his provident and dominant activity into constant exercise.

He arrived in Dublin two days afterwards, on the 15th of August, and was received with all possible demonstrations of joy. The population crowded out to welcome him, with mingled kindness and curiosity. When nearly in the heart of the city, where the concourse was greatest, he halted; and, rising in his carriage, with his hat in his hand, made a speech to the people. "He did not doubt," he said, "that, as God had brought him thither in safety, he would be able, by Divine Providence, to restore them all to their just liberties and properties; and," he added, "that all persons whose hearts' affections were real for the carrying on of this great work against the barbarous and bloodthirsty Irish and their confederates and adherents, and for propagating of Christ's Gospel, and establishing of truth and peace, and restoring of this bleeding nation of Ireland to its former happiness and tranquillity, should find favor and protection from the Parliament of England and him, and withal receive such rewards and gratuities as might be answerable to their merits." This speech was received by the people with shouts of "We will live and die with you!"[2] On the following day, a military and puritanic proclamation indicated the character of his

[1] Cromwell's Letters and Speeches, vol. ii. pp. 44, 45.

[2] Ibid. vol. ii. p. 48.

government; after reciting "the great mercies of God to the city of Dublin, particularly in the late defeat given to the rebels who encompassed it round about," he expressed his astonishment to learn that, "notwithstanding the goodness of God to them, yet by profane swearing, cursing, and drunkenness, his holy name is daily dishonored and blasphemed, contrary to the laws of God and the known laws of the land, and to the articles of war;" he enjoined the mayor and magistrates of the city, as well as the officers of the army, "to put in due execution the laws against such offenders;" and he finally declared that he would "punish the neglect and contempt of his proclamation with the severest penalties of the law."[1]

No sooner had his troops rested a few days than he entered the field, but with intentions very different from those he had professed at a distance, whilst his expedition was in preparation. As soon as he was in Ireland, on the theatre of war and in the midst of the combatants, Cromwell became convinced that the prejudices and animosities of the English against the Irish, of the Protestants against the Catholics, of the Republicans against the Royalists, were there fierce and uncontrollable passions, which might be used with powerful efficacy so long as they were allowed free course, but which permitted no politic calculations or wary compromises. He accepted this conclusion without hesitation, as a fact which admitted of no discussion, and determined to take full advantage of it. The instructions and examples which he received from London urged him rather to pursue this course than otherwise. The news from Ireland, and particularly Jones's victory at Dublin, and the confidence which it inspired, dissipated all the schemes of negotiation with the Irish and the Catholics, which had recently been in contemplation. The Parliament severely disavowed the suspension of hostilities

Whitelocke's Memorials, p. 423.

which Monk had concluded with O'Neil, and the political leaders who had secretly incited Monk to take this step, felt themselves obliged to be the first to blame his act, in order to succeed afterwards in getting him excused because of his intention. A few days later, the House voted that Sir Kenelm Digby and Sir John Winter—those ardent Catholics whom it had allowed, and almost invited, to come to London, that it might secure their co-operation in Ireland, at the price of the liberty of their faith and worship—were dangerous men, whom it was necessary to dismiss without delay; and they were ordered to leave England immediately on pain of death and the confiscation of their property if they ventured to return thither.[1] All tendency to compromise, from motives of either justice or prudence, had disappeared; and in the councils of England, as in the army in Ireland, religious and political fanaticism alone prevailed.

It was under these sombre auspices that Cromwell marched from Dublin, on the 31st of August, at the head of about ten thousand men, to lay siege to Drogheda, the most important town in the province of Leinster. Ormonde, on retiring from the siege of Dublin, had thrown into this town a garrison of three thousand men, nearly all English, commanded by Sir Arthur Ashton, an old wooden-legged officer, of tried courage and fidelity, in the hope that it would long arrest the progress of the enemy. After employing six days in preparing for the siege, Cromwell summoned the governor to surrender, and on his refusal, on the 10th of September, the storm commenced. The first attack, although vigorous, failed, with great loss to the assailants; Colonel Castle and several other officers were killed in the breach. Cromwell headed the second attack himself, and, notwithstanding the energetic resistance of the besieged, the entrenchments were carried in succession, as well as the towers and churches of the town,

[1] Commons' Journals, vol. vi. pp. 277, 289; Whitelocke, pp. 419, 422, 423.

to which the most obstinate had retreated. "In the heat of action," wrote Cromwell to the President of the Council of State and to the Speaker of the House of Commons, "I forbade our men to spare any that were in arms in the town; and, I think, that night they put to the sword about two thousand men, among whom were the governor, Sir Arthur Ashton, and divers considerable officers. The next day the two towers were summoned, in one of which was about six or seven score; but they refused to yield themselves; and we, knowing that hunger must compel them, set only good guards to secure them from running away until their stomachs were come down. From one of the said towers, notwithstanding their condition, they killed and wounded some of our men. When they submitted, their officers were knocked on the head, and every tenth man of the soldiers killed, and the rest shipped for the Barbadoes. I believe all their friars were knocked on the head promiscuously. I am persuaded that this is a righteous judgment of God upon these barbarous wretches, who have imbrued their hands in so much innocent blood; and that it will tend to prevent the effusion of blood for the future;—which are the satisfactory grounds to such actions, which otherwise cannot but work remorse and regret.

"P. S.—The following officers and soldiers were slain at the storming of Tredah: The governor, one colonel, two lieutenant-colonels, one major, eight captains, eight lieutenants, and eight cornets—all of horse; three colonels, with their lieutenants and majors, forty-four captains, and all their lieutenants, ensigns, &c.; 220 reformadoes and troopers; 2500 foot soldiers, besides staff-officers, surgeons, &c., and many inhabitants."[1]

According to other reports, by royalist and even parlia-

[1] Carlyle, Cromwell's Letters and Speeches, vol. ii. pp. 56—68; Old Parliamentary History, vol. xix. pp. 201—210; Whitelocke, pp. 424—427.

mentary writers, not only did the carnage last two days, but officers who were discovered after the lapse of five or six days, during which they had been concealed by the humanity of some of the soldiers, were put to death in cold blood; and at the moment of the massacre, women and children met with the same fate as armed men. "It was," says a contemporary panegyrist of Cromwell, "a sacrifice of three thousand Irish to the ghosts of ten thousand English, whom they had massacred some years before."[1]

The sacrifice did not produce the effect which Cromwell had anticipated would justify it; it did not suffice to prevent the further effusion of blood; another such example had to be made. Wexford, a month afterwards, defended itself with the same obstinacy as Drogheda, and witnessed a similar massacre. Other places, it is true, from intimidation or treachery, surrendered: Cork, Ross, Youghal, and Kilkenny, submitted without resistance; but other places again, Callan, Gowran, and Clonmel, made a bold defence; and some, Waterford for instance, resisted so vigorously that Cromwell was obliged to raise the siege. And, even where success seemed won most easily, it was sullied by acts of wanton cruelty: at Gowran the soldiers obtained their lives on surrendering the place, but on the condition of giving up their officers, who were all put to death. The Bishop of Ross was hanged in his episcopal robes, under the walls of a fortress defended by his troops. Clonmel made an heroic resistance, and when at length it surrendered, Cromwell found not a single man belonging to the garrison in it; whilst he was signing the articles of capitulation with the inhabitants, they had left the town by night with their arms and baggage, to recommence the war elsewhere.[2]

[1] Old Parliamentary History, vol. xix. p. 210; Clarendon's History of the Rebellion, vol. vi. p. 396; Ludlow's Memoirs, p. 129.

[2] Carlyle, Cromwell's Letters and Speeches, vol. ii. pp. 50—166; Commons'

It is the ordinary artifice of bad passions to impute the cruel satisfaction with which they glut themselves, either to some great idea whose accomplishment they are earnestly pursuing, or to the absolute necessity of success. History would be dishonored by admitting these lying excuses: it is her duty to refer evil to its source, and to render to the vices of mankind that which is their due.

Human fanaticism also lies, or allows itself to be deluded by pride, when it pretends to be the executor of the high decrees of Divine justice: it is not the office of man to pronounce upon nations the sentences of God.

Cromwell was not bloodthirsty; but he was determined to succeed rapidly and at any cost, from the necessities of his fortune, far more than for the advancement of his cause: and he denied no outlet to the passions of those who served him. He was an ambitious and selfish, though really great, man, who had narrow-minded and hard-hearted fanatics for his instruments.

His great and true means of success did not consist in his massacres, but in his genius, and in the exalted idea which the people had already conceived of him. Sometimes by instinct, sometimes from reflection, he conducted himself in Ireland towards both his friends and his enemies with an ability as pliant as it was profound; for he excelled in the art of treating with men, and of persuading, or seducing, or appeasing those even who naturally regarded him with the greatest distrust and aversion. At the same time that he gave up to murder and pillage the towns which fell into his hands, he maintained in other respects the severest discipline in his army, not suffering it to do the inhabitants any wrong, and taking care that it paid for all it consumed. That very man who boasted that at Drogheda "all the friars were

Journals, vol. vi. pp. 314, 323; Whitelocke, pp. 433, 434, 456; Godwin's History of the Commonwealth, vol. iii. pp. 151—161.

knocked on the head promiscuously," and who always pompously excepted the Catholics from his promises of Christian toleration, that very man maintained, by means of Irish monks, a most active police among his enemies, who kept him always well informed of their designs and movements, and were sometimes influential enough to procure their failure by promoting dissensions among them. He labored incessantly to detach all men of importance from the royal cause, and he even carried his attempts of this sort, unsuccessfully of course, as far as the Marquis of Ormonde himself, for whom he openly professed the highest esteem, and frequently asked: "What Lord Ormonde had to do with Charles Stuart, and what obligations he had ever received from him?" Towards the Parliament his behavior was very independent, but without vanity or bluster; his language, on the contrary, was deferential even to humility: after the capture of Ross, he wrote to the Speaker of the House of Commons: "Having given you this account, I shall not trouble you with particular desires. Those I shall humbly present to the Council of State. Only, in the general, give me leave humbly to offer what in my judgment I conceive to be for your service, with a full submission to you. We desire recruits may be speeded to us. The forces desired will not raise your charge, if your assignments already for the forces here do come to our hands in time. Wherefore I humbly beg that the moneys desired may be seasonably sent over; and those other necessaries, clothes, shoes, and stockings, formerly desired; that so poor creatures may be encouraged; and through the same blessed presence that has gone along with us, I hope, before it be long, to see Ireland no burden to England, but a profitable part of its Commonwealth."[1]

[1] Carlyle, Cromwell's Letters and Speeches, vol. ii. pp. 99—100; Clarendon's History of the Rebellion, vol. vi. pp. 427, 428; Whitelocke, p. 426; Godwin's History of the Commonwealth, vol. iii. p. 151.

It was not long before he discovered and put into practice the most effectual means for succeeding in this object. When he perceived that, notwithstanding some partial successes, he would never be able to disorganize the royalist party in Ireland, by depriving it of its leaders, he turned his attention towards the soldiers; they were numerous and brave, but for the most part utterly destitute and despondent. He published throughout the country that they were free to go and serve abroad; and that he authorized all the officers, or any other persons who chose to engage in the undertaking, to levy as many men as they could find, and to convey them out of Ireland for the service of the Continental powers. He communicated this permission to the Ministers of France and Spain in London. Numbers of royalist officers, both English and Irish, without employment or resources, saw a future thus opened to them, and offered their services to the foreign agents, for levying regiments and transporting them into France or Spain. Don Alonzo de Cardenas, the Spanish ambassador in London, and Cardinal Mazarin, eagerly availed themselves of this offer; in a few months, nearly twenty-five thousand Irish were enrolled for Spain, and twenty thousand for France, and that Catholic territory on which Ormonde found it very difficult to keep together a body of eight or ten thousand men, for the King's service, furnished more than forty thousand soldiers, hostile to the Parliament, for the service of France and Spain.[1]

So many successes, both military and political, gained so rapidly, and so skilfully extolled by his zealous friends, soon caused the Parliament almost as much alarm as they had won it security. Cromwell in London was, at every moment, a subject of embarrassment; but Cromwell, so powerful and glorious in Ireland, seemed more dangerous

[1] Clarendon's History of the Rebellion, vol. vi. pp. 428—431; Cromwell's Letters and Speeches, vol. ii. p. 163.

and threatening still. Moreover, a report was current that Charles Stuart, in consequence of fresh negotiations with the Scots, was on the point of proceeding to Scotland. Cromwell would probably be needed in that direction. On the 8th of January, 1650, it was determined that he should be recalled, and the Council of State was ordered to inform him of this resolution. He was then in winter-quarters, scarcely recovered from a rather severe illness. He suddenly re-entered the field, and vigorously recommenced his marches and sieges in various parts of Ireland. On the 25th of February, letters were read from him, in the House of Commons, announcing new successes. It was voted first, that a letter of thanks should be sent to him, and next that, on his return to London, he should "have the use of the lodgings called the Cockpit (a portion of the palace of Whitehall), of the Spring Garden and St. James's House, and the command of St. James's Park." Cromwell's wife and family, with considerable reluctance, made preparations for removing to their new abode; as for Cromwell himself, he continued to remain and conquer in Ireland. At length, on the 2d of April, he thus wrote to the Parliament:—

"I have received divers private intimations of your pleasure to have me come in person to wait upon you in England; as also copies of votes of the Parliament to that purpose. But considering the way they came to me was but by private intimations, and the votes did refer to a letter to be signed by the Speaker, I thought it would have been too much forwardness in me to have left my charge here, until the said letter came; it being not fit for me to prophesy whether the letter would be an absolute command, or having limitations with a liberty left by the Parliament to me, to consider in what way to yield my obedience. Your letter came to my hand upon Friday the 22d of March, the same day that I came before the city of Kilkenny. And I understood by Dr. Cartwright, who delivered it to me, that reason of cross winds, and the want of shipping in the West of England where he was, hindered him from coming with it sooner; it bearing date the 8th of January, and not coming to my hands until the 22d of March.

"The letter supposed your army in winter quarters, and the time of the year not suitable for present action; making this as the reason of your command. And your forces have been in action ever since the 29th of January; and your letter, which was to be the rule of my obedience, coming to my hands after our having been so long in action, with respect had to the reasons you were pleased to use therein, I knew not what to do. And having received a letter, signed by yourself, of the 26th of February, which mentions not a word of the continuance of your pleasure concerning my coming over, I did humbly conceive it much consisting with my duty, humbly to beg a positive signification what your will is; professing (as before the Lord), that I am most ready to obey your commands herein with all sincerity; rejoicing only to be about that work which I am called to by those whom God hath set over me, which I acknowledge you to be; and fearing only in obeying you, to disobey you. I most humbly and earnestly beseech you to judge for me, whether your letter doth not naturally allow me the liberty of begging a more clear expression of your command and pleasure; which, when vouchsafed unto me, will find most ready and cheerful obedience."[1]

He had gained as much time as he wished, and while he was delaying, the course of events was such as to render his return to London a new source of power and greatness to him.

When Charles II., after having left the Hague to pay a

[1] Cromwell's Letters and Speeches, vol. ii. pp. 157, 158.

visit to the Queen, his mother, at St. Germains, received certain information that Cromwell had assumed the government of Ireland, he hesitated more and more to proceed thither, as he was unwilling to risk his future and his life upon so dangerous a ground, and against so formidable an adversary. He spent three months at St. Germains, a monotonous residence, which the Court of France took little pains to render agreeable to him, and the ennui of which the imperious ill-temper of his mother did not tend to dissipate. At the news of Ormonde's defeat before Dublin, the young prince's first impulse was to set out at once for Ireland, and take his personal share in the struggle. To those who told him that it would be imprudent for him to go thither to share in defeat, he replied: "Then must I go there to die, for it is disgraceful for me to live anywhere else." "This speech appeared to proceed from a noble heart," says Madame de Motteville, who lived on almost as intimate terms with Queen Henrietta Maria as with Anne of Austria; "the greatest men of antiquity never spoke better; but young people pass easily from this rigid virtue into laxity; they afterwards endure with indifference those very evils which at first appeared to them the most insupportable in life, and the pleasures which they meet with in life are the cause of this. So it happened in the case of this prince."[1] His own courtiers were not long in estimating the character of their sovereign. "Foreign princes," wrote one of them to the Marquis of Ormonde, "begin to look upon him as a person so lazy and careless in his own business, that they think it not safe, by contributing anything to his assistance, to irritate so potent enemies as they fear his rebellious subjects are like to prove."[2] Charles soon experienced the effects of this feeling; Cardinal

[1] Mémoires de Madame de Motteville, vol. iii. pp. 329, 333; in Petitot's Collection.

[2] Carte's Ormonde Letters, vol. i. p. 319.

Mazarin gave him clearly to understand that his prolonged residence at St. Germains was becoming a source of embarrassment to the Court of France, which had no wish to quarrel with the Commonwealth of England. Queen Henrietta Maria herself, who stood in great need of Mazarin's favor, urged her son to take the Cardinal's hint, without requiring a more precise explanation of his wishes; and about the middle of September, 1649, Charles set out, through Normandy, for the island of Jersey, the only part of his dominions of which he still retained possession.[1]

No sooner had he arrived there than he received intelligence of the disaster of Drogheda, and almost at the same moment the Parliament of Scotland sent to request him to resume the negotiations which had been opened at the Hague for his return to his kingdom. Since the failure of that first attempt, the general feeling of the Scottish people in favor of the King had not ceased to manifest itself; several insurrections of the pure royalists had occurred in various parts of the kingdom; and although the Presbyterian Parliament had promptly repressed them, its leaders, Argyle amongst others, were convinced that they could not refrain from making another serious effort to induce Charles to return, or at least attempting a striking demonstration of their willingness to receive him. The propositions which their envoy, Lord Winram, of Liberton, brought to Jersey, were in substance the same, and to the full as harsh, as those which Charles had recently rejected at the Hague; but his position was now less advantageous; his enemies were triumphant in England and Ireland; from Paris and the Hague, his mother and brother-in-law urged him more strongly than ever to accept the proposition of the Scots, one writing to him that the Court of France, and the other that the people of Holland, were decidedly of opinion

[1] Clarendon's History of the Rebellion, vol. vi. pp. 351—354.

that he should do so. Charles wished to consult Ormonde. Ormonde replied that there was no possible ground for hope unless they could succeed in bringing about a war between England and Scotland, and thus operating a diversion which would enable the Irish royalists to take breath and attempt fresh efforts. Nearly all the most trusted counsellors of Charles, who were with him at the time, held the same opinion. He yielded to their unanimous advice, and, either because Jersey seemed an inconvenient place for negotiating, or in order to gain more time, he appointed the Scottish Commissioners to meet him at Breda, a town in the private domain of his brother-in-law, the Prince of Orange, where he felt himself perfectly free and safe. But as he felt neither satisfaction nor confidence in the negotiation to which he had submitted, he wrote to Montrose, who was then busy raising money and men in Germany: "I entreat you to go on vigorously, and with your wonted courage and care, in the prosecution of those trusts I have committed to you, and not to be startled with any reports you may hear, as if I were otherwise inclined to the Presbyterians than when I left you. I assure you I am upon the same principles I was, and depend as much as ever upon your undertaking and endeavors for my service."[1]

Montrose did not require to be stimulated to activity; passionately proud and devoted to his King, he had confidence in his cause, in himself, and in his destiny. A popular prediction had affirmed that he would restore the King to his throne; and he had been supplied by Charles with all the powers necessary to enable him to act. He travelled through the Netherlands, Germany, Denmark, and Sweden, seeking

[1] Laing's History of Scotland, vol. iii. pp. 441, 581; Clarendon's History of the Rebellion, vol. vi. pp. 399—401; Whitelocke, pp. 429, 430; Carte's Ormonde Letters, vol. i. pp. 338, 356.

the means of accomplishing his mission wherever he went, daily witnessing the failure of some of those on which he had relied, and daily returning to his work with the same conviction and the same ardor. That part of Europe, and especially Sweden, had then become the second fatherland of a large number of Scottish officers, who, after having served under Gustavus Adolphus in the Thirty Years' War, had settled there with the fortune or the fame which they had acquired. Montrose lived among them as a pleasant companion both in war and revel, attracting some by the brilliancy of his expectations, alluring others by his open-handed liberality; they had all promised him their personal support or influence for his great enterprise, and some had even furnished him with funds. The King of Denmark and several of the petty princes of Germany had given him similar assurances.[1] When he believed himself ready to enter upon action, he published from Copenhagen, a declaration in which he announced and justified his undertaking, and invited all faithful subjects of the King to join with him in Scotland for its accomplishment; he then appointed Hamburgh as the place of rendezvous for his recruits, and took up his own residence there, with greater pomp than his resources warranted, for the purpose of awaiting, organizing, and despatching his forces.[2]

Recruits arrived slowly and in small numbers; the Court of Denmark was zealous but poor; Queen Christina, of Sweden, who had at first appeared favorable, was suddenly seized with admiration for the English Commonwealth and for Cromwell. Montrose collected with great difficulty at Hamburgh and Gothenburgh, a body of twelve hundred

[1] Wishart's Memoirs of Montrose, Appendix xix. pp. 454—458.

[2] Clarendon's History of the Rebellion, vol. vi. pp. 408—410; Whitelocke, pp. 426, 430, 434—436; Wishart's Memoirs of Montrose, pp. 361—369.

men, poorly armed and equipped; a first division, which he sent off in September, 1649, perished at sea; the second, under the command of the Earl of Kinnoull, arrived safely at Kirkwall, the capital of Pomona, the principal of the Orkney islands, and fixed themselves there until the arrival of their general. Montrose on his side was awaiting fresh recruits, and the promised insurrections of the royalists in the Scottish Highlands. But the first attempt at insurrection, beginning too prematurely, had been too easily repressed;[1] no general rising took place; the friends of Montrose wrote to him that his presence was indispensable, and would certainly be efficacious. He set out, at length, and reached the Orkneys in the early part of March, 1650, with five hundred men, and a few Scottish nobles who were devoted to his person and fortune.

A short time before his arrival, and in answer to his declaration, the Kirk and Parliament of Scotland had published two other declarations against him, remarkable for their violence even in that age of unbridled passion. "It may seem strange," they said, "that we should think it worth the while to answer the slanders and groundless reproaches of that viperous brood of Satan, James Grahame, whom the Estates of Parliament have long since declared traitor, the church hath delivered into the hands of the devil, and the nation doth generally detest and abhor; yet, because our silence may be subject to misconstruction, and some of the weaker sort may be inveigled by the bold assertions and railing accusations of this impudent braggart, presenting himself to the view of the world, clothed with his Majesty's authority as Lieutenant-Governor and Captain-General of this Kingdom, we shall shortly answer what is said against us, take off the mask which he hath put on, and expose him

[1] Browne's History of the Highlands, vol. ii. pp. 26—28.

to public view in his own apparel."[1] All the old grievances of the dominant party, and the variations of conduct imputed to Montrose at the beginning of the civil war, and the acts of cruelty of which he had been accused during his campaign on behalf of Charles I., in 1645, were ably set forth in these two documents, which were read and commented upon from every Presbyterian pulpit; and at the moment when he set foot again in Scotland, the rage and terror of the people combined, against Montrose, with the hatred and alarm of his rivals.

On disembarking at the northern extremity of Scotland, he displayed somewhat pompously three banners, two in the name of the King, on one of which was painted the severed head of Charles I., with this motto: "Judge and revenge my cause, O Lord!"—on the third, which was his own standard, was a naked arm, holding a blood-stained sword, on a black ground, with this motto: "*Nil medium.*" He then advanced slowly through the counties of Caithness and Sutherland, expecting to be joined by recruits from the country itself. These recruits, however, did not appear; on the contrary, he learned that many chieftains, on whose support he had reckoned, had ranged themselves on the side of the Parliament; and he was visibly surprised and disappointed at the little sensation produced by his name and progress. The government at Edinburgh, whilst a larger body of troops were collecting under the command of David Leslie, sent forward some squadrons of cavalry under Lieutenant-Colonel Strahan, an impetuous sectary and valiant officer; five hundred infantry, collected by the Earl of Sutherland, joined Strahan's force, and they were lying together at Tain, on the eastern coast of Ross-shire, when they were informed that Montrose was encamped at a short distance, and care-

Wishart's Memoirs of Montrose, pp. 464, 465.

lessly guarded, as he did not know that the enemy was already so near him. It was Saturday, the 10th of April, and Strahan hesitated to march forward, as he was unwilling to run the risk of being obliged to fight on Sunday; but a movement made by Montrose brought the two troops still more closely together. Strahan then took his resolution, and advanced to within a league of Montrose's camp at Corbiesdale, which was still unaware of his proximity, and in considerable disorder. Strahan's squadrons charged it suddenly and in succession, as if they had been the vanguard of an army. Montrose tried to fall back upon a neighboring wood: the soldiers whom he had brought with him from Germany fought valiantly, but the recruits that he had raised in the Orkneys dispersed. With his accustomed bravery, he endeavored, but in vain, to rally them; his horse was killed under him, and he would have been taken on the field of battle, if his friend, Lord Frendraught, had not generously remounted him. The battle soon turned into a rout and massacre; ten officers, and more than three hundred soldiers, were slain; more than four hundred prisoners were taken, and a hundred Irish, who were found among them, were instantly shot. Montrose fled at full speed, and as soon as he was out of sight, he forsook his horse, threw away his George and his order of the Garter, changed clothes with a peasant, and betook himself across the fields in search of an asylum. He wandered for many days among the Highlands of Ross and Sutherlandshire, sometimes received with enthusiasm, sometimes repulsed with horror, frequently exhausted with fatigue and hunger, and vainly endeavoring to reach the coast. At length, on the 3d of May, either from mischance or treachery, he was discovered and arrested in a cottage on the estate of Neil Macleod, Laird of Assynt; from whence he was taken to the castles of Skild and Brane, until orders arrived for his immediate transfer to Edinburgh.[1]

He was now in the worst possible position; he had against him both the government and the people, the implacable hatred of his rivals, and the brutal fury of the multitude. They thronged on his route to load him with insults, but could not succeed in humbling him for a moment. He endured with the same firmness of soul the outrages of his enemies and the farewell meeting with his children, with whom he was allowed a brief interview at the house of his father-in-law, the Earl of Southesk. But marks of sympathy were not altogether denied him. At the Castle of Grange, where he lodged with his escort a short time before reaching Dundee, the Lady of Grange made an almost successful attempt to procure his escape during the night; and at Dundee itself, which in 1645 had suffered severely from his arms, the inhabitants, far from triumphing over him in his misfortune, treated him with the greatest respect, and, by their remonstrances, obtained permission from his guards to supply him with clothes suitable to his rank, instead of the tattered garments in which he had been captured, and which he had until then been insultingly obliged to wear.[2]

On the 17th of May he arrived at Leith, near Edinburgh. The Parliament met on the same day, and voted that "James Grahame should be brought on a cart, bareheaded, and bound to the cart by a rope—the hangman, in his livery, covered, riding on the horse that draws the cart—from the Watergate to the Tolbooth of Edinburgh, and from thence to the Parliament House; and there, in the place of delinquents, on his knees should receive his sentence, viz. to be hanged on a gib-

[1] Wishart's Memoirs of Montrose, pp. 372—377; Balfour's Annals of Scotland, vol. iii. p. 432, vol. iv. p. 9; Laing's History of Scotland, vol. iii. pp. 442—444; Browne's History of the Highlands, vol. ii. pp. 30—36.

[2] Wishart's Memoirs of Montrose, pp. 379—382.

bet at the Cross of Edinburgh, with his book and declaration tied by a rope about his neck, and there to hang for the space of three hours until he were dead; and thereafter to be cut down by the hangman; his head, hands, and legs to be cut off, and distributed as follows: his head to be affixed on an iron pole on the west pinnacle of the new prison of Edinburgh; one hand to be set on the gate of Perth, the other on the gate of Stirling; one leg and foot on the gate of Aberdeen, the other on the gate of Glasgow. If he was at his death penitent, and released from excommunication, then the trunk of his body should be interred in the Greyfriars; otherwise it should be interred in the Borrowmuir, by the hangman's men, under the gallows."[1] The manners of that age were still rude enough for the hatred of his enemies to take pleasure in such a spectacle, which was then calculated to inspire beholders with greater dread than disgust.

On the following day, at four o'clock in the afternoon, Montrose was conducted, on an old broken-down horse, from Leith to the Watergate of Edinburgh, where he was met by the magistrates of the city in their robes, escorted by the town-guard and hangman. A copy of his sentence was delivered to him; he read it, and returned it, saying with the greatest calmness and composure, "That he was ready to submit to it; only he was sorry that through him the King's majesty, whose person he represented, should be so much dishonored." The procession then moved forward; Montrose did not remove his hat, and the hangman knocked it off; thirty-four of his officers, his companions in captivity, walked, tied two and two together, before the cart. Along the whole route an immense crowd had collected for the purpose of assailing Montrose with abuse, and even with dirt and stones; but the tranquil firmness of his demeanor, the gravity of his

[1] Balfour's Annals of Scotland, vol. iv. pp. 12, 13.

looks, and the undaunted courage which he displayed, produced so powerful an impression upon the people that outrage ceased, silence reigned around the mournful cavalcade, or was broken at intervals only by expressions of compassion, and prayers on behalf of the illustrious prisoner. As the procession passed in front of the house of the Earl of Moray, the cart stopped for a moment; all looked up in surprise; the Marquis of Argyle was at the window, with his family and several friends; he had desired to feast his eyes upon the humiliation of that enemy before whom, five years previously, he had been forced to fly.[1] Although the distance was little more than a mile, three hours were spent in going from the gate of the city to the Tolbooth. On dismounting from the cart, Montrose gave the hangman some money, as a reward, he said, "for driving his triumphal chariot so well." The Parliament was in session; five commissioners were sent to the prison "to ask James Grahame if he had anything to say before he repaired to the House to receive his sentence." On their return to the Parliament, they reported that Montrose had refused to give any answer until he knew upon what terms they stood with the King, and whether they had come to any agreement with him. Seven commissioners were immediately sent to interrogate him, and to inform him that an agreement had been concluded with the King, who was on the point of returning to Scotland. Somewhat moved, doubtless, by this intelligence, Montrose declined giving any further answer, saying that he had made a long journey, and that after

[1] This fact is placed beyond doubt by a letter from the French agent Graymond to Cardinal Mazarin, dated 31st May, 1650. "Plusieurs prirent garde, et en ont bien discouru après, qu'on fit halte vis-à-vis la maison du Comte de Moray, où estoit entre autres M. le Marquis d'Argyle, que considéroit son ennemi par une fenestre entr'ouverte." Archives des Affaires Etrangères de France.

"the wearisome and tedious ceremony and compliment they had paid him that day," he desired some repose.[1]

Two days after, when he was brought to the bar of the Parliament, he allowed himself the pleasure of following his natural tastes, and appeared before his enemies in splendid attire. He wore a rich dress of black silk embroidered with silver, and over it a scarlet cloak, trimmed with silver lace, and lined with crimson taffety; and a beaver hat, with a broad silver band. On being placed on the raised platform appointed for criminals, he glanced proudly around him; his face was pale and careworn, but expressive of invincible courage and dignified resolution. The Chancellor, Lord Loudon, addressed him in a long and bitter speech, and concluded by saying, "that for the many horrible murders, treasons and impieties he had committed, God had now brought him to suffer condign punishment." When the Chancellor had terminated his harangue, Montrose obtained, with some difficulty, permission to say a few words in his own defence; he spoke with reserved hauteur, and considerable address, as if he had anticipated some result from his speech. "He considered the Parliament," he said, "as sitting by the King's authority; and therefore he had appeared with reverence, and bareheaded, which otherwise he would not willingly have done." He defended himself from the charges of cruelty which had been brought against him during the late war, saying, "that it was not in the power of the greatest generals to prevent disorders altogether in their army, but he had endeavored what he could to suppress them, and to punish them as soon as they were known; he had never spilt any blood—no, not of his most inveterate enemies—but on the field of battle; and even in the greatest heat of action, he had preserved the lives of many

[1] Wishart's Memoirs of Montrose, pp. 383—336; Balfour's Annals of Scotland, vol. iv. p. 14.

thousands. As to his late invasion, he had undertaken it at the command of his Majesty; and he might justly affirm that no subject ever acted upon more honorable grounds, nor by a more lawful power and authority than he had done. Wherefore," he said in conclusion, "he desired them to lay aside all prejudices, private animosity, and desire of revenge, and consider him, in relation to the justice of his cause, as a man and a Christian; as an obedient subject, in relation to the commands of his royal master, which he had faithfully executed; as their fellow-subject, and one to whom they lay under great obligations, for having preserved the lives and fortunes of many of them, at a time when he had the power and authority, and wanted only the cruel inclination, to have destroyed both. He entreated them not to be too rash in their judgment against him, but to judge him according to the laws of God, the laws of nature and nations, and particularly by the laws of the land; which if they refused, he appealed to the just Judge of the world, who must at last judge them all, and always gives righteous judgment." The Chancellor replied to him with anger and invectives. Montrose attempted to speak a second time, but he was stopped, and ordered to kneel down and receive his sentence; which he did.[1] His execution was fixed for the following day.

During the evening, the Presbyterian ministers and magistrates of Edinburgh besieged Montrose with their visits, in the hope of extorting from him some expression which would imply a recognition of the rightfulness of their Church and government. But their persevering endeavors only served to increase his enthusiasm. He told them "that he was much beholden to the Parliament for the great honor they had decreed him; for he was prouder to have his head fixed

[1] Wishart's Memoirs of Montrose, pp. 387—392; Balfour's Annals of Scotland, vol. iv. p. 16.

upon the top of the prison, in the view of the present and succeeding ages, than if they had ordered a golden statue to be erected to him in the market-place, or that his picture should be hung in the King's bedchamber. He thanked them for taking so effectual a method to preserve the memory of his loyalty and regard for his beloved sovereign, even to the latest posterity, by transmitting such lasting monuments of them to the four principal cities of the kingdom, and wished heartily that he had flesh enough to have sent a piece to every city in Christendom, as a testimony of his unshaken love and fidelity to his King and country." He spent the night in prayer, and in composing verses, in which he gave noble expression to the same sentiments. Early in the morning, the noise of drums and trumpets resounded through the town; he asked the captain of the guard what it meant, and was told that it was to call the soldiers and citizens to arms, because it was feared that some of the people might attempt to rescue him. "What!" said Montrose, "do I, who was such a terror to these good men, when alive, continue still so formidable to them now, when I am to die? but let them look to themselves, for even after I am dead, I will be continually present to their wicked consciences, and become more formidable to them than while I was alive." He then began to dress with great pains. Whilst he was at his toilette, Sir Archibald Johnstone, a member of Parliament, and one of his bitterest enemies, derisively expressed his surprise that a man in such a position should bestow so much care on the frivolous adornment of his person. Montrose answered with a smile, "that while his head was his own, he would dress and adorn it; but to-morrow, when it becomes yours, you may treat it as you please."

He dressed himself with great magnificence, and threw over his shoulders a handsome cloak of scarlet velvet, trimmed with gold lace, which his friends had sent him. As he walked from his prison to the place of execution, his grand air, and the proud and calm expression of his countenance, produced a more powerful effect than ever upon the spectators. He assisted the executioner to hang round his neck, in conformity with his sentence, the history of his wars, and his late declaration, and said "he reckoned himself more honored thereby, than when it had pleased his Majesty to create him a knight of the most noble Order of the Garter." He was not allowed to stand forward and address the people, but he addressed a few words to those who stood near him, expressive of his persistence in the sentiments which had guided his life hitherto, and of the utmost piety and tranquillity of soul. He requested permission to die with his hat on, it was refused; to retain his cloak—this also was denied him; upon which he desired the magistrates "to inflict what further degree of ignominy and disgrace they could possibly invent, for that he was ready to submit with the greatest cheerfulness to the highest indignities for the sake of that cause for which he suffered." His last words were, "May God have mercy upon this afflicted kingdom!"[1] It is said that the hangman himself wept, after having obeyed the fatal signal; that a murmur of indignant sorrow burst from the crowd; and that Argyle, on learning the particulars of his great rival's death, became agitated and melancholy, as if seized with regret, or struck by a presentiment of his own future fate.

The Commissioners of the Parliament had not deceived Montrose when they told him that they had treated with the King, and that he was about to return amongst them. At the very moment that Montrose began in Scotland his brief

[1] Wishart's Memoirs of Montrose, pp. 392—405; Balfour's Annals of Scottand, pp. 19—22; Laing's History of Scotland, vol. iii. pp. 444—447, 582.

and fatal campaign, Charles received the Scottish Commissioners at Breda, and resumed with them the discussion of their harsh propositions. Great difference of opinion existed among his advisers upon this subject. His most sensible and honest counsellors exhorted him not to submit to such thraldom, and supported their opinions by the authority of Hyde, in whom Charles had the utmost confidence, and whom he had just despatched on an embassy to Madrid. "If the King puts himself into the hands of the Scots," Hyde had written to Mr. Secretary Nicholas, "they cannot justly be accused of deceiving him, for, on my conscience, they will not use him worse than they promise, if he does all they require him to do in this last address. I wish, with all my heart, they who advise the King to comply and join with them, would deal as clearly, and say that the King should now take the Covenant, and enjoin it to others, and all observe it; but to say he should put himself into their hands, and hope to be excused taking it, and be able to defend others from submitting to it, or that he and we should take it and break it afterwards, is such folly and atheism, that we should be ashamed to avow or think it. Oh, Mr. Secretary! if I were now at Breda, I would fly to the Indies, rather than be involved in such councils."[1]

So long as there was any uncertainty as to the issue of Montrose's expedition, Charles hesitated. His good sense and dignity both led him to think with Hyde; but when he learned at Breda that Montrose was defeated, a fugitive, and, ere long, a prisoner, his frivolous and reckless counsellors carried their point. They had on their side the Queen-mother, the Prince of Orange, and that unwillingness to wait patiently, which is ever the result of exile. The friends of Hyde took

[1] Clarendon's State Papers, vol. iii. p. 14; Carte's Ormonde Letters, vol. i. p. 373; Clarendon's History of the Rebellion, vol. vi. pp. 401—408.

no part in the deliberations of the Council, and Charles consented to everything. He promised to swear fidelity to the Scottish Covenant, to disavow and annul every treaty of peace which had been concluded with the Irish, never to permit the free exercise of the Catholic religion in Ireland, or in any part of his dominions, to acknowledge the authority of the various Parliaments held in Scotland since the commencement of the war, and finally, to govern, in civil affairs, according to the advice of the Parliament, and in religious matters, according to that of the Church. And in order to give to his promise the sanction of an enormous falsehood, he wrote to the Parliament, that, as he had forbidden Montrose to engage in his expedition, he could not regret the defeat of a man who had dared to act in disobedience to his authority.[1]

It is said that Charles hoped by this means to save the life of Montrose, and that, when he was informed of his execution, he was on the point of breaking off all further negotiation. It is said, also, that at Edinburgh, when Montrose's expedition began, the violent party wished to recall the Commissioners of the Parliament from Breda, and to cease all negotiation with Charles; and that the immediate execution of Montrose was the bribe given by the moderate men to the fanatics, in order to induce them to concur in the King's return. No positive trace has remained of these mutual concessions: parties, like individual consciences, have their shameful secrets, which they employ all their arts to conceal. However this may be, no change was made in the existing state of things on either side; the Scottish Commissioners declared that they were satisfied with the King's promises; Charles acquiesced in Montrose's execution, as he had yielded

[1] Clarendon's State Papers, vol. iii. pp. 13—19; Balfour's Annals of Scotland, vol. iv. pp. 24, 25; Lingard's History of England, vol. xi. p. 51; Thurloe's State Papers, vol. i. p. 147.

to his own humiliation; and on the 2d of June, 1650, he embarked at Ter-Veere for Scotland, on board a flotilla which the Prince of Orange had placed at his disposal.[1]

He arrived three weeks afterwards on the coast of Scotland; but, before he was allowed to set foot on shore, he was required to sign the Covenant. The Scottish nobles who had advised him to consent to everything, Hamilton and Lauderdale among others, left him and retired to their estates; they were of the number of those whom, ever since the 22d of March, 1649, the Presbyterian Parliament had formally excluded from all participation in public affairs; and their presence with the King was not only compromising to him, but fraught with danger to themselves. Two days after his disembarkation, nearly all the English who had accompanied Charles were expressly sent out of the kingdom; the Duke of Buckingham, Lord Wilmot, and a few others of his household, the most frivolous and hypocritical of his courtiers, were alone authorized to remain with him. The Parliament had minutely arranged beforehand the route which he was to take to his palace of Falkland, near Edinburgh; and he was conducted thither with great marks of respect, but under the strictest guard and surveillance.[2]

At about the same time, Cromwell, yielding obedience at length to the wishes of the Parliament, returned from Ireland to England; on his disembarkation at Bristol, he was greeted with honors and acclamations by the whole town, who came out *en masse* to welcome him. As soon as it became known that he was near London, Fairfax and most of the officers of the army and members of Parliament went out to meet him at Hounslow Heath; at Hyde Park he found

[1] Laing's History of Scotland, vol. iii. p. 449; Clarendon's State Papers, vol. iii. p. 22.

[2] Godwin's History of the Commonwealth, vol. iii. p. 226; Clarendon's History of the Rebellion, vol. vi. pp. 436, 437.

the Lord Mayor and train-bands waiting for him; and from thence to St. James's Palace, where he was to lodge, it was, say the newspapers of the time, one vast tumult of salutation, congratulation, artillery-volleying, and human shouting. "What a crowd come out to see your Lordship's triumph!" said one of the bystanders to Cromwell; to which he replied, with his rough and frank good sense: "Yes; but if it were to see me hanged, how many would there be!"[1]

As soon as Montrose's expedition in the Highlands, and the arrangements concluded at Breda between Charles II. and the Scottish Commissioners, had become known in London, the Parliament had given the Council of State full powers to repel any invasion, and had voted a considerable increase of the army. Immediately on Cromwell's return from Ireland, Fairfax and he were appointed, the one Lord-General of the Forces, the other Lieutenant-General, to command what was vaguely called the "Northern Expedition." They both signified their acceptance of these appointments; but a few days after, the Council of State having decided that, instead of waiting until the Scots invaded England, the English army should take the initiative, and carry the war into Scotland, Fairfax manifested great reluctance to undertake such a command. His wife, a zealous Presbyterian, and the Presbyterian ministers by whom she was surrounded, had, it is said, suggested these scruples; but, perhaps, also, Fairfax was beginning to perceive that Cromwell and the republicans had used, and wished still to use, him as a cloak to cover, and an instrument to accomplish, designs utterly at variance with his feelings and wishes. In any case, his resistance was, in the eyes of the public, a cause of serious embarrassment, which could not be treated lightly, and to overcome which every effort should be made. Five com-

[1] Cromwell's Letters and Speeches, vol. ii. pp. 163, 164; Whitelocke, p. 457.

missioners — Cromwell, Lambert, Harrison, St. John, and Whitelocke—were appointed by the Council of State to wait upon Fairfax, to confer with him on the subject, and endeavor to remove his difficulties.

"My Lord General," said Cromwell, "we are commanded by the Council of State to endeavor to give your Excellency satisfaction on any doubts of yours which may arise concerning the command in Scotland, and the grounds of the resolution of the Council for the journey into Scotland."

FAIRFAX.—"I am very glad of the opportunity of conferring with this committee, where I find so many of my particular friends, as well as of the Commonwealth, about this great business; for I do acknowledge myself not fully satisfied as to the justice of our invasion of our Scottish brethren."

LAMBERT.—"Will your Excellency be pleased to favor us with the particular causes of your dissatisfaction?"

FAIRFAX.—"I shall very freely do it, and I think I need not make to you, or to any that know me, any protestation of the continuance of my duty and affection to the Parliament, and my readiness to serve them in anything wherein my conscience will give me leave."

HARRISON.—"There cannot be more desired nor expected from your Excellency."

FAIRFAX.—"Give me leave then, my Lords, with all freeness to say to you that I think it doubtful whether we have a just cause to make an invasion upon Scotland. With them we are joined in the National League and Covenant; and now for us, contrary thereunto, and without sufficient cause given us by them, to enter into their country with an army, and to make war upon them, is that which I cannot see the justice of, nor how we shall be able to justify the lawfulness of it before God or man."

CROMWELL.—"I confess, my Lord, that if they have given

us no cause to invade them, it will not be justifiable for us to do it. But, my Lord, they have invaded us, as your lordship knows they have done, since the National Covenant, and contrary to it, in that action of Duke Hamilton, which was by order and authority from the Parliament of that kingdom, and so the act of the whole nation by their representatives. And they now give us too much cause of suspicion that they intend another invasion upon us, joining with their King, with whom they have made a full agreement, without the assent or privity of this Commonwealth; and are very busy at this present in raising forces and money to carry on their design. I humbly submit it to your Excellency's judgment, whether these things are not a sufficient ground and cause for us to endeavor to provide for the safety of our own country, and to prevent the miseries which an invasion of the Scots would bring upon us? That there will be a war between us, I fear, is unavoidable. Your Excellency will soon determine whether it be better to have this war in the bowels of another country or of our own."

FAIRFAX.—"It is probable there will be war between us; but whether we should begin this war and be on the offensive part, or only stand upon our own defence, is that which I scruple. And although they invaded us under Duke Hamilton, who pretended the authority of the Parliament then sitting for it, yet their succeeding Parliament disowned that engagement, and punished some of the promoters of it. If we were assured of their coming with their army into England, I confess it were prudence for us to prevent them, and we are ready to advance into Scotland before they can march into England; but what warrant have we to fall upon them unless we can be assured of their purpose to fall upon us?"

HARRISON.—"I think, under favor, there cannot be greater

assurance or human probability of the intentions of any State than we have of theirs to invade our country."

FAIRFAX.—"Human probabilities are not sufficient grounds to make war upon a neighboring nation, to whom we are engaged in a solemn league and covenant."

ST. JOHN.—"But, my Lord, that league and covenant was first broken by themselves, and so dissolved as to cease, and the disowning of Duke Hamilton's action by their latter Parliament cannot acquit the injury done to us before."

CROMWELL.—"I suppose your Excellency will be convinced of this clear truth, that we are no longer obliged by the league and covenant which themselves did first break."

FAIRFAX.—"I am to answer only for my own conscience; and what that yields unto as just and lawful, I shall follow; and what seems to me, or what I doubt to be, otherwise, I must not do. Every one must stand or fall by his own conscience; those who are satisfied of the justice of this war may cheerfully proceed in it; those who scruple at it, as I confess I do, cannot undertake any service in it. I acknowledge that which hath been said to carry much weight and reason with it, and none can have more power upon me than this Committee, nor none be more ready to serve the Parliament than myself in anything wherein my conscience shall be satisfied; in this it is not, and therefore, that I may be no hindrance to the Parliament's designs, I shall willingly lay down my commission, that it may be in their hands to choose some worthier person than myself, who may upon clear satisfaction of his conscience undertake this business, wherein I desire to be excused."

CROMWELL.—"I am very sorry your lordship should have thoughts of laying down your commission, by which God hath blest you in the performance of so many eminent services for the Parliament. I pray, my Lord, consider all your faithful servants, us who are officers, who have served under you, and desire to serve under no other general. It would be a great discouragement to all of us, and a great discouragement to the affairs of the Parliament, for our noble general to entertain any thoughts of laying down his commission. I hope your lordship will never give so great an advantage to the public enemy, nor so much dishearten your friends as to think of doing so."

FAIRFAX.—"What would you have me do? As far as my conscience will give way, I am willing to join with you still in the service of the Parliament; but where the conscience is not satisfied, none of you, I am sure, will engage in any service; and that is my condition in this, and therefore I must desire to be excused."[1]

The Commissioners immediately reported this answer to the Council of State. "The Lieutenant-General," says Ludlow, "acted his part so to the life that I really thought him in earnest; which obliged me to step to him as he was withdrawing with the rest of the Committee out of the council-chamber, and to desire him that he would not, in compliment and humility, obstruct the service of the nation by his refusal; but the consequence made it sufficiently evident that he had no such intention."[2] Two days afterwards, Whitelocke and Lord Pembroke presented their report to the House, both on the main question of the invasion of Scotland, and on the conference between the Council of State and Fairfax. The House voted unanimously that it was both just and necessary that the English army should enter Scotland, and that it should be set in movement without delay. A declaration justifying this resolution was read and adopted. The House was informed that Mr. Rushworth, Secretary to the Lord-General, was at the door. He was at once admitted, and

[1] Whitelocke's Memorials, pp. 460—462; Old Parliamentary History, vol. xix. pp. 266—275.

[2] Ludlow's Memoirs, p. 135.

informed the House that the Lord-General had commanded him to present, from him, to the Parliament, the last commission he had received from the Parliament for the Scottish war, and likewise his first commission as Lord-General, if the Parliament pleased to desire it. A resolution was immediately passed, withdrawing all military command from Fairfax. This was the rupture of the Commonwealth with the only Presbyterian leader who had served it. Cromwell was at once appointed Captain-General and Commander-in-Chief of all the forces of England. Three days after, he left London to rejoin his army; and three weeks after, he crossed the Tweed, and entered Scotland at the head of about fifteen thousand men. On setting foot on Scottish soil, he harangued his troops. "As a Christian and a soldier, I exhort you to be doubly and trebly diligent, to be wary and worthy, for sure enough we have work before us! But have we not had God's blessing hitherto? Let us go on faithfully, and hope for the like still."[1]

If he had been aware of the proceedings in the councils of Scotland, and of the relation in which the Scots stood to the King whom they had recalled, Cromwell would undoubtedly have felt full confidence in his success. Neither demonstrations of public respect, nor the pomp of royalty, were wanting to complete the illusion of Charles's position; he had been voted an allowance of 9,000*l.* a month for the maintenance of his household; and he had been surrounded with a numerous retinue. In the absence of the Parliament, which then stood adjourned, the members of the intermediate committee, or Committee of Estates as it was called, with the Marquis of Argyle at their head, paid the King the most

[1] Commons' Journals, vol. vi. pp. 431, 432; Godwin's History of the Commonwealth, vol. iii. pp. 215, 221, 222; Cromwell's Letters and Speeches, vol. ii. p. 180.

assiduous homage. Argyle was a consummate courtier, careful to observe every point of etiquette, and to seize every opportunity of pleasing the King in small matters. At the same time, great preparations were being made for the impending war; the Parliament had taken measures for providing Scotland with an army of thirty thousand men; an experienced general, David Lesley, was to command it; and fortifications were in process of construction around the capital. But this show of zeal for monarchy ill concealed the forced nullity of the King, and the incoherence of the ideas and actions of the party who were desirous at once to support him and make him a nonentity. Charles was not present at the councils at which public affairs were discussed, and whenever he attempted to converse seriously with Argyle on the subject, that wily courtier respectfully eluded any such conversation. The theologians, on the other hand, attacked the young Prince whom the politicians took such pains to nullify; observances, remonstrances, and sermons, occupied the leisure which was forced upon him; and notwithstanding all his efforts to appear a hypocrite, he always passed, and deservedly, for a libertine. Although Presbyterians above all things, the Scots were sincere royalists; and Charles, who was but little inclined to indulge in illusions, knew perfectly well that, out of Scotland, he had neither kingdom nor army; but, on both sides, the distrust and dissatisfaction were profound, and although they were mutually necessary to one another, they differed too widely to come either to a thorough understanding or a lasting union.[1]

When it became known that Cromwell had passed the border, it was thought impossible to avoid showing the King to the army. He accordingly went to the camp, and the troops received him with demonstrations of joy, which soon

[1] Clarendon's History of the Rebellion, vol. vi. pp. 436—441; Whitelocke, p. 462; Laing's History of Scotland, vol. iii. p. 450.

aroused the suspicions of both ardent theologians and jealous politicians. Charles was gay, witty, and affable; his presence in the camp gave a great impulse to free conversation, occasioned many expressions of devotedness to his person, and probably led to some symptoms of insubordination and dislike of his keepers. The fanatics eagerly availed themselves of this opportunity; they loudly inveighed against the composition of the army, which contained, they said, a large number of malignants, old Hamiltonians, and episcopalian or libertine royalists. A purification was ordered; eighty officers were cashiered, and according to some authorities, several thousand soldiers were also disbanded. The King was not permitted to remain any longer in the camp. He was conducted with all haste to Leith, further north than he had yet been. But even these precautions were insufficient to calm the fears or satisfy the passions of the fanatics; they resolved to intimidate and compromise Charles more thoroughly still. They required him to sign an expiatory declaration, in which he should formally acknowledge and condemn the evil deeds of his father, the idolatry of his mother, and his own sin in consenting to a treaty with the Irish rebels; and should renew, against Popery and heresy, and in favor of free Parliament and the Presbyterian government of the church, all the protestations and promises which had already been obtained from him.[1]

Charles's first impulse was to refuse, saying that he would never again be able to look his mother in the face after signing such a document. He then requested time to take the advice of the council. The fanatics refused to wait; the Committee of Estates and that of the Kirk declared "that they espoused no malignant quarrel or party, nor acknow-

[1] Godwin's History of the Commonwealth, vol. iii. p. 226; Clarendon's History of the Rebellion, vol. vi. pp. 453, 454; Brodie's History of the British Empire, vol. iv. p. 280.

ledged the King or his interests, otherwise but in subordination to God; but they would vindicate themselves from the aspersion that they owned and supported his Majesty in all the proceedings of the late King."[1] Most of the officers of the army assured the Committee of Estates of their adherence to this declaration. Some of them even, including Colonel Strahan, the conqueror of Montrose, had secret communications with the English army and Cromwell on this subject; at which the royalists were justly alarmed. The Presbyterian ministers thundered from their pulpits that the King was the very root of malignancy, and that he had sworn to observe the Covenant without any intention of keeping his oath. Political reservations cannot withstand the contact of sincere passions. Charles was intimidated, yielded, and signed the expiatory declaration. Overjoyed at their triumph, the fanatics, and the people and army with them, celebrated a solemn fast in honor of this expiation; and more than one preacher assured his audience that "now the anger of heaven had been appeased, they would gain an easy victory over a blaspheming general and a sectarian army."[2]

A few months after this humiliation, Charles gave an audience to Dr. King, Dean of Tuam, who was about to return to the Marquis of Ormonde, in Ireland. "Mr. King," he said, "I have received a very good character of you, and do therefore give you asurance that however I am forced by the necessity of my affairs to appear otherwise, yet I am a true child of the Church of England, and shall remain firm unto my first principles. Mr. King, I am a true Cavalier. I understand you are willing to go into Ireland. My Lord

[1] Laing's History of Scotland, vol. iii. p. 455.

[2] Laing's History of Scotland, vol. iii. pp. 454—457; Whitelocke, pp. 468, 469; Cromwell's Letters and Speeches, vol. ii. p. 194; Lingard's History of England, vol. xi. pp. 59—60; Brodie's History of the British Empire, vol. iv. pp. 281—284; Burnet's History of His Own Time, vol. i. p. 99.

of Ormonde is a person that I depend upon more than any one living. I much fear that I have been forced to do some things which may prejudice him. You have heard how a declaration was extorted from me, and how I should have been dealt withal, if I had not signed it. Yet what concerns Ireland is no ways binding, for I can do nothing in the affairs of that kingdom, without the advice of my Council there, nor hath that kingdom any dependence upon this, so that what I have done is nothing; yet I fear it may prejudice my Lord of Ormonde, and my friends with him, so that if you would satisfy him in this, you would do a very acceptable service unto me; and tell him that I account it not only an error, but a misfortune that I came not into Ireland when he invited me thither."[1]

Cromwell was not ignorant of these dissensions in the Scottish government; but he soon found himself, with his army, in so difficult a position, that he was more occupied with escaping from his own dangers, than in taking advantage of the weakness of his enemies. As fast as he advanced into the Scottish territory, between the border and Edinburgh, the population retired before him with their cattle, furniture, and provisions, leaving in their villages only a few old women, who refused even to brew and bake for the English troops. This was in consequence of the orders of Lesley, and the sermons of the Presbyterian ministers, who were never weary of denouncing the republican sectaries, declaring that they would massacre all the inhabitants between the ages of sixteen and sixty—that they would cut off the right hand of all between six and sixteen years old—that they would burn the breasts of the women with hot irons—and destroy everything they found in their way. In vain had Cromwell published and distributed along his route, two proclamations addressed,

[1] Carte's Ormonde Letters, vol. i. pp. 391—393.

one "To the people of Scotland," and the other, "To all that are Saints and Partakers of the Faith of God's Elect in Scotland;" and intended, the first to dissipate the terrors of the people, and the second to satisfy their pious passions. In vain did he maintain the strictest discipline in his army, and sent back to Edinburgh, in his own carriage—in order to disprove the reputation for stern cruelty which was attributed to him—some Scottish officers, who had been taken prisoners in a skirmish: the feeling of terror and antipathy continued and increased. Cromwell was able to victual his troops only by keeping near the sea-coast, and obtaining supplies of provisions from England. Although it was the month of August, the weather was bad; it rained continually, and illness broke out in the English army. The Scottish general kept his men within their entrenchments, between Edinburgh and Leith, and was evidently determined to rest satisfied with covering the capital, and to avoid any general action, leaving the English to waste their strength in the solitude of the country, and the dearth of their camp. Cromwell more than once attempted to draw Lesley out of his lines, and to give him battle; he even risked his own person so openly in these skirmishes, that a Scottish soldier recognized him, and fired at him; upon which Cromwell shouted to him, "that if he had been one of his soldiers, he would have cashiered him for firing at such a distance." All these attempts, however, led to no result. Lesley remained steadily within his lines. "They hope," wrote Cromwell to Bradshaw, from Musselburgh, "we shall famish for want of provisions, which is very likely to be, if we be not timely and fully supplied."[1]

[1] Cromwell's Letters and Speeches, vol. ii. pp. 179—184; Whitelocke, p. 469; Old Parliamentary History, vol. xix. pp. 298—312; Brodie's History of the British Empire, vol. iv. pp. 278, 284—287; Godwin's History of the Commonwealth, vol. iii. p. 228.

His position soon became so critical, that Cromwell resolved to escape from it at any risk. It was decided in a council of war, that the army should fall back upon Dunbar, there to await supplies and reinforcements, and should retreat from thence, along the coast towards the English border, if reinforcements were not sent. On the following day, five hundred invalids were embarked at Musselburgh, and the retreat began. Lesley issued immediately from his camp, and closely followed the English army, harassing and attacking it at every step, without ever consenting to a general action. One of these attacks, during the night, was so vigorous, that "our rear-brigade of horse," writes Cromwell, "had like to have engaged with their whole army, had not the Lord, by his providence, put a cloud over the moon, thereby giving us opportunity to draw off those horse to the rest of our army." The English reached Dunbar in great distress, and on his arrival, Cromwell learned that Lesley had just occupied, with a considerable detachment, the pass of Cockburnspath, between that town and the English border; a narrow defile, "where," says Cromwell himself, "ten men to hinder are better than forty to make their way." As incapable of illusion as of discouragement, Cromwell wrote at once to Sir Arthur Haslerig, governor of Newcastle: "We are upon an engagement very difficult. The enemy hath blocked up our way at the pass at Copperspath, through which we cannot get without almost a miracle. He lieth so upon the hills, that we know not how to come that way without great difficulty; and our lying here clearly consumeth our men, who fall sick beyond imagination. I perceive your forces are not in a capacity for present release, wherefore, whatever becomes of us, it will be well for you to get what forces you can together, and the south to help what they can. The business nearly concerneth all good people. If your forces had been in a readiness to have fallen upon the back of Copperspath, it might have occasioned supplies to have come to us. But the only wise God knows what is best. All shall work for good. Our spirits are comfortable, praised be the Lord—though our present condition be as it is. And indeed we have much hope in the Lord, of whose mercy we have had large experience. Indeed, do you get together what forces you can against them. Set to friends in the South to help with more. Let H. Vane know what I write. I would not make it public, lest danger should accrue thereby. You know what use to make thereof."[1]

Great agitation, but of a very different character—the agitation of joy and pride—pervaded the Scottish camp. They saw retreating before them, "that Antichrist, that arrogant man, Cromwell, over whose head the curse of God hung for murdering the King and breaking the Covenant, who termed his guns his twelve apostles, and put his whole confidence in them." They held both his army and himself hemmed in between their mountains, their ocean, and their battalions. Lesley convoked his council; his own position was not exempt from difficulties; he could find neither water nor forage on the hills which were occupied by his troops; and it would be exceedingly dangerous to prolong his stay there. He persisted, however, in his opinion: they must, he said, continue to avoid any action, and to drive the English army, day by day, towards the border; what victory could be greater than to compel it to return home sick and humiliated, vanquished without a battle? Nearly all his officers were of the same opinion. But Lesley's council was not a simple council of war: delegates from the Committee of Estates and of the Kirk accompanied him; many ministers, and those most zealous fanatics, lived and preached in his camp; they taxed him with sloth, and urged him not to

[1] Cromwell's Letters and Speeches, vol. ii. pp. 198—201, 212, 213.

allow the escape of those enemies whom God had delivered into their hands. "They had disposed of us, and of their business," writes Cromwell, "in sufficient revenge and wrath towards our persons; and had swallowed up the poor interest of England, believing that their army and their King would have marched to London without any interruption." Although unconvinced, Lesley made but little resistance; he, also, had doubtless his illusions and temptations of pride. In a skirmish with an outpost, an English soldier, "a very stout man, though he had but a wooden arm," who had made himself conspicuous by his desperate resistance, was taken prisoner, and brought before Lesley, who asked him, "If the enemy intended to fight?" "What do you think we come here for?" answered the soldier; "we come for nothing else." "Soldier," said Lesley, "how will you fight, when you have shipped half of your men and all your great guns?" The man replied: "Sir, if you please to draw down your men, you shall find both men and great guns too." Lesley, more moved by the soldier's firmness than by his suggestion, sent him away free, and determined to seek the battle which he had until then so carefully avoided. "By seven o'clock to-morrow," he said to his officers, "we will have the English army, dead or alive."[1]

On the same day, in the morning, Cromwell, perplexed in spite of his firmness, had invited his most faithful friends to meet him, to pray together, and invoke the aid of God in their peril. "We lay very near the enemy," he writes, "being sensible of our disadvantage; having some weakness of flesh, but yet consolation and support from the Lord himself to our poor weak faith, wherein I believe not a few amongst

[1] Brodie's History of the British Empire, vol. iv. pp. 286—292; Lingard's History of England, vol. xi. pp. 61, 62; Cromwell's Letters and Speeches, vol. ii. pp. 202, 203; Carte's Ormonde Letters, vol. i. pp. 381—384.

us stand: That, because of their number, because of their advantages, because of their confidence, because of our weakness, because of our strait, we were in the mount, and in the mount the Lord would be seen; and that he would find out a way of deliverance and salvation for us; and, indeed, we had our consolations and our hopes.[1] When this devotional service was ended, at about four o'clock in the afternoon, Cromwell mounted his horse, and rode with Lambert, his major-general, about the neighborhood of Dunbar, in the park of Brocksmouth House, the residence of the Earl of Roxburgh. While looking towards the enemy from this point, he discerned through his glass an extraordinary movement in their camp: a portion, first of their cavalry and then of their artillery, marched from their left wing to their right, and descended the hills towards the sea, as if they intended more effectually to cut off all retreat for the English army, and to give it battle as soon as it began to move. "They are coming down," cried Cromwell; "the Lord hath delivered them into our hands!" He called Lambert's attention to this movement, and asked if it was not his opinion that they would now be able to attack the Scots with advantage. Lambert quite agreed with him, and Monk, coming up, likewise assented. A council of war was immediately convoked; Cromwell proposed that at daybreak the army should begin its march, and attack the Scots, who appeared determined to give battle, and to dispute their passage at every point. Monk energetically supported this proposition, and offered to lead the van, at the head of his brigade of foot.[2] The resolution was unanimously adopted, and the English spent the night in noiseless preparations for the combat.

[1] Cromwell's Letters and Speeches, vol. ii. pp. 213, 214.

[2] Burnet's History of His Own Time, vol. i. p. 100; Carte's Ormonde Letters, vol. i. p. 382; Laing's History of Scotland, vol. iii. p. 459.

The night was wild and wet, and just before daybreak, a thick fog arose, which caused the attack to begin a little later than Cromwell had intended. At the outset the English had the worst of it; their advanced guard of cavalry were vigorously received and repulsed by the Scottish artillery and lancers; the first regiment of English infantry restored the action, but did not decide it; and the fight continued hotly for some time, amid cries of "The Lord of Hosts!" from the English, and "The Covenant!" from the Scots. At about seven o'clock, Cromwell's own regiment of foot charged suddenly, and broke the Scottish lines. At this moment the fog dispersed, the sun shone brightly over hill and ocean. "Now, let God arise," exclaimed Cromwell, "and his enemies shall be scattered!" His words gave fresh courage to his men, and were repeated by all who stood near him. "He was a strong man," says one of his contemporaries; "in the dark perils of war, in the high places of the field, hope shone in him like a pillar of fire, when it had gone out in all the others." Enthusiasm is as contagious as discouragement; the English charged with redoubled vigor; the Scottish cavalry gave way; a body of infantry, which made a bold resistance, was broken through and scattered by the English squadrons; the cry arose, "They run! they run!" Disorder spread rapidly throughout the Scottish army, which took to flight in every direction. "After the first repulse," writes Cromwell, "they were made by the Lord of Hosts as stubble to our swords." At nine o'clock the battle was over; three thousand Scots had been slain; more than ten thousand prisoners, with all their artillery and baggage, and two hundred standards, were in the hands of the English. "I believe I may speak it without partiality," wrote Cromwell on the following day to the Parliament, "both your chief commanders and others in their several places, and soldiers also, acted with as much courage as ever hath been seen in any action since this war. I know they look not to be named, and therefore I forbear particulars."[1]

Two days afterwards, on the 5th of September, Cromwell resumed the offensive; and within four days he was master of Leith, of the whole country around Edinburgh, and of Edinburgh itself with the exception of the castle, which was occupied by a strong garrison. Charles II. and the whole Scottish government retired northwards, to Perth; Lesley, with the wreck of his army, westwards, to Stirling. The republican Parliament had attained its object: Scotland was invaded, and had fully enough to do to defend her own territory.

Amidst the general alarm, Charles rejoiced, in his heart, at the defeat of the fanatics, whose yoke he endured so impatiently. To them, to their malevolent exclusions and blind requirements, public opinion was beginning to ascribe these unexpected reverses. In vain did the six ministers who formed the Committee of the Kirk endeavor, in a sombre manifesto, to throw all the responsibility on the obstinate wickedness of their adversaries; maintaining that God would have given Lesley the victory, if the army and court had been thoroughly purged of all malignants. There is, even under the sway of the most ardent fanaticism, a degree of absurdity which, in presence of imperious and melancholy events, does not easily obtain credence. Charles deemed the moment favorable for escaping from his masters: by means of some of his officers, and particularly of Dr. Frazier, his physician, a determined enemy of Argyle, who had recently procured his banishment from court, he entered into secret negotiations with the royalist chiefs of the Scottish High-

[1] Carlyle's Letters and Speeches, vol. ii. pp. 206—216; Carte's Ormonde Letters, vol. i. pp. 380—384; Ludlow's Memoirs, p. 141; Whitelocke, pp. 470, 471; Brodie's History of the British Empire, vol. iv. pp. 292—294; Forster's Statesmen of the Commonwealth, vol. iv. pp. 286—290.

lands, among others with the Lords Huntly, Middleton, Ogilvy, and Dudhope, who promised to rise in arms as soon as he appeared among them. But at the very moment when his escape was finally arranged, the secret was communicated to Argyle, and the Committee of Estates immediately ordered all the Cavaliers, who still remained with the King, to leave the court within twenty-four hours, and the kingdom within twenty days. Three only were excepted from this order, and one of these was the Duke of Buckingham, who was suspected of having revealed the secret. Charles demanded that nine others of his friends should be excepted; his demand was refused. He did not press it; but, a week after, he left Perth at about one o'clock in the afternoon, in hunting costume, attended only by five servants; and as soon as he was out of sight, he set spurs to his horse, joined Lord Dudhope and Lord Buchan, who were waiting for him, and arrived at nightfall, escorted by a few Highlanders, at the house of the Laird of Clova, distant about fifty miles from Perth. He was sleeping quietly on a mattress, when, at break of day, entered Colonel Montgomery and three other officers sent from Perth by the Committee of Estates, who had discovered almost simultaneously the flight of the King and the place of his retreat. Charles parleyed with them; he had escaped, he told them, only because he had been informed that the Committee of Estates intended to give him up to the English, and to hang all his servants. Montgomery averred that this was a calumny. The chiefs who had escorted the King in his escape urged him to remain with them, assuring him that, some few miles further, he would find a numerous body of Highlanders ready to obey his orders. But the promise seemed vague, and Charles, like his father, had no great taste for hazardous adventures. Whilst he was hesitating, two squadrons of Scottish cavalry arrived to support Montgomery's representations. Seeing the house surrounded with troops, Charles yielded, and was immediately taken back to Perth.[1]

This ridiculous *Start*, as it was called, was not, however, lost to Charles. Argyle and the Committee of Estates became alarmed, both at the antipathy with which they inspired him, and at the facilities which he could find for escaping from them. In the Presbyterian church also, there were not wanting ministers more sensible than their fanatical colleagues, who said that they were not treating the King well, that they were unjust and harsh towards the moderate royalists, and that they should strive to rally all parties together, instead of perpetuating and exacerbating old dissensions. These opinions had their influence in the Parliament which met at Perth; it manifested as much zeal for the King's cause, and greater toleration of royalists of all shades; it voted all that was necessary for the reorganization of the army; and two resolutions, though violently opposed by the fanatics, were adopted—the one declaring that the expressions of repentance of the partisans of the late Duke of Hamilton should be accepted; and the other that, this done, they should be permitted to serve the King and defend the kingdom. A large number of moderate Presbyterians, and even of Cavaliers, hastened to profit by this permission: Hamilton and Lauderdale returned to court. Charles presided over the council, and gave his attention, without obstacle, to the affairs of the Parliament and army. Finally it was announced that, ere long, according to ancient usage, he would be solemnly crowned at Scone, and the preparations for this ceremony began. Argyle was not altogether free from anxiety at this movement, which brought his adversaries once more into contact with the King, and irritated his firm friends, the fanatics;

[1] Laing's History of Scotland, vol. iii. p. 464; Baillie's Letters, vol. ii. p. 356; Clarendon's History of the Rebellion, vol. vi. pp. 484—486; Lingard's History of England, vol. xi. pp. 64, 65.

but he felt the necessity of yielding, and Charles graciously took pains to quiet his distrust and calm his displeasure. He even went so far as to lead him to suppose that he might probably marry his daughter; and Captain Titus, a Presbyterian who was on good terms with Argyle, was sent into France to the Queen-mother, as if to obtain her consent.[1]

Cromwell, freed from the great care which had momentarily absorbed his whole attention, attentively observed these political resolutions of his adversaries, and anticipated much advantage from them. He was equally well able to address masses and individuals, to appeal to religious convictions, and to treat with material interests. The declaration which, on his arrival in Scotland, he had addressed "To all that are Saints and Partakers of the Faith of God's Elect in Scotland," had met with a vehement answer from the Scottish Kirk. Cromwell immediately seized upon this opportunity for entering into correspondence and controversy with them, discussing both their arguments and their acts, referring them to various passages of Holy Scripture in support of his own views, and inviting them to appeal to the general judgment of believers on the question at issue between them and himself. "You conceal from your own people," he says, "the papers we have sent you, as they might thereby see and understand the bowels of our affection to them, especially to such among them as fear the Lord." As soon as he was master of Edinburgh, he sent a letter to the governor of the Castle, in which most of the Presbyterian ministers had taken refuge, to inform them, "that they have free liberty granted them, if they please to take the pains, to preach in their several churches; and that he had given special commands both to officers and soldiers that they should not

[1] Clarendon's History of the Rebellion, vol. vi. pp. 487, 488; Laing's History of Scotland, vol. iii. pp. 464, 465; Burnet's History of his own Time, vol. i. p. 105.

in the least be molested." They refused to avail themselves of this permission, saying that they found nothing in his letter "whereupon to build any security for their persons while in the town, and for their return to the castle." He upbraided them for their pusillanimity in his reply, saying, "that if their Master's service (as they call it) were chiefly in their eye, imagination of suffering would not have caused such a return" to his proposal; and boldly affirming that "no man had been troubled in England or Ireland for preaching the Gospel; though none had liberty under pretence thereof, to overtop or debase the civil power."[1] He cared little about the strict accuracy of his assertions, provided that they produced, at the time when he spoke, and upon the public whom he addressed, the impression which he required.

A few months later, during a visit to Glasgow, he frequently attended at Presbyterian sermons, taking care to protect the liberty of the preachers, even when they attacked him, and always manifesting the greatest eagerness to enter into discussion with them. "He one day sent to them," says one of his officers, "to give us a friendly Christian meeting, to discourse of those things which they rail against us for; that so, if possible, all misunderstandings between us might be taken away. Which accordingly they gave us, on Wednesday last. There was no bitterness nor passion vented on either side; all was with moderation and tenderness. My Lord General and Major-General Lambert, for the most part, maintained the discourse; and on their part, Mr. James Guthrie and Mr. Patrick Gillespie. We know not what satisfaction they have received. Sure I am, there was no such weight in their arguments as might in the least discourage us from what we have undertaken."[2]

[1] Carlyle's Letters and Speeches, vol. ii. pp. 231—233; Old Parliamentary History, vol. xix. pp. 320—323; Thurloe's State Papers, vol. i. pp. 158—162.

[2] Cromwell's Letters and Speeches, vol. ii. p. 310.

Cromwell took as much care to conciliate individuals as to exercise a directing and favorable influence upon popular opinion. He found, among his prisoners, Mr. Alexander Jaffray, Provost of Aberdeen, and Mr. Carstairs, a Presbyterian minister of Glasgow, both intelligent and influential men; he conversed familiarly with them, and treated them so well that he succeeded in obtaining a strong hold upon their minds; upon which he made haste to exchange them for some English prisoners who were detained in Dumbarton Castle, and they became useful agents to him in the country. He never let slip any opportunity of showing politeness and confidence to the men who he knew were more favorable to the Commonwealth than to Charles Stuart; he was particularly attentive, for instance, to Sir Archibald Johnstone, who thenceforward became his secret friend, and ultimately his vigorous ally. Even under the most insignificant circumstances, from natural character or from calculation, he was careful to please those who were indifferent or hostile to him. Riding one day on a reconnoitering expedition in Lanarkshire, with some officers, he was in want of a guide, and could find none, "save one valetudinary gentleman," son of Sir Walter Stewart of Allertoun, a royalist and covenanter, another of whose sons had served as a captain in the Scottish army at the battle of Dunbar. When he had completed his survey, Cromwell called in at the house; Sir Walter had absconded; and his wife, who "was as much for the King and royal family as her husband," was alone to entertain the republican General. Cromwell entered into conversation with her, spoke with interest of her husband, her relatives and her children; and said that change of climate would be beneficial to her invalid son, and that Montpelier, in the south of France, would be the place for him. Another of her sons, a lad of ten years, went up to Cromwell, and began to handle the hilt of his sword: Cromwell patted him on the head, and said, "You are my little captain." On rising from table, he returned thanks to God for his repast in his usual manner, and prayed for a blessing upon the family. He then set off to rejoin the army, leaving the lady of the house full of admiration for his amiability and piety; "she was sure," she said, "that Cromwell was one who feared God, and had the true interest of religion at heart."[1]

Thus fomented by the able policy of Cromwell, division broke out among the Scots. In proportion as the Presbyterian leaders became more moderate, and manifested greater deference to the King, and tolerance of his friends, the fanatics became more violent, and separated more widely from him. They were especially incensed at certain resolutions of the Parliament, which, in consideration of a few expressions of repentance, had allowed the old royalists to resume their positions both in the court and the army. They addressed a violent remonstrance, on this subject, to the Committee of Estates, in which they openly attacked the King, regretted that he had ever been recalled; demanded that he should be excluded, for a time at least, from all participation in the government, and that his ministers, Argyle and Loudon among others, should be dismissed; and protested against all idea of an invasion of England, and even against the continuation of the war, as essentially unlawful, if it were to be carried on in the interest, and by the exertion of the libertine or hypocritical royalists. After the defeat at Dunbar, five counties of the southwest of Scotland, in which these opinions were predominant—Renfrew, Ayr, Galloway, Wigton, and Dumfries—had formed themselves into a separate association, and had demanded permission to levy troops on their own account, declaring that they would continue to resist the English sectaries, but that they would no longer serve under Lesley. The Parliament at Perth had weakly

[1] Cromwell's Letters and Speeches, vol. ii. pp. 311, 312.

consented to this; three or four thousand men had been levied in the remonstrant counties, and were under the command of Colonels Kerr and Strahan, the two most impetuous officers in the army, and both of them, or at least Strahan, in close correspondence with Cromwell. The fanatics, therefore, had both troops and leaders in that district. The Scottish government began to feel alarmed; the remonstrance was voted calumnious, treacherous, and dangerous: and Colonel Montgomery was sent, with two regiments of cavalry, to take the command of all the King's forces in the west. But the discussion had been long, and the execution was far from rapid; before it was possible to re-establish the authority of the government in the confederated counties, Cromwell sent Lambert thither with a body of troops, and eventually proceeded thither himself. Either by force of arms, or by the connivance of its leaders, the little army of fanatics was defeated and dispersed: and of its two commanders, one, Colonel Kerr, was wounded and taken prisoner without much resistance, and the other, Colonel Strahan, openly went over to Cromwell with several officers. "There is at this time," wrote Cromwell after this expedition, "a very great distraction, and mighty workings of God upon the hearts of divers, both ministers and people, much of it tending to the justification of our cause. And although some are as bitter and as bad as ever, making it their business to shuffle hypocritically with their consciences and the Covenant, to make it seem lawful to join with malignants, which now they do—as well they might long before, having taken in the head malignant of them: yet truly others are startled at it; and some have been constrained by the work of God upon their consciences, to make sad and solemn accusation of themselves; charging themselves as guilty of the bloodshed in this war, by having a hand in the treaty at Breda, and by bringing the King in amongst them. This lately did a lord of the session, and withdrew from the Committee of Estates. And lately Mr. James Livingston, a man as highly esteemed as any for piety and learning, who was a commissioner for the Kirk at the said treaty, charged himself with the guilt of the blood of the war, before their assembly; and withdrew from them, and is retired to his own house."[1]

Charles was as much rejoiced as Cromwell at this disorganization of the Presbyterian party, for at the same time, and by a natural coincidence, the royalist party became reconstituted; the moderate men daily allied themselves more closely with it, in order to escape from the yoke of the sectaries, who lost ground in the opinion of the quieter part of the population by their acts of violence and by their reverses of fortune; while the royalist nobles regained their former influence. The coronation took place in the cathedral church of Scone, on the 1st of January, 1651, with all the old regal solemnities; and notwithstanding the Presbyterian harshness of the sermon delivered on the occasion by Robert Douglas, the moderator of the general assembly of the Kirk —notwithstanding the unintelligent stringency of the oaths required from Charles—a feeling of serious and devoted loyalty animated the whole proceeding; the spectators, both lay and clerical, nobles and people, however ill-assorted their ideas in regard to government may have been, all sincerely desired a monarchical régime for their country, and Charles Stuart for their King.[2] Out of respect for his right they exposed themselves, by crowning him, to a very unequal conflict. Happy would it have been if they could have reckoned, on his part, upon a just return of sincerity and affection!

Almost at the very moment that Charles was crowned at

[1] Cromwell's Letters and Speeches, vol. ii. pp. 263—265; Baillie's Letters, vol. ii. pp. 348—369; Burnet's History of his own Time, vol. i. pp. 103—105; Laing's History of Scotland, vol. iii. pp. 461—466.

[2] Somers's Tracts, vol. vi. pp. 117—143.

Scone, the republican Parliament of England sent into Scotland a celebrated engraver, named Symons, to take the portrait of Cromwell, for the purpose of transferring it to a medal to be struck in commemoration of the battle of Dunbar. "It was not a little wonder to me," wrote Cromwell, "to see that you should send Mr. Symons so great a journey, about a business importing so little, as far as it relates to me; whereas, if my poor opinion may not be rejected by you, I have to offer to that which I think the most noble end, to wit, the commemoration of that great mercy at Dunbar, and the gratuity to the army; which might be better expressed upon the medal, by engraving on the one side the Parliament, which I hear was intended, and will do singularly well; and on the other side an Army, with the inscription over the head of it, *The Lord of Hosts!* which was our word that day. Wherefore, if I may beg it as a favor from you, I most earnestly beseech you, if I may do it without offence, that it may be so. And if you think not fit to have it as I offer, you may alter it as you see cause; only I do think I may truly say it will be very thankfully acknowledged by me, if you will spare the having my effigies in it."[1] The medal was struck without regard to this desire, and as it had been originally projected. No great man ever carried the hypocrisy of modesty so far as Cromwell, or so easily subordinated his vanity to his ambition.

Two incidents now occurred to give a new and unexpected direction to the progress of affairs and of the war. Cromwell fell seriously ill. Royalist plots broke out in England.

Ever since Charles II. had been in Scotland, the English royalists had been agitating in every direction to go to his assistance. He had sent blank commissions, with his signa-

[1] Cromwell's Letters and Speeches, vol. ii. pp. 290, 291; Harris's Life of Cromwell, p. 519.

ture, to many of them, giving them authority to raise men, to confer appointments, to make promises, in short, to act for him and in his name. Among the Cavaliers who resided in England, many were indiscreet, either from temerity or vanity; those who were living in safety on the Continent, in Holland, or at Paris with the Queen-mother, frequently compromised their friends at home by their correspondence or conversation; great jealousy and distrust existed among the different groups of these exiles, who were incessantly disputing for influence in their banishment, or quarrelling about their future hopes. Sometimes they refused to communicate or co-operate with one another; and sometimes they betrayed each other, from animosity or levity. The republican Council of State had organized, against them and among their own ranks, a very active police. One of its members, Scott, was specially entrusted with its management, and wanted neither ability nor funds for the proper discharge of his duty. During the years 1650 and 1651, four royalist plots were set on foot, either by old Cavaliers, or by Presbyterians, who were all the more zealous, because their conversion was both recent and sincere; but all failed, and in the space of thirteen months, twenty-seven royalists, military and civil, lay and ecclesiastic, known and obscure, were brought to the scaffold; some by sentence of court-martial, but most after trial by those High Courts of Justice which were erected, not for the purpose of judging in accordance with the laws, but in order to defend the Commonwealth against the opinions of the people, and the enterprise of its enemies. All these reverses, however, did not discourage the English royalists; they were devoted, harassed, and unoccupied; their King was in Scotland; his friends there were fighting for him; and thence they obtained, with regard to his danger, his strength, and his designs, vague notions which kindled both their animosities and their hopes. They could not make up their minds to remain quiet, when their cause was being so vigorously debated at their very gates; and, in their turn, they sent into Scotland reports of their attempts at insurrection, their illusions, and their promises.[1]

Whilst the royalist spirit was thus reviving in Scotland, and fermenting in England, Cromwell, on his return from a long winter's march at the head of his troops, through a heavy storm of hail, snow, and rain, was seized at Edinburgh with a violent attack of fever. This illness became serious; the Parliament and Council of State grew alarmed, and sent an express messenger to Cromwell, with the strongest assurances of their concern and solicitude; to which he thus replied in a letter to Bradshaw: "I do with all humble thankfulness acknowledge your high favor and tender respect of me, in sending an express to enquire after one so unworthy as myself. Indeed, my lord, your service needs not me; I am a poor creature; and have been a dry bone; and am still an unprofitable servant to my Master and you. I thought I should have died of this fit of sickness; but the Lord seemeth to dispose otherwise. But truly, my lord, I desire not to live, unless I may obtain mercy from the Lord to approve my heart and life to Him in more faithfulness and thankfulness, and to those I serve in more profitableness and diligence."[2] He soon got better, and resumed his ordinary mode of life. "The Lord General is now well recovered," was the news sent from Edinburgh to London; "he was in his dining-room to-day with his officers, and was very cheerful and pleasant; so that there is not any fear, by the blessing of God, but that he will be enabled to take the field when the pro-

[1] Milton's State Papers, pp. 33, 34, 37; Commons' Journals, vol. vi. pp. 504, 506; Whitelocke, pp. 484, 486; Carte's Ormonde Letters, vol. i. p. 414; Clarendon's History of the Rebellion, vol. xi. p. 490.

[2] Cromwell's Letters and Speeches, vol. ii. p. 302.

visions arrive."[1] And so, in fact, he did; but his disease soon broke out again, and three successive relapses bore witness to its obstinacy. The Parliament sent two celebrated physicians, Dr. Bates and Dr. Wright, to Edinburgh, without delay, and Fairfax gave them his own carriage for the journey. And finally, the House voted that "in regard to the Lord General's relapse, and present indisposedness, and the nature and sharpness of the air where he is, he be desired, in relation to his health, to remove himself into some part of England, until, by the blessing of God upon means used, he be restored into a condition of health and strength to return to the army; he disposing thereof, in the mean time, and the management of affairs there, into such hands as he shall think fit."[2]

When these votes reached Scotland, an important event had just occurred, which led to the expectation that fresh resolutions would be adopted by the royalist party. The moderate men, with Hamilton and Lauderdale at their head, had decidedly gained the ascendency in the Scottish Parliament. Argyle and his friends made vain efforts to oppose them; and Charles, while treating the rigid Presbyterians with courtesy and consideration, successfully employed all his address and influence to secure and enhance the triumph of their adversaries;-the army was reorganized in accordance with his wishes; in spite of violent debates, and the formal protest of the Chancellor, Lord Loudon, a number of old royalists, and those of the most obnoxious class, were appointed colonels. Finally, the Parliament invited the King to take the command in person,[3] and Charles actually became

[1] Cromwelliana, p. 101.

[2] Commons' Journals, vol. vi. p. 579; Cromwell's Letters and Speeches, vol. ii. p. 314; Whitelocke's Memorials, p. 494.

[3] Laing's History of Scotland, vol. iii. p. 467; Browne's History of the Highlands, vol. ii. p. 69; Godwin's History of the Commonwealth, vol. iii. pp. 246, 247.

the leader of his troops, as well as the head of his council, at the very moment when the English Parliament advised Cromwell, for the sake of his health, to leave Scotland, where he seemed on the point of death.

A month had scarcely elapsed, and, either from the vigor of his constitution or the energy of his will, Cromwell was convalescent, and had actively recommenced the campaign; manœuvring round about the Scottish army, which was again shut up within its intrenchments at Stirling; reducing to submission the adjacent counties; gaining possession, by storm or treachery, of most of the fortresses which still held out against him; defeating, either in person, or by his lieutenants, the detached bodies of troops which attempted to hamper his movements; and finally laying siege to Perth—thus threatening to deprive Charles, who lay encamped at Stirling with his army, of the seat of his government.

Charles then abruptly took the resolution which he had long been meditating; he announced to his council his intention of breaking up the camp, and carrying the war into England, where his partisans only awaited his presence to rise in insurrection against the Parliament. Many of the Scottish leaders, assuredly, though staunch royalists, were far from approving, in their hearts, of such a design; they had little inclination to compromise themselves so far with their formidable neighbors; sometimes even they had suggested to Charles that he would do well to content himself with the crown of Scotland, and to leave England to struggle, as long as it pleased, beneath the yoke of the Commonwealth, and of its revolutionary factions. The recollection of the invasion attempted in 1647, by the late Duke of Hamilton, and of its ill success, was still present to their minds. Nevertheless, most of them silently assented to the plan, being either intimidated by the will of the King, or carried away by the irresistible influence which is always exercised over men's minds by a bold resolution in critical circumstances. Argyle, almost alone, used every effort to dissuade the King from this step; out of jealousy for the loss of his power, perhaps, for it marked the triumph of his rivals, the Hamilton faction; but also from prudence and political sagacity. He estimated more correctly than the little court of Charles, the state of the public mind in England, the ardor of the young republican party, and the slight chances in favor of a royalist insurrection. Why run such risks, and leave Scotland destitute both of its army and its King, after it had shown so much devotion to his cause? Why plunge, with his little Scottish army, into the midst of his enemies, when he might, by remaining in Scotland on the defensive, waste and destroy the English army, and Cromwell himself, by the severities of a second winter? Charles gave no heed to his advice. Argyle insisted, declaring that, for his part, he would never share in such an undertaking, and requested permission to retire to his estates. Some persons advised Charles to have him immediately arrested; it was dangerous, they said, to leave so powerful a malcontent behind him in Scotland. Charles refused, however, either out of consideration for his recent intimacy with Argyle, or from fear of the consequences of an open rupture. Argyle set out at once for his seat at Inverary. The King publicly announced, by proclamation, his intention to begin his march for England on the following day, accompanied by those of his subjects who were willing to prove their loyalty to him by sharing his fortune; and on the following day, in fact, the 31st of July, 1651, he was on his road to Carlisle, at the head of an army of eleven, or according to some authorities, fourteen thousand men, with David Lesley for his lieutenant-general.[1]

[1] Clarendon's History of the Rebellion, vol. vi. p. 491; Whitelocke, p. 501; Laing's History of Scotland, vol. iii. p. 468; Godwin's History of the Commonwealth, vol. iii. pp. 253, 260.

Cromwell was encamped before Perth, of which he had just gained possession, when he learned this news. It is doubtful whether he was either surprised or grieved to hear it; he was strongly impressed with the difficulties and dangers, both to his army and himself, of the prolongation of the inconclusive war which he had been carrying on for a year in Scotland; and he thought himself far more certain to obtain prompt and decisive success in England. As early as the month of January preceding, he had intimated to the Parliament that the Scots might probably attempt an invasion; and his recent manœuvres, by placing him in the rear of the Scottish army, so clearly opened the way to England to the King, that they almost seemed to invite him to take it. He did not conceal from himself the impression of terror, anger, and distrust which would be produced in London by such a movement; all the more because, a week before, when he was marching on Perth, he had written, "The enemy's great expectation now is to supply themselves in the West with recruits of men, and what victual they can get; for they may expect none out of the North, when once our army shall interpose between them and Perth, to prevent their prevalency in the West, and making incursions into the borders of England."[1] With dignified and sagacious firmness, he immediately encountered the reproaches and suspicions which he anticipated, and wrote to the Parliament, on the 4th of August, "While lying before Perth, we had some intelligence of the enemy's marching southward, though with some contradictions, as if it had not been so. But doubting it might be true, we marched with all possible expedition back again, and have passed our foot and many of our horse over the Frith this day, resolving to make what speed we can up to the enemy, who, in his desperation and

[1] Cromwell's Letters and Speeches, vol. ii. p. 320.

fear, and out of inevitable necessity, is run to try what he can do this way. I do apprehend, that if he goes for England, being some few days' march before us, it will trouble some men's thoughts, and may occasion some inconveniences, which I hope we are as deeply sensible of, and have been, and I trust shall be as diligent to prevent, as any. And, indeed, this is our comfort, that in simplicity of heart as towards God, we have done to the best of our judgments; knowing that if some issue were not put to this business, it would occasion another winter's war, to the ruin of your soldiery, for whom the Scots are too hard in respect of enduring the winter difficulties of this country; and to the endless expense of the treasure of England in prosecuting this war. It may be supposed we might have kept the enemy from this, by interposing between him and England: which truly I believe we might; but how to remove him out of this place, without doing what we have done, unless we had had a commanding army on both sides of the river of Forth, is not clear to us!

"We pray, therefore, that (seeing there is a possibility for the enemy to put you to some trouble) you would, with the same courage, grounded upon a confidence in God, wherein you have been supported to the great things God hath used you in hitherto—improve, the best you can, such forces as you have in readiness, or as may on the sudden be gathered together, to give the enemy some check, until we shall be able to reach up to him; which we trust in the Lord we shall do our utmost endeavor in. And, indeed, we have this comfortable experience from the Lord, that this enemy is heart-smitten by God; and whenever the Lord shall bring us up to them, we believe the Lord will make the desperateness of this counsel of theirs to appear, and the folly of it also. When England was much more unsteady than now; and when a much more considerable army of theirs, unfoiled, invaded you; and we had but a weak force to make resistance at Preston, upon deliberate advice we chose rather to put ourselves between their army and Scotland; and how God succeeded that, is not well to be forgotten! This present movement is not out of choice on our part, but by some kind of necessity; and, it is to be hoped, will have the like issue. Together with a hopeful end of your work, in which it's good to wait upon the Lord, upon the earnest of former experiences, and hope of His presence, which only is the life of your cause."[1]

Cromwell had not deceived himself; the disturbance was great in London; fear concealed itself beneath the mask of anger; in the Parliament as in the city, and even in the interior of the Council of State, Cromwell was declaimed against and loaded with blame, and it was even suggested that he had treated with Charles Stuart to betray the Commonwealth. "Some," says Mrs. Hutchinson, "could not hide very pale and unmanly fears; and Bradshaw himself, stout-hearted as he was, privately could not conceal his fear."[2] But among the leaders at least, the alarm was of short duration; Vane, Scott, Robinson, and Henry Martyn were men of active and obstinate courage, passionately devoted to their cause, and moreover compromised to that point at which courage, without ceasing to be a virtue, becomes a necessity. They immediately took measures for making a bold stand against the invaders, and reviving public confidence. The army, to which they had recently added three thousand horse and a thousand dragoons, received a fresh augmentation of four thousand infantry. The militia were called out throughout the country. Three regiments

[1] Cromwell's Letters and Speeches, vol. ii. pp. 327—329; Godwin's History of the Commonwealth, vol. iii. p. 253; Old Parliamentary History, vol. xix. pp. 455, 498.

[2] Memoirs of Colonel Hutchinson, p. 356.

of volunteers were formed in London and its neighborhood, for the special purpose of serving as a guard to the Parliament. Several earnest and influential men, among others Colonel Hutchinson and John Claypole, Cromwell's son-in-law, raised similar troops by their own exertions; and the Parliament voted the necessary sums for defraying all these expenses. On entering England, Charles had published a proclamation of general amnesty, from which three men only, Cromwell, Bradshaw, and Coke, the three principal actors in the trial of the King his father, were excepted. The Parliament replied to this by ordering it to be burned, in London, by the common hangman, in presence of the militia regiments; and by declaring Charles Stuart, and his abettors, agents, and accomplices, rebels and traitors to the Commonwealth of England. They also voted the punishment of death against all who should, in any way, maintain any correspondence with him; imprisoned or banished all the old royalists; and, in fine, established so rigorous and minute a system of police that, among other provisions, all masters of families, in certain parts of the country, were enjoined to keep their children and servants within their houses, except at certain hours of the day, and if they remained absent from home for more than twelve hours, to notify their absence to the committee of the militia of the place, under penalty of being held responsible for their actions.[1]

Meanwhile Charles advanced with his army, through the north-western counties of England, without meeting with any opposition. On learning his departure, Cromwell had immediately detached Lambert and Harrison, with most of his light troops, to follow him, and either separately or together to harass his flanks and rear, so as to straiten his

Commons' Journals, vol. vi. pp. 557, 614, 619—622; vol. vii. pp. 3, 6, 7, 9.

quarters and impede his progress in every way, without risking a general action, in which they could not fail to be worsted, and which Cromwell wished to reserve for himself. "His Majesty," wrote Lord Lauderdale to his wife, from Penrith, "is thus far advanced into England with a very good army; I dare say, near double the number of those that the King of Sweden entered Germany with, if they be not more. As soon as we came into England, his Majesty was by an Englishman, whom he made King-at-Arms for that day, proclaimed King of England, at the head of the army, with great acclamation, and shooting off all the cannon. Yesterday he was proclaimed here in Penrith, and will be in all the market-towns where we march. Never was an army so regular as we have been since we came into England; I dare say we have not taken the worth of a sixpence; and whatever our enemies print or write, trust me this is the best Scots army that ever I saw, and I hope shall prove best. All those that were unwilling to hazard all in this cause with their King, have on specious pretence left us. This is a natural purge, and will do us much good. Nothing of action yet, except the driving of some small parties, with which I will not trouble you. One thing I cannot forget: this morning, my Lord Howard of Escrick's son came in to us from the enemy, with his whole troop; his Majesty received him graciously, and immediately knighted him. He is the first, but I am confident a few days will show us more that will return to their duty."[1]

Lord Lauderdale was deceived in his expectation. Few Englishmen joined Charles on his march: he was invading England at the head of an army of Scotsmen and Presbyterians, foreigners and sectaries. The national pride was

[1] Cary's Memorials of the Civil War in England, vol. ii. pp. 307—309; Cromwell's Letters and Speeches, vol. ii. p. 327; Whitelocke's Memorials, p. 501.

wounded, the adherents of the episcopal church were discontented and disquieted, and these feelings lent fresh influence to the fear inspired by the Parliament and its severities. Charles met with no more support than resistance: in most of the towns through which he passed, he was received with acclamations; but the population did not rise in his favor, and the royalist leaders themselves arrived only in small numbers, and with but few followers. On his departure from Scotland, Charles had sent information of his movement to one of his most devoted and bravest adherents, the Earl of Derby, who, since the termination of the civil war, had been living in retirement in the Island of Man, with Charlotte de la Tremouille, his wife, quite as royalist and heroic as himself. Derby hastened to rejoin the King with a small troop of chosen friends and servants, and Charles directed him to go through Lancashire for the purpose of rousing and collecting his partisans in that county. But whilst the earl was engaged in the performance of this mission, he was surprised and defeated at Wigan by Colonel Robert Lilburne, whom Cromwell, with his habitual prudence, had sent thither, to put down any royalist movements which might be attempted. Derby was taken prisoner, but contrived to escape, and made his way, a fugitive, and almost alone, to join the King once more at Worcester. Another of Charles's lieutenants, of a different religious and political creed, General Massey, an excellent officer, who had been a Presbyterian and Parliamentarian in the early part of his career, also received orders to rally the royalists in Lancashire and Cheshire, where he was supposed to have considerable influence; and he had met with tolerable success in his work, when the Scottish ministers, who attended the march of the royal army, perceived that he recruited among Episcopalians and Catholics, as well as among Presbyterians. Without saying anything to the King, they sent a declaration after him, which they required him to publish, to the effect that no one was to be admitted into the army who did not first subscribe the Covenant. Charles no sooner heard of this declaration, than he wrote to Massey to suppress it; but his letter was intercepted, and published by the Parliament, and only served to give another proof of the King's duplicity, and the internal dissensions of his party. Whilst the royalists manifested this timidity, the republicans displayed the utmost firmness: the commandant of the little town of Biggar, on being summoned to surrender, replied, "that he would keep it for the Parliament, from whom he held it." Charles had intended to make Shrewsbury the centre of his operations in the west, and he hoped that its governor, Colonel Mackworth, a lawyer who had turned soldier, would open its gates to him; but Mackworth refused to do so, and immediately received from the Parliament a chain of gold, in thanks for his fidelity. On arriving at Warrington, on the Mersey, the royal army perceived on its left a considerable body of troops. It was Lambert and Harrison, who had combined to prevent their passing the river, by destroying the bridge; but they did not succeed in this; the royal army passed over, and some squadrons of Cavaliers vigorously charged Lambert's vanguard with shouts of "Oh, you rogues, we will be with you before your Cromwell comes!" Lambert refused to give battle, and retreated in some disorder. Charles thought it inexpedient to pursue him—he was anxious to get forward. But at the very moment that the enemy were retiring before him, Charles observed his lieutenant-general, David Lesley, looking sad and melancholy, and keeping aloof from his officers. The King "rode up to him, and asked him with great alacrity how he could be sad, when he was at the head of so brave an army, which looked so well that day? to which David Lesley answered him in his ear, that he was melancholic indeed, for he well knew that army, how well soever it looked, would not fight."[1]

On the 22d of August, Charles arrived at Worcester, where he had promised his tired troops good quarters, and ample repose. For a moment he was tempted to start again immediately, and to march upon London without halting; but he was one of those men who have mind enough to conceive great designs, but too weak a will to execute them. Worcester was an important and well-situated town; the Council of State had made it a place of banishment for a number of gentlemen of the neighborhood, who thus found themselves collected there on the King's arrival, and who received him with transports of delight. The mayor and all the local authorities manifested equal devotedness to his cause; and measures were immediately taken for the provisioning of his army. Charles resolved to establish his head-quarters in the town, and on the 23d of August, 1651, exactly nine years, day for day, since the King his father had planted the royal standard at Nottingham, to begin the civil war, Charles set up his standard at Worcester, and summoned, by solemn proclamation, all his male subjects between the ages of sixteen and sixty, to join him at the general muster of his forces on the 26th of August, in the meadows between the city and the River Severn, which flows near it. Thirty or forty gentlemen only, with about two hundred followers, appeared at the rendezvous. The royal army was then found to consist of about twelve thousand men, of whom ten thousand were Scots, and scarcely two thousand English.[2]

[1] Clarendon's History of the Rebellion, vol. vi. pp. 494—498; Whitelocke, pp. 266, 501—503; Godwin's History of the Commonwealth, vol. iii. pp. 260—267; Lingard's History of England, vol. xi. pp. 76—78; Boscobel Tracts, pp. 27—29.

[2] Whitelocke, pp. 503, 504; Clarendon's History of the Rebellion, vol. vi. pp. 506, 507; Boscobel Tracts, pp. 173, 180; Cromwell's Letters and Speeches, vol. ii. p. 330; Lingard's History of England, vol. xi. p. 77.

A very strong movement, on the contrary, had taken place in the republican party, and even throughout the country generally, against those insolent neighbors who had come to impose a king upon England by force of arms, and those tyrannical Presbyterians who proposed to establish their creed upon the oppression of Christian consciences. All diversity of political ideas and desires disappeared almost entirely before this national feeling. The militia of a great many large towns—London, Bristol, York, Gloucester, Coventry, Hereford—rose with ardor to defend their homes, or even to join the army which was defending their country. Regiments of volunteers were formed in several counties for the same purpose. Fairfax, who had refused to invade Scotland, placed himself at the head of his neighbors in Yorkshire, and offered his services to Cromwell, to repulse the men who had dared to invade England. The Parliament, by the measures it adopted, and the rewards it distributed, and Cromwell, by the commands he issued, and the examples he made along his whole route, from the north-east to the south-west of England, unremittingly fostered this movement, and when, after a march of twenty-one days, Cromwell, who had left Scotland with ten thousand men, arrived before Worcester, on the 28th of August, he had under his command an army of thirty-four thousand men, of whom twenty-four thousand were infantry, and ten thousand cavalry.[1]

The royal army was much less numerous, less animated, and less ably commanded. It was not even accurately known who was to command it. At the time when it entered England, the ambitious, presumptuous, and restless Duke of

[1] Whitelocke, pp. 497, 502, 504; Commons' Journals, vol. vii. pp. 6, 8; Godwin's History of the Commonwealth, vol. iii. pp. 263, 268, 407, 408; Brodie's History of the British Empire, vol. iv. p. 307; Boscobel Tracts, p. 180.

Buckingham had told the King that it would be unwise to leave it under the command of a Scottish general, and had proposed himself as Lesley's successor. At Worcester, when the moment for decisive action drew near, he renewed his demand with such importunity that the King grew angry, and told him he could hardly believe he was in earnest, or that he could really consider himself fit for such a charge. The duke asked wherein his unfitness lay. "You are too young," replied Charles. "But, sire," urged Buckingham, "Harry the Fourth of France commanded an army and won a battle when he was younger than I am;" and he persisted so strongly in his request, that at last the King was compelled to tell him he would have no generalissimo but himself; "upon which the duke was so discontented that he came no more to the Council, scarce spoke to the King, and would not converse with anybody; nor did he recover this ill-humor whilst the army stayed at Worcester."[1] Misunderstanding prevailed among the other generals also. Lesley, who was dispirited and unpopular, detested Middleton, who was confident and beloved by the soldiers; Massey had been grievously wounded in an attempt to prevent the enemy from passing the Severn and taking up a position on both banks of the river, and was confined to his bed, incapable of active service. Charles was constantly employed in reconciling or pacifying his lieutenants, but he was himself frivolous and careless; he had but little authority, little faith in his own success; and traitors were not wanting within the walls of Worcester to inform Cromwell of the bad internal condition of the royal army—its dissensions, hesitations, movements, and projects.[2]

[1] Clarendon's History of the Rebellion, vol. vi. pp. 507—509.

[2] Boscobel Tracts, pp. 30, 125, 180, 220; Whitelocke, p. 505; Cromwell's Letters and Speeches, vol. ii. p. 335.

Cromwell did not hesitate a moment: without waiting for the slow results of a siege, he resolved to attack Worcester at once on both sides of the Severn, at both extremities of the town, and to carry it at all risks. He encamped on the left bank of the river, and on the very day of his arrival, in spite of the obstinate resistance of the royalists, he passed a body of troops to the right bank, under Lambert's orders; and five days after, during the evening of the 2d of September and the morning of the 3d, numerous reinforcements, commanded by Fleetwood, executed the same movement, with orders to attack the western suburb of Worcester, whilst Cromwell himself, at the eastern extremity, directed the principal attack against the city itself. Charles, whose information was very imperfect, did not expect any serious affair on that day, and was quietly resting his troops; but at about one o'clock in the afternoon, while on the tower of the cathedral with his staff, he noticed several of Cromwell's regiments crossing the river by a bridge of boats, and marching against the Scottish troops, who had been posted, under Major-General Montgomery, to defend the western approaches to the city. Almost at the same moment he heard, on the eastern side, the volleys of the republican artillery, which was beginning to batter the approaches to the place. Charles descended hastily from the tower, mounted his horse, and rode to the western suburb to support Montgomery. Cromwell was already there in person, warmly pushing the attack: before acting himself on the left bank, he had desired to make sure that the orders which he had given were well executed on the right. The Scots made a bold resistance. Charles thought that the bulk of the parliamentary army were engaged on this side, and returning immediately into the town, he put himself at the head of his best infantry and his squadrons of English cavalry, left the city by the eastern gate, and marched upon Cromwell's camp, hoping to find it weakly guarded, and to be able to destroy it. But Cromwell also had passed rapidly over to the left bank of the river, and reappeared at the head of the troops which he had left there. The battle, thus engaged at both extremities of Worcester, lasted for four or five hours—"as stiff a contest as I have ever seen," wrote Cromwell; but begun and maintained by the royalists in the midst of great confusion. The troops led by Charles himself charged the republicans so vigorously that they gave way at first, abandoning a part of their artillery; three thousand Scottish cavalry, commanded by Lesley were under arms behind the King, who sent them orders to follow up his movement, and charge in their turn. "Oh, for one hour of Montrose!" shouted the English Cavaliers; but Lesley remained motionless. Cromwell meanwhile rallied his troops, and resumed the offensive; the royal infantry, failing in ammunition, fell back; the Duke of Hamilton and Sir John Douglas were mortally wounded. Cromwell, everywhere present and full of confidence, carried the attack in person to the intrenchments of Fort Royal, which covered the city on that side, and summoned the commandant, who occupied it with fifteen hundred men, to surrender; a volley of artillery was his reply; but the fort was soon stormed, and the garrison put to the sword. Both royalists and republicans fought hand to hand up to the gates of the city; there the disorder was extreme—an ammunition wagon had been overthrown, and blocked the passage; Charles was obliged to dismount from his horse, and enter Worcester on foot; the republicans dashed through the breach after him. Meanwhile the conflict in the west had the same issue: Montgomery's Scots, after having exhausted their ammunition, fell back upon the town, pursued by Fleetwood's troops, who entered with them. The combat was renewed in the streets in the form of partial encounters, and intermingled with acts of pillage and heroism, devotedness and flight. Charles remounted on horseback, and endeavored to rally his men, but in vain. "Then shoot me dead!" he cried, "rather than let me live to see the sad consequences of this day." But ere long it became his most imperative duty not to fall into the hands of the enemy. About fifty royalists, led by Lord Cleveland, Colonel Wogan, Sir James Hamilton, and Major Careless, formed themselves into a compact body, and with ardent courage charged the republican troops in every direction, in order to cover the retreat of the King, who at length left Worcester by St. Martin's gate, and took the northern road. Before he had ridden far he came up with some of Lesley's cavalry, who were flying without having fought; for a moment he felt disposed to try once more to induce them to turn and renew the action. "But no," he said to himself, "men who deserted me when they were in good order, would never stand to me now they are beaten." So he left Lesley and his Scotsmen to effect their retreat as they best might, and concentrated his attention on providing for his own safety. The idea occurred to him of going to seek an asylum in London—the best place, perhaps, both for concealment and for taking advantage of any opportunity that might present itself for renewing the war. But he mentioned this plan only to Lord Wilmot, his most intimate confident; and, followed by about sixty devoted Cavaliers, he pursued his way towards the north, protected for the moment by the night, and anxiously consulting with his companions as to their means of safety for the morrow.[1]

[1] Boscobel Tracts, pp. 30—38, 123—130, 134; Clarendon's History of the Rebellion, vol. vi. pp. 510—514; Clarendon's State Papers, vol. iii. p. 30; Whitelocke, p. 507; Cromwell's Letters and Speeches, vol. ii. p. 337; Bates, Elenchus Motuum Nuperorum, part ii. pp. 219—225; Godwin's History of the Commonwealth, vol. iii. pp. 271—274; Lingard's History of England, vol. xi. pp. 77, 78; Cromwelliana, p. 115; Old Parliamentary History, vol. xx. pp. 59—68.

At about the same time, at ten o'clock in the evening, Cromwell, who had hardly made his entry into Worcester, which was still a prey to confusion and pillage, sent a short announcement of his victory to the Parliament, and a fuller account on the following day. "The battle," he wrote, "was fought with various success for some hours, but still hopeful on our part; and in the end became an absolute victory—and so full a one as proved a total defeat and ruin of the enemy's army. We took all their baggage and artillery. What the slain are, I can give you no account, because we have not taken an exact view; but they are very many: and must needs be so; because the dispute was long and very near at hand, and often at push of pike. There are about six or seven thousand prisoners taken here; and many officers and noblemen of very great quality: Duke Hamilton, the Earl of Rothes, and divers other noblemen—I hear, the Earl of Lauderdale; many officers of great quality; and some that will be fit subjects for your justice. . . . . The dimensions of this mercy are above my thoughts. It is, for aught I know, a crowning mercy. Surely, if it be not, such a one we shall have, if this provoke those that are concerned in it to thankfulness, and the Parliament to do the will of Him who hath done His will for it, and for the nation;—whose good pleasure it is to establish the nation and the change of the government, by making the people so willing to the defence thereof, and so signally blessing the endeavors of your servants in this late great work."[1]

When this letter was read, the Parliament called in Major Cobbett, who had brought it, and wished to hear from him a circumstantial narrative of the battle. Cobbett at the same time produced the Collar and Garter of the King, which had been found at Worcester, in the house which he had occupied.

[1] Cromwell's Letters and Speeches, vol. ii. pp. 339—341.

Two members of the House, Mr. Scott and Major Salwey, on their return from the camp to which they had been sent on a special mission, also satisfied, by numerous details, the curiosity of their colleagues. Every day brought the names of new and important prisoners: the Earls of Derby, Cleveland, Lauderdale, Shrewsbury, and Kelly, Generals Massey, Middleton, and Lesley, indeed, nearly all the royalist leaders fell, during their flight, into the hands of the republican authorities. It was truly, as Cromwell had said, a crowning victory. The Parliament was anxious to show its grateful joy by all means in its power. It ordered a solemn thanksgiving service throughout the three kingdoms, and gave a great banquet in Whitehall. Four members, Whitelocke, St. John, Lisle, and Pickering, were appointed to wait on Cromwell, to express to him, in terms officially voted by the House, the sense which Parliament entertained of his glorious services. The palace of Hampton Court was assigned to him for a residence, with an estate in land of the yearly value of 4,000*l.* His principal officers, and even the obscure messengers who had brought the news, received splendid rewards. But while favors were thus lavished on the victors, severities were not forgotten towards the vanquished. Nine of the principal prisoners were chosen to be tried by court-martial for high treason; one of them, the Duke of Hamilton, died of his wounds before judgment could be pronounced upon him; three, the Earl of Derby, Sir Timothy Fetherstonhaugh, and Captain Benbow, were tried at Chester, and condemned to death. They met their fate with the courage of martyrs. "For the cause in which I had a great while waded," said the Earl of Derby on the scaffold, "I must needs say, my engagement or continuance in it hath laid no scruple upon my conscience. It was on principles of law, and on principles of religion, that I embraced it; my judgment is satisfied, and my conscience rectified; for which I bless God. I will not presume to decide controversies. I pray God to prosper that side that hath right with it; and that you may enjoy peace and plenty, when I shall enjoy peace and plenty, beyond all you possess here."[1]

Either because such speeches from the vanquished seemed to the Parliament more dangerous than their punishment was useful, or because the completeness of its triumph inclined it to moderation, these painful spectacles were not multiplied. The other prisoners of mark remained confined in the Tower. The common soldiers were treated with severity, but their fate was kept as secret as possible; thousands of them were sold or given away to merchants or planters, and sent to work either in the colonies, or in the mines of Africa. Finally, it was decreed, and solemnly proclaimed all over the country, that a reward of one thousand pounds should be given to any person who should "bring in to the Parliament Charles Stuart, son of the late tyrant."[2]

Whilst the Parliament was passing this decree in London, its soldiers were traversing the western counties in all directions in search of the king, and finding traces of him everywhere, but himself nowhere. Five days after the battle, a detachment of infantry arrived suddenly at the old monastery of Whiteladies, the seat of a Catholic gentleman named Giffard, and required him, on pain of death, to tell them what had become of the king, who, they said, had recently been concealed in his house. Mr. Giffard resolutely denied having seen the fugitive, and begged, if he must die, that they would first give him leave to say a few prayers. "If

[1] Commons' Journals, vol. vii. pp. 12—16; Old Parliamentary History, vol. xx. p. 72; State Trials, vol. v. pp. 294—323; Boscobel Tracts, pp. 187, 193, 198; Clarendon's History of the Rebellion, vol. vi. pp. 515—518; Whitelocke, p. 508.

[2] Godwin's History of the Commonwealth, vol. iii. pp. 273—276; Commons Journals, vol. vii. p. 14.

you can tell us no news of the king," said one of the soldiers, "you shall say no prayers." He persisted in his silence, and the soldiers, after having carefully searched the whole house, rode off without doing him any further injury. Whiteladies, however, had been the first asylum of Charles; he had arrived there at daybreak on the 4th of September, scarcely twelve hours after having escaped from Worcester. He had immediately cut off his hair, stained his hands and face, and assumed the coarse and threadbare garments of a peasant; and five brothers Penderell, all of them laborers, woodmen or domestics in the service of Mr. Giffard, had undertaken to secure his safety. "This is the king," said Mr. Giffard to William Penderell; "thou must have a care of him, and preserve him as thou didst me." They accordingly took Charles to Boscobel House, and concealed him in the adjoining woods. It was raining heavily: Richard Penderell procured a blanket, and spread it for the king under one of the largest trees; while his sister, Mrs. Yates, brought a supply of bread, milk, eggs, and butter. "Good woman," said Charles to her, "can you be faithful to a distressed Cavalier?" "Yes, Sir," she replied, "and I will die sooner than betray you." Some soldiers passed on the outskirts of the wood, but did not enter it, because the storm was more violent over the wood than in the open fields. On the next day, the king concealed himself among the leafy branches of a large oak, and from this cover he could see the soldiers scouring the country in search of him. One night he left his hiding-place, to endeavor to cross the Severn, and take refuge in Wales; but as he was passing a mill with Richard Penderell, his guide, the miller called out, "Who goes there?" "Neighbors going home," answered Penderell. "If you be neighbors, stand," cried the miller, "or I will knock you down." They fled as fast as they could, and were pursued for some time by several men who came out of the mill with the miller. In another of their attempts to escape, while fording a small river, the King, who was a good swimmer, helped his guide across, as he was unable to swim. He wandered for seven days in this manner through the country, changing his place of refuge almost daily, sometimes hidden beneath the hay in a barn, sometimes concealed in one of those obscure hiding-places which served as a retreat to the proscribed Catholic priests; hearing or seeing, at every moment, the republican soldiers who had been sent in search of him. In concert with his faithful guards, and with Lord Wilmot, who had rejoined him, he resolved to make for the sea-coast, near Bristol, in the hope of being able to find a vessel to take him over to France. He now changed his disguise, assumed a servant's livery instead of his peasant's garb, and set off on horseback, under the name of William Jackson, carrying behind him his mistress, Miss Jane Lane, sister of Colonel Lane, of Bentley, his last place of refuge in Staffordshire. "Will," said the colonel to him at starting, "thou must give my sister thy hand to help her to mount:" but the King, unused to such offices, gave her the wrong hand. "What a goodly horseman my daughter has got to ride before her," said old Mrs. Lane, the colonel's mother, who was watching their departure, though unacquainted with the secret. They set off, but they had scarcely ridden two hours, when the King's horse cast a shoe, and they halted at a little village to get another shoe. "As I was holding the horse's foot," says the King in his narrative of his escape, "I asked the smith what news. He told me that there was no news that he knew of, since the good news of the beating of those rogues, the Scots. I asked him whether there were none of the English taken that had joined with the Scots. He answered that some of them were taken, but he did not hear that that rogue, Charles Stuart, had been taken yet. I told him that, if that rogue were taken, he deserved to be hanged more than all the rest, for bringing in the Scots. Upon which he said that I spoke like an honest man; and so we parted."[1]

On the 13th of September he reached Abbotsleigh, near Bristol, the residence of Mr. Norton, a cousin of Colonel Lane. He there learned, to his great sorrow, that there was not in the port of Bristol any vessel on board which he could embark; and he was obliged to remain in the house four days. Under pretence of indisposition, he was indulged with a separate chamber, and by Miss Lane's request, particular care was taken of him. He was really much harassed and fatigued, though but little inclined to endure patiently either hunger or ennui. On the morning after his arrival, he rose early, and went to the buttery-hatch to get his breakfast, where he found Pope, the butler, and two or three other servants; "and," he says, "we all fell to eating bread and butter, to which Pope gave us very good ale and sack. As I was sitting there, there was one that looked like a country fellow sat just by me, who gave so particular an account of the battle of Worcester to the rest of the company, that I concluded he must be one of Cromwell's soldiers. But I asking him how he came to give so good an account of that battle? he told me he was in the King's regiment; and on questioning him further, I perceived that he had been in my regiment of guards. I asked him what kind of a man I was? To which he answered by describing exactly both my clothes and my horse; and then looking upon me, he told me that the king was at least three fingers taller than I. Upon which I made what haste I could out of the buttery, for fear he should indeed know me, being more afraid when I knew he was one of our own soldiers, than when I took him for one of the enemy's."

[1] Boscobel Tracts, pp. 40—46; 134, 136—146, 190, 192, 218, 223—226, 239—241.

Charles had no sooner returned to his room, than one of his companions came to him in great agitation, and said: "What shall we do? I am afraid Pope the butler knows you, for he says very positively to me that it is you, but I have denied it." Charles had already learned that, in positions of danger, bold confidence is often no less a source of safety than a necessity; he sent for the butler, told him all, and received from him, during his stay at Mr. Norton's house, the most intelligent and most devoted care.

But attentions, even when shown most discreetly, sometimes prove most compromising; at the end of four days Charles had to seek a new asylum; and on the 14th of September, he left Abbotsleigh for Trent House, in the same county, the residence of Colonel Wyndham, a staunch royalist. In 1636, six years before the outbreak of the war between Charles I. and his Parliament, Sir Thomas Wyndham, the Colonel's father, when on the point of death, had said to his five sons—"My sons, we have hitherto seen serene and quiet times, but now prepare yourselves for cloudy and troublesome. I command you to honor and obey our gracious sovereign, and in all times to adhere to the crown; and though the crown should hang upon a bush, I charge you forsake it not." The injunctions of the dying man were obeyed; three of his sons and one of his grandsons fell on the battle-field, fighting for Charles I.; and Colonel Wyndham, who had also served with honor in the royal army, was, in 1651, a prisoner on parole in his own house. He received the king with the utmost devotedness, and set to work immediately to obtain some means of embarkation for him in one of the neighboring ports. He thought he had succeeded in doing so at Southampton; but the vessel which he had fixed upon was required by the agents of the Parliament to transport a body of troops to Jersey. A sea-captain of Lyme, named Limbry, under-

[1] Boscobel Tracts, pp. 54, 108—110, 146—150, 243.

took, not without considerable hesitation, to convey to St. Malo some royalist gentlemen who had been engaged in Worcester fight; every arrangement was made as to the price, the day, the hour, and the place of embarkation: on the 23d of September, the vessel was to set sail from Charmouth, a little port near Lyme, and during the night, the long-boat was to fetch the fugitive royalists, from an appointed place on the beach.

Guided by Colonel Wyndham, Charles proceeded to the spot agreed upon, where he was met by Lord Wilmot; they waited there all night, but the boat did not make its appearance. Limbry, at the moment when he was about to send his things on board, had been detained by the anger and despair of his wife. On that very day, at the fair of Lyme, proclamation had been made of the act of Parliament which offered a reward of a thousand pounds for the king's arrest, and at the same time menaced with the severest punishment all who should give him refuge. Limbry's wife, without suspecting that the king himself was concerned in the matter, declared to her husband that she would not suffer him to take on board his vessel any royalist, or to expose her children and herself to utter ruin for the sake of any lord, however high his rank; and with the help of her two daughters, she locked her husband in his room, threatening that, if he persisted in his design, she would denounce it immediately to Captain Macy, who commanded a company of the Parliament's troops at Lyme. Limbry yielded to the fears and violence of his wife. The king's position was now becoming dangerous; the presence of so many strangers at Charmouth had been remarked; Lord Wilmot's horse required shoeing; the smith to whom it was taken said that "he was sure his three shoes had been set in three several counties, and one of them in Worcestershire." Suspicions were aroused; the puritan minister of the place, a zealous republican, went to the hostess of the inn where Charles had been staying, and said to her, "Why, how now, Margaret, you are a maid of honor now." "What mean you by that, Mr. Parson?" said she. "Why, Charles Stuart lay last night at your house," he answered, "and kissed you at his departure; so that now you can't but be a maid of honor." The hostess grew angry, and told him he was a scurvy-conditioned man to go about to bring her and her house into trouble; "but," she added, "if I thought it was the King, as you say it was, I would think the better of my lips all the days of my life; and so, Mr. Parson, get you out of my house, or else I'll get those shall kick you out." Charles left Charmouth in all haste, but on arriving at Bridport, a neighboring town, he found the streets filled with soldiers; it was the regiment which the Parliament was about to send to take possession of Jersey. "What is to be done?" asked Colonel Wyndham, in great alarm; Charles, with his accustomed presence of mind, and still acting the part of a domestic, dismounted, took the bridles of the horses, and passing boldly among the troopers, with many a coarse jest and rough word, he went straight to the best inn of the place, and remained there until his party had quietly dined. In the meanwhile, at Charmouth and its neighborhood, the report that Charles Stuart had been there had assumed consistency; Captain Macy mounted his horse with some of his men, rode at full speed to Bridport, and, after making full inquiries there, set off immediately in pursuit of the fugitives; but at a short distance from the town, Charles and his companions had left the high road, and continued their journey across country. Macy lost all trace of them; and from village to village, they returned to Colonel Wyndham's house in Somersetshire, divided between feelings of increased perplexity, and the delight of finding rest after danger.

Charles remained for eleven days at Trent House, still seeking, but in vain, the means of transport to France. It then became necessary for him once more to change his residence. Colonel Wyndham was informed that his house was becoming more and more suspected; and ere long, troops arrived in the neighborhood. On the 6th of October, the King left the Trent House to take refuge at Hele House, the residence of Mr. Hyde, in Wiltshire; where he would be nearer the small sea-ports of Sussex, at one of which his friends hoped to be able to procure him a vessel. They at last succeeded in obtaining one, and on the morning of the 13th of October, Charles left his last hiding-place, escorted by a few faithful friends, who had brought their dogs, as if for a coursing expedition on the downs. They slept at Hambledon, in Hampshire, at the house of a brother-in-law of Colonel Gunter, one of the King's guides; and the master of the house, on his return home, was astonished to find his table surrounded by unknown guests, whose gayety exceeded the bounds of "decent hilarity." The King's cropped hair, and the reproof which he administered to the honest squire for a casual oath, redoubled his surprise; he bent towards his brother-in-law, and asked if that fellow were not "some roundheaded rogue's son." The colonel assured him that his suspicions were unfounded, upon which he sat down at table with his guests, and gayly drank the King's health "in a good glass of beer, calling him brother roundhead." On the following day, the 14th of October, they proceeded to Brighthelmstone, where they were to meet the master of the promised vessel, and the merchant who had engaged it for them. They all supped together at the village inn; during the meal, the captain, Anthony Tettersall, scarcely once took his eyes off the King; and after supper he took the merchant aside and told him "that he had not dealt fairly with him; for though he had given him a very good price for carrying over that gentleman, yet he had not been clear with him;—for," said he, "he is the King, and I very well know him to be so." The merchant assured him that he was mistaken, but he answered: "No I am not; for he took my ship, together with other fishing vessels at Brighthelmstone, in the year 1648, when he commanded his father's fleet; but be not troubled at it, for I think I do God and my country good service in preserving the King, and by the grace of God, I will venture my life and all for him, and set him safely on shore, if I can, in France." At about the same time, at another part of the room, the innkeeper came up to the King, who was standing by the fire, with his hand resting on the back of a chair, and kissed his hand suddenly. "God bless you wheresoever you go!" he said; "I do not doubt, before I die, to be a lord, and my wife a lady." Charles laughed, and went into another room, putting full trust in his host; and at five o'clock on the morning of the 15th of October, the King and Lord Wilmot were on board a little vessel of sixty tons, which only waited for the tide to leave Shoreham harbor. As soon as they were at sea, Captain Tettersall came into the cabin where the King was lying, fell on his knees, kissed his hand, and protesting his entire devotedness, suggested that, in order to prevent all difficulty, he should himself persuade the crew, who imagined that they had embarked for the English port of Poole, to sail towards the coast of France, by representing himself to them as a merchant in debt, who was afraid of being arrested in England, and wished to recover some money that was owing to him at Rouen. Charles willingly acceded to this proposition, and contrived to ingratiate himself so thoroughly with the sailors, that they joined him in requesting the captain to turn aside from his course in favor of his passengers. The weather was fine and the wind favorable, and at one o'clock in the afternoon of the 16th of October, the ship's boat landed the King and Lord Wilmot in the little port of Fécamp. They proceeded on the following day to Rouen, clothed so wretchedly and looking so disreputable, that when they presented themselves at an inn, the host hesitated to give them admittance, taking them "to be thieves, or persons that had been doing some very ill thing." Charles sent for an English merchant who resided at Rouen, to supply his immediate necessities; and wrote at once to the Queen his mother, who was in the utmost anguish as to his fate. The most contradictory reports had been spread regarding him: some stated that he had been captured by Cromwell's soldiers, others that he had succeeded in making his escape to Holland. As soon as it became known that he was at Rouen, the English refugees flocked to meet him; he left that city on the 29th of October, and on the 30th, he met his brother, the Duke of York, at Magny, and afterwards at Monceaux, near Paris, the Queen his mother, the Duke of Orleans his uncle, with a large number of French and English gentlemen who had come out on horseback to welcome him. He proceeded that same evening to the Louvre, saved from all peril, but conquered and without hope.[1]

He had wandered about England for forty-two days, and had been concealed successively in eight different hiding-places; forty-five persons of all ranks in life, whose names have reached us, and doubtless many others of whom we have no information, had known who he was and where he was. Not one of them betrayed, even by an indiscretion, the secret of his presence or of his movements. Sincere devotedness can inspire the most simple-minded with sagacity, and the weakest with virtue.

Whilst Charles was thus experiencing at once the severest trials of his destiny and the fidelity of his friends, Cromwell had returned in triumph to London, preceded by the prison-

[1] Boscobel Tracts, pp. 67—73, 119—122, 156—163, 251—259; Clarendon's State Papers, vol. iii. pp. 30, 31; Bates, Elenchus Motuum Nuperorum, pp. 226—266.

ers whom he had taken, and surrounded by the officers who had shared in his victory. The four commissioners who had been delegated by the Parliament went, on the 11th of September, beyond Aylesbury to meet him. "We come," they said to him, "in the name of the Parliament, to congratulate your Lordship on your good recovery of health, after your dangerous sickness. Your unwearied labors and pains, in the late expedition into Scotland, for the service of this Commonwealth; your diligence in prosecution of the enemy, when he fled into England; the great hardships and hazards you have exposed yourself unto, and particularly in the late fight at Worcester; your prudent and faithful managing and conducting throughout this great and important affair, which the Lord from heaven hath so signally blessed, and crowned with so complete and glorious an issue; —of all these things the Parliament have thought fit, by us, to certify to your Lordship their good acceptance, and great satisfaction therein; and for the same, to return to you in the name of the Parliament and Commonwealth of England, their most hearty thanks; as also, to the rest of your officers and soldiers, for their great and gallant services. And since, by the great blessing of God upon your Lordship's and the army's endeavors, the enemy is so totally defeated, and the state of affairs, as well in England as in Scotland, such as may very well dispense with your Lordship's continuance in the field, the Parliament do desire your Lordship, for the better settlement of your health, to take such rest and repose as you shall find most requisite and conducing thereunto; and for that purpose, to make your residence at or near London; whereby also, the Parliament may have the assistance of your presence, in the great and important consultation for the further settlement of this Commonwealth, which they are now upon." On his entry into London, Cromwell was met by the Speaker and a large number of members of the House of Commons, by the President of the Council of State, the Lord Mayor and aldermen of the city, and many thousands of notable citizens, who accompanied him to Whitehall, amid salutes of artillery and popular acclamations; and when, four days afterwards, he made his appearance again in the House, the Speaker reiterated to him the solemn thanks of the Parliament and country.[1]

Cromwell received all these honors with pious modesty, saying but little of himself, and ascribing, first to God and then to his soldiers, the whole merit of his success. Through his humility, however, glimpses of an irrepressible internal exultation occasionally manifested themselves: his affability towards the commissioners whom the Parliament had sent to meet him wore an air of magnificence and grandeur; he presented to each of them a fine horse and some of the prisoners of rank whom he brought with him, and who would certainly redeem their liberty at a high price. To Whitelocke he gave two of them, and he liberated them without ransom. Cromwell proceeded slowly towards London, receiving the homage of the population on his route, and sometimes even halting to share in the hawking expeditions of the gentlemen whom he met. At Aylesbury, it was remarked that he remained long in private conversation with the Chief Justice St. John, one of the Parliament's commissioners, and also one of Cromwell's most intimate confidants. His air, his language, and his manners, seemed to undergo a natural transformation; and Hugh Peters, a clear-sighted sectarian preacher, who had long been used to understand and serve him, said, as he noticed his altered appearance: "This man will be king of England yet."[2]

[1] Commons' Journals, vol. vii. pp. 13, 14, 18; Whitelocke's Memorials, p. 509.

[2] Whitelocke, p. 509; Ludlow's Memoirs, p. 189; Cromwell's Letters and Speeches, vol. ii. p. 343.

His good fortune extended to his lieutenants; on leaving first Ireland, and then Scotland, he had delegated the command in the former country to Ireton, and in the latter to Monk—the one a republican, the other a royalist at heart, but both of them sensible, capable, rough-mannered men, well fitted to carry on a work of war, and of government by the sword when the victory was won. Both of them obtained complete success. Monk met with desperate resistance at several places, and especially at the siege of Dundee; Ireton continued the system of cruel severity which Cromwell had put in practice, and died of the plague, it is said, after the siege and capture of Limerick. But at the end of the year 1651, both Ireland and Scotland were in entire subjection; Ormonde had returned to the Continent; the Scottish Highlanders, unable to undertake any serious enterprise, had great difficulty in maintaining some remnant of independence in their rude mountain fastnesses. At the same time, the fleet and troops of the Parliament had regained possession of the islands of Guernsey, Jersey, Scilly, and Man, the last refuges of the royal dominion: the chief colonial dependencies, New England, Virginia, and Barbadoes, had either hastened or been compelled to accept the new government of the home country;[1] and a few months after that battle which had consummated the defeat of royalty in England, the republican Parliament was master of all the English territories, in both hemispheres.

[1] Commons' Journals, vol. vii. pp. 31, 35, 62, 90, 124, 172; Whitelocke, pp. 523, 527; Clarendon's History of the Rebellion, vol. vi. pp. 545—554.

BOOK III.

IMPRESSION PRODUCED ON THE CONTINENT BY THE TRIAL AND EXECUTION OF CHARLES I.—ASSASSINATION OF DORISLAUS AT THE HAGUE, AND OF ASCHAM AT MADRID—ATTITUDE OF THE CONTINENTAL STATES TOWARDS THE COMMONWEALTH OF ENGLAND—DEVELOPMENT AND SUCCESSES OF THE ENGLISH NAVY —FOREIGN POLICY OF THE REPUBLICAN PARLIAMENT—RIVALRY BETWEEN FRANCE AND SPAIN IN THEIR RELATIONS WITH ENGLAND—RECOGNITION OF THE COMMONWEALTH BY SPAIN—RELATIONS BETWEEN ENGLAND AND THE UNITED PROVINCES—ENGLISH AMBASSADORS AT THE HAGUE—DUTCH AMBASSADORS IN LONDON—THEIR WANT OF SUCCESS—NEGOTIATIONS OF MAZARIN IN LONDON—LOUIS XIV. RECOGNIZES THE ENGLISH COMMONWEALTH—WAR BETWEEN ENGLAND AND THE UNITED PROVINCES—SUCCESSES OF BLAKE—EFFECTS OF THE WAR IN ENGLAND.

THOUGH victorious over its enemies at home, the Commonwealth was, as yet, neither at peace nor at war with the States of the Continent.

The trial and execution of Charles I. had produced the deepest emotion throughout Europe. It was the second time, within a period of sixty years, that royalty had fallen, in England, beneath the axe of the executioner. It was the first time that the sovereignty of the people and a republican form of government had been proclaimed and established in a great Christian country. The surprise, anxious curiosity, pity, and indignation which these occurrences awakened were universal. Protestant countries felt the necessity of clearing the Reformation from the reproach of having instigated or contributed to so great a crime. In Germany, in Denmark, in Sweden, and most of all in Holland, the ministers of religion hastened loudly to express their reprobation; the pulpits resounded with maledictions against the anarchical and sacrilegious sectaries; and the clergy of the Hague waited in a body upon Charles II., and solemnly expressed to him their grief and horror, in a Latin oration. The feelings of the people corresponded with these manifestations on the part of the Church; the details of the trial and death of Charles I. were collected and published with pious respect; a woman at the Hague fell into travail and died with terror at hearing the news. The representatives or partisans of the regicides were treated with aversion and insult in the streets: from popular instinct, or Christian conscientiousness, or political wisdom, Protestant and republican Holland shrank from any manifestation of indulgence for so unprecedented an act, considering it as full of social danger as of moral iniquity.[1]

In Catholic countries—Spain, Portugal, Italy, and Southern Germany—the impression was equally strong, but of a different nature. Both clergy and people regarded the fate of Charles I. as the natural consequence of heresy, and as an exhibition of the justice of God, who punishes peoples and kings by one another, when they separate from his Church. The crime excited deep aversion, but it was accompanied by less surprise than in Protestant Europe, and perhaps also by less sympathy and sorrow.

In France the impressions were of a more mingled character. At the very moment when pure monarchy was on the point of predominating in that country, the spirit of reform and of political liberty had attempted a sincere and earnest, but superficial and vain, effort to arrest its progress. The English Parliament found many admirers among the partisans of the Fronde; its maxims were welcomed, and its

[1] Clarendon's History of the Rebellion, vol. vi. pp. 267, 268; Wicquefort's Histoire des Provinces Unies, vol. iv. p. 155; Whitelocke, pp. 386—390.

acts observed, with eager curiosity; and more than one pamphlet pointed out the House of Commons and the city of London as models for the Parliament and bourgeoisie of Paris. But the trial of Charles I., the violent mutilation of the House of Commons, the abolition of the House of Lords, and the tyrannical establishment of the Commonwealth, gave the royalist opinion in France, with regard to the affairs of England, an ascendency in harmony with the course of French affairs, and which the prolonged disorders of the Fronde, and the relations of its leaders with the English republicans, strengthened rather than diminished. The revolution of England, far from alluring, excited only mingled reprobation and alarm; it was attacked in a multitude of pamphlets; Joan of Arc was represented as exhorting the French to take arms to avenge the cause of royalty upon the English parricides; and the monarchical opinion with regard to England soon prevailed among the French people, always eager spectators of public events.

Two tragical incidents which occurred at this time, give a striking proof of the state of public opinion in Europe.

On the 3d of May, 1649, Dr. Isaac Dorislaus, a native of Holland, who had long been settled in England, and had been appointed one of the counsel to conduct the prosecution of the King, arrived at the Hague, having been sent by the Parliament in the capacity of an assistant to Walter Strickland, the Commonwealth's resident ambassador to the United Provinces. He was quietly supping in the evening, with several other persons, at the Swan inn, when six men in masks arrived at the house; two of them remained outside to guard the door; the others entered, put out the lights in the hall, and presenting themselves suddenly, in the dining-room, told those who were at table not to stir, for there was no harm intended to any but the agent that came from the rebels in England, who had recently murdered their King.

"They then dragged Dorislaus from the table, and put him to death; and quietly sheathing their swords, they left the room, rejoined their companions in the street, and quitted the Hague, before any one had either time or inclination to arrest them."[1]

About a year afterwards, in the early part of May, 1650, Anthony Ascham, an author of small reputation, who had taken part in the overthrow of the monarchy and the trial of the King, disembarked at Cadiz, on a mission from the Parliament to the King of Spain. Before he left London, his thoughts had dwelt much on the fate of Dorislaus, and he had expressed his anxiety on the subject to M. de Croullé, the French Chargé-d'affaires.[2] On his arrival at Cadiz, the governor, the Duke of Medina Celi, placed him under the care of Colonel Don Diego de Moreda, and two other officers, who were ordered to escort him to Madrid, and not to leave him until he was safely established in that city. They arrived there on the 5th of June, and either from negligence or ill-will, the Spanish officers, after having taken Ascham to a little inn, left him there alone, and went in search of a lodging for themselves elsewhere. On the following day, at noon, Ascham was at table with his secretary, Rivas, a renegade Franciscan monk; a man entered; Ascham advanced to meet him, taking him for a friend; but on catching sight of three other strangers who entered at the same time, he started quickly back to seize his pistols, which lay on a table near him; when the first comer, calling him a traitor, caught him by the hair, and struck him dead with his stiletto. His

[1] Wicquefort's Histoire des Provinces Unies, vol. iv. p. 157; Leclerc's Histoire des Provinces Unies, vol. ii. p. 271; Clarendon's History of the Rebellion, vol. vi. pp. 297, 298; Whitelocke, pp. 368, 401; Commons' Journals, vol. vi. p. 206.

[2] Letters from M. de Croullé to Cardinal Mazarin, June 30, 1650; in the Archives des Affaires Etrangères de France. See Appendix II.

secretary, Rivas, attempting to escape and shouting for help, was also killed on the spot; one English domestic alone escaped, and spread the alarm. The four murderers left the room, returned to their companions who were awaiting them at the street-door, and proceeded without hindrance to seek sanctuary, one in the house of the Venetian ambassador, and the other five in a church adjoining the hospital of St. Andrew.[1]

At Madrid and at the Hague, the public excitement, and the anxiety of the two governments, Dutch and Spanish, were very great. The republican Parliament resented, as was anticipated, these bloody outrages; it manifested its sympathy for the two victims by public honors; Vane presented a solemn report on the assassination of Dorislaus; his body was brought to London, and buried in Westminster Abbey; and the whole Parliament attended the funeral. Similar respect, though in a less degree, was paid to Ascham. Pensions and employments were bestowed on both their families. Urgent and even threatening demands were made at the same time, and frequently renewed, at the Hague and at Madrid, to obtain justice upon the assassins. Both governments promised redress, and attempted to give it. The murderers were well known; those of Dorislaus were dependents of Montrose; those of Ascham were English Cavaliers who had taken refuge at Madrid, and one of them was a servant in the house of Lord Cottington and Sir Edward Hyde, who then resided at Madrid, as the ambassadors of Charles II. But at the Hague no one was arrested. At Madrid, although the civil authorities removed the murderers from their asylum, the Church asserted its privileges, and the prolonged conflict between the two jurisdictions ended in the impunity

[1] Thurloe's State Papers, vol. i. pp. 148—153, 202—204; Clarendon's History of the Rebellion, vol. vi. pp. 441—444; Old Parliamentary History, vol. xix. p. 285; Commons' Journals, vol. vi. pp. 407, 428.

of the assassins; one only, who was found to be a Protestant, was delivered over to the secular arm and hanged. Both in Holland and Spain public feeling protected them; they had, it was said, only punished by murder men guilty of more heinous murder; and far from showing any repentance for their action, they gloried in it: those who had killed Ascham told the magistrates of Madrid that they would have killed him in presence of the King of Spain, if they had not found a more convenient opportunity. And the secret indulgence of the governments connived with the popular feeling; they pursued the crime from complaisance or fear, but without any serious desire to punish the criminals. A few weeks after the assassination of Ascham, in a conversation with Lord Cottington and Hyde, the prime minister of Spain, Don Luis de Haro, did not hesitate to say: "I envy those gentlemen for having done so noble an action, how penal soever it may prove to them, to revenge the blood of their king. If the king my master had such resolute subjects, he would never have lost his realm of Portugal, for want of one brave man to take away the life of the usurper."[1]

But far more in the seventeenth century than in our own times, politicians cared little to act in accordance with their real feelings and their private speeches; and whilst the public on the Continent gave free vent to their ill-will towards the republican judges of Charles I., the governments, either from calculation or fear, manifested either indifference or reserve. The Dutch ambassadors who had been sent to London to attempt to save the King, demanded, after his death, that their negotiations with the Parliament should

[1] Commons' Journals, vol. vi. pp. 209, 211, 313; Old Parliamentary History, vol. xix. pp. 286, 287; Leclerc's Histoire des Provinces Unies, vol. ii. p. 272; Wicquefort's Histoire des Provinces Unies, vol. iv. p. 158; Clarendon's History of the Rebellion, vol. vi. pp. 444—450; Papers from the Archives of Simancas in Appendix III.

not be published; and though one of them, Adrian Pauw, left England immediately, the other, Albert Joachim, continued to reside there. Anne of Austria and Cardinal Mazarin thought it fitting that the young King of France should make some effort to save the life of the king his uncle; and Louis XIV., accordingly, wrote two solemn letters to Cromwell and Fairfax;[1] but before M. de Varennes, who was appointed to deliver them, had left Paris, Charles I. was executed. M. de Bellièvre, then ambassador of France in London, made no attempt on his behalf; he did not even ask permission to see him. Some surprise was manifested at this at Paris, in the king's council; but Bellièvre was warmly defended and approved. "I see the necessity which I have for your protection," he wrote to M. Servien, "and the kindness with which you have extended it to me. I thought that it was better to be blamed for not having taken a step which any one might have seen could produce no advantage to the King of England, than to be guilty of the harm which that step might have done to the affairs of the king my master. For, as you know very well, they are so suspicious here with regard to everything that proceeds from France, that that which would pass unnoticed from others is declared criminal when it comes from us; and as, of foreign powers, they fear us alone, they pay such attention to our actions and our words that the least expression of the resentment which we must feel for that which they have done, might be enough to lead them to make alliance with Spain; and the knowledge of this fact, combined with the general instructions which I have always received not to irritate these fellows (*ces gens-ci*), made me resolve to act as I have done. I cannot repent of having

[1] See Appendix IV.

been too circumspect, as I now find myself supported by your approval."[1]

After the King's death, Bellièvre persisted in his circumspection. "If there were a Court here," he wrote, "I should need no other rule as to the time for putting on mourning, and the manner of wearing it; but as there is none, I think it right to wait the orders it may please you to send me."[2] He was ordered to go into mourning and leave the country; for Mazarin was as little inclined to recognize the English Commonwealth as to irritate it. Bellièvre quitted London, but not till after a delay of three months, and leaving behind him his secretary, Croullé, who was directed to watch over the interests of France, though not in any official character. The last relations of the ambassador with the Parliament were somewhat difficult; he attempted, but in vain, to obtain his passports without taking leave; and he was obliged to wait upon the Speaker, who reported his visit to the House. "Here," wrote Bellièvre, "no affair is unimportant, and no despatch prompt, especially where France is concerned; and at this time, when those who govern are so jealous of their newly-acquired authority, and so unaware of how much they may obtain or preserve in regard to strangers, that everything gives them umbrage; and they forget that which is due, out of fear of doing too much. . . . . Moreover, so uncertain are they in their resolutions that they are capable of passing in a moment from a compliment to an insult, or from an offensive action to an excess of civility."[3]

[1] Wicquefort's Histoire des Provinces Unies, vol. iv. p. 162; MSS. de Brienne, in the Bibliothèque Impériale, Paris; Archives des Affaires Etrangères de France.

[2] M. de Bellièvre to M. Servien; Archives des Affaires Etrangères de France.

[3] Ibid.

The Court of Madrid treated the new Commonwealth with even greater consideration than that of Paris, for it left its ambassador, Don Alonzo de Cardeñas, in London, without at first renewing his credentials, but confidentially authorizing him to continue his relations with the republican Parliament. This was a less difficult position for Don Alonzo than for any other person, as he had for a long while displayed great coolness, and even malevolence, towards Charles I., and had assiduously cultivated the favor of the revolutionary leaders; so that between them and him an interchange of friendly feelings and good offices had been established, from which Spanish policy hoped to gain great advantage.[1]

The Emperor and Princes of Germany, the King of Denmark, and the Queen of Sweden, were less reserved in their manifestation of the feelings with which they were inspired by the republican Parliament and its acts; but, alone among the sovereigns of Europe, the Czar of Russia, Alexis Michaelowitz, the father of Peter the Great, broke off all connection with the revolutionary Commonwealth, and expelled the English merchants from his dominions.[2]

But all was not done by the powers of the Continent when they had assumed an uncertain and expectant attitude towards the republican Parliament; they had also to regulate their conduct towards the exiled King, and here their perplexities and the inconsistent weaknesses of their policy were still greater. Charles II. resided among the sovereigns of Europe, sometimes with the Prince of Orange, his brother-in-law, and sometimes at the Court of the King of France,

[1] Letter of Cardeñas to King Philip IV., February 18, 1649; Deliberations of the Council of State at Madrid on the Letters of Cardeñas, March 13, 1649; in the Archives of Simancas: see Appendix V. Clarendon's History of the Rebellion, vol. vi. p. 328.

[2] Wicquefort's Histoire des Provinces Unies, vol. iv. p. 156; Clarendon's History of the Rebellion, vol. vi. pp. 248—250; Whitelocke, p. 466.

his cousin-german; the Queen of Spain, Elizabeth of France, was his aunt. He was everywhere able to invoke, and he did in fact invoke, the ties of consanguinity, as well as the common interest and honor of kings. He sent Lord Cottington and Hyde to Madrid, Sir John Colepepper to Moscow, Lord Wilmot to Ratisbon, and Mr. Crofts to Poland. Sovereigns and their ministers found themselves incessantly in presence of his rights, his hopes, his demands, his complaints, and his agents. Nothing is more offensive to power than the sight of misfortunes which it will not succor, but which it is bound to respect; it has, however, many ways of ridding itself, at small cost, of such burdens. William of Orange alone was a warm and active friend of Charles Stuart; he was an ambitious and imperious young prince, inclined to violent enterprises and to absolute power, but of a noble and sincere heart; to restore the fortunes of his brother-in-law, he wasted his strength in efforts and sacrifices which were too limited to be effectual, and to which his unexpected death soon put an end. Excited by the Stadtholder and by the popular feeling of Holland, the States-General of the United Provinces bestowed on Charles great marks of interest and respect: on the news of the death of the King his father, they waited on him in a body to express their condolence; and the Grand Pensionary, Van Ghent, in his harangue called him Sire, and your Majesty; but those words were pronounced with some embarrassment, and in a low voice, as though he were unwilling to compromise himself too deeply with the rising Commonwealth by recognizing the new King in too pointed a manner. The Court of France considered that it was quite enough to give an asylum and a pension to the widow and children of Charles I.; it abstained from any other expression of feeling, and Charles Stuart received from it, on his father's death, neither letter nor message—indeed no mark whatever of sympathy or support. The King of Spain, who had not to answer for the presence of the Stuarts in his dominions, thought it his duty to write a letter of friendly condolence to Charles II., in which he gave him the title of King; but he long delayed sending it. When Charles, on leaving the Hague for Paris, passed through the Spanish Netherlands, he was received with great honors at Antwerp and Brussels; a splendid carriage and six fine horses were presented to him; he was even supplied with a loan of money; the Archduke Leopold and the Spanish ambassador in Holland, Anthony Lebrun, gave him encouragement in their private conversations; but at the same time they took the most minute precautions to deprive these demonstrations of all political value, and to represent them as mere acts of politeness. The Court of Madrid absolutely forbade any act or speech on their part which might be regarded in London as a positive declaration in favor of the King; they were even ordered to antedate certain letters which seemed to present this character.[1] The crowned heads of Europe were willing to treat Charles II. with respect and to do him service, provided that no meaning could be attached to their conduct which might be incompatible with the maintenance of strict neutrality between him and the republican Parliament.

To this political coolness were added acts of cynical indifference in private life. The furniture and pictures of Charles I., who loved the arts, and had patronized them with taste,

[1] Clarendon's History of the Rebellion, vol. vi. pp. 310—313, 323—333, 470, 569; Leclerc's Histoire des Provinces Unies, vol. ii. p. 270; Letter from the Archduke Leopold, Governor of the Netherlands, to King Philip IV., March 4, 1649; Letter of Condolence from King Philip IV. to his Majesty King Charles of England, April 5, 1649: a first draft had been prepared in the month of March preceding; Letters from the Conde de Penaranda and the Archduke Leopold to King Philip IV., July 4—8, 1649; Deliberations of the Council of State at Madrid on the Title to be given to Charles II., August 2, 1649: in the Archives of Simancas. See Appendix VI.

were sold in London. Cardeñas and Croullé gave full information of this to Don Luis de Haro and Cardinal Mazarin, who, either for their sovereigns or for themselves, eagerly purchased, often at low prices, these spoils of the royal martyr. "If the pictures are sold at the prices marked in the list which you have sent me, I think them very dear," wrote Mazarin to Croullé; "that, however, will not prevent me from sending some intelligent person to buy several for me." Queen Christina of Sweden, and the Archduke Leopold, governor of the Spanish Netherlands, also purchased several; and when, in 1651, in the middle of winter, the King of Spain requested Lord Cottington and Hyde to leave his dominions, one of the secret causes of that resolution was the expected arrival of eighteen mules from Corunna, laden with pictures and curiosities belonging to Charles I., which had been purchased in London for Philip IV., and which he thought he could not decently display in his palace, so long as the ambassadors of Charles II. were at Madrid.[1]

Both great and small, at home and in exile, the English royalists were offended and indignant at this eager readiness to profit by their disasters, while rendering them so little help. "The neighbor princes," says Clarendon, "joined in this manner to assist Cromwell with very great sums of money, whereby he was enabled to prosecute and finish his wicked victory; whilst they enriched and adorned themselves with the ruins and spoils of the surviving heir, without applying any part thereof to his relief, in the greatest necessities which ever king was subject to." And Graymond, the agent of Cardinal Mazarin in Scotland, wrote to him: "The servants of the King of Great Britain here utter imprecations against

[1] Clarendon's History of the Rebellion, vol. vi. pp. 249, 458—460; Letters from Croullé to Mazarin, February 11 and May 23, 1650; and from Mazarin to Croullé, June 17, 1650: in the Archives des Affaires Etrangères de France. See Appendix VII.

the kings and sovereigns of the earth, and principally against His Majesty (Louis XIV.), if he does not assist their King, after whose ruin they desire that of all others; and they do not scruple to say they will contribute with all their power to their destruction, which will be, they say, very easy to effect, when once the people have, in imitation of England's example, breathed the sweetness of popular government. They already point to Cromwell as the author of this great design, and the reformer of the universe . . . . and they say that he will begin with us, and that we well deserve it, because we do not endeavor the restoration of the King of England, though we are under the greatest obligations to do so."[1]

Such anger was very natural on the part of earnest and devoted adherents of a persecuted cause. But they ill understood the political state of Europe, and did not appreciate the general causes which rendered the kings of the Continent so cold and inert in presence of events which seemed to affect them so nearly.

The progress of affairs in England was watched with the closest attention by the European powers, but it did not inspire them with any serious alarm. Though they regarded the English revolutionaries with the utmost antipathy, they did not feel themselves really menaced by them, and their own position did not furnish any necessity for engaging in a direct and open struggle against them. At precisely the same period when royalty was tottering to its fall in England, it was gaining strength on the Continent; in all the great States of Europe, feudal and municipal liberties, the independent aristocracy, and the turbulent democracy of the Middle Ages, were disappearing, or giving way before it; the ne-

[1] Clarendon's History of the Rebellion, vol. vi. p. 249; Letters from Graymond to Mazarin, October 23, 1649: in the Archives des Affaires Etrangères de France.

cessity for order in society, and for unity in the supreme power, everywhere predominated; the general tendency of ideas, as well as of events, was towards monarchy. The Commonwealth appeared a singular fact, purely local in its character, and the contagious influence of which was not greatly to be dreaded on the Continent, even in those States which were still agitated by civil dissensions.

The name of Commonwealth, or Republic, moreover, was not then necessarily a cause of distrust and alarm; although that form of government had, until then, prevailed only in secondary States, it had maintained its place in Europe without disturbing European order by its presence; the great European monarchies had lived on good and peaceable terms with the Republics of Italy, Switzerland, Germany, and the Netherlands. Europe had not yet contracted the habit of considering the republican form of government as the precursor and promoter of revolutions and anarchy.

The English revolution furthermore presented itself as much in a religious as in a political character. The great wars of religion were now at an end; the Treaty of Westphalia had just laid the foundation of a new European order; the Catholic States and the Protestant States had mutually come to an understanding, and among the latter, the most recent and most opposed, the United Provinces, had at length conquered their position and tranquillity. The prevalence of peace between the various Christian communions, if not in the interior of every State, at least in the external relations of countries with one another, had been definitely established; and although religious prejudices and animosities were far from being extinct, neither government nor people were willing to renew a conflict by which all had cruelly suffered, and in which neither party could any longer hope to crush its rival. It is by exhaustion and necessity that God imposes justice and good sense upon nations.

Religious peace restored liberty to politics; religious passions and creeds no longer regulated the designs and alliances of States; the spirit of ambition or of resistance to ambition, of preponderance or independence, of aggrandizement or equilibrium, became the principal motive of the conduct of governments in their international relations; they sought to obtain thereby means of attack or defence in their temporal hopes or fears, and weapons to serve them in their rivalries. The English revolution profited by this new and purely lay character of continental politics. Of the two great powers, France and Spain, which then contested for the ascendency in Europe, neither wished to quarrel with the young Commonwealth; they both did their best either to draw it into their camp, or keep it from joining the enemy; and two systems of alliance, more or less complete, and more or less openly avowed between France, England, and the United Provinces on the one side, and between Spain, England, and the United Provinces on the other, were the constant thought of Mazarin and Don Luis de Haro, at Paris and Madrid, and the object of the unceasing labors of their agents in London.[1]

The republican Parliament had a just, though confused and incomplete consciousness of its position. It understood that it was detested, but in no respect menaced, by the great European monarchies, and it conducted itself towards them with caution and dignity, but without uneasiness or angry feeling. It showed no anxiety to be recognized by them, neither did it hasten to accredit representatives of the Commonwealth to their courts. Not that it felt no impatience on this subject;

[1] Letters of Antony Lebrun, Spanish Ambassador in Holland, to Don Alonzo de Cardeñas, November 29, 1649; of Cardeñas to Philip IV., January 23 and February 15, 1652; and of the Archduke Leopold to Philip IV., February 6, 1652: in the Archives of Simancas. Letters of Croullé to Mazarin, January 10, 1650; and of Servien to Croullé, January 28, 1650: in the Archives des Affaires Etrangères de France. See Appendix VIII.

it frequently sounded the foreign agents who still remained in England, Bellièvre, Croullé, Cardeñas, and Joachim; sometimes in order to learn from them what sort of a reception would be given at their respective courts to the ministers whom the Commonwealth might send, and sometimes to intimate to them that they could not themselves continue to reside in London unless they received from their governments fresh credentials accrediting them to the Parliament.[1] This strong desire to be formally recognized was exhibited from time to time by indirect means. "It has been printed here," wrote Croullé to Mazarin, "that the State-councillors of France had treated with the English merchants on the subject of the business they transact, and had thereby recognized the Parliament as representing the Commonwealth. I hope they will rest contented with this imaginary recognition."[2] The Parliament was not thus easily satisfied; it continued, on the contrary, to prove itself at once exacting and impatient in this respect; determined to wait for the recognition of the Commonwealth so long as it was not complete and satisfactory; and deliberating, on various occasions, and with jealous susceptibility, upon the formalities to be observed in the relations of the Commonwealth with foreign governments.[3] But its attitude was calm and dignified at the same time; it publicly declared its intention to maintain all the existing treaties between England and other States;[4]

[1] Letters from Croullé to Mazarin, November 15 and December 6, 1649, and November 7, 1650; and from Servien to Croullé, November 6, 1649; in the Archives des Affaires Etrangères de France. Letters from Cardeñas to Philip IV., June 20 and August 13, 1649; and Deliberations in the Council of State at Madrid on the Recognition of the Commonwealth of England, October 9, 1649, and May 7, 1650: in the Archives of Simancas. See Appendix IX.

[2] Archives des Affaires Etrangères de France.

[3] Commons' Journals, vol. vi. pp. 416, 517, 618; vol. vii. p. 64.

[4] Thurloe's State Papers, vol. i. p. 135.

it recommended the Council of State to employ consuls in all foreign countries, in order that friendly commercial relations might not be broken off;[1] it retained in France an officious agent, named Angier, who actively watched over English interests;[2] and it remained in frequent and courteous communication with some of the foreign ministers in London, particularly the Spanish envoy Cardeñas and the Dutch ambassador Joachim, who had not yet received fresh letters of credence, but who were known to be well disposed towards the Commonwealth. In spite of numerous marks of inexperience, and some tendency to arrogance, the conduct of the republican leaders, in regard to foreign policy, was characterized by dignified reserve and intelligent prudence, and by a desire to remain at peace abroad, so as not to aggravate the difficulties and burdens of their government at home.

On one point only they engaged unreservedly and at all risks, in a bold and even violent course of action. In the month of June, 1648, a considerable portion of the fleet, eleven vessels, had revolted from the Parliament, and sailed over to Holland to place themselves under the orders of the Prince of Wales, for the service of the imprisoned King. In the month of October following, Prince Rupert was appointed admiral of this royal fleet; though until then unused to the sea, he was a man of dashing bravery, fond of adventure, fearless of a life of hardship and uncertainty, familiar and liberal towards his inferiors; he soon became as popular with the sailors as with the soldiers, and he continued on sea, against the Commonwealth, the same determined, wandering, and predatory warfare which he had waged on land against the Parliament. Charles II. was then living in a state of deep distress; he was in want of money to help his partisans,

[1] Commons' Journals, vol. vi. p. 333.
[2] Ibid. pp. 132, 494.

to pay his servants, to send messages to the Queen his mother, and even to undertake a journey himself. His brother-in-law, the Prince of Orange, could not, notwithstanding his generous friendship, supply all his wants; some few of the princes of the Continent, the Duke of Lorraine, the Queen of Sweden, the King of Poland, and the Czar of Russia, made him occasional loans or presents; his faithful friends in England sent him a part of what was left them after confiscations and sequestrations; but these supplies were speedily exhausted; Charles had no permanent or certain income. He sought and found, in the fleet commanded by Prince Rupert, precarious though sometimes abundant resources; it sailed up and down the Channel, in the North Sea, and all round England, making numerous and rich prizes from the mercantile fleet of the Commonwealth, and often, at hap-hazard, from that of any country: it was a fleet of corsairs under a royal flag, sent out to provide for the expenses of a proscribed king. Many private ship owners, English, Scotch, French, and Dutch, requested permission to share in this life of adventure and profit, by equipping ships at their own cost; leave was readily granted or sold to them; orders were issued by Charles II. for the regulation of this service, and the division of the booty; a fifteenth part of the value of all the prizes taken was allotted to the King, and a tenth to the admiral; the remainder was divided into three parts, one for the owners of the vessel, one for the purveyors of provisions and stores, and the third for the crew, among whom it was distributed in proportion to the rank and position of every man, from the admiral down to the common sailor. All commercial and personal security disappeared from the British waters; they became an arena of incessant depredations—of a privateering warfare, in which the vessels even of the King of France, and of the

States-General of Holland, disguising their flags, did not fail frequently to engage.[1]

Against this ruinous and insulting danger, the republican Parliament immediately took the most vigorous measures. No sooner had it acceded to power than it reorganized and augmented, by all available means, the fleet which remained at its disposal. On the 2d of February, 1649, thirty merchant vessels were engaged for the service of the State, and equipped for war; the naval forces voted in March, 1650, for the campaign of the following summer, amounted to sixty-five ships and 8150 men; and during the winter of 1650–1651, thirty-nine vessels, manned by 4190 sailors, and carrying 954 guns, were specially set apart for the protection of the English coasts. The impressment of sailors was rigorously carried on. Large provision was made for all the expenses of the naval forces, for the payment and promotion of the officers, and for the wages, maintenance, and rewarding of the sailors. Vane was president of the committee of the navy, and introduced his spirit of intelligent and zealous activity into all the departments of the service. Blake, Dean, Popham, Ayscue, Penn, and Baddeley were placed in command of various squadrons, and sent to cruise in the Channel or the North Sea, off the coasts of Ireland, France, Holland, Portugal, and Spain, and even in the Mediterranean, the Levant, and the West Indies. Most of them were officers of the land army, without nautical experience, but of tried boldness and capacity, devoted to the Commonwealth, eager for success and glory for their country and themselves, caring little what it might cost either themselves or their country, and firmly

[1] Clarendon's History of the Rebellion, vol. vi. pp. 23, 31, 140, 148—152; Granville Penn's Memorials of the Life of Sir William Penn, vol. i. pp. 260, 266; Hepworth Dixon's Life of Admiral Blake, pp. 114—118; Warburton's Memoirs of Prince Rupert and the Cavaliers, vol. iii. pp. 250, 266, 286—297; Whitelocke, pp. 308, 349, 447.

resolved to maintain everywhere, and at any price, the honor and safety of the English name and flag.[1]

To these well-provided and ably commanded material forces, the Parliament added legislative measures no less efficacious for the protection of the national commerce. It regulated the laws relating to maritime prizes in the way most calculated to excite the ardor and to recompense the efforts of its seamen.[2] It called home all those who were serving in foreign fleets; and to such English merchants as had suffered heavy losses at sea by visits from foreign vessels, it secured the means of obtaining redress for their injuries.[3] A declaration of Louis XIV. had recently prohibited the introduction into France of all woollen stuffs or silks manufactured in England; the Parliament directed the Council of State to prepare a report upon the different treaties which had hitherto regulated the commercial relations of the two countries, and on the ground that the recent prohibition was illegitimate, it forbade in its turn the introduction into England of wines, woollen stuffs, and silks from France.[4] "And to those who told them that this exclusion would not be effectual, and that they could not do without our wines," wrote Croullé to Mazarin, "they answered jocosely that men soon got accustomed to anything, and that, as they had without inconvenience dispensed with a king, contrary to the general belief, so they could also easily dispense with our French wines."[5]

Success attended these vigorous measures, ordered by an imperious government, and executed by bold and able agents. The republican fleet sailed into every sea, sometimes convoy-

[1] Commons' Journals, vol. vi. pp. 129, 134, 148, 149, 156, 375, 467; Memorials of Sir William Penn, vol. i. pp. 294—297, 302—304.

[2] Commons' Journals, vol. vi. pp. 202, 204.

[3] Ibid. pp. 379, 397.

[4] Ibid. pp. 284, 285.

[5] Archives des Affaires Etrangères de France.

ing the English merchant ships, sometimes making rich prizes of foreign traders, chasing the flag of Charles II. everywhere to the death, and inspiring wherever it went that mingled fear and respect which is always felt for a power which acts with rapidity and energy. Prince Rupert, towards the end of the winter of 1649, was cruising off the eastern and southern coast of Ireland, with a view to second the operations of the royal army in that Island, and to seize the merchant vessels which were always numerous in those waters. Blake sailed thither in pursuit of him, and blockaded him in the port of Kinsale. Rupert managed to escape with his fleet; but he lost three of his ships, and repaired with the rest to the coast of Portugal, to resume his random life of freebooting and adventure. Blake followed him thither by order of the Parliament, taking with him Charles Vane, a brother of Sir Harry Vane, who had been commissioned to lay before the King of Portugal the complaints and demands of the Commonwealth. Both fleets anchored opposite each other at the mouth of the Tagus, and both began negotiations with the Court of Lisbon—Rupert that it should continue to support him, and Blake that it should cease to do so. Rupert found great favor both at the Court and among the people of Portugal: on his arrival, King John IV. had sent several of his officers to meet him, and conduct him in state to the palace; and whenever he came on shore, the populace of Lisbon thronged around him with noisy acclamations. Blake, on the contrary, was an object of deep antipathy both to the Court and people, who were ardently royalist and Catholic in their opinions: whenever his sailors left their ships, they were insulted, and sometimes maltreated, either by Prince Rupert's men, or by the Portuguese themselves. Paying but little attention to these manifestations of ill-will, Blake demanded of King John to rid his dominions of pirates who had robbed the Commonwealth of England of a portion of its fleet by debauching its sailors; and stated that he had orders to pursue and destroy them as enemies of all regular commerce between civilized nations; but if the King of Portugal would not himself undertake to drive the pirates from his ports, he desired that at least he would not take it ill that the English admiral should enter the harbor with his squadron, and execute the commission which he had received from his government. The indignation which this demand produced at Lisbon was immense; the Queen and the Prince Royal sustained the somewhat tottering courage of the King, who was advised by some of his ministers to yield. A nobleman of high rank was sent to Blake with complimentary messages and presents, but with orders to repulse his pretensions, and to refuse him admittance into the harbor. Blake tried to force an entrance, but without success; his ships were fired on by the forts at the mouth of the river, and he was obliged to desist. He then began to make reprisals upon the commerce of Portugal; no ships, either royal or mercantile, were allowed either to enter or leave the port of Lisbon; Blake seized first five, and then nine, and he afterwards destroyed a rich fleet of twenty-three vessels from Brazil, declaring that he would not cease hostilities until the royalist pirates were either delivered up or ordered away. The Court of Lisbon alternated between anger and fear; it ordered the arrest and imprisonment of the English merchants resident in that capital; and Charles Vane, finding it impossible to obtain the restoration of their liberty and property, re-embarked on board the fleet, and returned to England. But at the same time, the King of Portugal urged Prince Rupert to withdraw, unless he considered himself strong enough to attack Blake's fleet, and deliver the kingdom of his presence. Rupert one day appeared disposed to give battle; but Blake had received a reinforcement of eight vessels under Admiral Popham, and he manifested such eagerness to begin the attack himself, that Rupert retired beneath the protection of the forts, and at last contrived to escape, with great difficulty, from the port of Lisbon, to seek fortune and safety in the Mediterranean. Blake pursued him along the Spanish coast as he had done along that of Portugal; and the same hesitations between favor and disfavor, the same alternations of anger and fear which had agitated the Court of Lisbon when in presence of these two rival fleets, disturbed, though more remotely, the Court of Madrid. As soon as Prince Rupert appeared off Malaga, the two ambassadors of Charles II. in Spain, Cottington and Hyde, informed the Spanish government of his arrival, and claimed a favorable reception for the cousin and fleet of their King. Don Luis de Haro readily promised it, as much from disquietude at the presence of so formidable a foreign force, as from favor to a royal fleet. But it was learned soon after at Madrid that the republican fleet was also off the coast of Spain, pursuing that of King Charles, and demanding as at Lisbon, admittance into the Spanish ports, in order to attack and destroy it. Equally violent and imperious claims were asserted by both parties simultaneously: Rupert, after having sunk several English merchant vessels before Malaga, demanded of the governor to arrest on shore, and deliver into his hands the master of one of those ships, who had taken an active part against King Charles, that "he might boil him in pitch." This the governor refused to do. Blake, on his side, learning that Prince Rupert had landed, urged the Spanish authorities to deliver him up to him, as a leader of pirates, and an enemy of all nations. The Court of Madrid took refuge against these impetuous demands, in delay and inactivity. The war between the two fleets continued for some months longer on the Spanish coast; at length, Blake destroyed the greater part of the royal fleet in an engagement off Malaga; and Rupert, left with two vessels only, wandered for some time in the Mediterranean, and then, passing through the Straits, sailed to the Atlantic, and along the Western coast of Africa, in search of opportunities for making new prizes without having to fight the fleet of the Commonwealth. The republican navy remained predominant in the seas of south-western Europe; Penn and Lawson were sent out in pursuit of Rupert, of whose whereabouts nothing was known; and Blake was recalled to England, to resume, in concert with Dean and Popham, the command of the fleet in the Channel and the North Sea. There the republican navy was in presence of more formidable rivals; but there also it had already given abundant proof of its vigor and daring. French commerce especially had paid dear for the prizes which its privateers had made at first upon the English. In the month of September, 1651, the Parliament declared that, as it could not obtain justice from the King of France, it had determined to do itself justice; six French ships, arrested by captains of vessels in the service of the State, were definitively confiscated, and no satisfaction was given to the remonstrances which arrived from Paris on the subject.[1] At sea the Parliament felt its strength, and had made it felt; its flag floated proudly on the breeze, feared by its enemies, and respected by its rivals.

But its success and skill, in matters of foreign policy, extended only thus far: though, in its maritime affairs, it displayed great ability and energy, in its diplomatic relations and undertakings it was equally deficient in sagacity and good sense, in moderation and resoluteness.

It was in the presence of two powers, at ardent rivalry

[1] Memorials of Prince Rupert, vol. iii. pp. 288—388; Clarendon's History of the Rebellion, vol. vi. pp. 270, 390—395; vol. vii. pp. 65, 66; Thurloe's State Papers, vol. i. pp. 134, 137, 138, 140—142, 154—158; Whitelocke, pp. 410, 429, 446, 449, 458, 463, 470, 471, 475, 476, 484—486, 515, 520; Dixon's Life of Blake, pp. 122—165.

with each other, but placed in very different positions and animated by very different tendencies. Spain, yet glorying in her recent greatness, of which Europe still stood in dread, was rapidly declining; the empire of Germany belonged to her no longer; notwithstanding protracted and sanguinary efforts, she had lost the United Provinces; her dominion in Italy was limited: a conspiracy had in one day robbed her of Portugal: afar off, and in the New World only, her possessions continued immense: she was, to use the pithy phrase of Sully, " one of those States which have strong arms and legs, but a weak and debilitated heart."[1] Amid the splendor of its court, and the pomposity of its language, the Spanish government felt itself really weak, and sought to conceal its weakness by immobility. Philip IV. and Don Luis de Haro, both of them sensible and moderate men—the one from idleness, and the other from prudence—and tired of conflicts which resulted only in defeat, aspired solely to the security of peace, and devoted their utmost care to avoiding all questions and circumstances which would have imposed upon them efforts of which they did not feel themselves capable. Divided and enervated, the House of Austria retained perhaps less ambition than power, and, except in cases of absolute necessity, pompous inertness was the policy of the successors of Charles V.

France and the House of Bourbon, on the contrary, were advancing together with bold and rapid progress: a potent spirit of activity and ambition animated both the councils of the crown and the various classes, more especially the superior classes of citizens; a taste for great designs and striking enterprises everywhere prevailed, without any fear of the labors and responsibilities which they entail. Thus, notwith-

[1] Sully to President Jeannin, in the Négociations du Président Jeannin, p. 261.

standing civil dissensions and fruitless endeavors for political liberty, the State grew stronger and more extended; the national unity and the royal authority received simultaneous development. As persevering as he was supple, and by turns a conqueror and a fugitive, but always a favorite and first minister, whether in exile or at Paris, Mazarin pursued the work of Henry IV. and of Richelieu, through alternate successes and reverses in war and at court. The government and the country displayed at once the characteristics of youth and age, were guided by powerful traditions in the midst of an entirely new movement, and yet were full of strength and thirsting for greatness.

Between these two powers, England might either have chosen an ally at her will, or have firmly maintained the balance: notwithstanding their repugnance to the regicide Commonwealth, they were so passionate in their jealousy and fear of one another that they subordinated all other feelings to the desire of mutually depriving each other of so important a supporter. The republican Parliament adopted neither of these courses: imperfectly appreciating the real strength and future prospects of the two powers, and swayed by old habits of routine, it remained wavering, but not impartial, between Spain and France—affecting neutrality without knowing either how to abandon it opportunely, or to maintain it unimpeachably.

Spain had some slight claims to preference: it was not from Madrid that Queen Henrietta Maria, the constant object of the antipathy and hostility of the Parliamentarians, had come; it was not at Madrid that she still found an asylum and the means of support. At the time of the King's trial, Don Alonzo de Cardeñas, on being urged by the royalists to make some demonstration in his favor, had formally refused to do so, saying that he had no instructions from his Court on the subject.[1] After the proclamation of the Commonwealth, he had remained in London on very good terms with the republican leaders, and he had solicited from his Court the renewal of his letters of credence, giving it to understand that he would turn them to good account, both for the political interests of Spain, and for the religious interests of the English Catholics.[2] Philip IV. and Don Luis de Haro were less hasty than Cardeñas; they would have preferred to declare neither for nor against Charles II. or the Commonwealth, to take secret advantage of the favorable tendencies of the one, to give some underhand expressions of sympathy with the other, and to wait events in complete inaction. Such was the constant drift of the opinions of the Spanish Council of State, when consulted by its King, sometimes upon the despatches of Cardeñas, and sometimes on those of Charles II. and his ambassadors. For more than a year, this policy of indifference and inertness was pursued at Madrid: no fresh instructions, no new powers were sent to Cardeñas; an attempt was made to prevent Cottington and Hyde from coming to Madrid, and as that failed, no heed was taken of their presence.[3] When they learned that Anthony Ascham was about to arrive in Spain, on a mission from the Parliament, they expressed their indignant surprise "that his Catholic Majesty should be the first Christian Prince that would receive an ambassador from the odious and execrable murderers of a Christian King, his brother and ally; which no other prince had yet done, out of the detestation of that horrible parricide."[4] The Council of State

[1] Letter from Cardeñas to King Philip IV., February 15, 1649; in the Archives of Simancas. See Appendix V.

[2] The same to the same, February 18, 1649. See Appendix V.

[3] Deliberations of the Council of State at Madrid, March 13—29, May 4, June 6, and August 2, 1649; in the Archives of Simancas. See Appendices V. and VI.

[4] Clarendon's History of the Rebellion, vol. vi. p. 442; Note from Lord

deliberated upon their remonstrance; and again, some months after, upon their request that Prince Rupert and his fleet might be well received in all the ports of Spain.[1] A direct answer either to their demands or complaints was sedulously avoided: both in regard to the republican Commonwealth and the proscribed King, the chief desire of the Court of Madrid was to say nothing, and to remain in inactivity.

But their relative positions gradually altered: the Parliament became more exacting; Cardeñas wrote to his King that they refused to treat with him, and that he would be obliged to leave England, unless he received fresh letters of credence, in which the Commonwealth was expressly recognized.[2] The assassination of Ascham, and the perseverance of the Parliament in its endeavors to obtain justice upon his murderers, plunged the Court of Madrid into great embarrassment. Charles II., on his side, treated Spain with ill humor; he went to Paris, under the pretext of visiting the Queen his mother, but in reality, it was said, for the purpose of receiving the advice and directions of Mazarin; and he bestowed the name of *brother* on the King of Portugal, who in Spain was always termed a *tyrant* and *usurper*.[3] The republican Parliament, on the other hand, was rough in its treatment of the House of Braganza, and had almost made war on it, because of the support it had given to Prince Rupert and his fleet. After hesitating twenty-one months, the Court of Madrid at length came to a decision; it dismissed from Spain

Cottington and Hyde to Philip IV., May 10, 1650; in the Archives of Simancas. See Appendix X.

[1] Deliberations of the Council of State at Madrid, May 10 and October 22, 1650; in the Archives of Simancas. See Appendix XI.

[2] Cardeñas to King Philip IV., June 20, 1649. See Appendix VI.

[3] Antoine Lebrun to Cardeñas, from the Hague, November 29, 1649; and Cardeñas to King Philip IV., December 14, 1649; in the Archives of Simancas. See Appendix XII.

the two ambassadors of Charles II., and sent fresh letters of credence to Cardeñas, accrediting him to the Parliament of the Commonwealth. At the same time Juan de Guimaraes arrived in London, sent by the King of Portugal to put an end to the misunderstanding between the two countries. The Parliament made Guimaraes wait fifteen days before giving him permission to come to London; and even then it was carried by a majority of one vote only, and it was decided that he should be received without public ceremony by a committee of eleven members.[1] But only two days after Cardeñas had announced the arrival of his new letters of credence, he was received by the entire Parliament in solemn audience.[2] Three Commissioners, one of whom was the Earl of Salisbury, went to fetch him from his house in a carriage belonging to the State; thirty or forty other carriages accompanied him, filled with Spanish and English gentlemen; two regiments of cavalry were drawn up before Whitehall as he passed; and he was escorted by a regiment of infantry. On his entrance into the hall in which the Parliament was assembled, he took his seat in an arm-chair which had been prepared for him, delivered to the Speaker his letters of credence, which were written in the Latin language, and pronounced a long speech in Spanish, in which he congratulated himself on being the first who came, in the name of the greatest prince of Christendom, to recognize that House as the supreme power in the nation, and narrated with much detail the steps taken by the King his master to secure the punishment of the murderers of Ascham, and to make Prince Rupert withdraw from the ports of Spain. Republican pride took pleasure in receiving with such pomp this striking homage from a monarch; a few austere Puritans alone were dissatisfied by it. "I fear," wrote Bradshaw to

[1] Commons' Journals, vol. vi. pp. 504, 510, 511, 516, 519, 522, 529, 530.

[2] Ibid. vol. vi. pp. 513, 515.

one of Cromwell's officers, "our impatient haste to ingratiate with neighboring nations hath done us neither honor nor profit. God grant we may depend upon Him, and seek aright for His owning of us, and that we may be independent enough as to all others! But in these things I have many dissenting brethren, and I write to one much abler to judge, and therefore abstain."[1]

At the same time that the Parliament was bestowing upon, and receiving from, the Spanish ambassador these striking marks of mutual good-will, the house of the French Chargé-d'affaires, Croullé, was broken into by a band of soldiers, and he was himself arrested, taken before the Council of State, and ordered to leave England within ten days. "Although Messieurs les Espagnols have waited till the last moment," he wrote immediately to Cardinal Mazarin, "they have not failed to be well received; and as it cannot have been without conditions that they have resolved to take this step, the principal of which conditions would be to be on bad terms with France, they thought fit to precede that ceremony by an action which would prove their desire to disoblige that country. Yesterday when, in accordance with the permission I have received from Court to keep a priest in my service, he was saying mass before an audience of several Frenchmen and a very few English, a company of soldiers came into my house, secured the doors, and, having entered, began to beat and maltreat all whom they met, and I was of the number. A French gentleman and I, by opposing ourselves to the violence which they were about to do to the altar, gave sufficient time to the officiating priest to divest himself of his robes and to mix with the crowd, whence I found means to take him, and to shut him up in my cabinet, so that he was not seen. The soldiers having made them-

[1] Milton's State Papers, p. 40.

selves absolute masters of everything, I went with an English nobleman and two French gentlemen to lay my complaint before the President of the Council, who, without deigning to hear me, had me arrested and confined in the guard-house and in a wretched inn until nightfall. At about six o'clock I was summoned before the Council of State, where, having given a simple and truthful narrative of the affair, it was resolved to order me to leave the country; which having been communicated to me by the President, I told him that I was here by the command of the King my master, whom I would inform of what he had stated to me, and that as soon as I had received his Majesty's orders, I would obey them without delay. To which the President having replied, that what I had then said evinced more contempt of the Council than anything I had said before, that no kings had authority to give orders in that country, and that, if I did not obey, they would proceed against me in the usual course; I answered that when I had spoken of his Majesty's commands, I had understood them as referring only to myself, who, wherever I was, received no other, and that they had in their hands the power and the force to do what they pleased, but not to make me do anything contrary to my duty; upon which I withdrew. This morning a messenger from the Council of State has brought me their orders, with a passport for me to leave the country within ten days, with which I must comply. I shall, however, wait the commands which it shall please your Eminence to send me."[1]

Mazarin felt the utmost displeasure at this incident; he had long been disturbed by the intrigues of Cardeñas in London, and by the preference given to Spain, by the English Government. On the 6th of August, 1649, he had written

[1] Letter from Croullé to Mazarin; Archives des Affaires Etrangères de France.

to Croullé, by M. Servien: "I beg you not to lose any opportunity for filling the Parliament with the greatest distrust of the Spaniards, which I doubt not you will do vigorously and adroitly upon all occasions;" and a few months later he wrote: "It would be well for the Parliament of England to furnish us secretly with some assistance in men or money, to enable us to defend ourselves against the great preparations which the Spaniards are making to attack us on all sides in the coming campaign. . . . At least you must always make it your object to prevent them from giving any help to the enemy, on the false representations which Cardeñas will make to them."[1] The information which Croullé transmitted to Mazarin had never been calculated to allay his anxieties; at one time he sent him an account of the marks of favor which the Parliament was bestowing on Cardeñas; at another, the announcement, well or ill founded, that a hundred thousand pounds sterling had been sent from London to Madrid, to help Spain in the war against France. MM. de Bouillon and Turenne, who were then the leaders of the Fronde, had, it was said, written to Cromwell to request his support, and the Republican Council of State contemplated sending part of the fleet which was cruising off Lisbon to assist the insurgent Frondeurs at Bordeaux.[2] A report was spread that Cromwell, after having subjugated Ireland, would make a journey into France: by a singular misapprehension, Mazarin at first saw in this only a friendly intention, and Servien immediately wrote to Croullé: "If, at the close of his expedition in Ireland, Mr. Cromwell comes into France, being, as he is, a person of merit, he will be well received

[1] Letters from Servien to Croullé: Archives des Affaires Etrangères de France.

[2] Letters from Croullé to Mazarin, January 10, May 16, July 4, and September 12, 1650; in the Archives des Affaires Etrangères de France. See Appendix XIII.

here; for assuredly every one will go to meet him at the place where he disembarks."[1] But Croullé's letters quickly disabused the Cardinal: "I know of no persuasion strong enough," he wrote, "to remove from the minds of all that, as soon as Cromwell has done in Ireland, he will pass into France with his army. . . . . All that is said about his design proceeds from those who desire it from different motives of interest; and from this cause he is made to say a quantity of things which I have always neglected to write, as being destitute of certainty and likelihood; as, among other things, that, looking at his hair, which is already white, he said that, if he were ten years younger, there is not a king in Europe whom he would not make to tremble, and that, as he had a better motive than the late King of Sweden, he believed himself still capable of doing more for the good of nations than the other ever did for his own ambition."[2]

Whether true or false, these rumors and sayings gave Mazarin great anxiety; the declared hostility of England would have seriously aggravated the difficulties of his precarious position at home, and the embarrassments of his foreign policy, which he obstinately pursued, in spite of all personal inconveniences. By his side, Colbert, as yet a mere councillor of State and intendant of the Cardinal's household, but already passionately devoted to the maintenance of the national prosperity, unremittingly denounced the sufferings and losses which were inflicted upon French commerce by the prohibitive measures of the republican Parliament, and the underhand and irregular warfare waged between the navies of the two States. Mazarin absolutely needed powerful allies in Europe; Colbert required security for French

[1] Letter from Servien to Croullé; in the Archives des Affaires Etrangères de France.

[2] Letters from Croullé to Mazarin; Archives des Affaires Etrangères de France.

commerce, both on land and sea. For a moment, Mazarin indulged the hope of being able to conclude an effectual alliance with the United Provinces against Spain and England: the Count d'Estrades, who had long been an ambassador in Holland, was in 1650 governor of Dunkirk; and on the 2d of September the Prince of Orange wrote to him: "The confidence which I have in your friendship, and in that which you entertained for my late father, leads me to hope that you will not refuse me the request which I make to you to come and visit me at the Hague as soon as possible, as I have very important affairs to communicate to you." This communication was a project of a treaty by which Louis XIV. and the Prince of Orange were to bind themselves "to make war in common against Spain, and at the same time to break with Cromwell, by endeavoring, by all sorts of means, to restore the King of England to his kingdom." D'Estrades sent for instructions to Mazarin, who immediately replied: "The Queen has commanded me to give you orders to proceed without delay into Holland, to the Prince of Orange; and in order that you may be in a position to treat with him, if you find him disposed to break with Spain, I send you the King's authority to conclude the treaty; and it would be the greatest service you could possibly render his Majesty. For my own part, I shall be very grateful to you if you induce that Prince to break with Spain; which would frustrate all the measures of my enemies, and dissipate the cabals and factions which are appearing at Court and in the Parliament against me. I beg you to neglect no effort to secure the success of this affair, which is most important."[1]

The affair did not succeed: the Prince of Orange died on the 6th of November, 1650; and towards the end of the

[1] Lettres, Mémoires et Négociations de M. le Comte d'Estrades, vol. i. pp. 99—103.

same year, Mazarin found himself standing alone, in presence of Spain, which still continued hostile, of the British Commonwealth, which had been officially recognized by Spain, of the United Provinces, which had been detached from the cause of monarchy by the death of their Stadtholder; and without any relations, even officious, with England, from whence his agent had been expelled.

From character as much as from policy, it was impossible for him to remain in this position; as impatient as he was crafty, and making small account of mortifications, he was one of those men who rush into action in order to escape from embarrassment, and who expose themselves to a fresh repulse rather than make no attempt to repair those which they have suffered. The French merchants insisted strongly upon the renewal of pacific relations with England; they attempted themselves to enter into direct correspondence with the republican Parliament and Council. Salomon, Vicomte de Virelade, wrote in their name from Paris, to the British Council of State, to request a safe-conduct to come to London and negotiate on their behalf: "No one here," replied Walter Frost, the Secretary of the Council of State, "could treat with you concerning these affairs, excepting only the sovereign power, or those whom it might depute; and that power will receive no address from any but the sovereign power of France, which alone can give the necessary authority for treating of such affairs. I cannot therefore obtain for you a passport to come hither in the capacity which you indicate. . . . . But if the State of France will, by you, make overtures of a public address to this Commonwealth regarding these affairs, in the manner usual between sovereign States, I have no doubt that this State will be glad to receive any honest and just propositions which will tend to terminate differences, and restore freedom of trade for the common advantage."[1]

Colbert now came to the assistance of the merchants: he drew up a statement in which, after laying down the principle that "for the restoration of trade two things were necessary—safety and liberty," he proceeded to enumerate the facts which deprived all trade between France and England of these two conditions of existence, and indicated, without hesitation, the means by which they might be recovered. "The point on which the English most strongly insist," he said, at the close of his report, "is the recognition of their Commonwealth, in which the Spaniards have preceded us. A closer union is consequently to be feared as the result of the negotiations of the Spanish ambassador in England. It is for our lords, the ministers, to prescribe the form of this recognition, how far it should extend; in which France will be excusable before God and men, if she be compelled to proceed to a recognition of that Commonwealth, in order to prevent the leagues and evil designs of the Spaniards, who are guilty of all kinds of injustice, and submit to all imaginable meannesses, in order to injure us."[2]

If he alone had had to decide, Mazarin would probably have acted with promptitude and thoroughness; but he had also to consult Anne of Austria, her council, and her confidants. He presented to her a report, in which the question of the recognition of the Commonwealth of England, was carefully discussed. "It seems at first sight," he says, "that if we are guided by the laws of honor or justice, we ought not to recognize this Commonwealth; as the King could do nothing more prejudicial to his reputation than to consent

[1] Documents Inédits sur l'Histoire Diplomatique de France, Revue Nouvelle, vol. v. pp. 413—416. See Appendix XIV.

[2] Documents Inédits sur l'Histoire Diplomatique de France, in the Revue Nouvelle, vol. v. pp. 409—413. See Appendix XV.

to a recognition by which he would abandon the interest of the legitimate king, his near relative, neighbor, and ally; and nothing more unjust than to recognize usurpers who have imbrued their hands in the blood of their sovereign. . . . . But as the laws of honor or justice should never lead us to do anything contrary to the dictates of prudence, it must be considered that all the demonstrations which we might now make in favor of the King of England, would not lead to his restoration; that a longer refusal to recognize the Commonwealth will serve in no way to augment or confirm the rights of the King; . . . . . that whatever the necessities of the time and of our affairs may compel us to do in favor of the Commonwealth, will not prevent us from afterwards being able to take advantage of any favorable conjunctures that may present themselves, when we shall be in a better condition to attempt some great enterprise; . . . . . that, moreover, there is reason to fear that, if the Spaniards once become more intimately allied with the English, as they are ardently laboring to be, they will prevent them from consenting to any accommodation with us, and will persuade them, if not to make open war upon us, at least to give them powerful assistance against us. There accordingly remains no room for doubt that we should without delay enter into negotiations with the Commonwealth of England, and give it the title which it desires. One condition is, nevertheless, absolutely necessary; and without it, it would be useless to pledge ourselves to grant this recognition; and that is, to be assured beforehand that we shall derive from it some utility, capable of counterbalancing the prejudice which may accrue by it to our reputation; . . . . . it would be doubly prejudicial to condescend to an act of meanness, if, after we had done it, the English should continue in a state of indifference and coolness towards us; and if our advances only served to make them more haughty and unyielding, in the conditions of the treaty which must be made with them for the accommodation of the differences which exist between us."[1]

To escape from this danger, and not "expose themselves to public disgrace with no profit," it was resolved first of all to send to London a secret agent, M. de Gentillot, a man of talent, well acquainted with England, and who had already been employed more than once on similar missions. "His Majesty," it was stated in his instructions, "has thought fit that the Sieur de Gentillot, as he is going into England, should labor adroitly and quietly, by means of the friends and connections which he has in that country, to obtain accurate information whether there is a real disposition to put an end, by a fair accommodation, to the difference which exists between the two nations, and to re-establish a good correspondence between them. He must be assured above all things that the Parliament of England has not made any private treaty with the Spaniards against France, and that it is not so far pledged to them that it will be unable to enter into all the accommodations and confederations which may be judged useful for the two kingdoms. The English will not fail to demand whether the King will openly recognize their Commonwealth by letters and other public demonstrations; in answer to which the Sieur de Gentillot will represent that there will be no difficulty upon that head, and that it is a point which the Parliament may consider as conceded in accordance with its desire; but that it is important for us to be assured that, after the recognition has taken place, we shall not relapse into any rupture or bad understanding, and that hostilities shall entirely cease. This assurance can be no other than the agreement, at the same time, upon a plan

[1] Documents Inédits sur l'Histoire Diplomatique de France, in the Revue Nouvelle, vol. v. pp. 416, 419; MSS. de Brienne, in the Bibliothèque Impériale, Paris. See Appendix XVI.

of accommodation of the differences which exist between the two nations." Here followed an enumeration of these differences, and of the precise conditions of the treaty which was to terminate them; and the instructions ended thus: "The Sieur de Gentillot may even intimate that, if the Commonwealth of England desires any closer engagement with France, especially against Spain, we are entirely disposed towards such an alliance. . . . In case the said Sieur de Gentillot should find such a disposition on the part of the English, on his giving information thereof, the ambassador who will be sent into England, will be instructed, and will have full powers, to treat of such an alliance."[1]

In taking this step, Mazarin had forgotten to give due con sideration to two things—the weakness of his own position, and the pride of the English republicans. At the moment when M. de Gentillot arrived in London, the Frondeurs were victorious in Paris: the Cardinal, obliged to fly, had found an asylum, with great difficulty, first at Havre, and then at Sedan; and the British Parliament, on its side, wishing to be recognized by France as it had recently been by Spain, openly and without further delay, refused to listen to, and even admit into London, any secret and officious agent. "I regret above all things in the world," wrote M. de Gentillot to M. Servien, "that I did not rightly understand matters before I undertook this journey: these people have too much cause for complaint; they wish to be addressed in due form, and to be treated with in the same way as other powers. I have done everything that was possible to be done; but all has been of no avail. It was thought that you had sent me hither only to act as a spy upon their affairs. Either from that or some other reason, or to show us that they cannot

[1] Documents Inédits sur l'Histoire Diplomatique de France; Revue Nouvelle, vol. v. pp. 419—422. See Appendix XVII.

admit any kind of negotiation which evades a recognition of their power, it is certain that very abruptly they sent for me on Friday, as a private individual, to come to them: six deputies of the Council of State examined me a little, went away to make their report, and shortly afterwards sent a secretary to give me an act which ordains that I must leave London within three days: in obedience to which, I leave this to-day, which is my third day; and I shall cross over to Calais to await an answer to this despatch."[1] No further orders were given to M. de Gentillot; he returned to Paris, and the rest of the year 1651 passed away, without any fresh attempt at an accommodation being made between the Court of France and the republican Parliament.

This was thought of very little consequence in London, for the Commonwealth and its leaders were in one of those periods of good fortune and hope which deceive governments, and especially new governments, as to their real strength, and give manifestation to all the dreams of their pride. At the same time that its recognition by Spain introduced the young Commonwealth into the society of European States, the death of William, Prince of Orange, laid open to the influence of England the United Provinces, the very one of those States to which it was bound by the most natural links of position and interest. Both of them Protestant and republican, the one hardly victorious, and the other still engaged in the struggle for the defence of its faith and liberties, the two nations had the same cause to maintain, in the name of analogous ideas, and frequently against the same enemies. Everything invited them to a close alliance. A serious obstacle opposed this at the outset: two great parties —the patrician burghers of the towns on the one side, and

[1] Documents Inédits sur l'Histoire Diplomatique de France; MSS. de Brienne, in the Bibliothèque Impériale, Paris.

on the other, the House of Nassau, supported by the remains of the feudal nobility, and by the masses—disputed for the government of the United Provinces: both were powerful and worthy of respect, for both had gloriously fought and suffered for the independence of their country. When the victory was won, they immediately began a secret as well as an open conflict; the one party aspiring to found an aristocratic and federal republic, the other tending to transform, under the name of a Stadtholderate, the confederation of the United Provinces into a sole and hereditary sovereignty; a deplorable disunion, in which both parties, obeying noble impulses, and sustaining legitimate interests, aggravated beyond measure, by their passions, the importance of their disagreements, and were, in turn, equally regardless of what their strength could effect, and of what their country desired. As long as the Prince of Orange lived, he secured the preponderance, in the councils of the United Provinces, of a policy hostile to the British Commonwealth, not, however, without great efforts, or with complete success. He would have desired to engage the confederation in the cause of Charles II., even at the cost of war: this was evidently more than was consistent with the welfare or the public feeling of the country. The province of Holland, in which commercial interests and the patrician burghers predominated, energetically supported a peaceful and neutral policy; it maintained friendly relations, on its own account, with the English Parliament, taking care to keep on good terms with its merchants, and to show it particular respect on all occasions; it even sent and maintained for some time in London, a special agent, Gerard Schaep, whom the Parliament received and treated with great distinction.[1] A rupture between the two States was thus prevented, but this was the

[1] Commons' Journals, vol. vi. pp. 414, 421, 422, 425.

limit of the influence of the province of Holland and its magistrates; they could not prevent the Prince of Orange, seconded by the jealousies of the other provinces, and by the popular feeling of the country, from securing the preponderance of a royalist policy in the general conduct of affairs. Not only did the States-General bestow on Charles II. all such marks of interest, and all such indirect support as would not absolutely pledge them to his service, but they admitted him to confer with them, to explain to them his position and views, to ask their advice; and at the same time, they refused to grant any audience to the Resident of the English Commonwealth, Walter Strickland, who had remained at the Hague after the murder of his colleague, Dorislaus, and neither his repeated demands, nor the formal protest of the States of the province of Holland, could overcome their refusal.[1] Strickland returned to London, and in giving an account of his mission to Parliament, with the bitterness of a disappointed diplomatist, made it aware of the deep-rooted enmity with which it was regarded by the Prince of Orange, and the States-General, over which he had complete control.[2]

On the death of the Prince of Orange, a complete change took place in this state of things. Notwithstanding that great marks of respect and affection were shown towards his family, neither his dignities nor his power were transmitted to the child to whom his widow, the Princess Mary Stuart, gave birth a few days after his death, and who afterwards became William III., King of England. The magistrates of the principal towns, the families of De Witt, Bicker, De Waal, Ruyl, Voorhout, and others, resumed the functions of

[1] Leclerc's Histoire des Provinces Unies, vol. ii. p. 272; Commons' Journals, vol. vi. pp. 295, 315; Thurloe's State Papers, vol. i. pp. 113—115; Clarendon's History of the Rebellion, vol. vi. p. 470.

[2] Commons' Journals, vol. vi. p. 452.

which the prince had violently deprived them; the municipal aristocracy and the province of Holland, in which its chief strength resided, regained their ascendency in the central government; an extraordinary assembly of the States-General restored to vigor the republican traditions of the confederation; everything announced that a pacific and even friendly policy towards the Commonwealth of England would be substituted for the royalist and hostile policy of the Prince of Orange. Never could a more favorable opportunity have presented itself for the conclusion, between the two Protestant republics, of that intimate alliance which their position seemed to indicate to them.[1]

The Parliament hastened to seize it, and determined that ambassadors extraordinary should be sent to the Hague to settle all differences, and treat of an alliance, between the two States. In order to give this embassy greater authority, it was intrusted to the Chief-Justice, Oliver St. John, one of the ablest leaders of the Parliament during the civil war, and of the Commonwealth since its victory, and, moreover, an intimate friend and councillor of Cromwell. St. John refused at first, on the ground of ill-health. He was a selfish, arrogant, and timid revolutionist, satisfied with his judicial position and his indirect influence in the government, and unwilling to compromise either his self-respect or his safety in a mission which would certainly be difficult, and might perhaps be dangerous. The House would not accept his refusal, appointed Walter Strickland as his colleague, gave them their instructions, and despatched them on their mission, which was surrounded with unusual splendor. Forty gentlemen, and a retinue of about two hundred servants, accom-

[1] Wicquefort's Histoire des Provinces Unies, vol. iv. pp. 200—220; Leclerc's Histoire des Provinces Unies, vol. ii. pp. 288—303; Wagenaar's Vaderlandsche Historie, vol. xii. p. 118, *et seq.*

panied them. St. John took Thurloe with him as his secretary. On their arrival in Holland, first at Rotterdam, and then at the Hague, they were received with no less attention and solemnity. A deputation from the States-General came to meet them, attended by twenty-seven carriages; they expressed great regret that they could not lodge them in the house devoted by the State to the reception of foreign ambassadors, as it was already occupied by the French ambassador, M. de Bellièvre; they were therefore established in a private house, and most of their suite were lodged in the neighborhood, going and coming through the streets incessantly, but always in parties of three or four, and carrying their swords in their hands or under their arms, as though they thought themselves in a hostile country, and surrounded by the murderers of Dorislaus. The English royalists were indeed very numerous at the Hague, in the train of the Princess of Orange and of the Duke of York, and very much inclined to insult the ambassadors of the Commonwealth. The Dutch population itself was also ill-disposed towards them, and followed them about with offensive curiosity, ridiculing their attitudes, and saying that they were doubtless afraid.[1]

The feelings of the men who were then at the head of the government of Holland were of a very different character. From position as well as from prudence, for their own sakes no less than for the sake of their country, they sincerely desired to be on good terms, and even to form a true alliance, with the Commonwealth of England. Three days after their arrival at the Hague, St. John and Strickland were received by the States-General in solemn audience, with the most

[1] Commons' Journals, vol. vi. pp. 525, 527, 528, 541, 543; Whitelocke, pp. 487, 488, 490; Clarendon's History of the Rebellion, vol. vi. pp. 594—596; Wicquefort's Histoire des Provinces Unies, vol. iv. p. 287; Leclerc's Histoire des Provinces Unies, vol. iii. pp. 307, 308.

distinguished marks of friendly consideration, and seven commissioners were appointed to confer with them. They were instructed to declare to the ambassadors "that the United Provinces offered their friendship to the Commonwealth of England, and that they were inclined, not only to renew and maintain inviolably the affection and friendly relations which had at all times existed between the English nation and themselves, but also to make a treaty of common interest with the Commonwealth." The first words of the two ambassadors made it evident that such offers would not suffice them. "We propose," they said, "that the amity and good correspondence which hath anciently been between the English nation and the United Provinces, be not only renewed and preserved inviolably, but that a more strict and intimate alliance and union be entered into by them, whereby there may be a more intrinsical and mutual interest of each in other, than has hitherto been, for the good of both."[1]

What was this "more strict and intimate alliance" to be? What was the meaning of the "more intrinsical and mutual interest?" For six weeks, St. John and Strickland refused to give any more definite explanation of their meaning; it was, they said, for the States-General to explain, with precision and detail, their views in this negotiation; as for themselves, they did not consider the first offer which had been made to them at all satisfactory; and as the Parliament had appointed a fixed and limited term for the duration of their embassy, they insisted that a clear and peremptory answer should be promptly given to their general proposition.[2]

A design of vast and chimerical ambition, one of those designs which men hesitate to acknowledge even while they are laboring to accomplish them, was entertained in the secret

[1] Wicquefort's Histoire des Provinces Unies, Preuves, vol. ii. pp. 379—391.
[2] Ibid. vol. ii. pp. 392—394.

souls of St. John and the Parliamentary leaders who had sent him on his mission. At once presumptuous and restless, they were under the influence of that exuberance of rash activity, that necessity of gaining strength by extension, which characterizes new powers when intoxicated by their first successes. The reports spread about Cromwell's plans for an expedition into France had no other origin; sensible, even in the midst of the utmost revolutionary ferment, Cromwell probably never entertained such an idea; but in the army, in the Parliament, everywhere throughout republican England, ideas of this kind formed the theme of passionate discussion among men of bold and unquiet minds, who imagined everything would be possible to their country and themselves, after what they had already done. The United Provinces were not like France; there was no necessity to conquer them by war; half the work was done already; all moral and material ties, religion, institutions, politics, commerce, connected and assimilated the United Provinces with England. Why should not the assimilation be carried as far as union? Why should two republics so similar and so near to one another remain separated? "*Faciamus eas in unam gentem*—let us make of them one nation," was the idea of the republican leaders in England. Strickland, during his first mission to the Hague, had already expressed it in a letter to Walter Frost, the Secretary of the Council of State; it inspired the embassy of St. John, and swayed the entire negotiation.[1]

It was a dream as full of imprudence as of pride. The union into a single State, and under the same government, of the two great Protestant republics would assuredly have met with desperate resistance in Europe, and might perhaps have rekindled the wars of religion. The population of Hol-

[1] Thurloe's State Papers, vol. i. p. 130; Clarendon's History of the Rebellion, vol. vi. p. 594; Godwin's History of the Commonwealth, vol. iii. p. 372; Leclerc's Histoire des Provinces Unies, vol. ii. p. 309.

land would have indignantly rejected any such proposal; it was the loss of their national existence, and their absorption into the more powerful State of England, which was already exceedingly unpopular in the United Provinces, as their former protector, their present rival, and probably their future enemy. Satires, songs, and other small compositions in prose and verse, expressive of deep hatred and violent threats against the English, were already in circulation among the people; even the heads of the Dutch government, the men most decidedly in favor of a good understanding with England, were too high-minded not to place the independence of their country far above all other considerations, and their good-will in the negotiation diminished as soon as they caught a glimpse of the ambitious design of the foreign envoys. Deploring, some years later, the Orangist intrigues and popular passions which had led to the rupture between the two countries, John de Witt said, with patriotic bitterness: "To this must be added the insupportable humor of the English nation, its continual jealousy of our prosperity, and the mortal hatred of Cromwell to the young Prince of Orange, the son of the sister of that banished king, who was the person he most feared in the world."[1]

Various incidents, some of them natural and almost unavoidable, others the result of deliberate design, occurred still further to augment the difficulties of the negotiation. The populace of the Hague frequently exhibited the coarsest ill-feeling towards the ambassadors; in the streets and suburbs of the town, their servants were insulted and maltreated by the servants of the Princess of Orange, or by the Cavaliers in the train of the Duke of York, who was then residing with his sister. The Prince and Princess themselves often passed

[1] Leeven en Dood der Gebroeders Cornelis en Johan de Witt, pp. 26, 27, 35; Histoire de Corneille et Jean de Witt, vol. i. p. 64.

and repassed, slowly and with a brilliant cavalcade, in front of the residence of the ambassadors, as if to brave them; puerile pleasures, in which party hatreds and humors indulge in order to obtain consolation and recreation in the time of their impotence. One day Prince Edward, a younger brother of Prince Rupert, seeing the ambassadors pass in their carriage, shouted after them: "O you rogues! you dogs!" On another occasion, St. John, while walking in the park at the Hague, met the Duke of York, on foot like himself, and they did not recognize one another until they were almost face to face. As the ambassador of the Commonwealth would not give way, the Prince snatched his hat off his head, and threw it in his face, saying: "Learn, parricide, to respect the brother of your King." "I scorn," answered St. John, "to acknowledge either you or him of whom you speak, but as a race of vagabonds." They both laid their hands on their swords, but the gentlemen who were with them surrounded them, and prevented an encounter. A Colonel Apsley boasted, it is said, that he would go and strangle St. John in his house. The ambassadors complained of these affronts to the States-General. The magistrates instituted prosecutions, took measures of police, and placed guards all round their residence. Official satisfactions were not wanting; but the animosities of the royalists and of the populace continued to exist, and constantly found some new form and fresh opportunity for manifesting themselves.[1]

The ambassadors sent a report to London of the almost equally perilous and difficult position in which they were

[1] Commons' Journals, vol. vi. pp. 560, 568; Whitelocke, pp. 491, 493, 494; Clarendon's History of the Rebellion, vol. vi. pp. 594—596; Old Parliamentary History, vol. xix. p. 473; Carte's Ormonde Letters, vol. i. p. 447, vol. ii. p. 2; Raguenet's Histoire de Oliver Cromwell, p. 261; Leclerc's Histoire des Provinces Unies, vol. ii. pp. 308—310; Wicquefort's Histoire des Provinces Unies, vol. iv. p. 289; Thurloe's State Papers, vol. i. p. 179.

placed; they even sent Thurloe to give a detailed explanation of the state of affairs in Holland, and to inquire whether they should continue to negotiate or return home.[1] The Parliament, which clung strongly to its plan, authorized them to prolong their stay; but at the same time, to give the States-General a proof of their dissatisfaction and power, it ordered the arrest at sea of nine merchant vessels belonging to Amsterdam, and bound for Portugal; and sent to the Hague for explanation of the attitude of Admiral Tromp, who was cruising with his squadron off the Scilly Islands, as though he intended to take possession of them. The States-General explained the instructions which had been given to Tromp, and complained of the seizure of the nine ships.[2] Neither country was willing to take the initiative in the rupture; but the temper of both parties daily became more unfriendly, and was displayed even in the actions and words of courtesy which were intended to conceal it.

After more than two months had been spent in useless conference—months wasted by the English ambassadors in not stating what they were endeavoring to effect, and by the Dutch in not giving an answer to what was asked of them thus indirectly, although they understood it quite well—St. John and Strickland at length decided to announce with precision some of their pretensions, in seven articles.[3] These alone would have resulted in the complete connection of the policy and fate of the United Provinces with the policy and fate of England in all matters of peace, war, and alliance; and they moreover bound the States-General to abdicate, in certain cases, on their own territory, the rights and free ex-

[1] Commons' Journals, vol. vi. p. 568.

[2] Thurloe's State Papers, vol. i. p. 177; Whitelocke, pp. 491, 492; Wicquefort's Histoire des Provinces Unies, Preuves, vol. ii. pp. 397—402; Leclerc's Histoire des Provinces Unies, vol. iii. p. 311.

[3] Thurloe's State Papers, vol. i. p. 182; Wicquefort's Histoire des Provinces Unies, Preuves, vol. ii. pp. 410—414.

ercise of sovereignty. And to indicate that their mission was far from being limited to even these extreme terms, the two ambassadors hastened to add that, if their first demands were acceded to, "the Parliament had given them power to propound and bring to effect on their part, matters of greater and higher concernment to the good of both commonwealths."[1]

Evidently, with such after-thoughts, nothing was possible; no further explanation was necessary to produce a complete mutual understanding. From politeness, the negotiation was continued a few days longer; but on the 29th of June, 1651, St. John and Strickland announced that the Parliament had recalled them, and requested an audience to take leave, which was granted to them on the following day. In presence of the States-General, the official language of St. John was moderate and courteous, but on separating from the Dutch commissioners, with whom he had been negotiating for three months, he said to them: "I perceive that their High Mightinesses are waiting the issue of affairs in Scotland, that they may regulate their carriage to our government accordingly, and that for that reason they have slighted the generous overtures with which we were charged. It is true that some members of our Parliament dissuaded this embassy, and advised that we should first finish our war in Scotland, and then expect your representatives on our shores. But I thought more honorably of you. I was wrong: and I now confess that these cautious advisers understood you better. Take my word for it, however, our Scottish campaign will soon be terminated as our warmest friends would wish, and you will then repent your having so lightly treated the proposals we have made."[2] Two days afterwards, the English

[1] Thurloe's State Papers, vol. i. p. 188; Wicqueforte's Histoire des Provinces Unies Preuves, vol. i. pp. 415—418.

[2] Histoire de Corneille et Jean de Witt, vol. i. p. 63; Wicquefort's Histoire

ambassadors left Holland, refusing, in obedience to the express commands of the Parliament, the rich presents which were offered them by the States-General; and on the 7th of July, Whitelocke announced to the House that they had returned to London, and were ready to give a report of their mission.[1]

Two decisive measures promptly followed the presentation of this report. On the 5th of August, Whitelocke proposed to Parliament the famous bill known as the Act of Navigation, which provided that no foreign ships should be allowed to bring into England any commodities which were not the proper produce or manufacture of the countries to which they respectively belonged. This was the hardest blow which could possibly be struck at Holland, whose prosperity mainly depended upon its carrying trade. Before the end of the year, the bill was definitively adopted, and put into operation.[2] At the same time, letters of marque were granted to many English merchants, to enable them, it was said, to indemnify themselves for the losses which had been inflicted on them by the Dutch Navy. The United Provinces had refused to allow themselves to be conquered by negotiation: war was now proposed against them.

The victory of Worcester carried to a climax the proud confidence of the republican Parliament; and the States of the Continent, by their attitude and conduct after that great defeat of the royalist party, served only to justify and increase it. From all parts there came to London declarations of recognition of the Commonwealth, overtures of official

des Provinces Unies, Preuves, vol. ii. p. 428; Heath's Brief Chronicle, pp. 524—527; Thurloe's State Papers, vol. i. pp. 189—192.

[1] Commons' Journals, vol. vi. pp. 593, 595; Whitelocke, p. 496; Leclerc's Histoire des Provinces Unies, vol. ii. p. 313.

[2] Commons' Journals, vol. vi. p. 617; vol. vii. p. 27; Leclerc's Histoire des Provinces Unies, vol. ii. pp. 313, 314.

relations, and almost even diplomatic congratulations and compliments. Tuscany, Venice, Geneva, the Hanseatic Towns, the Swiss Cantons, and the petty princes of Germany, sent and received agents.[1] From Sweden, Denmark, and Portugal, extraordinary ambassadors brought letters from their sovereigns to the Parliament, were presented to it in solemn audience, and commenced eager negotiations with it, either to put an end to existing differences, or to enter into immediate alliance.[2] Wonderstruck by the success of the Commonwealth, all Europe took measures to live on good terms with it, whether it believed or not in its future stability.

Mazarin could not remain passive amid this movement, for no one was readier than he to bend before power, either to attract and use it for his advantage, or to conceal from it his real views. He renewed his attempts to resume friendly relations with the English Commonwealth; M. de Gentillot made a fresh journey to London, where Mazarin maintained numerous secret agents, both French and English, partly for the purpose of collecting information, and partly to form connections which he hoped some day to turn to his profit. His anxiety became still more intense when he learned that Sir Harry Vane had been to Paris, and had an interview with Cardinal de Retz. "On my return home at about eleven o'clock in the evening," says De Retz, "I found a certain Fielding, an Englishman, whom I had known formerly at Rome, who told me that Vane, a great Parliamentarian and intimate confidant of Cromwell, had just arrived in Paris, and had orders to see me. I found myself somewhat embarrassed by this; however, I thought I ought not to re-

[1] Commons' Journals, vol. vii. pp. 19, 28, 96, 142, 256.

[2] Commons' Journals, vol. viii. pp. 77, 103, 104, 130, 135, 136, 137, 230, 234, 243, 177, 178, 182, 185, 186, 187, 190, 191, 194, 203, 223, 229, 149, 159, 165, 245, 252, 261, 269, 270, 273, 276, 277.

fuse this interview, at a conjuncture when we were not at war with England, and when the Cardinal himself was making both base and continual advances to the Protector. Vane gave me a short letter from him, which was only a letter of credence. The substance of his discourse was that the sentiments which I had expressed in defence of public liberty, combined with my reputation, had inspired Cromwell with a desire to make friendship with me. This was adorned by all the courtesies, all the offers, and all the temptations that you can imagine. Vane appeared to me a man of surprising capacity. I answered with all possible respect: but assuredly I neither said nor did anything that was not worthy both of a true Catholic and of a good Frenchman."[1] Mazarin judged otherwise, and from his place of exile at Bruhl he wrote thus to the Queen: "The Coadjutor has always spoken with veneration of Cromwell, as of a man sent by God into England, saying that he would raise up similar men in other kingdoms; and once, in jovial company when Ménage was present, hearing some one extol the courage of M. de Beaufort, he said in express terms: 'If M. de Beaufort is Fairfax, I am Cromwell.'"[2]

Mazarin excelled in the art of ruining his enemies by exaggerating the meaning of their actions or words, and by immediately appropriating to his own use, with the utmost effrontery, their tactics and weapons. Whilst he thus represented to the Queen as a crime in the Coadjutor the sentiments which he entertained with regard to Cromwell, he was himself laboring to enter into intimate relations with Cromwell: too sagacious not to perceive that in him were centred all the power and ability then existing in England, it was to the future master of the Commonwealth, and no longer to

[1] Mémoires du Cardinal de Retz, p. 211.

[2] Lettres du Cardinal Mazarin à la Reine Anne d'Autriche, publiées par M. Ravenel, pp. 5, 6.

the republican Parliament, that his advances were addressed. Cromwell willingly received them; he also was busily engaged in securing to himself powerful friends in every direction. "He adroitly leaves to others the conduct and care of everything unpopular," wrote Croullé to M. Servien, as early even as 1650, "and reserves to himself such things as give satisfaction; or at least he spreads a report to this effect, in order that, if they succeed, they may be attributed to him, and if not, that it may be thought that it was in his will to do them, but that their realization was prevented by others."[1] On the 5th of February, 1652, the Comte d'Estrades, who was still governor of Dunkirk, wrote to Mazarin, who had then returned into France, and had just rejoined the Queen at Poitiers: "The Protector Cromwell has sent to me Mr. Fitz-James, his colonel of guards, to propose to me to treat about Dunkirk, that he would give me two millions for it, and that he would engage to furnish fifty vessels and fifteen thousand foot-soldiers, to declare against Spain, and against the enemies of the King and of your Eminence, with whom he would wish to make a close friendship. I replied to Mr. Fitz-James that, if the troubles and civil war which existed in France did not oblige me to send to the Queen and your Eminence, I would have had him thrown into the sea for having supposed me capable of betraying my King, but that the present state of affairs obliged me to detain him with me until I had received an answer from the Court." Mazarin replied to D'Estrades: "My opinion was that we should accept Cromwell's proposition; but M. de Châteauneuf opposed it, and carried the Queen with him, so that she would not consent to it. . . . I leave it for the Sieur de Las to express to you the sentiments which I feel towards you: your interests are as dear to me as my own." D'Estrades understood his

[1] June 20, 1650; Archives des Affaires Etrangères de France.

wishes, and did not lose a moment; five days afterwards he wrote to Mazarin: "As soon as I had received from M. de Las the letter which acquainted me with the intentions of your Eminence touching the proposition of England, I communicated the same to my friend in London, and begged him to give me an answer on the point contained in my letter, as speedily as possible. He arrived in this town this morning, and told me, on the part of Mr. Cromwell, that what the Commonwealth demands is that the King should recognize them, and send an ambassador as soon as possible, and that he should pay their subjects that which has been taken from them at sea. . . . He told me afterwards that Mr. Cromwell had charged him to tell me that, if your Eminence could not remain in France, and your enemies should oblige you to leave your country, he assured me that you would be well received in England if you should wish to retire thither, and treated by the Commonwealth with all kinds of honor; that they would give you a good house to live in, entire safety for your person, and the free exercise of your religion; and that whenever you wished to go to Rome, you should be furnished with vessels to convey yourself and all your train whithersoever you might wish."[1]

Mazarin now thought himself near the accomplishment of his wishes: powers were immediately sent to the Comte d'Estrades "to treat of a new alliance with the Commonwealth of England. . . . In judging," Louis XIV. was made to say, "that the Sieur Cromwell might send some one to us to be better informed of our good intentions, you will have to acquaint him with them, and to open yourself in all confidence, not only respecting any treaty with the Common-

[1] Lettres, Mémoires et Négociations du Comte d'Estrades, vol i. pp. 103—107; Letter from the Comte d'Estrades to Cardinal Mazarin, in the Archives des Affaires Etrangères de France.

wealth, but also with the said Sieur Cromwell personally, for the common welfare of the two kingdoms as well as for his private interests; as I give you, by these presents, power to act, negotiate, treat, and promise in my name all that you may judge fitting with regard to the said Cromwell, and I will ratify and execute all that you shall have promised in my name."[1] D'Estrades, however, did not leave Dunkirk: it was not until a month after the date of his powers, that he received precise instructions, and a letter from Mazarin with comments upon them. The Cardinal wished to sell dearly the recognition of the Commonwealth, and to grant it only in exchange for an immediate treaty which should not merely put an end to all differences between the two states, but should secure to France the alliance, or at least, the secret support, of England against Spain. In this hope, he even authorized D'Estrades to resume the question of the cession of Dunkirk to the English.[2] Being doubtless informed by his friends in London that he would have but little chance of success, D'Estrades never went on this mission. In his stead, almost identical instructions were given to M. de Gentillot, who furthermore had orders to deliver to Cromwell a letter from Louis XIV. himself, to the following effect: "Mr. Cromwell, as I am sending expressly to London the Sieur de Gentillot, a gentleman of my chamber, with letters of credence to the Parliament of the Commonwealth of England and to the Council of State, in order to acquaint them with my good intentions; and as it is advantageous to both States to live in good neighborhood, peace, and amity, I have charged him with this letter for you, to assure you of my good-will and entire disposition to do whatever may conduce

[1] Letter from Louis XIV. to the Comte d'Estrades; MSS. de Brienne, in the Bibliothèque Impériale, Paris.

[2] MSS. de Brienne, in the Bibliothèque Impériale, Paris. See Appendix XVIII.

to the security and liberty of the trade, well-being, and mutual advantage of the two nations; and feeling assured that you will contribute willingly to so good a result, I leave it to the said Sieur de Gentillot to tell you more, begging you to give him credence as a person in whom I place entire confidence."[1] Whether it was never carried out, or whether it failed obscurely, the mission of Gentillot produced no more result than that of D'Estrades. Both parties were feeling their way, without advancing. Meanwhile, Mazarin became more and more anxious and hurried. Some months previously, at the very moment when he had commenced these negotiations, the Prince de Condé and the Frondeurs of Bordeaux had also sent to London two agents, MM. Barrière and De Cugnac, with instructions to solicit the support of the Commonwealth, and to offer in return free trade with Guienne, certain favors towards the French Protestants, and even the cession of the island of Oleron. These agents had, in the first instance, no public character; they addressed themselves to all the men of importance, and particularly to Cromwell, stating their demands and offers to all whom they thought able to help them. But on the 31st of March, 1652, the Speaker informed the Parliament that he had received a letter signed "Louis de Bourbon," and addressed "Au

[1] The text of this letter is as follows: "Monsieur Cromwell, envoyant exprès à Londres le Sieur de Gentillot, gentilhomme de ma chambre, avec lettres de créance au Parlement de la République d'Angleterre, et au Conseil d'Etat, pour leur faire entendre mes bonnes intentions, et comme il est avantageux à l'un et à l'autre Etat de vivre en bon voisinance, paix et amitié, je l'ai chargé de cette lettre pour vous, pour vous assurer de ma bonne volonté et disposition entière à faire ce qui servira à la sureté et liberté du commerce, bien et utilité réciproque des deux nations; et m'assurant que vous contribuerez volontiers à un si bon effet, je me remets au dit Sieur de Gentillot de vous en dire davantage, vous priant de lui donner créance comme en une personne en qui je prends une confiance entière." MSS. de Brienne, in the Bibliothèque Impériale, Paris.

Parlement de la République d'Angleterre," accrediting M. de Barrière. This letter was read and referred to the Council of State, who received Barrière and heard his propositions. Whitelocke presented a report on the subject to the Parliament. The mission now appeared to assume a definite character; the Spanish ambassador warmly supported it; the Comte de Daugnon, governor of Brouaye, and an ally of the Prince de Condé, also sent agents and promises to London. Finally the city of Bordeaux itself, in its own name, despatched two special deputies, MM. de Blarut and de Trancons, "to demand of the Commonwealth of England, as of a just and powerful State, assistance in men, money, and ships to support the city and commons of Bordeaux, now united with our lords the Princes; and not only to shelter them from the oppression and cruel vengeance which is in store for them, but also to effect their restoration to their ancient privileges, and to enable them to breathe a freer air than they have hitherto done. And as the said lords of the Parliament of the Commonwealth of England," continued their instructions, "will probably demand of them reciprocal advantages, they will let them first explain their pretensions, and afterwards, if necessary, they may grant them a port in the river of Bordeaux, where their vessels may find retirement and safety, such as Castillon, Royau, Talmont or Paulhac, or that of Arcachon if they wish, which they may fortify at their own expense. We may even permit them to besiege and capture Blaye, in which our troops will help them as much as possible. They may also make a descent upon La Rochelle and capture it, if they please."[1]

The alarm was great, both at Court and in the Council. Whilst, in the southern provinces, civil war thus invited a

[1] Commons' Journals, vol. vii. pp. 112, 117, 129, 133; Documents inédits sur l'Histoire Diplomatique de France, in the Revue Nouvelle, vol. v. pp. 381—393; Thurloe's State Papers, vol. i. pp. 216, 224, 226, 250.

foreign army into France, foreign war still continued in those of the north: the Spaniards were vigorously pushing the siege of Gravelines; Dunkirk was expected shortly to fall, and the news arrived suddenly that seven vessels, which had left Calais for the purpose of conveying thither provisions and reinforcements, had been arrested and captured at sea by the English squadron, under the command of Admiral Blake. In vain did all the French authorities make the most urgent remonstrances; in vain did the Duke de Vendôme, Grand Admiral of France, write to Blake, to the republican Council of State, and even to the Parliament;[1] they replied that the letters of marque issued by the French government had caused, and still continued to cause, the greatest injury to English commerce, for which they had resolved to obtain or take reparation, and they refused to release the ships which had been seized.[2] Evidently, the Parliament was resolved not to purchase the recognition of the Commonwealth at the price which Mazarin wished to make it pay: it was determined to maintain its wavering neutrality between France and Spain, and inclining always rather towards Spain, it willingly seized upon all opportunities for making France feel its power to do her harm. Don Alonzo de Cardeñas had carefully fostered this tendency in London: the proceedings and messengers of Mazarin had caused him the utmost anxiety, and he had sent minute information of all that had passed to his Court, urging it to make to the Parliament, on its side, the advances and concessions necessary to prevent any alliance between England and France. Sometimes he labored to induce Spain to enter into an intimate alliance with the two Protestant republics of London and the Hague,

[1] MSS. de Brienne, in the Bibliothèque Impériale, Paris. See Appendix XX.

[2] Commons' Journals, vol. vii. pp. 175, 195, 224; Dixon's Life of Blake, pp. 208—210.

against France and Portugal; sometimes he urged his Court to second the English in an enterprise against Calais, on condition that they should aid the Spaniards in the siege of Gravelines, Dunkirk, and Mardyke. Finally, he undertook to conclude between Spain and the Commonwealth of England, a formal treaty of friendship, which should securely bind both States; and on the 20th of September, 1652, he sent to Madrid a draft in twenty-four articles, which he had already submitted, on the 12th, to the republican Council of State, who had manifested a strong disposition to accept it.[1]

Urged by these dangers, Mazarin at length determined to recognize the Commonwealth, without deriving any immediate advantage from the step. On the 2d of December, 1652, M. de Bordeaux, Councillor of State and Intendant of Picardy, received directions to convey a letter from the King to the Parliament, and to re-establish official relations between the two States. This resolution was adopted and executed without either boldness or gracefulness, with an air at once haughty and embarrassed. The instructions of M. de Bordeaux formally stated that he was not an ambassador, and he was ordered to declare as much on his arrival; they seemed to make the commercial interests of the two countries, and the restitution of the seven vessels captured on their way to Dunkirk, the almost entire object of his mission; they recommended him, it is true, "to say nothing which might lead to a rupture, or offend the English, so as not to give them any pretext for declaring themselves enemies of the crown, as it appears to His Majesty that it is better for a time that they should rove the seas and practise the piracy with which they reproach others, than that they should do anything worse,

[1] Letters from Cardeñas to Philip IV., January 23, February 5, 15, 25, July 19, September 12, 20, 1652; Deliberations of the Council of State at Madrid on the Despatches of Cardeñas, August 14, 1652; in the Archives of Simancas. See Appendix XXI.

namely, join their forces with the Spaniards, and take the rebels under their protection;" but at the same time, Bordeaux was enjoined, "if he could obtain no satisfaction regarding the special business with which he was charged, to return to France without waiting for further orders," whilst, if he found the Parliament favorably disposed and ready to appoint commissioners to examine the old treaties with him, he was to wait, "and send at once to His Majesty, to receive his commands, together with the necessary powers and instructions." In reality, the step was decisive, and carried with it the full recognition of the Commonwealth; but either from natural hesitation, or from complaisance to the scruples of the Queen and Court, Mazarin had attempted to give it the appearance of an experimental mission of a limited and conditional character, and one which could be receded from at any time without discredit.[1]

Republican pride quickly detected and frustrated this petty artifice. When the Speaker announced to the Parliament that he had received a letter from the King of France, its superscription was first of all examined: it was addressed, "A nos très chers et grands amis les Gens du Parlement de la République d'Angleterre." The master of the ceremonies was directed to state to M. de Bordeaux, that this was not the style in which foreign princes wrote to the Parliament, and that a letter thus addressed could not be received. Two days afterwards, Bordeaux sent back the letter with this new address: "Au Parlement de la République d'Angleterre;" it was immediately admitted, and the 21st of December following was fixed for the reception of M. de Bordeaux, but he was informed that "as he was not an ambassador, he would have audience neither of the Parliament, nor of the Council

[1] Archives des Affaires Etrangères de France; MSS. de Brienne, in the Bibliothèque Impériale, Paris. See Appendix XXII.

of State, but of a Committee." When admitted before this committee, "The King of France, my master," he said, "having judged it fitting, for the good of his service, to send me to the Parliament of the Commonwealth of England, has commanded me to greet it on his part, and to assure it of his friendship, from the confidence which he has of finding in it a mutual correspondence to his good intentions. The union which should exist between neighboring states is not regulated by the form of their government; wherefore, though it has pleased God, in His providence, to change that which was formerly established in this country, there does not cease to be a necessity for trade and friendship between France and England. This kingdom may have changed its aspect, and from a monarchy have become a Commonwealth, but the position of places does not change; people always continue neighbors, and remain interested in one another, for trading purposes; and the treaties which exist between nations are not so much binding upon princes as upon peoples, as they have for their principal object their common advantage." Having thus formally recognized the Commonwealth, Bordeaux proceeded at once to the special object of his mission, and after a few phrases against the intrigues of Spain, and upon the power of France, he ended by demanding the restitution of the seven vessels, and by giving the Parliament full assurance that "His Majesty, who regards justice as the principal support of his sceptre, and the solid foundation of legitimate empires, will not fail to have compensation given to all those of this State who may have just claims against his subjects; and that, having obtained the satisfaction which is his due, he will embrace all means likely to maintain a perfect correspondence between the two States."[1]

[1] Commons' Journals, vol. vii. pp. 228, 230, 233; Archives des Affaires Etrangères de France; MSS. de Brienne, in the Bibliothèque Impériale.

On learning that this step had been taken by the King of France towards the republican Parliament, the Queen of England, Henrietta Maria, wrote to her second son, the Duke of York: "My son, this letter is to inform you that, as they have sent from here to England to recognize those infamous traitors, notwithstanding all the reasons which we could give against the measure, the King, your brother, has resolved to leave this place, and has already communicated his intention to the Queen. He has not yet taken any resolution with regard to you. Wherefore you must still act as if you were ignorant of this embassy, and in case any one should mention it to you, you must say that you cannot believe it. . . . I confess to you, since my great misfortune, I have never felt anything equal to this. May God take us under His holy protection, and give us the patience which we shall need to support this blow!"[1] Charles II., however, did not leave Paris—he was not asked to do so; and the pension of six thousand livres a month, which he received from Louis XIV., was continued; but his position became more and more isolated and melancholy, and his most faithful advisers urged him thenceforth to seek an asylum elsewhere.

The Commonwealth seemed equally triumphant both at home and abroad—in European diplomacy as well as in the civil war; but the fatal effects of its imprudent and arrogant policy towards the United Provinces had begun to manifest themselves, and far overbalanced the advantages which accrued to it from its recognition by Louis XIV., and its imperfect neutrality between France and Spain.

When the Dutch leaders had rejected the propositions of the English ambassadors, and refused to connect the fate of their country with that of a Commonwealth so dangerous

[1] MSS. de Brienne, in the Bibliothèque Impériale, Paris; Clarendon's History of the Rebellion, vol. vi. p. 605; vol. vii. p. 49.

and tottering, they had done a deed of equal patriotism and courage, and had discharged their duty towards the dignity as well as the safety of the State which they governed. But they were sincerely desirous of peace, and even of an alliance, with England; the victory of the Parliament at Worcester and its Act of Navigation, by showing them that war was at once most probable and most perilous, determined them to attempt a last effort to avoid it. As soon as they learned the flight of Charles II. after his defeat, a decree was proposed in the States-General, enacting that no foreign prince should be allowed to enter their territory without their formal consent; and shortly afterwards they sent three ambassadors to London, with orders to resume the negotiations which St. John and Strickland, on leaving the Hague, had so abruptly broken off. At their first audience, the principal of the three ambassadors, Jacobus Catz, formerly Grand Pensionary of the United Provinces, endeavored, in a long speech, which was too flattering to be adroit, to conciliate the friendly feeling of the Parliament. Their reception had been attended with great pomp; the master of the ceremonies had been ordered to fetch them from Gravesend, in barges decorated with official ensigns; three members of Parliament had met them at Greenwich, and conducted them on the following day to Westminster. On their entrance into the hall, the Speaker and all the members rose, and took off their hats: the English republicans were anxious to treat the republic of the United Provinces with distinction, and to diffuse among both nations the conviction that they regarded it with sincere sympathy: but at the same time, swayed by mingled feelings of pride and rancor, they received and discussed its propositions with the haughty obstinacy of a power confident in its own strength, and burning to avenge a misapprehension which it regarded as an insult. In both countries the popular feeling was in accordance with this disposition of the English government: in Holland, either from an Orangist spirit, or from national rivalry, the people expected a war, and manifested a greater inclination to desire than to fear it; the fishermen of the Meuse related, with patriotic confidence, their visions of great navies, which had appeared in the air, just above their coasts, engaging in mighty conflicts, from which they prognosticated the victory of the Dutch flag. In London, the populace were still more animated: they daily received news of hostile proceedings at sea, between English and Dutch ships, sometimes relating to the affronts and losses which English commerce had experienced, and sometimes to the bold reparation which it had taken for itself at the expense of its rivals; and more than once, on hearing such news, whether true or false, the mob thronged round the house which the Dutch ambassadors occupied at Chelsea, and showed so strong a tendency to insult them, that Parliament was obliged to assign them a guard for their protection.[1]

Among the negotiators themselves the difficulties daily grew more insurmountable; unexpected questions arose; old or new pretensions were put forward on both sides. The Dutch, having become a powerful nation, were also anxious to establish their entire independence at sea, and to free themselves from the admissions of inferiority which England had been, or assumed to be, entitled to impose upon them. The English accused their kings of the House of Stuart of having abandoned, or allowed to fall into desuetude, those external tokens of their empire over the sea, which in former days, and especially during the glorious reign of Elizabeth, their sailors had possessed, or laid claim to. The salute of their flag, the right of visiting, and the right of fishery, became the

[1] Commons' Journals, vol. vii. pp. 45, 53, 54, 56, 58, 64; Whitelocke, pp. 512, 518, 521, 533; Leclerc's Histoire des Provinces Unies, vol. ii. p. 314; Wicquefort's Histoire des Provinces Unies, vol. iv. pp. 307—310.

subject of animated debates; the more they were prolonged, the haughtier became the demands and tone of the English; they even began to speak, without evasion, of their sovereignty over the seas which surrounded their island; the Dutch ambassadors, from royalty as much as from prudence, declared that their government was equipping a large fleet to protect their trade in those waters. The English commissioners almost contested their right to do this, saying that they would themselves maintain the police of the sea for the common advantage of all. Whilst quarrels about principles were thus growing in bitterness, actual hostilities spontaneously commenced between the two nations; their ships never met without exchanging some mark of enmity; it was soon learned that an embargo had been laid in the ports of Holland upon all English ships; and that a Dutch merchant fleet, returning from the Mediterranean, had refused to lower its flag to the English squadron, upon which Commander Young had attacked it, to compel it to do so. Explanations were demanded and given on both sides; the embargo in Holland was raised; but the ill-feeling which it had excited in England continued. The Dutch negotiators did their best to extenuate grievances, and to resolve questions pacifically; but they were not all three animated by this desire to an equal extent; their dissensions were remarked, and they were called, ironically, "The disunited ambassadors of the United Provinces." They insisted in vain upon the abolition, or at least the temporary suspension, of the Act of Navigation; the Parliament was inflexible on this point; and, both from external incidents and from the turn taken by the negotiations themselves, the maintenance of peace daily became more doubtful and more difficult.[1]

[1] Commons' Journals, vol. vii. pp. 103, 135, 139; Whitelocke, pp. 512, 517, 522, 529, 530; Dixon's Life of Blake, pp. 189—191; Wicquefort's Histoire des Provinces Unies, vol. iv. pp. 310—318; Leclerc's Histoire des Provinces Unies, vol. ii. pp. 314—316; Heath's Brief Chronicle, p. 585.

In the midst of these diplomatic agitations, it suddenly became known that, on the 12th of May, in the Downs, not far from Dover roadstead, the Dutch fleet, under the command of Tromp, and the English fleet, under Blake, had met and fought. Informed that Tromp was cruising in that part of the Channel, and suspecting that some hostile design was in contemplation on his part, Blake had immediately sailed thither, and on his arrival, he had, by firing three signal-guns in succession, summoned the Dutch admiral to lower his flag in presence of the English squadron. Tromp kept on his course without taking any notice of his summons. Soon after he fell in with a ketch coming from Holland, which evidently brought him important orders, for he suddenly veered round and made towards Blake, who lay to, and repeated his summons. According to the account given by the English admiral, Tromp's only answer was to send a broadside into the *James*, Blake's flag-ship, which caused it considerable damage. "Well," said Blake, "it is not very civil in Van Tromp to take my flag-ship for a brothel, and break my windows;" and in his turn, he opened a vigorous cannonade upon the *Brederode*, Tromp's own vessel. The action thus unexpectedly begun, lasted more than four hours; Tromp had forty-two ships, and Blake only twenty-three. The English admiral had more than fifty men of his own crew killed or wounded; the Dutch lost one of their ships. When night fell, Tromp made sail towards the coast of Holland; and on the following day at dawn, Blake, who had remained on the scene of action, could discover no trace of his enemy.[1]

Two sensations of a very different character, in London anger, and at the Hague anxiety, were excited by this news.

[1] Whitelocke, pp. 523, 524; Dixon's Life of Blake, pp. 191—195; Memorials of Sir William Penn, vol. i. pp. 419—423; Leclerc's Histoire des Provinces Unies, vol. ii. pp. 315—317; Wicquefort's Histoire des Provinces Unies, vol. iv. pp. 318—320.

"Tromp came to brave us on our own seas," said the English; "he wished to surprise our fleet, that he might attack and destroy it by treachery." "Tromp was driven towards the English coast by stress of weather," answered the Dutch; "he was returning, and about to salute the English fleet, when he was violently summoned and attacked; he merely stood on the defensive, and withdrew as soon as he could do so honorably; with his superior force, he could easily have destroyed the English fleet, if such had been his design." These explanations, and especially the last, were received with ironical derision, as falsehoods almost equivalent to fresh insults. The populace manifested their furious ill-feeling towards the ambassadors more strongly than ever. A fourth ambassador extraordinary arrived suddenly from the Hague—Adrian de Pauw, Pensionary of the Province of Holland, already well known and esteemed in England, attached to a pacific policy, and of a prudent and conciliating character. He brought, on the part of his government, the strongest denials of any hostile or offensive intention towards England; he declared that Tromp had neither received any instructions, nor entertained any purpose, to attack the English fleet, and that what had happened had only been the result of unfortunate misconceptions and accidents; he demanded that an inquiry should be instituted into the facts, and into the conduct of the two admirals, offering the dismissal of Tromp from his command, if the charges imputed to him were substantiated; and, in the meanwhile, he insisted that the negotiations should be pursued and brought to a conclusion. Pauw was received with great consideration; but, in their suspicions as in their desires, the Parliament and the Council of State proved inflexible; and, after several conferences, feeling somewhat embarrassed by the urgency of the Dutch negotiators, they suddenly set up, as a preliminary condition, the claim that the United Provinces should indemnify them for the expenses which the prospect of a war had already forced them to incur; which being granted, they would pursue the negotiations. It would be impossible, I think, carefully to examine these facts and documents without coming to the conclusion that, in spite of the intrigues of the Orangist party, the rulers of the United Provinces were sincerely desirous of peace, whereas, either from passion or premeditation, the English republicans, both Parliament and people, obstinately clung to every cause of war, in the hope of establishing their supremacy at sea, and even of carrying out, by force of arms, those ambitious designs upon the United Provinces, which negotiation had failed to crown with success. Perceiving the inutility of further efforts, Pauw and his colleagues at length requested an audience to take leave; on the following day they were received with great marks of official respect by the Parliament, to which, before their departure, they delivered a series of documents in which their propositions and conduct were, in their point of view, faithfully stated and fully justified. Five days afterwards, on the 7th of July, 1652, the Parliament published its declaration of war, with an exposition of its motives; and fifteen days afterwards, the manifesto of the States-General also appeared, accepting, with spirit, though with regret, the defiance which had been offered them.[1]

Although with forces, in reality, very unequal, the two nations entered upon the conflict with the same ardor, and almost with the same confidence. The navy of the United Provinces was, at that time, superior to that of England, both in reputation and ability; it had been formed, for nearly

[1] Commons' Journals, vol. vii. pp. 140, 141, 142, 147, 149, 150, 152; Whitelocke, pp. 537—538; Dixon's Life of Blake, pp. 195—197; Wicquefort's Histoire des Provinces Unies, vol. iv. pp. 322—324; Leclerc's Histoire des Provinces Unies, vol. ii. pp. 318—320.

a century, by commercial enterprise with distant lands, by the conquest and administration of remote possessions in America and the Indies, and in difficult and dangerous fisheries; its sailors were numerous and practised; its admirals had begun to introduce, into the command of great fleets, the art of executing scientific and connected manœuvres, which was almost unknown at that period, according to their own historians, to the best English seamen. The latter, on their side, possessed vessels generally of a larger size, manned by more numerous crews, and furnished with heavier guns; they were, moreover, thoroughly under the influence of the most energetic human passions, patriotism, pride, ambition, and jealousy; and they had, to back them, a country far more populous and wealthy than the United Provinces, and placed, not under the feeble and mutable direction of a confederation of States, but under the sole authority of a revolutionary assembly, proud of its triumphs at home, and accustomed to lavish men and money for the successful accomplishment of its designs. A month after his encounter with Tromp off Dover, Blake had under his command a fleet of 105 ships of war, carrying 3,961 guns, and manned, in addition to their crews, by two regiments of infantry. The Dutch had not been less vigilant in their preparations; they had hired, on account of the State, all the merchant ships of large tonnage which they could obtain; sixty men-of-war, of immense size, were in process of construction; a multitude of expert foreign sailors were lured into their service by the promise of high wages; and when Tromp put to sea, he had under his command a fleet of 120 ships, which, in the opinion of every Dutch patriot, would be able to sweep the English navy from the face of the ocean.[1]

On the 21st of June, before even the Dutch ambassadors

[1] Dixon's Life of Blake, pp. 197—202; Memorials of Sir William Penn, vol. i. pp. 395—432.

had left London, or war had been officially declared, Blake set sail from Dover with sixty vessels, leaving one of his lieutenants, Sir George Ayscue, to defend the Channel, whilst he himself sailed northwards, either to protect the numerous English merchantmen who were returning from the Baltic, or to destroy the Dutch fishing-boats, which thronged in vast numbers to the coasts of Scotland and the neighboring islands for the herring fishery. This fishery had become an important feature in Dutch trade; a host of small vessels, called busses, were engaged in it, each manned by a family of fishermen, for even the women and children took part in the adventure. It was an unfailing means of subsistence to the poorer classes, and to the State the source of an extensive trade, and a nursery of hardy seamen. More than six hundred barques of all sizes, protected by twelve Dutch men-of-war were collected in the seas of the north of Scotland when Blake arrived there. Falling suddenly upon them with infinitely superior forces, Blake, notwithstanding their courageous resistance, sank three of the men-of-war, captured the other nine, and seized the six hundred herring-busses; after taking a tenth of the produce of their fishery as a tribute, from a feeling of generous humanity he sent them home with the remainder, ordering them never again to fish in those waters without having first obtained permission of the Council of State. Meanwhile Tromp, informed by the Dutch ambassadors, on their return, of the English admiral's plan of campaign, came out of the Trexel as soon as he knew that Blake was on his way to the north, and made all sail towards the British Channel, with seventy-nine men-of-war and ten fire-ships, in the hope that he would be able to destroy Ayscue's very inferior fleet, and afterwards to effect a landing, or to commit great ravages, along the coast of England. The alarm was great in London and the adjacent counties; the militia of Kent rose in arms to repel the menacing invader; batteries were hastily erected on several points along the coast; courier after courier was sent to Blake to inform him of what was going on in the Channel, and to urge his return. Nature lent the Parliament the aid which Blake could not have had time to afford. In the very midst of the Channel, Tromp's fleet was delayed by a dead calm which rendered all movement impossible, and when the wind returned, it blew from the land, and with such violence, that, notwithstanding the skill and perseverance of the Dutch sailors, they found it impossible to get near enough to the English coast to attack Ayscue, who lay in safety under the cliffs. Immediately renouncing a project which he saw he could not accomplish, Tromp set out with his whole fleet for the North, where he would be sure to fall in with Blake, separated from Ayscue, and distant from any place which might have supplied him with reinforcements; and he promised himself that he would inflict, on the English admiral himself, the defeat which his lieutenant had just escaped. On the 5th of August, the English and Dutch fleets fell in with one another between the Orkneys and the Shetland Isles; the English were considerably weakened, for, on receipt of the news from London, Blake had despatched eight of his best frigates southwards, to reinforce Ayscue; he did not attempt, however, to avoid a battle, and he was making every preparation on board his flag-ship, the *Resolution*, to attack Tromp, when he perceived in the sky signs of an approaching tempest. Feeling certain that, on that day, any engagement would be impossible, he signalled his captains to shelter their ships as they best could in the little archipelago of the Shetland Isles, and so to await the morrow. The storm burst ere long, and lasted all night with unusual violence even for those seas; the wind, rain, thunder, and darkness rendered any concerted manœuvre, and almost all communication, impossible between the ships; the Dutch fleet was dispersed and cruelly damaged; many vessels were wrecked either at sea or on the coast; others fled for refuge to Norway; the fire-ships were dashed in pieces; and when morning broke, instead of the noble squadron which he had brought with him, Tromp, as he stood on the deck of the *Brederode*, could only see a few vessels drifting at hap-hazard, dismasted, with their sails in tatters, and still struggling with great difficulty against a sea which was covered with wrecks. He could succeed in collecting only forty-two of his ships, with which he returned in despair to Scheveling in Holland, where he was received with surprise, sorrow, and unjust indignation by his countrymen. Blake, whose fleet had suffered much less severely, pursued the Dutch to their retreat, and as he was unable to come up with them, and bring them to an engagement, he ravaged and insulted their western coasts from Wadden to Zealand, and then ran across to Yarmouth with the ships he had captured, and nine hundred prisoners.[1]

Tromp was proud and sensitive: wounded and disgusted by the clamors which assailed him because a calm and a tempest had by turns prevented him from engaging the enemy, he resigned his command. He was moreover inclined towards the Orangist party, and the republican aristocracy, who were then predominant, made no efforts to retain his services; they thought they could give him a successor worthy to fill his place. Not long before, they had appointed to the command of part of their naval forces Michael Ruyter, a man of obscure origin but great popular reputation, beloved by the sailors, a stranger to all political parties, and always ready to serve his country with equal modesty and heroism.

[1] Dixon's Life of Blake, pp. 202—207; Memorials of Sir William Penn, vol. i. pp. 432—435; Whitelocke, pp. 538, 542; Heath's Chronicle, pp. 597—599; Leclerc's Histoire des Provinces Unies, vol. ii. pp. 320, 321; Wicquefort's Histoire des Provinces Unies, vol. iv. pp. 331—333.

No sooner had he embarked on board his ship the *Neptune*, than Ruyter entered the Channel with thirty vessels, fell in with an English fleet off Plymouth under the command of Ayscue, consisting of forty vessels larger and better equipped than his own, attacked it suddenly, and compelled it to retire into Plymouth harbor, leaving the Dutch masters of the open sea. Ruyter himself was humbly astonished at this success: "It is only," he wrote, "when it pleases God to inspire courage that victories are gained: this is a work of Providence for which men could not possibly account." The Parliament, dissatisfied with Ayscue, who was moreover suspected of royalism, deprived him of his command, but not discourteously, and gave him a pension of three hundred pounds, and a landed estate of the same annual value in Ireland; his squadron was placed under the command of Blake. The States-General, on their side, being resolved to carry on the war with energy, had, immediately after Tromp's retirement, fitted out a new squadron; and one of the boldest of the leaders of the aristocratic party, Cornelius de Witt, had been appointed its admiral. He was brave to excess, and thoroughly experienced in nautical matters, but stern, passionate, obstinate, and short-sighted, and no favorite with the sailors, who feared his severity, without having confidence in his good fortune. This choice was regarded as political rather than military, and gave great dissatisfaction to the friends of Tromp, who were numerous in the fleet. Before putting to sea, at the very moment when he embarked, Cornelius de Witt was compelled to inflict severe punishment on some mutineers. Ruyter was ordered to join him, and serve under him. Their forces, which effected a junction on the 2d of October, 1652, between Dunkirk and Newport, amounted to sixty-four sail. Blake had for some time been cruising in the neighborhood, with a fleet of sixty-eight ships, in search of the enemy, and in the hope of an engagement.

Being informed on the 8th of October, that the Dutch fleet was in sight to the north-east of Dover, he pushed rapidly in front of his squadron, signalled all his ships to rally, and gave the order to the crew of his own vessel: "As soon as some more of our fleet comes up, bear in among them!" In a council of war held the previous evening on board the Dutch admiral, Ruyter had given his opinion that a battle should be avoided rather than invited; he had found that several ships in the squadron were in a bad state, and scantily provided with ammunition; perhaps also he had not entire confidence in the good-will of all the crews, and even of all the officers. Cornelius de Witt absolutely insisted upon fighting; and although, during the previous night, a storm had separated from him several of his ships, which were slow in rejoining him, he accepted Blake's attack with an ardor which five hours of unsuccessful conflict did not abate for for an instant. Two of the Dutch vessels foundered at the first onset; two others were boarded and taken; and several captains executed the admiral's orders without the zeal and alacrity which are essential to victory. Just before the action began, De Witt wished to remove his flag to the *Brederode*, Tromp's old flag-ship; but the unwillingness of the crew to receive him was so evident that he gave up the idea, and remained on board his own vessel, a huge and unwieldy Indiaman. Ruyter, with his vanguard division, performed prodigies of skilful and devoted valor: De Witt, by his indomitable courage, gained the admiration even of his enemies. But their efforts were vain; the advantage everywhere remained with the English; and when night fell upon the two fleets, very different feelings swayed the combatants: on board the English ships reigned the activity of satisfaction and hope; both officers and sailors labored cheerfully to repair their damages, to collect their ammunition, and to prepare for the renewal of the battle on the morrow; in the Dutch fleet, on the contrary, extreme discontent and anxiety prevailed. De Witt once more assembled his council of war; he wished to recommence the fight at daybreak; but he was informed that twenty of his captains, without waiting any orders, or giving any intimation of their purpose, had separated, under cover of the darkness, from the main body of the fleet, and sailed no one knew whither. Ruyter and all the other captains declared that a second action was impossible; De Witt was obliged to yield, and to consent to return to Holland to refit his squadron in its ports, and to receive fresh instructions from the States-General. Blake followed the Dutch in their retreat, without hanging too closely on their rear, and cruised for some days along their coast, proud of his victory, and jealously determined to make it unquestionable.[1]

Misfortune and impending danger teach nations justice: the eyes of all Holland turned once more towards Tromp; he had not done all that had been expected of him, but he had not been defeated; he had yielded to calm and tempest, not to the English. It was he who, for twenty years, had commanded the fleets of Holland against those of Spain, and conquered the independence of his country at sea. He was known to be an implacable enemy of the English navy, by one of whose cruisers he had been taken prisoner in his youth, and detained more than two years on board his captor. The voice of the people urged the States-General to restore him to his command. The King of Denmark, alarmed at the maritime preponderance of England, employed his influence at the Hague to the same purpose. Tromp was recalled; all the naval forces of the State were placed once more under

[1] Dixon's Life of Blake, pp. 208—215; Memorials of Sir William Penn, vol. i. p. 435; Commons' Journals, vol. vii. p. 166; Whitelocke, pp. 542, 543; Leclerc's Histoire des Provinces Unies, vol. ii. pp. 321—324; Wicquefort's Histoire des Provinces Unies, vol. iv. pp. 333—336; Gerard Brandt's Life of Ruyter, pp. 18—23.

his command; Cornelius De Witt, Ruyter, Evertz and Floritz, the most renowned sea-captains of Holland, were appointed his vice-admirals. De Witt declined, on the ground of ill-health; he was really ill of fatigue, chagrin, and anger; Ruyter accepted without hesitation. An ally more brilliant than powerful, Charles II., offered the States-General to serve, as a simple volunteer, on board their squadron; he was sure, he said, that many captains in the English fleet were only waiting for an opportunity to come over to him, and would do so as soon as they knew he was near at hand. By the advice of John De Witt, then Pensionary of the Province of Holland, the States-General declined this offer; they had already refused to link their destiny with that of the regicide Commonwealth; and they were equally unwilling to connect their cause with that of the proscribed King. With a staff thus composed, Tromp set to work with earnest energy to refit the fleet with all possible speed; all the ports and arsenals of the United Provinces put forth their utmost resources. The Parliament and Blake believed they would not need to make any fresh efforts for some months: a naval campaign in winter then appeared, even to the bravest seamen, almost an impossibility: several divisions of the English fleet had been sent to their special stations, in the Baltic, the north of Scotland, and the western entrance to the Channel. Blake, modest even in success, and always impressed with a deep sense of his responsibility, had requested the Parliament to associate with him, in the naval command, two experienced generals who would aid him in bearing its weight. Monk and Dean had been appointed to this service; but both were still occupied in completing the subjection of Scotland; and while waiting their arrival, Blake was cruising with his squadron from port to port between Essex and Hampshire, when a report reached him that a large Dutch fleet had put to sea under the command of Tromp, and a few days afterwards, from the out-look of his vessel the *Triumph*, he perceived their ships in full sail between Dover and Calais. Tromp's fleet consisted of seventy-three sail, and Blake had only thirty-seven. He convoked a council of war without delay, to give his captains his instructions rather than to consult them, for he was determined to fight; he inspired them with his own confident ardor, and the battle took place on the following day, with equal impetuosity on both sides. It was a series of individual combats, the brunt of which was chiefly borne by Ruyter, Evertz, and Tromp for the Dutch, and by Blake for the English. Blake was for some time surrounded by a number of the enemy's ships, who boarded him thrice, and were thrice repulsed; but for the obstinate fidelity of two of his own vessels, the *Sapphire* and the *Vanguard*, which stood by him with unwavering steadiness and devotion, the English admiral must have fallen before the overwhelming numbers of his foes. Thick fog and darkness at length separated the two squadrons; but Blake's fleet was *hors de combat;* two of his ships, the *Garland* and the *Bonadventure*, after a desperate resistance, had fallen into the hands of the Dutch; several others, with their sails in shreds, their masts shattered, and their crews disabled, could no longer keep the sea; and Blake accordingly retired into the Thames to repair damages, recall the other divisions of his scattered fleet, and await their arrival in a safe anchorage. Tromp meanwhile sailed up and down the Channel as a conqueror, with a broom at his mast-head, thus braving the English navy in those very seas in which she claimed unrivalled sovereignty; and the States-General, prouder even than their admiral, officially informed the European powers of their victory, and prohibited all correspondence or communication with the British Isles, fancying themselves strong enough to place them in a state of naval blockade.[1]

Blake unreservedly declared his reverse, with firm and sorrowful disinterestedness. "I am bound," he wrote to the Council of State, "to let your honors know that there was much baseness of spirit, not among the merchantmen only, but in many of the State's ships. And therefore I make it my earnest request that your honors would be pleased to send down some gentlemen to take an impartial and strict examination of the deportment of several commanders, that you may know who are to be confided in, and who are not. It will then be time to take into consideration the grounds of some other errors and defects, especially the discouragement and want of seamen. . . . . And I hope it will not be unseasonable for me, in behalf of myself, to desire your honors that you would think of giving me, your unworthy servant, a discharge from this employment as far too great for me; so that I may spend the remainder of my days in private retirement, and in prayers to the Lord for blessings on you and on this nation." The Council of State did everything that Blake proposed, except granting his petition to be allowed to retire; three of its members were sent on board the fleet, and subjected the conduct of the officers to a strict examination; several were dismissed, and some even arrested; the admiral's own brother, Benjamin Blake, being found guilty of some neglect of duty, was cashiered and sent on shore. At the same time, all the disposable ships in the neighboring ports were required to form the fleet; a resolution was carried to raise the effective marine

[1] Dixon's Life of Blake, pp. 216—225; Memoirs of Sir William Penn, vol. i. pp. 556—560; Whitelocke, p. 551; Clarendon's History of the Rebellion, vol. vi. pp. 601—606; Leclerc's Histoire des Provinces Unies, vol. ii. p. 324; Wicquefort's Histoire des Provinces Unies, vol. iv. p. 336; Brandt's Life of Ruyter, p. 24; Heath's Chronicle, p. 611.

force to thirty thousand men; the stores necessary for equipping and repairing the ships were provided without delay; Monk and Dean were ordered to hold themselves ready to embark, and take their share in the responsibility and dangers of the ensuing campaign. And as to Blake himself, the Council of State wrote to him, "to acquaint him with what they had done for the giving him an addition of strength, and to let him know that they do leave to him, upon the place, to do what he may for his own defence and the service of the Commonwealth."[1]

Two months after his reverse off the Naze, Blake sailed from the mouth of the Thames with sixty men-of-war; the two most experienced seamen of his country, Penn and Lawson, commanded his van and rear guard; and he was accompanied by two of the most valiant generals of the land army, Monk and Dean, with twelve hundred veteran soldiers. Twenty other ships from Portsmouth joined him in the Straits. It was the most numerous, the best equipped, and the most ably commanded fleet the Commonwealth had ever put to sea. Blake sailed westward down the Channel, full of impatience and hope that he would soon meet the enemy; he knew that Tromp would, at that period, be probably on his return from the western coast of France, whither he had gone to meet a large fleet of traders which had been ordered to rendezvous at the Isle of Rhé, and which he was ordered to convoy to Holland. On the 18th of February, at daybreak, between Cape La Hogue and Portland Bill, the Dutch fleet came in sight; and Blake himself, from his flag-ship the *Triumph*, was one of the first to perceive its advance. Seventy-five men-of-war, and two hundred and fifty merchantmen, sailing under their escort, covered the sea far and wide.

[1] Memorials of Sir William Penn, vol. i. pp. 456—466; Dixon's Life of Blake, pp. 225—228; Whitelocke's Memorials, p. 551; Commons' Journals, vol. vii. p. 222.

Blake at that moment was fortunately within call of his two vice-admirals, Penn and Lawson, though not of his whole fleet; Monk, among others, was some miles astern with a division. Tromp perceived the temporary superiority of his forces, and giving orders to his convoy to keep to windward, he resolved to begin the engagement at once. At that very moment Blake bore down upon him, and the *Triumph* sent a broadside into the *Brederode*. Tromp received the fire without returning it at first; but as soon as the two vessels were within musket-shot of each other, he poured his first tremendous broadside into the English flag-ship, then, suddenly tacking round, gave her a second, and quickly reloading his batteries, and passing under his enemy's stern, he discharged into her a third broadside, which took terrible effect on the crew and tackling of the *Triumph*. On seeing the flag-ship surrounded with fire and wreck, Vice-Admiral Penn dashed gallantly in, and attacked Tromp in his turn. The entire English squadron arrived successively, and a furious battle was engaged on all sides. It lasted all day long, with alternations of success and defeat which hourly redoubled the ardor of the combatants, making each in turn hope that the victory would remain on his side. Tromp, Ruyter, De Wildt, Kruik, and Severs, among the Dutch captains, and Blake, Penn, Lawson, and Barker, among the English, performed prodigies of valor and skill; Ruyter, surrounded by the English just as he had boarded and taken one of their ships, narrowly escaped being made prisoner. None of the English vessels suffered so severely as that of the admiral himself; his flag-captain, Andrew Ball, and his secretary, Sparrow, were killed by his side; more than half his crew fell before the fire of the Dutch; Blake himself was at last wounded in the thigh, and the same bullet, after hitting him, tore away part of General Dean's buff coat. At the approach of evening, however, Blake, believing himself in possession of the advantage, ordered some of his ships to sail towards the Dutch convoy and prevent it from escaping. Tromp perceived this manœuvre, and immediately fell back with the main body of his fleet, to cover his convoy. Night fell and put an end to the action. The next day at dawn, Tromp, dispersing his squadron so as to guard his whole convoy, crowded sail and stood up the Channel. Blake followed him with his whole force, came up with him about noon, and the battle was renewed with the utmost fury. Ruyter, on all occasions the boldest and most resolute of the Dutch, was again very near falling into the hands of the English; he owed his safety entirely to the vigilance of Tromp, who, seeing him in imminent peril, sent a ship to support and extricate him from his position. But the efforts of the Dutch admiral were various and divided; whilst fighting, he was incessantly obliged to protect his convoy, and get gradually near the coast of Holland in order to place it in safety. The second day of the battle was less advantageous to him than the first: four or five of his ships were taken or destroyed. Either from party animosity or from weakness, some of his captains sent, in the evening, to inform him that they had no more powder, and could no longer take part in the fight; he ordered them to withdraw during the night, fearing they might on the morrow be guilty of some treasonous act, or some contagious example of cowardice. On the following day Blake perceived that the Dutch fleet was reduced in number, and with fresh ardor he immediately renewed both the attack upon Tromp and the pursuit of the convoy. Neither the ability nor the energy of the Dutch admiral slackened for a moment; he maintained the fight, rallying with great difficulty his disordered convoy, and gradually retiring along the French coast in order to reach that of his own country. He succeeded in this design on the fourth day after his encounter with Blake, by dint of persevering and intelligent courage, but after having lost, according to the statements of the Dutch, nine ships of war and twenty-four merchantmen, and, according to the English reports, seventeen ships of the first class and more than forty of the second. The States-General, in this emergency, proved themselves worthy of being so faithfully served, for they acted with justice: not only did they express their gratitude to Tromp, Ruyter, Evertz, and Floritz, but, in order to give them an unmistakable proof of their approbation, they made them rich presents, to which the particular States of the province of Holland added gifts of their own. The Parliament, on its side, gave way, somewhat noisily perhaps, to transports of joy; not only did it address official thanks to the commanders of the squadron, and take measures, first by opening a subscription, and afterwards, in the name of the State, to provide for the families of the men who had fallen in the action; but it appointed the celebration of a solemn service of thanksgiving throughout the dominions of the Commonwealth. Wherever the Dutch prisoners landed, they were escorted to London by troops of horse, and in all the towns through which they passed, the bells rang merry peals in celebration of a victory, which had been preceded by such intense anxiety, and which had cost such desperate efforts.[1]

It was at once real and futile; it was an additional vicissitude in a struggle already full of vicissitudes, but not one of those triumphs which definitively settle questions, and decide the fate of nations. Victorious not long before, the United Provinces were now defeated, but not despondent; it soon became known that a new fleet was in preparation in their

[1] Whitelocke, p. 551; Dixon's Life of Blake, pp. 230—244; Old Parliamentary History, vol. xx. pp. 116—121; Memorials of Sir William Penn, vol. i. pp. 472—485; Wicquefort's Histoire des Provinces Unies, vol. iv. pp. 336—339; Leclerc's Histoire des Provinces Unies, vol. ii. pp. 128—333; Brandt's Life of Ruyter, pp. 28—32.

ports: whoever was the victor, the war only became more ruinous and desperate after every battle.

The Catholic powers of the Continent, France and Spain especially, watched with secret satisfaction this ardent conflict between the two Protestant republics; which, in spite of all their expressions of courtesy, they regarded, in reality, with distrust and ill-will. The English Parliament had found it impossible either to remain really neutral between the Courts of Paris and Madrid, or to secure, by a decided choice, an alliance with either of them; in its indecision, it had always inclined towards Spain, whose inert and feeble policy could lend it no effectual assistance, and had constantly manifested a kind of hostile coolness towards France, whose ambitious activity and increasing strength might have rendered her a most useful ally. Both Courts remained motionless, seeking rather to aggravate than to terminate the war. The Protestant Courts of the North, on their side—Sweden and Denmark, among others—were divided between the two rival republics. The King of Denmark, Frederick III., after having first made the most marked advances in London, took the side of the United Provinces, with which he was connected by commercial interests and prior treaties; Queen Christina of Sweden showed some favor rather towards the British Commonwealth, but did not declare herself on its side, or lend it any assistance.[1] The ambitious and short-sighted arrogance of the republican Parliament had thrown all the foreign relations of England into disorder, and forced it to adopt a policy which set it at variance with its natural friends, without anywhere providing it with other allies.

At home, this policy imposed enormous burdens on the nation, and necessitated an increase of tyranny on the part of

[1] Leclerc's Histoire des Provinces Unies, vol. ii. pp. 326, 327; Wicquefort's Histoire des Provinces Unies, vol. iv. pp. 352—361; Commons' Journals, vol. vii. pp. 103, 104, 119, 133, 135, 137, 149, 182, 190, 191, 194, 203, 234.

the new government. It was requisite to maintain the army constantly on a war-footing, to defend the Commonwealth against the disaffection of the country; and incessantly to augment the fleet, to defend the country against foreign foes. In December, 1652, the Parliament voted 120,000*l.* per month for this double defence during the coming year—80,000*l.* for the army, and 40,000*l.* for the fleet; and new acts of a special character were passed on several occasions, during the course of 1653, to supply the deficiencies of this inadequate budget. And as the public taxes, although very heavy, were not enough to meet such necessities, recourse was constantly had, either to further sales of crown or church lands, or to fresh confiscations either of the revenues, or of the entire property, of delinquent royalists. In November, 1652, the Parliament voted that the parks and palaces of Windsor and Hampton Court, Hyde Park, Greenwich Park, and Somerset House, should be sold, and that the proceeds should be devoted to the expenses of the navy; bills were also proposed for the sale of the royal forests, and even of several cathedrals, which it was doubtless intended to demolish. Many of these measures were either not carried into effect, or were afterwards revoked; but the confiscations and fines inflicted on the royalists were always rigorously levied. In 1651, at the time when the negotiations with the United Provinces were broken off, seventy wealthy Cavaliers were condemned to the confiscation of all their property, both real and personal. During the following year, amid the exigencies of the war, twenty-nine others suffered the same fate; and six hundred and ninety-two others were allowed to ransom their sequestrated possessions only by paying one-third of the value to the Commonwealth within four months.[1] Civil tyranny thus

[1] Commons' Journals, vol. vi. p. 604; vol. vii. pp. 160, 211, 212, 216, 222, 224; Old Parliamentary History, vol. xx. pp. 103—113; Scobell's Collection of Acts, pp. 156, 210.

undertook to supply the necessities which an unwise foreign policy had created.

A united and unopposed government would have found it exceedingly difficult to endure such a burden for any length of time. The republican Parliament, with all its feverish enthusiasm, was weak and tottering; for it was rent by violent internal dissensions, and Cromwell, at once powerful and at leisure, made it his sole business to turn its faults to his own advantage, and to undermine the ground beneath its feet.

BOOK IV.

CONFLICT BETWEEN CROMWELL AND THE PARLIAMENT—ATTEMPTS TO OBTAIN A REDUCTION OF THE ARMY—PROPOSITION OF A GENERAL AMNESTY AND A NEW ELECTORAL LAW—PROJECTS OF CIVIL AND RELIGIOUS REFORM—CONVERSATION BETWEEN CROMWELL AND THE PRINCIPAL LEADERS OF THE PARLIAMENT AND ARMY—PETITION OF THE ARMY IN FAVOR OF REFORM, AND FOR THE DISSOLUTION OF THE PARLIAMENT—CHARGES OF CORRUPTION AGAINST THE PARLIAMENT—IT ATTEMPTS TO PERPETUATE ITS EXISTENCE BY SANCTIONING NEW ELECTIONS—URGENCY OF THE CRISIS—CROMWELL DISSOLVES THE PARLIAMENT.

On the 9th of September, 1651, three days after the Parliament had appointed four of its members to wait upon Cromwell, and offer him their most thankful congratulations upon the victory of Worcester, it voted that the charges of the Commonwealth should be lessened without delay, and directed the Council of State and the Committee of the Army to furnish it with a return of all the forces then on foot, that it might consider how the army might be most conveniently reduced, and the expenses of the State diminished. On the following day it was resolved that four thousand cavalry and four thousand infantry should be disbanded. Six days afterwards, Cromwell, on resuming his seat in the House, received the solemn thanks of the Speaker, a gift of lands of the yearly value of four thousand pounds, and the palace of Hampton Court as a residence; but at the same time the House referred it to the Council of State to consider what forces were necessary to be kept up for the safety of the country; and in consequence, on the 2d of October, it determined that five regiments of foot and three regiments of horse should be dismissed, that a large number of garrisons should be reduced, and that the army should be left at an establishment of about twenty-five thousand men, whereby a saving of thirty-five thousand pounds per month would be effected.[1]

These measures were evidently dictated by a regard for the public interest; the country groaned beneath the weight of taxation, and it was to be expected that victory would remove at least a part of the burdens imposed by war. But apart from these considerations, the attitude of the Parliament disclosed the prevalence of other feelings and other motives; in its anxiety to disband the troops, its chief object was to weaken a dangerous rival. Such an attempt must be perilous, however necessary and legitimate; revolutionary governments are never welcome to break the sword which has saved their life; the service is so great that they can never adequately reward or forget it, and their prudential measures to check ill-satisfied ambition are regarded as evidences of ingratitude and fear. Those powers only, which are based upon right, and sanctioned by time, can recompense and disarm great conquerors without fear of making them their masters.

Cromwell made no resistance, no objection even; the measure was too natural, and too indisputably necessary to admit of opposition. He was, moreover, greatly pleased at the dismissal of the militia regiments, whose independent habits, and patriotic rather than military spirit, were by no means agreeable to him. But too clear-sighted to mistake the intentions of the Parliament, he hastened, in his turn, to take precautions, and prepare to be avenged upon it. At his instigation, and with his support, two propositions, both popular in the country, although with different parties, were imme-

[1] Commons' Journals, vol. vii. pp. 15, 18, 19, 23.

diately revived, and carried with all expedition through the House: these were a general amnesty, and an electoral law to regulate the period of the dissolution of the Parliament, and the nomination of its successors. Neither of these propositions was a new one; for more than two years they had figured among the number of those questions which the Parliament announced its intention to determine, and which it made some show of taking into consideration. On the 25th of April, 1649, it had decided, upon the report of Ireton, that an Act of amnesty should be prepared—the basis of such an Act had been indicated by the House. The bill was produced, read a first and second time on the 5th of July, and referred to a committee, which was to meet on the following day; after which, nothing more was heard of it. At about the same period, on the 15th of May, 1649, a committee had been appointed to prepare a law for the election of future Parliaments. On the 9th of January, 1650, Vane made a long report on this subject, in which the principles of the new electoral system were set forth: the House resolved that it would meet once a week to discuss the measure; and during the years 1650 and 1651, forty-eight sittings were actually held, or at least convoked, for this purpose. But neither the amnesty nor the electoral law made any real progress; the Parliament's only serious occupation was to maintain itself in power, and defend itself against its enemies. As soon as, by Cromwell's influence, the two measures were again brought forward, their supporters allowed the House no rest. The Act of amnesty was revived on the 17th of September, 1651, and reported on the 27th of November; and, after being vigorously debated during sixteen sittings, it was at length adopted on the 24th of February, 1652, with certain modifications and restrictions. The country took so lively an interest in it, that, on ordering its publication, the House directed the Council of State to take care that it was not abusively and incorrectly reprinted, so that no mischief or inconvenience might arise thereby. The discussion of the electoral law was carried on with even greater heat and expedition; it occupied the committee appointed to draft it, and the House itself, from the 17th of September, 1651, to the 18th of November following; special meetings, frequent divisions, and very small majorities attested both the keenness of the debate and the importance of the question; forty-nine votes against forty-seven decided that the moment had come for fixing a term to the duration of the existing Parliament; and in all the divisions, we find Cromwell at the head of the most ardent supporters of the dissolution. They at length gained their point, but the realization of their triumph was deferred to a long date: on the 18th of November, 1651, the Parliament voted that it would not continue its sittings beyond the 3d of November, 1654.[1] Thanks to Cromwell's victories, the civil war between the Parliament and the King had ceased, and yet it was attempted to assign a duration of three years to the duel which was about to commence between Cromwell and the Parliament.

From good sense, rather than from moderation or patience of character, Cromwell could wait; under all circumstances, he judiciously estimated how much was possible, and attempted nothing more, although his desires and intrigues had a much wider range. He had succeeded in obtaining the fixation of a term to the existence of the Parliament; he did not attempt to abridge that term to suit his pleasure; but indirect means presented themselves to him for harassing, and more speedily exhausting, the power with which he had to contend; and he set them in operation, sometimes with passionate earnestness, and sometimes with profound astuteness, according as occasion suggested or allowed.

[1] Commons' Journals, vol. vi. pp. 195, 250, 210, 344; vol. vii. pp. 19, 44, 96, 36, 37; Ludlow's Memoirs, p. 189.

At that period the spirit of innovation in England was not confined to questions of government and political order alone; it extended to civil order also, and demanded, in the laws and judicial procedure, reforms in which the daily interests of the entire population were concerned. On these subjects, numerous ideas were in fermentation, which, though still obscure, vague, and incoherent, were always powerful, because of the rude necessities to which they corresponded, and the unbounded prospects which they opened to view. It was proposed to abolish burdensome taxes, to render the administration of justice less tedious and costly, to simplify the laws relating to property, to lessen the weight of the public debts, to remove the restraints which pressed upon the condition of persons and the ordinary relations of life, and to supply the necessaries of existence at a cheaper rate, and with less difficulty. Among the higher and more enlightened classes, whether from selfishness, or from a love of order and a just understanding of the conditions of the social state, these ideas obtained but little credit; the lawyers, especially, obstinately rejected them, and rallied numerous and respectable interests to resist them. But among the inferior classes, the Levellers, the Mystics, the honest dreamers, or the men of perverse and ill-regulated mind, indeed, all that section of the people, in whom just feelings and bad passions, practical instincts and chimerical absurdities are so closely associated, welcomed with enthusiasm the hope of such reforms, and loudly demanded their immediate accomplishment.

In religious matters, also, desires at once ardent and confused, acute sufferings and grave disorders, excited and maintained a continual agitation. The Anglican Church had fallen; there were no more bishops, no more chapters, no longer an exclusive and official ecclesiastical establishment. But the English nation retained an earnestly religious character; it required an assured form of worship, regular practices of devotion, and an assiduous preaching of the gospel. The sects satisfied these wants of the soul as far as their own particular adherents were concerned; but the sects formed only a small minority; beyond the sectaries, the proscribed Catholics, and the infidels (who were more numerous at that period than is commonly believed), was the mass of the people, sorrowful and indignant sometimes at being unable to find ministers of their faith, and sometimes at being deprived of those in whom they had confidence, and compelled, by destitution if not by force, to listen to others in whom they placed no reliance, and whom they regarded with no respect. The Presbyterians had come forward, and towards the close of 1649, the Parliament had given them permission to organize their ecclesiastical establishment, under the title of a National Church;[1] but they met with only very incomplete success, for they were thought to be as exclusive and tyrannical as the Anglican Church had been, and the other dissenting sects rejected them as utterly as the Anglicans themselves. The result of all this, in regard to religion, was a state now of abandonment and death, and now of persecution and anarchy, which giving rise to endless clamors, recriminations, disputes, and complaints, which were invariably addressed to the Parliament, as the source of all evils as well as of all remedies, and which it was at a loss for means how either to stifle or to satisfy.

With regard to all these questions of organization, both civil and religious, Cromwell had no fixed principles, and no unalterable determination: no mind could have been less systematic than his, or less governed by general and preconceived ideas; but he had an unerring instinct of popular feel-

[1] Neal's History of the Puritans, vol. iii. pp. 248—250; Grant's Summary of the History of the English Church, vol. ii. p. 413.

ings and wishes; and without much caring to inquire how far they were legitimate or capable of satisfaction, he boldly became their patron, in order to make them his allies. He had long ago perceived with what favor any ideas of reform in civil suits would be welcomed, and he had lent them his support. In 1650, writing to the Parliament after the victory of Dunbar, he said: "Relieve the oppressed, hear the groans of poor prisoners in England. Be pleased to reform the abuses of all professions; and if there be any one that makes many poor to make a few rich, *that* suits not a Commonwealth."[1] When, after the termination of the civil war, he took up his residence in London, with nothing to do but attend to what was passing among the people, or in the Parliament, he became the centre of all projects of this nature, and the hope of their promoters and partisans. On the 27th of October, 1651, certain prisoners confined in the prisons of London addressed him to the effect—"That the law was the badge of the Norman bondage, and that prisons were sanctuaries to rich prisoners, but tortures to the poorer sort, who were not able to fee lawyers and jailers. They, therefore, pray the General, into whose hands the sword is put, to free them from oppression and slavery, and to restore the nation's fundamental laws and liberties, and to gain a new Representative; and that the poor may have justice, and arrests and imprisonments may be taken away." Six weeks after, numerous petitions arrived from the country, addressed to the General and his officers, and demanding of them "the abolition of tithes, of the excise, and of the managing and unlawful using of the laws of the land, through the number, pride, subtlety, and covetousness of lawyers, attorneys, and clerks, whereby the poor countrymen find the cure worse than the malady." The movement of the people, in this respect, to-

[1] Cromwell's Letters and Speeches, vol. ii. p. 217.

wards the army and its leaders was so universal, that, in several places, officers received authority from the General to sit as judges, and decide suits, "wherewith the people were much satisfied for the quick despatch they received with full hearing."[1]

When religion and the Church were concerned, Cromwell was somewhat more embarrassed; for, in reference to these matters, he had, not inflexible resolutions, but engagements and allies which he had no wish to abandon. The enthusiastic sectaries of the army, the soldiers of the fifth monarchy (which was to be the reign of Jesus Christ), had constituted his strength, first against the King, and afterwards against the Presbyterian party in the Parliament. He knew all that was to be apprehended or expected from them; from their military fidelity and their mystical fanaticism, they were, in critical moments, his most necessary and surest instruments; and he carefully kept up his intimacy with them. But he required, in the religious order of things, a more elevated and extensive influence: this he sought and obtained from two sources—the regular preaching of the Gospel, and liberty of conscience: he became the avowed protector of these two interests; by the first he conciliated the Presbyterians, who alone, after the ruin of the Anglican Church, could supply the country with any considerable number of learned, pious, and honored ministers; whilst in the name of liberty of conscience he became the man most necessary to all under persecution, even to the Episcopalians and Catholics, who were denied the free exercise of their faith, but who promised themselves that they would obtain from him tacit toleration and secret support. Among all ranks of society, and within the pale of every Christian community, he thus maintained relations and inspired hopes,

[1] Whitelocke's Memorials, pp. 512, 517, 519.

which furnished him sometimes with grievances, and sometimes with weapons, against the Parliament.

He did not, however, confine himself to this indirect opposition, or rest satisfied with the slow progress which it enabled him to achieve; he was as full of passionate energy as of cautious artifice, and as eager to strike a decisive blow, when it became possible, as he was persistent in secretly pursuing his object, when it was necessary to wait for opportunities of success. He was anxious to know with some degree of certainty what were the views of those men whose co-operation was necessary to him, and how far he might reckon upon their friendly support. On the 10th of December, 1651, he "desired a meeting with divers members of Parliament, and some chief officers of the army," at the house of the Speaker, Lenthall; on the one side were Fleetwood, Desborough, Harrison, and Whalley, his old companions in war and victory; on the other, Whitelocke, Widdrington, St. John, and Lenthall, the civil leaders of the revolution. The conversation is thus reported by Whitelocke.

Cromwell.—"Now that the old King is dead, and his son defeated, I hold it necessary to come to a settlement of the nation. And in order thereunto, I have requested this meeting that we together may consider and advise, What is fit to be done, and to be presented to the Parliament."

Speaker Lenthall.—"My Lord, this company were very ready to attend your Excellence, and the business you are pleased to propound to us is very necessary to be considered. God hath given marvellous success to our forces under your command; and if we do not improve these mercies to some settlement, such as may be to God's honor, and the good of this Commonwealth, we shall be very much blameworthy."

Harrison.—"I think that which my Lord General hath propounded, is, To advise as to a settlement both of our civil and spiritual liberties; and so, that the mercies which the Lord hath given in to us may not be cast away. How this may be done is the great question."

WHITELOCKE.—"It is a great question indeed, and not suddenly to be resolved! Yet it were a pity that a meeting of so many able and worthy persons as I see here, should be fruitless. I should humbly offer, in the first place, Whether it be not requisite to be understood in what way this settlement is desired? Whether of an absolute republic, or with any mixture of monarchy."

CROMWELL.—"My Lord Commissioner Whitelocke hath put us upon the right point; and indeed, it is my meaning that we should consider, Whether a republic, or a mixed monarchical government will be best to be settled? And, if anything monarchical, then, In whom that power shall be placed?"

SIR THOMAS WIDDRINGTON.—"I think a mixed monarchical government will be most suitable to the laws and people of this nation. And if any monarchical, I suppose we shall hold it most just to place that power in one of the sons of the late King."

FLEETWOOD.—"I think that the question, Whether an absolute republic, or a mixed monarchy, be best to be settled in this nation, will not be very easy to be determined."

LORD CHIEF JUSTICE ST. JOHN.—"It will be found, that the government of this nation, without something of monarchical power, will be very difficult to be so settled as not to shake the foundation of our laws, and the liberties of the people."

SPEAKER LENTHALL.—"It will breed a strange confusion to settle a government of this nation without something of monarchy."

DESBOROUGH.—"I beseech you, my Lord, why may not this, as well as other nations, be governed in the way of a republic?"

WHITELOCKE.—"The laws of England are so interwoven with the power and practice of monarchy, that to settle a government without something of monarchy in it, would make so great an alteration in the proceedings of our law, that you will scarce have time to rectify it, nor can we well foresee the inconveniences which will arise thereby."

COLONEL WHALLEY.—"I do not well understand matters of law; but it seems to me the best way, Not to have anything of monarchical power in the settlement of our government. And if we should resolve upon any, whom have we to pitch upon? The King's eldest son hath been in arms against us, and his second son likewise is our enemy."

SIR THOMAS WIDDRINGTON.—"But the late King's third son, the Duke of Gloucester, is still among us, and too young to have been in arms against us, or infected with the principles of our enemies."

WHITELOCKE.—"There may be a day given for the King's eldest son, or for the Duke of York his brother, to come in to the Parliament. And upon such terms as shall be thought fit and agreeable both to our civil and spiritual liberties, a settlement may be made with them."

CROMWELL.—"That will be a business of more than ordinary difficulty! But really I think if it may be done with safety and preservation of our rights, both as Englishmen and as Christians, that a settlement with somewhat of monarchical power in it would be very effectual."[1]

The conversation continued for some time in this strain, but no other result was arrived at than to make the leading men in the Parliament and army aware of the designs of Cromwell, and to acquaint him with their feelings and wishes. He also perceived that he might find a dangerous opponent in the young Duke of Gloucester, who was at that time in England, and in the hands of the Parliament. A few months

[1] Whitelocke's Memorials, pp. 516, 517.

after, the Prince's tutor, Mr. Lovel, received secret encouragement to request that the Duke of Gloucester might be liberated from prison, and sent into Holland to the Princess of Orange, his sister. He had no difficulty in obtaining this permission, together with a sum of five hundred pounds for the expenses of the voyage, on condition that the Prince should embark at the Isle of Wight, the place of his confinement, and should not touch at any point on the English coast on his way to Holland.[1] Thus a royal competitor was removed, under a show of generosity and kindness.

The republican leaders of the Parliament were not ignorant of the views and intrigues, which Cromwell took so little pains to conceal, and they used their utmost efforts to thwart him. For a considerable period they had attempted to give some satisfaction, or at least to excite hopes that satisfaction would be given, to the desires for reform which were rife all over the country. A committee had been appointed to inquire into the changes necessary to be introduced into the civil law, and the Parliament had more than once urged this committee, which went languidly to work, to proceed with greater energy and assiduity.[2] But these recommendations, which probably were not of a very forcible character, had produced but little effect, and only one important result had emanated from the deliberations of the Committee. It had proposed, and Parliament had adopted, an Act ordaining that in future all the laws, and all proceedings before all Courts of Justice, should be conducted in English, and not in French or Latin; and to secure the execution of this really popular measure, the Parliament had carefully gone into the minutest details.[3] Some abuses had also been reformed in the practice of the Court

[1] Clarendon's History of the Rebellion, vol. vii. pp. 87, 88; Heath's Brief Chronicle, p. 614.

[2] Commons' Journals, vol. vi. pp. 280, 328, 485.

[3] Ibid. vol. vi. pp. 487, 488, 490, 493, 500.

of Chancery, and the expense of lawsuits considerably diminished.[1] But either from professional obstinacy, or from a just dread of the consequences of innovation, the lawyers, who predominated in the committee, had strenuously opposed nearly all the plans of the reformers, and it had relapsed into its former languor when the struggle between Cromwell and the Parliament occurred to revive its activity. As soon as it found that Cromwell was seeking this kind of popularity, the Parliament ordained, "That the committee for regulating the law be revived, and sit to-morrow in the afternoon, and so *de die in diem:* with power to confer with what persons they shall think fit, and to send for persons, papers, witnesses, and what else may conduce to the business; and to report to the House from time to time, as often as they shall think fit."[2] But this was only a promise, that had been renewed several times already, and had always proved unproductive; it was felt necessary to do something more novel, and better calculated to inspire the partisans of reform with fresh confidence. It was determined that a commission should be appointed of persons not members of the House, "to take into consideration what inconveniences there are in the law, and how the mischiefs that grow from the delays, the chargeableness, and the irregularities in law proceedings, may be prevented, and the speediest way to reform the same;" and that they should report their opinions and suggestions to a Parliamentary Committee.[3] Twenty-one persons, nearly all of them eminent for rank or learning, were selected to form this commission, and the celebrated jurisconsult, Matthew Hale, was the first on the list.[4] The most important questions of civil legislation were fully discussed: the registration of marriages,

[1] Commons' Journals, vol. vi. pp. 509, 525.
[2] Ibid. vol. vii. p. 26.
[3] Ibid. vol. vii p. 58; Whitelocke, p. 519.
[4] Ibid. vol. vii. pp. 71, 74.

births, and deaths, the transfer of property and its registration, the abolition of fines upon bills, declarations, and original writs, the speedy recovery of rents, and other matters of equal importance; on all these subjects, the commission drafted schemes of reform for the consideration of the House, several of which were actually submitted to it by Whitelocke, who, according to his estimation of the chances of success, became by turns the opponent or the reporter of innovations.[1] A general work, "containing the system of the law," was also prepared by this Commission and laid before the House, which heard it read, and ordered that three hundred copies of it should be printed, "to be delivered to members of the Parliament only."[2]

In religious matters, also, the Parliament would have been glad to obtain some popularity, and gain for itself, as Cromwell had done, clients and friends among all denominations. In the year 1650, it had abolished the laws passed during the reign of Queen Elizabeth to enforce uniformity of faith and worship;[3] but at the same time, it had continued and even aggravated the persecution of the Catholics and Episcopalians, and promulgated new laws against immorality of conduct, "obscene, licentious, and impious practices," and "atheistical, blasphemous, and execrable opinions;"[1] attempting by this means to give satisfaction at once to religious animosities, to liberty of conscience, and to austerity of character. Such a task cannot possibly be performed by the power whose duty it is to put all the laws into daily application, and which, even in the eyes of the people whose passions it has adopted, must bear the punishment of their inconsistencies and iniquities. Cromwell, carefully keeping himself aloof from the

[1] Commons' Journals, vol. vii. pp. 107, 110.
[2] Ibid. vol. vii. pp. 249, 250.
[3] Ibid. vol. vi. p. 474.
[4] Ibid. vol. vi. pp. 410, 423, 430, 453.

Government, was able to protect by turns, and with greater or less reserve, sectaries of all sorts, Episcopalians, Catholics, and even freethinkers of the worst kind; whilst the Parliament, whose duty it was to govern, found itself taxed sometimes with harshness for repressing them, and sometimes with laxity for tolerating them, and gained only enemies where Cromwell recruited partisans.

High-minded and high-spirited men, and Vane especially, were unable patiently to endure this position, and earnestly strove to rise above it. Some great event or some important act could alone achieve their deliverance; they stood in need of some splendid success, which should not be gained for them by Cromwell. This was probably one of the causes which, either from reflection or instinct, instigated them to their project for a close alliance between England and Holland, and to the war which the failure of this attempt occasioned between the two States. Just about this period, another prospect, not wanting in grandeur, presented itself before them, Scotland was subjugated. Monk was governing it with soldier-like sternness, but sensibly and justly. Argyle alone retained, in his domains, some remnant of independence; but it was fraught with no danger to the conquerors. Why should they not incorporate Scotland with England? Great Britain would then form only a single State, as it already formed a single island; and the Commonwealth would have the glory of accomplishing that which England's greatest kings had attempted in vain to effect. On the 9th of September, 1651, scarcely six days after the battle of Worcester, this design was mooted in the Parliament, and before the year was at an end, it was transformed into an express declaration of the entire union of the two countries. Eight commissioners, with Vane and St. John at their head, set out for Scotland, with detailed instructions for its execution. They arrived at Edinburgh on the 20th of January, 1652, and took up their residence at Dalkeith, whither they summoned delegates from all the counties and boroughs of Scotland, in order to obtain their consent to the union. The undertaking was attended with great difficulty; and had it not been for the authority of Monk and his garrisons, all Vane's eloquent persuasiveness would probably have failed of success. The Scottish people were indignant at the idea of losing their nationality; the Presbyterian clergy protested against any infraction of the independence of their church, and abjured any admission of the spiritual power of the Parliament. The vassals of Argyle refused to obey the orders of the English commissioners. The Provost of Edinburgh attempted in vain to induce the ministers of the town to preach in favor of the union; he only obtained this answer—"that they knew better what to preach than the Provost could instruct them."[1] The counties and boroughs which refused to send delegates, or whose delegates refused to accede to the union, were deprived of their franchises; and yet, even according to the computation most favorable to the English, twenty counties and thirty-five boroughs only, out of ninety, gave their consent. But victorious force does not need even so much as this to proclaim that its right is recognized. Argyle, on receiving a promise that his domains should be protected, and that he should be paid whatever was due to him, consented at length to come to terms. Vane returned to London, on behalf of the commissioners, to report to Parliament their success. It was agreed that twenty-one Scottish delegates should proceed thither soon afterwards, to discuss the definitive terms of the union; and, on the 13th of April, 1652, on

[1] Cromwell's Letters and Speeches, vol. ii. pp. 345—347; Burnet's History of His Own Time, vol. i. pp. 112—115; Guizot's Life of Monk, pp. 39—42; Commons' Journals, vol. vii. pp. 14, 21, 30, 31, 53, 85, 96, 110, 118, 129; Whitelocke, pp. 519, 521—523, 528, 529; Balfour's Annals of Scotland, vol. iv. p. 350; Ludlow's Memoirs, p. 172.

the report of Whitelocke, in the name of the Council of State, a bill was brought forward to decree the abolition of royalty in Scotland, and the union of the two countries under the sole authority of the Parliament, into whose body a certain number of Scottish representatives were to be admitted.

A few weeks afterwards, either because this imperfect success had inspired the Parliament with greater confidence, or because the necessity of providing for the expenses of the naval war with Holland appeared to it a favorable opportunity, the question of the reduction of the army was revived. The House resolved, "that it be referred to the Council of State (upon conference with the Lord General and such other persons whom they shall think fit), to take into consideration both the garrisons and forces in England and Scotland; and how some considerable retrenchment may be made of the charge, with safety to the Commonwealth; and report the same to the House on to-morrow se'ennight." This resolution had no sooner been passed than the Speaker received a letter from Cromwell, which was read to the House; it has not been inserted in the journals, but it evidently referred to the desire for a reduction of the army which the House had expressed; for, twelve days after, the expenses of the army in England and Scotland were voted without any reduction.[1]

The Parliament anticipated, and indeed appeared to obtain, better success with regard to the army in Ireland. Although several parts of that island were still in a state of insurrection, or at least of insubordination, the war there was virtually at an end; all the places of any importance had surrendered, and the enemies of the Commonwealth were nowhere able to make any stand against its soldiers. Another operation, more cruel even than war, had begun, namely, the expropriation and transplantation, either completely or

[1] Commons' Journals, vol. vii. pp. 136, 138, 139, 142.

partially, of all the Catholic population of Ireland, for the purpose of paying, in the first place, the adventurers in the loan contracted in 1642, with the Irish confiscations as security; and secondly, the arrears due to the disbanded soldiers. Such a prospect could not fail to render the reduction of this part of the army more easy of accomplishment. As soon as this terrible remodelling of landed property and the population was effected, the Parliament proposed to incorporate Ireland, as well as Scotland, with England, by granting it also a small amount of influence in the general assembly in which the government of the Commonwealth was vested; and it hoped to exercise a decisive preponderance in a country where it was thus able to dispose everything at its pleasure.[1]

But Cromwell, ever careful to allow no opportunity to escape which might be made conducive to his fortune, had been furnished, by a frivolous incident, with the means of extending his influence to Ireland, and he had hastened to avail himself of them. After the death of Ireton, who, under the title of Lord Deputy, had commanded in Ireland as the lieutenant of Cromwell (who still retained the rank of Governor-General of that kingdom), Lambert, who was then serving in Scotland, was appointed to succeed him, under the same name and with the same powers. Vain and fond of display, he left Scotland in all haste to take possession of his new honors, and made his entry into London with a large and magnificent train; having, it is said, spent five thousand pounds on his equipage. A few days after, Lady Lambert, his wife, who was as vain as himself, met Ireton's widow, Cromwell's daughter Bridget, in St. James's Park, and pompously took precedence of her. Notwithstanding her piety

[1] Commons' Journals, vol. vii. pp. 79, 123, 161, 229; Ludlow's Memoirs; Leland's History of Ireland, vol. iii. pp. 387—397.

and sorrow, Lady Ireton felt this insult keenly. Fleetwood, Cromwell's lieutenant-general in the command of all the forces of the Commonwealth, happened by chance to be present at this scene; he was himself a widower, and he offered Lady Ireton first his sympathy and condolence, and ultimately his hand. She accepted without hesitation; the wife of the Lieutenant-General of the Commonwealth would, of course, take precedence on all occasions of the wife of the Lord Deputy of Ireland. This marriage met with Cromwell's entire approval; Fleetwood belonged to a wealthy and important family, and could not fail to prove a useful son-in-law. An opportunity soon presented itself for turning this new connection to profit; Cromwell's commission as Governor-General of Ireland was nearly expired; a proposition was made in the House for its renewal, but Cromwell himself declined this favor, saying that he had enough honors and authorities already. The office of Lord-Lieutenant or Governor-General was therefore suppressed. A Lord-Deputy without a Governor-General was held to be a solecism; and another title, with various compensations, was offered to Lambert; but he would not accept what he considered a diminution of his glories, and resigned his office. It was then decided that the Commander-in-chief of the forces of the Commonwealth should appoint some officer to the command in Ireland, and Cromwell named Fleetwood. But careful to heal the wound that he had inflicted, he attempted, and successfully, to persuade Lambert that the ill-will of the Parliament alone had deprived him of the title of Lord Deputy, which he, Cromwell, would have been delighted that he should retain; and with a thorough comprehension of the meanness which may lie hid under a show of vanity, he expressed to Lambert his regret that his brief dignity should have involved him in such enormous expenses, and requested permission to make up his loss from his own purse; to which

Lambert consented, thus placing himself, in his misadventure, under obligation to Cromwell, who, by this means, made his son-in-law the commander in Ireland, and converted the man whom some had attempted to set up as his rival in the army, into a deadly enemy of the Parliament.[1]

He excelled in thus vigorously pushing his advantages. The House, notwithstanding the check which it had just received, persisted in its design of reducing the army. Cromwell resolved openly to engage in the conflict between the army and the Parliament, in the name of all the grievances, real or imaginary, and all the desires, practicable or chimerical, which were rife in the country, and to which the House was continually promising, though it never gave, satisfaction. On the 12th of August, 1652, the House ordered the Council of State, with all convenient speed, to report to it what had been done touching the retrenchment of the forces, particularly in the three garrisons of Exeter, Gloucester, and Bristol. On the same day, a general council of officers met at Whitehall; and on the day following, six of the leaders, Commissary-General Whalley, Colonels Hacker, Barkstead, Okey, and Goffe, and Lieutenant-Colonel Worsley, presented themselves at the door of the House with a petition in which all these grievances and desires, in reference to both civil and religious matters, were summed up in twelve articles, in respectful but peremptory terms, and insisting, at the close, on the enactment of "such qualifications for future and successive Parliaments, as should tend to the election only of such as were pious, and faithful to the interest of the Commonwealth."[2]

The House felt some surprise at this proceeding; such

[1] Ludlow's Memoirs, p. 177; Hutchinson's Memoirs, pp. 360, 361; Whitelocke, pp. 523, 533, 536.

[2] Commons' Journals, vol. vii. pp. 163, 164; Whitelocke, p. 541; Cromwell's Letters and Speeches, vol. ii. p. 372.

petitions had formerly been used against the Crown; but, since the establishment of the Commonwealth, the army had ceased thus to interfere in the government. Cromwell himself had contributed to lull the fears of the House, for, without any scruple about contradicting or belying himself, at the very moment when he was thus secretly instigating the officers to urge the Parliament to dissolve, he had appeared desirous of diverting them from this step, and had given his word to the House that if it should order the army to break their swords and throw them into the sea, they would obey without hesitation.[1] The petition was received with great respect, and referred to a special committee, which was ordered to inquire how many of its particulars were already under consideration, how far they had been proceeded in, and what method might be adopted for their more speedy expedition. The Speaker, on behalf of the House, thanked the officers for their constant affection to the Parliament, and for the vigilant care for the public interest expressed in their petition. But, when these official demonstrations were over, the principal members of the House unreservedly expressed their dissatisfaction at a proceeding, and at language, "so improper, if not arrogant, for the officers of the army to use to the Parliament their masters." "You had better stop this way of petitioning by the officers of the army with their swords in their hands," said Whitelocke to Cromwell, "lest in time it may come too home to yourself."[2] But Cromwell made light of his anxiety; no one cared less for the embarrassments which success might one day entail upon him.

About six weeks after this, meeting Whitelocke walking one evening in St. James's Park, Cromwell saluted him "with more than ordinary courtesy," and desired him to

[1] Ludlow's Memoirs, p. 191.

[2] Commons' Journals, vol. vii. p. 164; Whitelocke, p. 541.

walk aside with him that they might have some private discourse together. The following conversation then ensued.

CROMWELL.—"My Lord Whitelocke, I know your faithfulness and engagement in the same good cause with myself, and the rest of our friends; and I know your ability in judgment, and your particular friendship and affection for me; and, therefore, I desire to advise with you in the main and most important affairs relating to our present condition."

WHITELOCKE.—"Your Excellency hath known me long, and I think will say that you never knew any unfaithfulness or breach of trust by me; and for my particular affection to your person, your favors to me, and your public services, have deserved more than I can manifest. Only there is, with your favor, a mistake in this one thing, touching my weak judgment, which is incapable of doing any considerable service to yourself or this Commonwealth; yet to the utmost of my power, I shall be ready to serve you, and that with all diligence and faithfulness."

CROMWELL.—"I have cause to be, and am, without the least scruple of your faithfulness, and I know your kindness to me, your old friend, and your abilities to serve the Commonwealth; and there are enough besides me that can testify it. I believe our engagements for this Commonwealth have been and are as deep as most men's; and there never was more need of advice and solid hearty counsel, than the present state of our affairs doth require."

WHITELOCKE.—"I suppose no man will mention his particular engagement in this cause, at the same time when your Excellency's engagement is remembered; yet to my capacity, and in my station, few men have engaged further than I have done; and that, besides the goodness of your own nature and personal knowledge of me, will keep you from any jealousy of my faithfulness."

CROMWELL.—"I wish there were no more ground of suspicion of others than of you. I can trust you with my life and the most secret matters relating to our business, and to that end I have now desired a little private discourse with you. Really, my Lord, there is very great cause for us to consider the dangerous condition we are all in, and how to make good our station, to improve the mercies and successes which God hath given us, and not to be fooled out of them again, nor to be broken in pieces by our particular jarrings and animosities one against another, but to unite our councils, and hands and hearts, to make good what we have so dearly bought, with so much hazard, blood, and treasure; and that, the Lord having given us an entire conquest over our enemies, we should not now hazard all again by our private janglings, and bring those mischiefs upon ourselves which our enemies could never do."

WHITELOCKE.—"My Lord, I look upon our present danger, as greater than ever it was in the field; and, as your Excellency truly observes, our proneness is to destroy ourselves, when our enemies could not do it. It is no strange thing for a gallant army, as yours is, after full conquest of their enemies, to grow into factious and ambitious designs; and it is a wonder to me that they are not in high mutinies, their spirits being active, and few thinking their services to be duly rewarded, and the emulation of the officers breaking out daily more and more, in this time of their vacancy from their employment; besides, the private soldiers, it may be feared, will in this time of their idleness, grow into disorder; and it is your excellent conduct which, under God, hath kept them so long in discipline, and free from mutinies."

CROMWELL.—"I have used, and shall use, the utmost of my poor endeavors to keep them all in order and obedience."

WHITELOCKE.—"Your Excellency hath done it hitherto even to admiration."

CROMWELL.—"Truly God hath blessed me in it exceedingly, and I hope will do so still. Your Lordship hath observed most truly the inclinations of the officers of the army to particular factions and to murmurings that they are not rewarded according to their deserts, that others who have adventured least, have gained most, and they have neither profit, nor preferment, nor place in government, which others hold, who have undergone no hardships nor hazards for the Commonwealth. And herein they have too much of truth; yet their insolency is very great, and their influence upon the private soldiers works them to the like discontents and murmurings. Then, as for the members of Parliament, the army begins to have a strange distaste against them, and I wish there were not too much cause for it. And really their pride and ambition, and self-seeking, engrossing all places of honor and profit to themselves; and their daily breaking forth into new and violent parties and factions; their delays of business, and design to perpetuate themselves, and to continue the power in their own hands; their meddling in private matters between party and party, contrary to the institution of Parliaments, and their injustice and partiality in those matters; and the scandalous lives of some of the chief of them;—these things, my Lord, do give too much ground for people to open their mouths against them, and to dislike them. Nor can they be kept within the bounds of justice, and law or reason; they themselves being the supreme power of the nation, liable to no account to any, nor to be controlled or regulated by any other power, there being none superior or co-ordinate with them. So that, unless there be some authority and power so full and so high as to restrain and keep things in better order, and that may be a check to these exorbitances, it will be impossible in human reason to prevent our ruin."

WHITELOCKE.—"I confess the danger we are in by these

extravagances and inordinate powers is more than I doubt is generally apprehended; yet, as to that part of it which concerns the soldiery, your Excellency's power and commission is sufficient already to restrain and keep them in their due obedience; and, blessed be God! you have done it hitherto, and I doubt not but by your wisdom you will be able still to do it. As to the members of Parliament, I confess the greatest difficulty lies there, your commission being from them, and they being acknowledged the supreme power of the nation, subject to no control, nor allowing any appeal from them. Yet I am sure your Excellency will not look upon them as generally depraved; too many of them are much to blame in those things you have mentioned, and many unfit things have passed among them; but I hope well of the major part of them, when great matters come to a decision."

CROMWELL.—"My Lord, there is little hope of a good settlement to be made by them—really there is not; but a great deal of fear, that they will destroy again what the Lord hath done graciously for them and us. We all forget God, and God will forget us, and give us up to confusion; and these men will help it on, if they be suffered to proceed in their ways. Some course must be thought on to curb and restrain them, or we shall be ruined by them."

WHITELOCKE.—"We ourselves have acknowledged them the supreme power, and taken our commissions and authority in the highest concernments from them; and how to restrain and curb them after this, it will be hard to find out a way for it."

CROMWELL.—"What if a man should take upon him to be King?"

WHITELOCKE.—"I think that remedy would be worse than the disease."

CROMWELL.—"Why do you think so?"

WHITELOCKE.—"As to your own person, the title of King would be of no advantage, because you have the full kingly power in you already, concerning the militia, as you are General. As to the nomination of civil officers, those whom you think fittest are seldom refused; and, although you have no negative vote in the passing of laws, yet what you dislike will not easily be carried; and the taxes are already settled, and in your power to dispose the money raised. And as to foreign affairs, though the ceremonial application be made to the Parliament, yet the expectation of good or bad success in it is from your Excellency, and particular solicitations of foreign ministers are made to you only. So that I apprehend indeed less envy, and danger, and pomp, but not less power and real opportunities of doing good, in your being General, than would be if you had assumed the title of King."

CROMWELL.—"I have heard some of your profession observe, that he who is actually King, whether by election or by descent, yet being once King, all acts done by him as King are lawful and justifiable, as by any King who hath the crown by inheritance from his forefathers; and that, by an Act of Parliament in Henry the Seventh's time, it is safer for those who act under a King (be his title what it will) than for those who act under any other power. And surely the power of a King is so great and high, and so universally understood and reverenced by the people of this nation, that the title of it might not only indemnify in a great measure those that act under it, but likewise be of great use and advantage in such times as these, to curb the insolences and extravagances of those whom the present powers cannot control, or at least are the persons themselves who are thus insolent."

WHITELOCKE.—"I agree in the general with what you are pleased to observe as to this title of King; but whether for your Excellency to take this title upon you, as things now are, will be for the good and advantage of yourself and friends, or of the Commonwealth, I do very much doubt, notwithstanding that Act of Parliament of 11 Henry VII., which will be little regarded or observed to us by our enemies, if they should come to get the upper hand of us."

CROMWELL.—"What do you apprehend would be the danger of taking this title?"

WHITELOCKE.—"The danger, I think, would be this. One of the main points of controversy betwixt us and our adversaries, is whether the government of this nation shall be established in monarchy, or in a free State or Commonwealth; and most of our friends have engaged with us upon the hopes of having the government settled in a free State, and to effect that, have undergone all their hazards and difficulties—they being persuaded (though I think much mistaken) that, under the government of a Commonwealth, they shall enjoy more liberty and right, both as to their spiritual and civil concernments, than they shall under monarchy; the pressures and dislike whereof are so fresh in their memories and sufferings. Now, if your Excellency shall take upon you the title of King, this state of our cause will be thereby wholly determined, and monarchy established in your person; and the question will be no more whether our government shall be by a monarch or by a free State, but whether Cromwell or Stuart shall be our king and monarch. And that question, wherein before so great parties of the nation were engaged, and which was universal, will by this means become in effect a private controversy only. Before it was national, what kind of government we should have; now it will become particular, who shall be our governor, whether of the family of the Stuarts, or of the family of the Cromwells. Thus, the state of our controversy being totally changed, all those who were for a Commonwealth (and they are a very great and considerable party), having their hopes therein frustrated, will desert you; your hands will be weakened, your interest straitened, and your cause in apparent danger to be ruined."

CROMWELL.—"I confess you speak reason in this; but what other things can you propound that may obviate the present dangers and difficulties, wherein we are all engaged?"

WHITELOCKE.—"It will be the greatest difficulty to find out such an expedient. I have had many things in my private thoughts upon this business, some of which, perhaps, are not fit or safe for me to communicate."

CROMWELL.—"I pray, my Lord, what are they? You may trust me with them. There shall no prejudice come to you by any private discourse betwixt us; I shall never betray my friend. You may be as free with me as with your own heart, and shall never suffer by it."

WHITELOCKE.—"I make no scruple to put my life and fortune in your Excellency's hand; and so I shall, if I impart these fancies to you, which are weak, and perhaps may prove offensive to your Excellency; therefore, my best way will be to smother them."

CROMWELL.—"Nay, I prithee, my Lord Whitelocke, let me know them. Be they what they will, they cannot be offensive to me; but I shall take it kindly from you. Therefore I pray do not conceal those thoughts of yours from your faithful friend."

WHITELOCKE.—"Your Excellency honors me with a title far above me; and since you are pleased to command it, I shall discover to you my thoughts herein, and humbly desire you not to take in ill part what I shall say to you."

CROMWELL.—"Indeed I shall not; but I shall take it, as I said, very kindly from you."

WHITELOCKE.—"Give me leave, then, first to consider your Excellency's condition. You are environed with secret enemies. Upon your subduing of the public enemy, the officers of your army account themselves all victors, and to have had an equal share in the conquest with you. The success which God hath given us, hath not a little elated their minds, and many of them are busy and of turbulent spirits, and are not without their designs how they may dismount your Excellency, and some of themselves get up into the saddle. They want not counsel and encouragement herein, it may be, from some members of the Parliament, who may be jealous of your power and greatness, lest you should grow too high for them, and in time overmaster them; and they will plot to bring you down first, or to clip your wings."

CROMWELL.—"I thank you that you so fully consider my condition. It is a testimony of your love to me and care of me; and you have rightly considered it; and I may say without vanity that in my condition yours is involved and all our friends; and those that plot my ruin will hardly bear your continuance in any condition worthy of you. Besides this, the cause itself may possibly receive some disadvantage by the strugglings and contentions among ourselves. But what, sir, are your thoughts for prevention of those mischiefs that hang over our heads?"

WHITELOCKE.—"Pardon me, sir, in the next place, a little to consider the condition of the King of Scots. This prince being now, by your valor, and the success which God hath given to the Parliament, and to the army under your command, reduced to a very low condition; both he and all about him cannot but be very inclinable to hearken to any terms, whereby their lost hopes may be revived of his being restored to the crown, and they to their fortunes and native country. By a private treaty with him, you may secure yourself and your friends, and their fortunes; you may make yourself and your posterity as great and permanent, to all human probability, as ever any subject was, and provide for your friends. You may put such limits to monarchical power, as will secure our spiritual and civil liberties; and you may secure the cause in which we are all engaged (and this may be effectually done) by having the power of all the militia continued in yourself, and whom you shall agree upon after you. I propound therefore for your Excellency to send to the King of Scots, and to have a private treaty with him for this purpose. And I beseech you to pardon what I have said upon this occasion; it is out of my affection and service to your Excellency, and to all honest men; and I humbly pray you not to have any jealousy thereupon of my approved faithfulness to your Excellency and to this Commonwealth."

CROMWELL.—"I have not, I assure you, the least distrust of your faithfulness and friendship to me, and to the cause of this Commonwealth; and I think you have much reason for what you propound. But it is a matter of so high importance and difficulty, that it deserves more of consideration and debate than is at present allowed us. We shall therefore take a further time to discourse of it."[1]

Cromwell could at his pleasure postpone a conversation with Whitelocke, when it took a turn which was not agreeable to him, but he could not adjourn the impending conflict between the Parliament and himself, which was made manifest, and hastened onwards, by such confidential communications; it was war, and one of those wars which do not admit of a pacific settlement. Notwithstanding the hypocrisy displayed in the personal relations and language of the antagonists, the conflict was thenceforward avowed and active. Irritated and paralyzed at once by the intrigues of its enemy, the Parliament introduced into its management

[1] Whitelocke's Memorials, pp. 548—551.

of public affairs the consciousness of its own danger—and the precautions requisite for its own defence. Never had it manifested so much anxiety to give satisfaction to the wishes of the country; law reform, the alleviation of the condition of the poor, the measures necessary for securing the preaching of the Gospel, and the maintenance of its ministers in every part of the empire—indeed all questions of a popular character, whether civil or religious, were the subjects of repeated discussion and deliberation; and those great political acts which were calculated to throw lustre on the ruling power, such as the union of England and Scotland, the settlement of the affairs of Ireland, and the necessities of the war with the United Provinces, were incessantly under debate. The Government strove hard to obtain a little dignity or favor from every available source. But most of these attempts resulted in nothing; debates were indefinitely prolonged and resumed, conferences and reports of committees were multiplied to no effect, resolutions which seemed decisive were revoked or called in question. The Parliament was evidently under the sway of a continuous perplexity, which urged it to redouble its efforts, at the same time that it doomed them to unproductiveness.

Cromwell, on his side, was not exempt from anxiety and hesitation; he had frequent conversations, sometimes with the officers only, sometimes with the officers and members of Parliament together, and sometimes even with Presbyterian or other ministers, whom he consulted as it were upon a case of conscience, in order to bring them over to his views: but he sometimes met with opposition as frank and decided as his own words were indiscreet and passionate. At one of these conferences, Dr. Edmund Calamy, a preacher of great eminence in the city, boldly opposed the system of a sole ruler as unlawful and impracticable. Cromwell answered readily upon the first head of unlawful, and appealed to the safety of the nation being the supreme law. "But," said he, "pray, Mr. Calamy, why impracticable?" Calamy replied: "Oh! 'tis against the voice of the nation; there will be nine in ten against you." "Very well," said Cromwell; "but what if I should disarm the nine, and put a sword into the tenth man's hand, would not that do the business?"[1] This bold language on the part of a conqueror whose prowess had so often been tried, proved sufficiently seductive to most of the bystanders, but filled others with alarm. The enthusiastically mystical sectaries, with Harrison at their head, were entirely devoted to Cromwell; the Parliament was, in their eyes, only a profane power which held the place of the government of Christ, the only legitimate king; and they anticipated, from the piety of Cromwell, the advent of the reign of the saints, and from his valor the overthrow of Antichrist as personified in the Pope and the Turks. Men of unbiased mind, the secular politicians, clearly understood that the struggle between their General and the Parliament could not be long continued, and that the moment of its termination was at hand. Numerous letters arrived from the army in Scotland, to assure the English army of their sympathy and support. In the army of Ireland the feeling was less unanimous; Ludlow, who had served there for many years with great distinction, possessed considerable influence, which he employed wholly to keep up the republican spirit. Three officers, Colonel Venables, Quartermaster-general Downing, and Major Streater, went to London to oppose the designs which they saw were in contemplation. Cromwell either gained over or silenced Downing and Venables; but Streater remained firm, and even went so far as to say in a conference: "That the General intended to set up himself, and that it was a betray-

[1] Forster's Statesmen of the Commonwealth, vol. v. p. 52; Life of Oliver Cromwell (London, 1743), p. 225; Neal's History of the Puritans, vol. iv. p. 374.

ing of their most glorious cause, for which so much blood had been spilt." Harrison denied this accusation, saying: "That he was assured the General did not seek himself in it, but did it to make way for the rule of Jesus, that he might have the sceptre." "Well," replied Streater, "Christ must come before Christmas, or else he will come too late."[1]

The danger was not so pressing as Streater imagined. Cromwell had the sense to perceive the obstacles which stood in his way, and to take time to surmount them. In the midst of the conflict in which he was so hotly engaged, and doubtless with a view to moderate it by lulling suspicions, he suddenly withdrew his opposition to the plan for a fresh reduction of the army, which had been thrown out by his influence, five months previously; and on the 1st of January, 1653, by agreement between the Parliament and the General, this reduction was positively ordered—about three thousand infantry, and a thousand cavalry were disbanded, several garrisons were reduced, and a saving of 10,000*l.* a month was effected in the charges of the Commonwealth.[2]

Cromwell could afford to make the House this sacrifice; it had already received from him, and more especially from itself and from time, the fatal blows beneath which it was finally to succumb. For more than twelve years, in its entire or mutilated state, this Parliament had held the reins of power, and was responsible, in the eyes of England, for events, as well as for its own acts, for what it had failed to foresee, as well as for what it had decreed, for what it had not prevented, as well as for what it had done. And not only for twelve years had the Parliament governed, but it

[1] Forster's Statesmen of the Commonwealth, vol. v. p. 44; Life of Oliver Cromwell, p. 228; Whitelocke, p. 553.

[2] Commons' Journals, vol. vii. p. 241.

had absorbed into itself all powers; it alone treated and decided on a multitude of questions which, before its time, would have devolved upon the Crown or its agents, the magistrates and the local authorities: confiscations, sequestrations, sales of royal and ecclesiastical domains, the disputes which arose upon these questions, appointments to public offices, the conduct of war by land and sea—the whole revolutionary administration and government—were in the hands of the Parliament, which was thus charged with an infinite number of private as well as public interests. The journals of the House give evidence, on every page, of this monstrous centralization of affairs of every kind daily debated and decided either by the House itself, or by its committees; and this was carried to such an extent, that, from time to time, the House was obliged to determine that for one or two weeks, it would set aside all private affairs, and attend only to the public business of the country.[1] A deplorable state of confusion, truly, in which the Parliament lost not only its time, but its virtue. Neither the good sense nor the honesty of the majority of mankind could stand against this prolonged enjoyment of power in the midst of chaos: abuses, vexations, malversations, and unlawful transactions sprang up and multiplied, as the natural fruit of such a state of things; and the Parliament, absolute master of the fortune and fate of a host of citizens, as well as of the fate and fortune of the State, soon became notorious as a den of iniquity and corruption.

Politically, this accusation was unjust. The political leaders of the republican Parliament, Vane, Sidney, Ludlow, Hutchinson, and Harrington, were men of spotless integrity, passionately devoted to their cause, but pledged to no other interest than the triumph of their cause and passion. The

[1] Commons' Journals, vols. vi. and vii. *passim;* Whitelocke, p. 551.

cause itself, though incompatible with common sense, and regarded with antipathy by the country, was a noble and a moral one; the principles which presided over it were a firm faith in truth, and affectionate esteem for humanity, respect for its rights, and a desire for its free and glorious development. But among the secondary, though active ranks of the party, in the minds of a large number of members, both of the Parliament and of the local committees connected with it, and under the influence either of political disappointments, or personal temptations, a spirit of greedy selfishness, license, and indifference, a tendency to despise or doubt the virtues of justice and probity, had made frightful progress, and given rise to disorders which had entailed upon the party and the Parliament, universal disrespect and dislike.

Several disgraceful scandals occurred to justify and exasperate this public feeling. Lilburne, ever rapid to maintain his rights, and satisfy his animosities, had, on behalf of one of his uncles, claimed the proprietorship of certain mines in the county of Durham, held unlawfully (as he said) by Sir Arthur Haslerig, who was as stirring and popular in the Parliament, as Lilburne in the city. The demand was twice rejected by the committee appointed to inquire into the case. Lilburne accordingly published against his judges a pamphlet,[1] in which he termed them "four of the most unjustest and unworthiest men that ever the Parliament made judges, fit for nothing but to be spewed out of all humane society by all ingenuous rational men, and deserving to have their skins flayed over their ears, stuffed full of straw, and hung up in some public place." He also addressed to the Parliament itself a petition no less insulting to Haslerig. The Parliament ordered that it should be examined by a committee of

[1] This pamphlet is entitled: "A just Reproof to Haberdasher's Hall," and was published in August, 1651.

fifty members; and, after a long investigation, Lilburne was condemned to pay a fine of 3,000*l.* to the State, 2,000*l.* as damages to Haslerig, and 500*l.* a piece to the four members of the committee which had decided upon his claim, and to be banished from England for life.[1] Whether Lilburne's claim was a just one or not, and whatever may have been the violence of his complaint, such a sentence pronounced, not by judges, but by political enemies, revolted the public by its excessive rigor. The popular feeling became still stronger when this severity was compared with an even more glaring act of indulgence. Lord Howard of Escrick, a member of the House, had been expelled from his seat in Parliament, imprisoned in the Tower, and condemned to pay a fine of 10,000*l.*, for a notorious act of corruption;[2] but his fine was afterwards remitted, and he was set at liberty.[3] In reference to some business about naval prizes, a merchant, named Jacob Stainer, was brought to the bar of the House, and examined with regard to certain letters, in which, alluding either to the Parliament, or to the Council of State, he had written to his correspondent at Antwerp: "We have made a great many friends amongst the great ones, to speak for us in the business, when it comes before them." He gave a rather confused explanation, and was set at liberty on bail a fortnight afterwards.[4] Mr. Blagrave, a member of Parliament, was formally accused, by a person who gave his name, and offered to prove his charge, of having received money for certain appointments: the matter was referred to a special committee, and there remained.[5] The disgraceful avidity of private interests, and sometimes even the dis-

[1] Commons' Journals, vol. vii. pp. 71, 72, 74.
[2] Ibid. vol. vi. p. 591.
[3] Ibid. vol. vi. p. 318; vol. vii. p. 274.
[4] Ibid. vol. vii. pp. 223, 229.
[5] Ibid. vol. vii. p. 257.

honesty of certain members, were thus screened, if not by the complicity, at least by the timorous complaisance of the entire Parliament.

These excessive severities and favors were equally odious on the part of an assembly worn out by its prolonged existence as much as by its numerous mistakes, mutilated by its own hands, still full of discord, notwithstanding the smallness of its numbers, which even the defeat of its enemies at home had not strengthened, and which abroad was daily involving the country more deeply in a ruinous war against the only Protestant and republican nation among its neighbors. The public weariness and disgust were manifested on every side; a multitude of pamphlets, which daily became more insolent in their tone, were in circulation; contempt was mingled with hatred; ironical refutations were published of the declarations "of the imaginary Parliament of the unknown Commonwealth of England;"[1] and it was loudly called upon to make way for an assembly of better men. The House, in great irritation, ordered the Council of State "to suppress the weekly pamphlets, or any other books, that go out to the dishonor of the Parliament and prejudice of the Commonwealth," and gave it powers "to imprison the offenders, and to inflict such other punishment on them as they shall think fit."[2] But neither the anger of the House, nor the powers of the Council of State, were any longer sufficient to repress the hostility of a public who felt they had Cromwell for their ally. The Parliament struggled in vain to live; it was wanting at once in moral force and in material strength; united at length in a common antipathy, neither the people nor the army would any longer tolerate its existence.

Under the pressure of this position, the republican leaders were preparing with much debate the bill of dissolution,

[1] Commons' Journals, vol. vii. p. 195. [2] Ibid. vol. vii. pp. 236, 244.

which had so long been demanded of them, when an event occurred which suddenly modified their intentions.[1] The great victory which, about the middle of February, 1653, Blake gained over Tromp in the Channel, appeared to them a favorable circumstance; it threw lustre upon their government; and soon after overtures of peace arrived from Holland. In the private conclaves of his party, Vane strongly urged them to renounce all dangerous slowness of action. One of his friends, Roger Williams, who was then staying at his house, wrote to a correspondent in New England: "Here is great thoughts and preparations for a new Parliament. Some of our friends are apt to think a new Parliament will favor us and our cause more than this has done."[1] It was determined that the existing Parliament should dissolve on the 3d of November in that same year—that is, a year sooner than had previously been intended; and the House began seriously to discuss the provisions of the Act which was to regulate the election of its successors."[2]

This Act has been lost; it does not exist on the registers of the House, and has been found nowhere else; its essential provisions are, however, known. It established a system almost identical with that which, on the 20th of January, 1649, the general council of officers of the army had submitted to the Parliament: an assembly of four hundred members, to be elected in the counties by all the possessors of an annual income of two hundred pounds in real or personal property, and in the boroughs by all the inhabitants who paid a certain rent, the amount of which was not yet fixed. The schedule of the boroughs to be invested with electoral rights was minutely debated, and it suppressed many ancient privileges. But the electors were called upon only to make

[1] Forster's Statesmen of the Commonwealth, vol. iii. p. 149.

[2] Commons' Journals, vol. vii. pp. 244, 261, 263, 265, 268, 270, 273, 277.

up the number of the existing Parliament, and not to renew it entirely; the members then sitting, to the number of about one hundred and fifty, remained *de jure* members of the new Parliament, for the counties or boroughs which they had until then represented. More than this: they alone formed the committee invested with the right of pronouncing upon the validity of the new elections, and the qualifications of the persons elected—so that, far from running any risk of being excluded from the future Parliament, they continued to be its permanent and predominant nucleus.[1]

This assuredly was not the kind of dissolution which the country and the army expected: the falsehood was gross and palpable. Cromwell, however, grew anxious, and resolved in himself not to suffer such an Act to pass into a law. He was well aware of the powerful influence of legality, and the weaknesses of factions; and he knew how many people there are who, when the crisis approaches, are ready to be satisfied with a little. His intimate confidants, the preachers who were devoted to his person, went about in all directions repeating, even from the pulpit, that the Parliament decidedly was determined not to dissolve, and that, in one way or another, it would be necessary to force it to do so. Cromwell himself appeared to be more than ever undecided and perplexed. "I am pushed on," he said one day to Quarter-master-general Vernon, "by two parties to do that, the consideration of the issue whereof makes my hair stand on end. One of these is headed by Major-General Lambert, who, in revenge of the injury the Parliament did him in not permitting him to go into Ireland with a character and conditions suitable to his merit, will be contented with nothing less than their dissolution. Of the other Major-General Harrison is

[1] Cromwell's Letters and Speeches, vol. ii. pp. 379, 380; Godwin's History of the Commonwealth, vol. iii. p. 448; Forster's Statesmen of the Commonwealth, vol. iii. pp. 157—162; Commons' Journals, vol. vii. pp. 273, 752.

the chief, who is an honest man and aims at good things, yet, from the impatience of his spirit, will not wait the Lord's leisure, but hurries me on to that which he and all honest men will have cause to repent."[1] He sought out all the men of any importance, whether as soldiers or civilians, sometimes assembling them in conference at his house, sometimes sounding them in private conversations, and varying his confidential communications or his falsehoods, according as he wished to divert the suspicions of those whom he addressed, or hoped to gain them over to his design.

On the 19th of April, 1653, a more than usually numerous meeting was held at Whitehall; all the leading officers, the most eminent lawyers, Whitelocke, Widdrington, and St. John, and some twenty other members of the House, among whom were Sir Arthur Haslerig and Sir Gilbert Pickering, had been summoned or had come thither, either to concert together on what was to be done, or to explain their views. It had become known that the Parliamentary leaders, Vane especially, wished to press the adoption of the proposed bill. Cromwell urged the meeting to seek out some means of putting an end to the existing Parliament, and of providing for the government of the Commonwealth until a new Parliament should be called. He proposed that, as soon as ever the Parliament was dissolved, forty persons, selected from among the members of the House and of the Council of State, should be provisionally invested with the administration of public affairs. He had often declared that, "if they should trust the people in an election of a new Parliament according to the old constitution, it would be a tempting of God; and that his confidence was that God did intend to save and deliver this nation by few, as he had done in former times; and that five or six men, and some few more, setting them-

[1] Ludlow's Memoirs, p. 190; Whitelocke, p. 553.

selves to the work, might do more in one day than the Parliament had done or would do in a hundred, as far as he could perceive; and that such unbiased men were like to be the only instruments of the people's happiness." The discussion was animated and long; the bill which the Parliament then had under consideration was attacked as delusive, and destined, not to dissolve, but to perpetuate the Parliament, and as dangerous to the Commonwealth, for it opened the doors of the House to the Presbyterians, its mortal enemies. Widdrington and Whitelocke expressed themselves strongly against any plan for dissolving the Parliament against its own will, and instituting a provisional government in its stead; in their opinion, such a proceeding was warrantable neither in conscience nor in wisdom. "The work you go about is accursed," cried Haslerig, "it is impossible to devolve this trust." St. John maintained, on the other hand, that, in one way or another, the existing state of things must be brought to an end, and that the power of the Parliament could not be prolonged. Nearly all the officers were of this opinion. Cromwell reproved those who used violent language, and the conference broke up about midnight, without adopting any resolution. It was agreed, however, that they should meet again on the next day, and that the members of the House should take care that no abrupt decision was arrived at upon the bill in question, in order that they might still have time to consult together on the course they intended to pursue.[1]

The next day, the conference was less numerously attended: irritated or alarmed, several of those who had been present on the previous evening did not return, and others went to the House to watch its proceedings, and report to Cromwell.

[1] Whitelocke, p. 554; Heath's Flagellum, p. 130; Cromwell's Letters and Speeches, vol. ii. p. 380.

Whitelocke returned to the General's house, and renewed his objections to a dissolution of the Parliament, and the formation of a provisional government; foreseeing that he would be appointed a member of it, and, as he would not dare to refuse to serve, that he would be thereby compromised. While the discussion between them on this point was in progress, Cromwell was informed that the Parliament was sitting, and that Vane, Martyn, and Sidney were pressing the immediate adoption of what they called the dissolution bill. The members of the House who were with Cromwell at Whitehall went off immediately to Westminster; but Cromwell himself remained with his officers, determined still to wait, and not to act unless forced to do so by extreme necessity. Presently, Colonel Ingoldsby arrived, exclaiming, "If you mean to do anything decisive, you have no time to lose." The House was on the point of coming to a vote; Vane had insisted with such warmth and earnestness on passing the bill, that Harrison had deemed it necessary "most sweetly and humbly" to conjure his colleagues to pause before they took so important a step. Cromwell left Whitehall in haste, followed by Lambert and five or six officers; and commanded a detachment of soldiers to march round to the House of Commons. On his arrival at Westminster, he stationed guards at the doors and in the lobby of the House, and led round another body to a position just outside the room in which the members were seated. He then entered alone, without noise, "clad in plain black clothes, with gray worsted stockings," as was his custom when he was not in uniform. Vane was speaking, and passionately descanting on the urgency of the bill. Cromwell sat down in his usual place, where he was instantly joined by St. John, to whom he said, "that he was come to do that which grieved him to the very soul, and that he had earnestly with tears prayed to God against. Nay, that he had rather be torn in pieces than do it; but there was a necessity laid upon him therein, in order to the glory of God and the good of the nation." St. John answered, "that he knew not what he meant; but did pray that what it was which must be done, might have a happy issue for the general good;" and so saying, he returned to his seat. Vane was still speaking, and Cromwell listened to him with great attention. He was arguing the necessity of proceeding at once to the last stage of the bill, and with that view, adjured the House to dispense with the usual formalities which should precede its adoption. Cromwell, at this, beckoned to Harrison. "Now is the time," he said; "I must do it!" "Sir," replied Harrison, anxiously, "the work is very great and dangerous." "You say well," answered Cromwell, and sat still for another quarter of an hour. Vane ceased speaking; the Speaker rose to put the question, when Cromwell stood up, took off his hat, and began to speak. At first, he expressed himself in terms of commendation of the Parliament and its members, praising their zeal and care for the public good; but gradually his tone changed, his accents and gestures became more violent; he reproached the members of the House with their delays, their covetousness, their self-interest, their disregard for justice. "You have no heart to do anything for the public good," he exclaimed; "your intention was to perpetuate yourselves in power. But your time is come! The Lord has done with you! He has chosen other instruments for the carrying on His work, that are more worthy. It is the Lord hath taken me by the hand, and set me on to do this thing." Vane, Wentworth, and Martyn rose to reply to him, but he would not suffer them to speak. "You think, perhaps," he said, "that this is not parliamentary language; I know it; but expect no other language from me." Wentworth at length made himself heard; he declared that this "was indeed the first time that he had ever heard such unbecoming language given to the Parliament; and that it was the more horrid, in that it came from their servant, and their servant whom they had so highly trusted and obliged, and whom, by their unprecedented bounty, they had made what he was." Cromwell thrust his hat upon his head, sprang from his seat into the centre of the floor of the House, and shouted out: "Come, come, we have had enough of this; I'll put an end to your prating—Call them in!" he added briefly to Harrison; the door opened, and twenty or thirty musketeers entered, under the command of Lieutenant-Colonel Worsley.

"You are no Parliament," cried Cromwell; "I say, you are no Parliament! Begone! Give way to honester men." He walked up and down the floor of the House, stamping his foot, and giving his orders. "Fetch him down," he said to Harrison, pointing to the Speaker, who still remained in his chair. Harrison told him to come down, but Lenthall refused. "Take him down," repeated Cromwell; Harrison laid his hand on the Speaker's gown, and he came down immediately. Algernon Sidney was sitting near the Speaker. "Put him out," said Cromwell to Harrison. Sidney did not move. "Put him out," reiterated Cromwell. Harrison and Worsley laid their hands on Sidney's shoulders, upon which he rose, and walked out. "This is not honest," exclaimed Vane, "it is against morality and common honesty!" "Sir Harry Vane! Sir Harry Vane!" replied Cromwell; "you might have prevented this extraordinary course; but you are a juggler, and have not so much as common honesty. The Lord deliver me from Sir Harry Vane!" And, amidst the general confusion, as the members passed out before him, he flung nicknames in the face of each. "Some of you are drunkards!" he said, pointing to Mr. Challoner; "some of you are adulterers!" and he looked at Sir Peter Wentworth; "some of you are corrupt unjust persons!" and he glanced at Whitelocke and others; then, turning to Henry Martyn, he said, "Is a whoremaster fit to sit and govern?" He went up to the table on which the mace lay, which was carried before the Speaker, and called to the soldiers, "What shall we do with this bauble? here, take it away." He frequently repeated: "It is you that have forced me to this, for I have sought the Lord night and day, that he would rather slay me than put me upon the doing of this work." Alderman Allen told him, "That it was not yet gone so far, but all things might be restored again; and that, if the soldiers were commanded out of the House, and the mace returned, the public affairs might go on in their course." Cromwell rejected this advice, and called Allen to account for some hundred thousand pounds, which, as Treasurer of the army, he had embezzled. Allen replied, "That it was well known that it had not been his fault that his account was not made up long since; that he had often tendered it to the House, and that he asked no favor from any man in that matter." Cromwell ordered him to be arrested, and he was led off by the soldiers. The room was now empty; he seized all the papers, took the Dissolution-Bill from the Clerk, and put it under his cloak; after which he left the House, ordered the doors to be shut, and returned to Whitehall.[1]

At Whitehall, he found several of his officers, who had

[1] Whitelocke, p. 554; Leicester's Journal, pp. 139—141; Ludlow's Memoirs, pp. 193, 194; Old Parliamentary History, vol. xx. p. 128; Heath's Chronicle, p. 628; Bates, Elenchus Motuum Nuperorum, part ii. p. 284; Echard's History of England, vol. ii. p. 744; Peck's Memoirs of Oliver Cromwell, pp. 34—36; Clarendon's History of the Rebellion, vol. vii. pp. 1—7; Burton's Parliamentary Diary, vol. iii. pp. 98, 209.

In giving an account of the expulsion of the Long Parliament to M. Servien, in a letter dated May 3, 1653, M. de Bordeaux gives some details which I have not thought it right to insert in the text, as I find them mentioned by no contemporary English writer. They, moreover, appear to me very improbable, as they are at variance both with the general character of the event, and with all other accounts of it. But the letter which contains them deserves publication, and will be found in Appendix XXV.

remained there to wait the event. He related to them what he had done at the House. "When I went there," he said, "I did not think to have done this. But, perceiving the Spirit of God so strong upon me, I would not consult flesh and blood." A few hours later, in the afternoon, he was informed that the Council of State had just assembled in its ordinary place of meeting, in Whitehall itself, under the presidency of Bradshaw. He went to them immediately, followed only by Harrison and Lambert. "Gentlemen," he said, "if you are met here as private persons, you shall not be disturbed; but if as a Council of State, this is no place for you; and since you can't but know what was done at the House this morning, so take notice that the Parliament is dissolved." "Sir," answered Bradshaw, "we have heard what you did at the House in the morning, and before many hours all England will hear it. But, Sir, you are mistaken to think that the Parliament is dissolved; for no power under heaven can dissolve them but themselves. Therefore take you notice of that." All then rose and left the room. On the following day, the 21st of April, this announcement appeared in the *Mercurius Politicus*, which had become Cromwell's journal: "The Lord-General delivered yesterday in Parliament divers reasons wherefore a present period should be put to the sitting of this Parliament, and it was accordingly done, the Speaker and the members all departing. The grounds of which proceedings will, it is probable, be shortly made public." And, on the same day, a crowd collected at the door of the House to read a large placard which had probably been placed there during the night by some Cavalier who was overjoyed at finding his cause avenged on the republicans by a regicide; it bore this inscription:—

"This House to be let, unfurnished."[1]

[1] Ludlow's Memoirs, p. 194; Mercurius Politicus, No. 50, p. 238; Forster's Statesmen of the Commonwealth, vol. v. pp. 56—59.

APPENDIX.

APPENDIX.

APPENDIX I.

(Page 71.)

M. DE CROULLÉ TO CARDINAL MAZARIN.

Londres, 21 Juin, 1649.

. . . . Il s'était proposé de conférer quelques dignités dans le festin qui a été fait par la ville au Parlement et aux officiers de l'armée, ce qui a été remis à un autre temps. Lorsque le *speaker* y arriva, le maire de Londres vint au-devant de lui, et comme reconnaissant la souveraineté de l'Etat en sa personne, en qualité de chef du Parlement, lui remit la masse et l'épée, ainsi qu'il s'est toujours ci-devant pratiqué aux rois . . .

(Archives des affaires étrangères de France.)

APPENDIX II.

(Page 190.)

M. DE CROULLÉ TO CARDINAL MAZARIN.

Londres, 30 Juin, 1650.

After having given an account of the assassination of Ascham, at Madrid, he goes on to say:—

La nouvelle en fut sue dès hier matin; et ce jourd'hui l'ambassadeur d'Espagne en a reçu un exprès dont il a donné avis au conseil d'Etat, qui lui a envoyé le maître des cérémonies pour en savoir le détail et remercier le roi Catholique de la diligence dont il a usé pour trouver les coupables, et de la justice que l'on mande qu'il en fera faire. Si le dit roi eût fait autant d'état de l'envoyé de ses messieurs ici qu'euxmêmes en ont fait de celui de la province de Hollande, il n'eût pas éte logé dans une misérable hôtellerie, ni abandonné de sorté que, si le remords d'une mauvaise action n'eût aveuglé ceux qui l'ont commise, il n'y en aurait point eu de témoins. Je le rencontrai un peu avant qu'il partît d'ici, et parce que je le connaissais assez familièrement, lui dis que j'avais regret de ce que nous l'allions perdre, que est un terme assez ordinaire à notre langue en pareil cas; ce qu'il expliqua comme si je lui eusse prédit la même destinée qu'à Dorislaüs, qui lui est arrivée; dont il fut tout échauffé, jusqu'à, ce que je lui eus fait entendre ma pensée. . . . . Cet accident ne saurait rien altérer de la bonne intelligence que l'on suppose être entre cet Etat et l'Espagne, mais plutôt fournir moyen de la cimenter dans les remercîments et les compliments qui se feront réciproquement sur ce sujet. Je sais qu'en toutes choses ces gens-ci la favorisent au préjudice de la France.

(Archives des affaires étrangères de France.)

APPENDIX III.

(Page 192.)

I.—DELIBERATION ON THE STATE COUNCIL OF SPAIN ON THE CONSEQUENCES OF THE ASSASSINATION OF THE ENGLISH RESIDENT, ANTHONY ASCHAM.

Madrid, June 29, 1650.

SIRE: The Council of State, at which were present the Duke of Medina de la Torres, Don Francisco de Melo, the Marquis of Castel Rodrigo, and the Marquis of Valparaiso, has taken into its serious consideration the evil effects which may accrue to your Majesty's interests in consequence of the death of the Resident sent to this court by the Parliament of England, and of the person who served as his interpreter. Although this event was of such a character that it was impossible either for your Majesty, or for your ministers, to prevent it, for no one could have believed that it could have occurred at your Majesty's court and under your eyes, and no suspicion of it was awakened by any indication whatever—nevertheless, the Council of State is of opinion that the crime is of the utmost gravity on account of the circumstances which accompanied it, as the Resident had come hither under the favor of the shelter and protection of your Majesty. If such a crime were left unpunished, or did not receive exemplary chastisement, no one would believe himself in safety at your Majesty's court. Moreover, the Parliament of England might be filled with great resentment, and take some serious measure to obtain satisfaction, as it is to be feared it will do. Although your Majesty has already sent orders to the Court of Alcaldes to proceed as expeditiously as possible in this affair, that justice may be promptly done, the Council is of opinion that they are acting with greater slowness than the case requires; for it is an affair in which your Majesty's service and authority are deeply interested—one of those affairs, indeed, which should, without neglecting the requirements of justice, be despatched more quickly than is now the case, for it cannot admit of any negotiations whatever. For all these reasons, the Council considers it to be its duty to represent this to your Majesty, and to say that it will be necessary, as speedily as possible, to send a new order to the President of the Council, to declare to him that your Majesty's service requires that this affair should be proceeded with, within the strict limits of justice, and with as much haste and vigor as it is possible to apply to it. All that is done must be immediately reported to your Majesty, for the affair requires to be expedited and decided. Your Majesty will order whatever it may please you to command.

II.—RESOLUTIONS ADOPTED BY HIS MAJESTY THE KING, IN PURSUANCE OF THE ADVICE GIVEN BY THE COUNCIL OF STATE, ON THE OCCASION OF THE ARRIVAL OF THE RESIDENT OF THE PARLIAMENT OF ENGLAND, AND WITH REGARD TO THE PUNISHMENT OF HIS ASSASSINS.

Madrid, October, 1650.

1. In pursuance of the deliberations of the 3d of April, on the receipt of letters from the Duke of Medina Celi, in which he announced the arrival of the Resident of the Parliament in the port of Cadiz, his Majesty ordered that the duke should send him forward to Madrid, taking all necessary measures for his safety, and causing him to travel by the roads not infested by brigands. Letters to this effect were sent to the duke, who directed that the Resident should be accompanied by Don Diego de Moreda.

2. At another deliberation, on the 7th of June, his Majesty was informed of the arrival of the Resident at Madrid, and of his death, as well as that of his interpreter. On the same day the letters of credence were examined which the Resident was to have delivered to his Majesty, and information was received of the arrest of the five Englishmen who had assassinated him. His Majesty ordered that letters should be written to Don Alonzo de Cardeñas, to inform him of the occurrence and of the promptitude with which the assassins would be brought to trial, and to direct him to declare to the Parliament, that if they would send another person in the place of the assassinated Resident, they might do so. At the same time, his Majesty decided that an answer should be sent to the Parliament on the occasion of this event, and that this answer should serve Don Alonzo as his credentials on other occasions. All this was done conformably to the resolutions of his Majesty.

3. At another deliberation, on the 8th of the same month of June,

the Council met *in pleno* to discuss the form of address to be used in letters destined for the Parliament. On this point, his Majesty coincided with the opinion of the Marquis of Castel Rodrigo.

4. On the 15th of June another deliberation was presented to his Majesty, on the subject of a report from the President of the Council, stating that the aggressors demanded that, at their trial, the scutcheon and insignia found on the dead body underneath his clothes, should be produced, as well as the books which he had at his house. On this subject the Council represented to his Majesty that this should not be done until the said objects had been, in the first instance, handed over to the secretary who accompanied the Resident, for public faith could be observed only in this manner. The Council was of opinion that the trial of the culprits should be regularly conducted, but that the proceedings should be abridged as much as possible; as to the papers which might be made public and produced at the trial, it was for the criminal tribunal to decide, without any supreme action or secret interference on the part of his Majesty. These are the principles according to which it was judged fitting to proceed in this affair, and his Majesty was pleased to give them his sanction and approval.

5. At another deliberation, on the 8th of August, the Council, by its own movement, brought under his Majesty's consideration certain acts of maritime warfare on the part of the Parliament; and reminded him how powerful and irresistible the naval forces of the Parliament are; on this occasion also, the Council remarked that it had received no information as to the progress of the proceedings against the assassins who had murdered the Resident of the Parliament. It appeared to the Council that there had been great delay in pronouncing upon this affair, and executing his Majesty's orders: it was an affair which must not be lost sight of, on account of the reasons which have been already adduced at several deliberations; and the Council considered that these delays might inspire the Parliament with some resolution that would compel his Majesty sooner or later to take measures which he could now adopt without any embarrassment. The Council was of opinion that his Majesty should order the President of the Council to terminate this affair without further delay. To which his Majesty deigned to reply in these words: "The affair is diligently pursued, and rapidly advancing."

6. Another deliberation took place on the 3d of September, on the subject of letters received from Don Alonzo de Cardeñas, dated in the months of June and July, as well as of a letter which the Parliament had written to his Majesty to express their feelings with regard to the assassination of the Resident, and their hope that his Majesty would loyally execute justice on the murderers; for, they said, if such crimes

could be committed with impunity, in his Majesty's dominions, on any pretext whatever, they would inevitably be compelled to break off all relations between the two countries. These letters were read *in pleno concilio*; and, after having reflected on Don Alonzo's statements with regard to the forces of the Parliament, and the feeble condition of the royalist party in England: the Council, among other recommendations on the subject of the punishment to be inflicted on the Englishmen who have been arrested as guilty of the assassination, represented to his Majesty that the letter of the Parliament appeared to be an honest and respectful declaration that war would ensue unless, in some way or other, satisfaction were given them by the exemplary punishment of the crime which had been committed. This letter appeared to merit particular attention on the part of the Council, for it was evidently written under extra-judicial and incomplete notions of the affair, as Don Alonzo had not yet taken measures for placing in the hands of the Parliament the letter which his Majesty had addressed to them on the subject. The Council, therefore, deemed it expedient to remind his Majesty of what they had already expressed more than once, namely, that by this assassination the royal authority and dignity of his Majesty had received a serious injury, inasmuch as the Resident had come into Spain, under the safeguard of the public faith, and the protection of his Majesty; for which reasons it would be inexcusable to let the offenders go unpunished.

7. Another deliberation took place on the 7th September, on the subject of a letter from Don Alonzo de Cardeñas, dated on the 4th of August, in which he informed the king that the news had been published in London that the assassins of the Resident of the Parliament had been restored to the sanctuary of Church; in his letter Don Alonzo stated that the English Government was highly indignant at this, and made loud complaints, threatening to enforce satisfaction if it were not immediately given. On this occasion, the Council of State again represented to his Majesty how important it was, for all sorts of reasons set forth in the deliberation, to punish the assassins of the Resident; it can only repeat to his Majesty that it would be well for his Majesty to deign to decide this affair as speedily as possible, by sending the letter which Don Alonzo had just written on the subject, to the tribunal before which this affair is pending.

8. On the 9th of September there was another deliberation of the Council *in pleno*, and they transmitted to his Majesty the two deliberations above mentioned, as well as a third adopted after a special meeting. The Council discussed the question whether they should send to Don Alonzo an acknowledgment of the reception of his despatches, particularly of that in which he mentions the demands made by the Parliament in regard to the title and protocol which should be used in

addressing it. The Council was of opinion that it would be advisable for the punishment of the assassins of the Resident to precede the despatch of an answer to Don Alonzo. To which his Majesty replied as follows: "Act in conformity to the opinion of the Council, but send no answer to Don Alonzo until I give orders to that effect."

9. Finally, after the deliberation of the 15th of the present month of October, *in pleno concilio* on the subject of the despatches recently received from Don Alonzo, to the end that his Majesty should answer the Parliament and give it the titles which it demands, or else permit his ambassador to leave his post, and also in order to press the conclusion of the trial of the assassins of the Resident of England, his Majesty deigned to decide as follows:—

"In regard to the affair of those persons who have assassinated the Resident of the Parliament, I have given the necessary orders that they shall be proceeded against with all possible attention and as speedily as may be, without any contravention of the rules of justice; for at the same time I have recommended that everything shall be done according to the law, that there shall be no hurry, and that no reason of State shall cause more to be done than is just and right. I would rather lose my dominions than fail in doing that which is my first duty, and my Council of State will never advise me to do otherwise. If, as is probable, there should be any delay in pronouncing the sentence, Don Alonzo shall be informed of the state in which the affair stands, and we will send him a statement in the form proposed by the Council."

III.—DON ALONZO DE CARDEÑAS TO DON GERONIMO DE LA TORRE.

London, December 20, 1650.

Dear Sir: I was very much in want of the favor which you did me in writing to me what you wrote in your letter of the 25th of October, which reached me with his Majesty's Despatch of the 24th, for, judging from what I see, I shall have still to wait and endure a great deal. The people here are impatient at finding so many delays in receiving the satisfaction which they have demanded, and I have no human means of appeasing them. . . . What gives me most pain is to see that all my efforts will have been purely thrown away; that the interests of his Majesty will have been compromised, and that we shall lose the great advantage of maintaining disunion between this government and our enemies; when a remedy is sought for the evil, then it will be perceived that the opportunity has slipped away, and that the orders have come too late. I greatly fear that that unfortunate occurrence, the assassination of Ascham, may be the cause of much embarrassment and unpleasantness, unless punishment be immediately inflicted on the culprits, who so voluntarily and so blindly exposed themselves to such evident danger, and deprived us of all the advantages which we might otherwise have gained from England. It is truly extraordinary that in so atrocious a case means have not yet been found to bring it to an end, and that there should be members of the clergy in Spain who justify the crime, without making any distinction between particular cases and a crime so public and serious—a crime by which his Majesty's authority is outraged, and the interests of the State compromised, and from which immense inconveniences may probably result.

As to the war with Scotland, I may tell you that independently of the siege of the citadel of Edinburgh, which is already very far advanced, news have been received here of another defeat which General Cromwell has inflicted on the Scots, who have lost three thousand men, killed, wounded, and prisoners. The news from Ireland is, that the Catholics, finding it impossible to maintain their position, propose to send delegates to the Parliament to attempt an accommodation with it, and to obtain the best conditions possible.

(Archives of Simancas.)

APPENDIX IV.

(Page 193.)

I.—LOUIS XIV. TO CROMWELL.

Saint-Germain, 2 Février, 1649.

Monsieur Cromwell, j'ai le cœur si touché du mauvais état auquel est réduit mon frère, oncle et cousin, le roi de la Grande-Bretagne, que je ne puis plus longtemps dissimuler, sans être éclairé des véritables intentions de ceux qui ont sa personne royale en leur pouvoir, ne pouvant pas m'imaginer que ce qui s'est dit ici puisse avoir autre fin que de justifier son innocence, afin de faire honte à tous ses accusateurs; et comme vous êtes un de ceux qui y pouvez beaucoup contribuer, je vous écris celle-ci en particulier, de l'avis de la reine régente notre dame et mère, qui vous sera rendue par le sieur de Varenne, conseiller de mon conseil d'État et l'un de mes gentilshommes ordinaires, que j'envoie exprès pour vous faire connaître que vous avez en main une occasion de vous signaler, en faisant une action juste en faveur de votre souverain; en usant bien du pouvoir que les armes vous ont donné sur lui, pour le remettre dans sa dignité et dans ses droits, ce qui vous serait avantageux par la récompense que vous auriez méritée, et par le bien qui en reviendrait à votre patrie, le repos de laquelle vous devriez procurer: et ce faisant, je vous en serai obligé, et vous donnerai de solides effets de ma bonne volonté. Je veux bien juger de votre intérieur, et croire que vous vous servirez de l'occasion pour redonner à votre prince les marques de la grandeur et l'autorité qui lui appartiennent, faisant une chose fort glorieuse et qui vous rendra digne de toutes les grâces et faveurs, particulièrement de la royauté, et qui vous seront assurées par la parole que je vous ai donnée, et par ce que mes intentions vous seront plus particulièrement expliquées par M. de Bellièvre, mon ambassadeur, et par ledit Sieur de Varenne, en qui vous prendrez toute créance. Je m'en remets à eux de s'étendre davantage sur ce sujet, et cependant je prierai Dieu qu'il vous ait, etc.

II.—LOUIS XIV. TO FAIRFAX.

2 Février, 1649.

Monsieur le général Fairfax, nous avons toujours cru que vous aviez pris le commandement des armées d'Angleterre avec cette seule intention d'assurer le repos des peuples sous la juste et légitime domination de leur roi, et nous ne pouvons pas nous imaginer que sa personne royale, étant tombée sous votre pouvoir, puisse davantage être maltraitée, et que, si vous avez quelques raisons qui vous aient engagé d'en venir si avant, vous serez maintenant plus éclairé, et, après avoir reconnu ce qui est seul de sa dignité, ne perdrez pas l'occasion d'agrandir votre fortune en rétablissant la sienne. En quoi, si mes prières peuvent être efficaces, et qu'il se traite quelque accommodement en la conjoncture présente, non-seulement je vous en saurai gré, mais je veux être le garant de l'exécution des promesses qui vous seront faites par ledit roi, mon frére, oncle et cousin; et faisant réflexion sur ce qui vous sera plus particulièrement exposé par M. de Bellièvre et par le Sieur de Varenne, je prends sujet de bien espérer de votre humeur généreuse, qui donnera beaucoup d'éclat à sa réputation, si l'innocence du roi est manifestée; et ne pouvant m'imaginer qu'on voulût mépriser mes instances en une chose si juste et si raisonnable, et qui me tient au cœur par le lien du sang et de la fraternité, aussi je me persuade qu'après avoir ouï ce que j'ai mis en créance sur mon ambassadeur et sur ledit Sieur de Varenne, vous prendrez des résolutions conformes à l'honneur de votre profession, et à ce que doit un sujet à son roi et à sa patrie. Sur vos assurances, je prierai Dieu qu'il vous ait, etc.

(Manuscrits de Brienne.—Bibliothèque Impériale, Paris.)

APPENDIX V.

(Pages 195, 213.)

I.—DON ALONZO DE CARDEÑAS TO THE KING (PHILIP IV.) OF SPAIN.

London, January 15, 1649.

SIRE: In my despatch of the 18th December, I informed your Majesty of what the army of the Independents had done up to that day, since their arrival in London. Matters have since proceeded with great rapidity, to terminate in the position in which the affairs of the king (Charles I.) are at this moment. He has been transferred from Hurst Castle to Windsor, distant about twenty miles from this place; there he is kept confined under a strong and trusty guard; no one is allowed to speak to him; he has been refused the materials necessary for writing; and the small number of servants who have been left him, have been forbidden to kneel when they serve him, and to observe in their treatment of him the customary ceremonies and forms of respect with which he was formerly attended: in the printed publications, issued to-day, he is named simply Charles Stuart, without any other titles. Apart from the insolence of this proceeding, there is in it an infringement of his rights, for even if he should be deprived of the crown of this kingdom, there would still remain to him the crowns of Scotland and Ireland, of which the Parliament cannot strip him. .

The Queen of Great Britain has written to the Parliament and to General Fairfax, and the ambassador of France has received letters addressed to the Parliament. It is said that it (the Parliament) has not opened them on the ground that the address was not couched in the form prescribed; and it is rumored that they contained a request for a safe-conduct to take leave of the king before his Majesty is brought to trial.

For some days, a report has been current here that an ambassador will be sent from France to interpose on behalf of the king; but as yet it is not stated who this ambassador will be, for the Prince of Condé, who was mentioned as the probable envoy, will have enough to do at home. According to the last news received here, there have been tumults in Paris, which compelled their most Christian Majesties to escape from that capital, on the eve of the Epiphany. In the same manner there has been a report here—propagated, as I believe, by persons who are friendly to the king—that your Majesty was about to send an extraordinary ambassador for the purpose of making intercessions of the same character; and two days ago, when it became evident that the king's cause was becoming more and more desperate, a person, sent by other persons belonging to the royal and presbyterian parties, came to me to persuade me that, as the cause of all kings was at stake, and as it was important that monarchy should be preserved in the person of King Charles I., it was my duty, in your Majesty's interest, and to make good the expressions of friendship which your Majesty has always used towards King Charles—it was my duty, I say, to demand an audience of both Houses of Parliament and of the Council of War, and to employ my good offices with the promptitude which circumstances required, by declaring that your Majesty would strongly resent the proceedings which have been taken in regard to the king, and by making use even of threatening language; he added, that such a step would afterwards be appreciated by the king's sons, the probability being that the crown will revert to one of them. While expressing my sorrow at seeing matters brought to such an extremity, and dwelling very forcibly on the impression which the news would cause your Majesty, I replied that I had no doubt that your Majesty would, if necessary, appoint an extraordinary ambassador to represent you here, or would deign to give me special orders to take the steps suggested; but that, without such orders, I did not venture to undertake a matter of such a nature and of so much weight and importance. This same person told me that he believed that the Queen of Great Britain would write to me, to beg me to employ my good offices; but I doubt whether she will do so, for it is probable that she will have understood that, as my excuses may rest on want of instructions, I should not fail to allege that excuse to her; especially as the queen cannot be ignorant that, whatever exertions may be used, nothing will prevent the Parliament and army from pursuing the course which they have adopted towards the king. The Independents, either with a view to conciliate the English Catholics and to prevent them from making any demonstration in favor of the king, or because such conduct is in accordance with the great principle of that sect, liberty of conscience, have led the Catholics to hope for such liberty, and they have great expectations of obtaining it, or at least of obtaining permission to practise their worship, and the abrogation of those penal laws which are now in force against them. This is all I have to communicate to your Majesty. . . .

II.—DON ALONZO DE CARDEÑAS TO THE KING OF SPAIN.

London, February 18, 1649.

SIRE: In my despatch of the 12th of this month, I informed your Majesty of the melancholy end of the King of Great Britain. I have reserved for my present letter an explanation of the turn which the affairs of this country are likely to take. The general opinion is that the monarchical government will give place to a popular government, by the establishment of a republic, the plan of which, as I have been assured, has already been prepared for some time, and will be published ere long. It is also stated that the present Parliament will only last until the end of the month of April following; it will then dissolve, leaving a committee of twenty-five persons, or more, invested with the supreme authority, until the first Thursday in June, at which period it will resign its powers to a new government, composed of a national Representative of four hundred persons, appointed by the counties and towns of England; each electoral district will have to elect a certain number of delegates, in conformity to the Act which the Parliament is to pass before its dissolution; these delegates will be, as it were, the proxies of the town or county which may choose them, as were those who up to this time formed the House of Commons. By this arrangement, there will no longer be a Parliament, and the body which it is proposed to create, will differ from Parliament by the fact of its sitting permanently; but those who compose it will be elected for only two years. It is believed that this plan has been invented for the purpose of excluding from the government of the country all the nobility and persons of title, unless they are elected by some county or town. As the Independents did not think this sufficient, the House of Commons decided by vote, on the 16th of this month, that in future there should be no Upper House or House of Lords. This is part of a system they have adopted with a view to efface from the minds of many the grief caused by the execution of the king, by making it appear that, when the House of Lords is once removed from all share in the government, the affairs of the country will remain altogether in the hands of the people, whose power and authority will thereby be largely increased. In consequence of these resolutions, there will be great changes made in the laws, which, hitherto, have been framed in accordance with the monarchical constitution of the country; these changes are already under discussion, and statutes are being prepared abrogating the ancient laws. It is hoped that, among the laws destined to be thus abrogated, will be included the penal laws concerning the Catholics; a matter which, if it really occurs, must be ascribed to the special decrees of God, who has desired to manifest the immutability of his designs by affording relief, in ways so mysterious and unexpected, to the poor Catholics, who have suffered such terrible persecution. Even now, thanks to the Independents, the Catholics can appear freely in this capital and throughout the country, without any one doing them any harm; although it may be feared that this is only a ruse of the Independents, in order to conciliate the Catholic party, by modifying the severities with which they have been treated by the Presbyterians.

As the king is no longer living, and his descendants are excluded from the throne, it appears that the credentials of all the ambassadors are expired, and that every sovereign will have to grant new letters of credence to his envoy, to accredit him not only to the present Parliament so long as it lasts, but also to the government which it is proposed to introduce. It appears that these credentials must be preceded by a recognition of this Government as a lawful power, and that it will be necessary to use appropriate formalities in addressing it, and to treat it as a sovereign, to which title it will lay claim. As this is a point of great importance, I have thought it my duty to call your Majesty's attention to this subject, that you may be pleased to give me such instructions as you may think fit. Through having anticipated these inconveniences, I thought it my duty to represent to your Majesty, in my despatch of the 20th of August of last year, which I transmitted through the Secretary Geronimo della Torre, that it would be to the interest of your Majesty's service, that there should be no ambassador here from your Majesty, but only an agent who might give an account of all that occurred, until such time as matters resumed their stability, and it became possible to perceive in what this Government was likely to end. Now, I am inclined to believe that, if your Majesty adopted this resolution, we should avoid the embarrassment which could not fail to arise in case your Majesty should not deign to recognize the Government which it is proposed to create, and to renew my credentials; if that Government were to demand them of me, and I could not present them, it would cease to regard me as invested with a public character, and as the ambassador of your Majesty.

The States of Holland had sent two ambassadors to the Parliament to intercede on behalf of the late king; they arrived here on the 5th of this month, during the night preceding the day on which sentence was pronounced against the king. On the 8th, they had an audience of the Parliament, and proposed various combinations: they offered their mediation on behalf of the king, who, they said, should appear for trial whenever required, and the States engaged to give sureties for the performance of the promise; but as this proposition was not accepted, the ambassadors begged the Parliament to rest satisfied with deposing the king, and sparing his life, and to accept the Prince of Wales as king in his stead; they offered the same mediation, and the same sureties in relation to the accomplishment of any agreement that might be made with the prince. But the Parliament, before even giving an answer to the ambassadors, ordered the execution of the sentence, and forbade all persons to proclaim the Prince of Wales, king of England and Ireland. The ambassadors are consequently in a state of much dissatisfaction and irritation; one of them is Adrian de Pauw, our old friend in Holland—the same who was plenipotentiary for Holland at Munster, at the conclusion of the general peace. I have seen them already, and have been on terms of friendship and correspondence with them; yesterday they paid me a visit, and manifested great affection and satisfaction.

The archduke wrote me a letter on the 6th of this month; I received it on the 10th, the day after the execution of the king; in it he ordered me to employ my good offices with all the earnestness necessary, in requesting a delay in the king's trial until the arrival of a person whom his sovereign had resolved to send specially on his behalf. But even if the archduke's letter had not arrived too late, it is certain that no human efforts could have prevented the Independents from pursuing, towards the king, the course they had once adopted: their obstinacy in procuring his death was incredible; it was based on their fears, for his death alone could secure them against the consequences of the offence of which they had been guilty against him, and his existence was an obstacle to the plans which they wish to put in execution. This was very evident, not only from the strange and violent manner in which his trial was conducted, but also from the rapidity with which its conclusion was hastened. On the 23d of January the king arrived during the night in London; on the following day he was brought to trial; on the 6th of the present month of February he was condemned, and on the 9th he was executed; without the loss of a single hour either for his trial or for his execution. And, indeed, nothing less was to have been expected from his judges, for, not only were they perfectly illegal, and without any authority to sit in judgment upon him, but they were his enemies, and the men most interested in his ruin. No titled personage or baron took part in his trial; on the contrary, most of them have left London; a great many have not yet returned, and others keep themselves out of sight. The ambassadors of France and Holland have put themselves and their households into mourning; I have done the same; it was a mark of respect due to the memory of the king; and besides, any one who neglected to do so would be looked upon unfavorably. May God keep your Majesty! . .

III.—DELIBERATION OF THE SPANISH COUNCIL OF STATE CONCERNING THE AFFAIRS OF ENGLAND.

Madrid, March 13, 1649.

(At this meeting of the Council of State, the Count of Castrillo, and the Marquises of Castel Rodrigo and Valparaiso, took part in the proceedings.)

Summary.—The Council expressed its opinion on the contents of the despatches of Don Alonzo de Cardeñas regarding the affairs of England, and the projects of the French against Ireland. Then follows a decision docketed in the king's handwriting, and to the following effect: "No answer shall be returned (to Don Alonzo) in reference to the excuse which he has used for not interceding with the Parliament on behalf of King Charles I.; but his conduct shall be approved in the negotiation with Abbé ——, and in his efforts to create a diversion from the projects of the French; no new powers, however, shall be given him, for after an event so important and extraordinary as the one in question, it is necessary, before adopting any resolution, to see the change which will take place in the affairs of England, and to examine what it will best suit us to do."—Executed on the 15th of March. GERONIMO DE LA TORRE.

SIRE: The letters of Don Alonzo de Cardeñas, brought by the last courier to your Majesty, and to the Secretary Geronimo de la Torre, have been laid before the Council, in conformity with your Majesty's direction. These letters give your Majesty a detailed account of the state of things in England, of the danger to which the king was exposed in consequence of the nomination of the judges who were to inquire into the charges brought against him, and of the fears entertained that he would be deprived of life. They mention the rumour which prevailed of the arrival of an extraordinary ambassador from France to intercede with the Parliament in favor of the king; and they state that, in consequence of this rumour, certain persons belonging to the royal and Presbyterian parties spoke to Don Alonzo to induce him—since it was important to the cause of all kings that monarchy should be preserved in the person of the King of England, as well as a duty arising from the friendship which your Majesty has always manifested for that prince—to demand an audience of the Parliament, and to employ his good offices in your Majesty's name, stating that your Majesty would be offended if the king were brought to trial; to which Don Alonzo replied that he deplored the danger to which the king was exposed, that your Majesty would feel deep grief on learning all that had occurred, and that he had no doubt that you would send, if necessary, an extraordinary ambassador to employ his good offices, or would send to him personally, orders to make the representations suggested; but that, without such orders, he did not dare to engage in a matter of such a nature and of such great importance. The despatches of Don Alonzo further state that the Independents have given hopes to the Catholics in relation to liberty of conscience, with a view to secure their support, and to prevent them from making any demonstration in favor of the king.

Don Alonzo then relates the manner in which he set to work to place Abbé ——, an Irishman, who came from Paris, in communication with the Parliament. This Abbé gave them to understand, in certain conferences which he had with a committee of five persons specially appointed to treat this question, that the French had designs on foot against Ireland, of which the members of the committee already had some inkling; he also communicated to them certain papers concerning this affair, and supplied them with copies of the same. . . .

. . . . At that conference, the means were discussed of concluding an alliance with your Majesty, either for an offensive and defensive war, or for a defensive war only; and the members of the conference saw no hindrance to it, except in the embarrassment of their home affairs, which did not allow them to act as they could wish abroad. .

Don Alonzo observes that, in case there is a convention to be concluded, it will be necessary for your Majesty to send him full and sufficient powers, and a supply of money—which is indispensable, especially when one has to deal with so interested a nation as the English.

Don Alonzo next reports that he has done his best to induce the English Parliament to maintain friendly relations with the Parliament of France, and to encourage it in its resolutions; he was told that a letter would be written to direct the English Resident in Paris to offer the assistance of the fleet, as well as other succors. Finally, Don Alonzo ends by saying that it would be advisable for your Majesty to send some assistance in money to the party of the Irish clergy, as by that means we should gain certain persons in that country; and he adds, that Abbé —— is striving with the greatest zeal to bring about an agreement between the English Parliament and the kingdom of Ireland, in order that their united forces may drive out the Scots and Irish who are marching together under the protection of France. Don Alonzo says that he will lend his assistance to this plan, which will prove most advantageous to the interests of God and of your Majesty. He enters most fully into this subject in his despatches, which the Council lay before your Majesty, with their present deliberation.

The Council, after having conferred on the contents of these despatches, expressed the following opinions:—

The Count de Castrillo: The first part of the despatch which has been laid before the Council, and which was sent by Don Alonzo, contains reports of what is passing in England, especially on the subject of the imprisonment and trial of the king, and of the catastrophe which is expected to occur: this is an affair which, for several reasons, may, and must give rise to profound considerations, although it no longer requires any order or resolution on the part of your Majesty, for it appears that any intervention or remonstrance whatever with the Parliament, or with the tribunal appointed to judge this case, would be inopportune if what was anticipated has already been accomplished; it is even said that the king of England has already been beheaded. The efforts of your Majesty would, therefore, be fruitless, and the Count de Castrillo does not think that Spain has taken any such step on other occasions, that is, when other Kings of England have been deposed. Besides, when the affair has once been placed on a judicial footing, it was easy to elude any interference. Only the Count de Castrillo could have desired that Don Alonzo should not have said that he had no orders from your Majesty, but rather that he should have given his questioners to understand that he was expecting orders. There will be great need for reflection as to the answer to be sent him; but in order not to fall into either extreme, we might, alleging as our reasons the reports and conjectures which are current on the subject of Don Alonzo's statement, reply that his interference would be inopportune; or we might pass this point entirely in silence. This would not be the worst plan to adopt.

The other part of the despatch concerns the machinations of the French, as well as the parley, negotiations, and parties of the kingdom of Ireland—the journey which Abbé —— has recently made—the steps taken by Don Alonzo to obtain his entrance into London, and the report of this business and of his conduct in it. In the first place, he must be approved; and as it is important, as much as possible, to procure the failure of the projects of the French, we might reply to Don Alonzo that he must act with this end in view, and maintain, as he seems determined to do, for your Majesty's advantage, his friendly relations with the members of the clergy and with the old Irish, as well as with those who belong to their party, in all that concerns religion, for that is your Majesty's principal interest.

In the remainder of the despatch, Don Alonzo demands of your Majesty full powers, in case it were possible, to conclude an alliance with England. Setting aside the fact that your Majesty is not greatly disposed to conclude treaties with heretics (for this point is well deserving consideration), the Count de Castrillo does not think that your Majesty should now send the full powers which are requested by Don Alonzo. The order of things in England is not yet firmly established; affairs are still in a period of crisis; causes of great disturbance may yet arise; to all which must be added the affairs of France. It appears, therefore, more becoming not to decide this matter at this moment, and to reply to Don Alonzo that full powers shall not be wanting as soon as circumstances shall render them necessary. Let him still continue to open the way for negotiations advantageous to your Majesty, by thoroughly examining all things, and let him continue to report whatever occurs.

The Marquis de Castel Rodrigo: Although the King of England (Charles I.) behaved very ill towards your Majesty in the affair of Portugal, and under other circumstances, all princes cannot but deeply resent that which has happened to him, on account of the affront offered thereby to royal dignity generally. On the other hand, the

Marquis thinks that great advantages will result therefrom to your Majesty, by reason of the hatred and distrust which must necessarily spring up between the Independents and France, not only on account of the ties of relationship of the king's widow with France, but also because of the fall of the Presbyterians, who belonged to the French party. The men now in power will always seek to put down the patrons of the Presbyterians; and as the power of France is great, they must apply themselves to raise up embarrassments to her policy, and to sow divisions in her midst; this they will be better able to do than any others, on account of their vicinity, and of their understanding with the Huguenots. In this manner, and by this means, we may do a great deal without appearing to do anything, as the Marquis has already suggested to Don Luiz de Haro. And the Marquis even feels no scruple that your Majesty should assist the Huguenots of France, for the war which their king has waged against them, was not a war of religion, but of politics; he waged it only against the walls of their towns, which he destroyed, leaving them the free exercise of their religion; besides, *liberty of conscience is admitted* all over France. To this must be added the great prejudice which the internal tranquillity of France has occasioned to all Christendom, for thereby the Catholic religion has perished in Germany, and the island of Candia has fallen into the power of the Turks; so that all that can possibly be done to embarrass the French seems to the Marquis to be absolutely necessary. . . . .

In the opinion of the Marquis, therefore, we should be obliged to Don Alonzo for what he has done in this respect, and should give him express orders to continue to act thus, and to foment these discords by all means in his power, keeping always in communication with the Count de Penaranda, for, even if peace should be made, it would be necessary to act thus in order to preserve it. . . . .

. . . . When circumstances prove favorable, full powers may properly be sent to Don Alonzo. For the present, it will be best to tell him that they are not sent now for the reasons explained above; unless your Majesty should think fit to transmit them to the Count de Penaranda to be forwarded to Don Alonzo when the opportune moment arrives.

The Marquis thinks, with the Count de Castrillo, that, in the answer to be sent to Don Alonzo, we should pass over in silence all that concerns the intervention he was requested to attempt in favor of the king (Charles I.).

THE MARQUIS DE VALPARAISO concurred in the opinions expressed by his colleagues.

. . . . As to Don Alonzo's statement that the Parliament of England intends to offer aid to that of France, we must encourage it to do so, and afterwards seek, by all possible means, to procure its failure, even if it should be necessary to spend money on the matter. Don Alonzo also should be recommended, as he has such detailed information,·from such reliable sources, regarding them ovements and proceedings of France, to continue to inform your Majesty of everything without neglecting any opportunity for doing so. However, your Majesty will ordain whatever may seem good to you.

APPENDIX VI.

(Page 197.)

(Page 197.)

I.—THE ARCHDUKE LEOPOLD (GOVERNOR OF THE NETHERLANDS) TO THE KING OF SPAIN (PHILIP IV.)

Brussels, March 4, 1649.

HENRI DE VIC, Resident of the late King of England, being on the point of returning to the Hague, has requested me to write to his master to express my feelings of condolence with him on the death of his father (Charles I.), and thus to reply to two letters which he wrote me while he was styled the Prince of Wales. There was no difficulty about treating with this prince until the moment when England, after having taken the life of her king and legitimate sovereign, decided by act of parliament that she would no longer be governed by a king, and at the same time stripped the descendants of the defunct monarch of their lawful inheritance. As there is at this moment in London an ambassador from your Majesty, who has not yet received instructions as to the manner in which he is to act towards the Parliamentarians, I felt unwilling to be the first to decide the question, how the prince is to be treated, who has been so unjustly and unlawfully despoiled of his kingdom and dominions. I have heard it stated that the Dutch have sent delegates to express their condolence to the prince, and that these envoys called him *Sire* in French, and that once even they styled him *Your Majesty*, but pronounced the word indistinctly, and decline to put in writing what they had said verbally. Wherefore, I have directed the Secretary of State to explain to the English Resident the reasons which prevented my answering the prince's letters, and determined me to wait until my master the Emperor and your Majesty should have first arranged this matter with his master; I added that, if I were not here as governor of these provinces, I should not, in my quality of a son of the Emperor and an Archduke of the empire, refuse the prince a title conferred on him by his birth and descent from so long a line of kings. The Resident appeared satisfied with my answer, and sent to me to request me to write officially to his Majesty the Emperor, and to your Majesty, to beseech you not to fail of performing this pious duty towards his master, seeing that all Europe is in suspense regarding the resolution which the two greatest sovereigns in the world are likely to adopt on this matter. Your Majesty will be pleased to acquaint me with your orders as to the manner in which I must act under these circumstances. Until then, I shall defer any communications with a prince so unfortunate in every respect. God keep your Majesty!

II.—FIRST DRAFT OF A LETTER FROM THE KING OF SPAIN (PHILIP IV.) TO THE NEW KING OF ENGLAND.

Madrid, March 10, 1649.

News of the death of King Charles, your Majesty's father, has reached me here from various quarters. I was filled by it with deep feelings of grief, on account of the relationship and close friendship which united us. I express my great grief at it to your Majesty, and, as is just, I communicate to you the pain which that event has caused me, as your Majesty will easily understand, by the Councillor Anthony Brun, my ambassador in the United Provinces, who will deliver these presents to your Majesty, whom may God have in his holy keeping!

[This draft was afterwards modified, and sent in the following terms:—]

THE KING OF SPAIN TO THE KING (CHARLES II.) OF ENGLAND.

Condolence on the occasion of his father's death.

April 5, 1649.

News of the sad event of the death of his Majesty King Charles, your Majesty's father, has reached me here from various quarters: I have been afflicted by it with the pain and sorrow which could not fail to be provoked by circumstances so extraordinary and deplorable; for even if there had not existed, to produce these sentiments, either the ties of relationship or the intimate friendship which united us, I should have found sufficiently powerful motives to grief in the excellent qualities which were combined in the person of the king, and with which God, in his goodness, had been pleased to endow him. I can conceive what affliction your Majesty will have felt, both on account of your loss, and of the manner in which it occurred; I can assure your Majesty that the affliction which I have experienced, both on account of the event and of all its circumstances, is not inconsiderable. I beg to express my condolence with your Majesty, and I am sure that, thanks to your wisdom and firmness, your Majesty will be resigned to the will of God, who disposes all things for the best; and this is what I beg your Majesty to do. For this and for all the rest, I depend upon what your Majesty will hear from the mouth of my councillor, Anthony Brun, who will deliver this letter to your Majesty.

(Inside the letter is written: to the new King of England.)

III.—DELIBERATION OF THE SPANISH COUNCIL OF STATE UPON THE DESPATCHES OF THE SPANISH AMBASSADOR IN LONDON, AND UPON THE POLICY TO BE PURSUED TOWARDS ENGLAND.

29th March, 1649.

SIRE: Your Majesty has deigned to command that a meeting of the Council of State *in pleno* be summoned for Sunday evening to take cognizance of the letters of Don Alonzo de Cardeñas of the dates of the 12th, 18th, and 26th of February, as well as of a letter from the Archduke Leopold of the 4th instant. In these letters an account is given of what has occurred to the King of England, of all the circumstances that have taken place until the hour of his death, of the turn that affairs are about to take in England, of the resolution of the English to allow themselves no longer to be governed by a king, of the exclusion of the offspring of the late king, and of their deliberations upon the form of Government to be adopted in future. . . . . Don Alonzo begs to be informed how he is to act in these circumstances, considering that his mission has expired; he also explains in these letters why he has not employed his good offices with the Parliament in favor of the king, as had been demanded of him; he states that he has gone into mourning for the king because the representatives of France and Holland have done so; and speaks of the proclamation of the Prince of Wales as king by the Scotch. Monseigneur, the archduke, begs likewise to be informed in what manner he should treat the Prince of Wales, considering that the representative of that Prince has begged him to reply to two letters which he had sent him on his behalf, and to address some words of consolation to him in so sad and deplorable a conjuncture.

The Count de Monterey, the Duke of Medina de la Torres, and the Marquises of Castel Rodrigo and Valparaiso have taken part in the Council; the Count de Castrillo has excused himself on the plea of ill health. The Council, after a lengthened discussion upon the contents of the said despatches, sets forth the following considerations to your Majesty.

The matter concerning the King of England is a very extraordinary event, and one worthy of mature consideration, seeing that it is the subjects themselves of the King of England who have deprived him of life by such detestable means, and with no other motives than those given by Don Alonzo in his despatches. The Council regards this event as so evil an example, that it would be a just thing for all princes to unite together to inflict an exemplary punishment on the English Parliament. At the same time the Council thinks, on the other hand, that your Majesty would not be able to embark in it, on account of the numerous embarrassing affairs with which you are surrounded, and of so many pressing wars in which your Majesty is engaged both in Spain and abroad: the other princes, who ought equally to take part in it, are occupied with their own concerns, especially the King of France, who is embarrassed by the war he has himself stirred up, and by discords and dissensions among his own subjects, as everybody knows; the English Parliament is so powerful that no one could now overthrow what it has done; this same Parliament has testified the intention of maintaining favorable relations with your Majesty, in which, far from failing your Majesty, it has rendered you service; further, it would serve to foment the bad understanding between the Parliament and the French, and would accord with the old maxim according to which it is always of the greatest advantage to Spain to live in peace with England and preserve her friendship. Guided by these motives, the Council is of opinion that at present, and until time should reveal some other combination, it would not be suitable for your Majesty to introduce any change in your policy, but that, on the contrary, it would be more advisable to maintain good relations with the Parliament. The Council adds that your Majesty owed very little to the late King of England, who, immediately after the insurrection of Portugal, had received the ambassador of the tyrant, forgetting the intimate friendship which bound him to your Majesty. All that can be done at present (in the opinion of the Council) is to reply to the archduke, by telling him that he can answer the letters addressed to him by the Prince of Wales, giving him the title of "your Majesty" and all his other titles; the Council is also of opinion that, in order to act prudently towards the Parliament who might take offence at it, it would be well that the letter (of the archduke) should be predated, so that it might be said that it had been written before the news was received that the Parliament had excluded the posterity of the late king from the throne.

The Council thinks that, in the same manner, your Majesty might address a letter to the Prince of Wales predated, expressing to him the grief which the death of his father had occasioned your Majesty, and telling him that this news had reached your Majesty from various quarters, and that you were unwilling to lose a single moment in testifying your sentiments; the Council thinks that it would be well to send this letter to the archduke, to the end that he should confide it, together with that which his Highness shall himself write, to the Councillor Brun, who ought to be already in Holland, or nearly there; it would be desirable that, on the part of your Majesty, as well as on that of the Emperor, there was an expression of condolence in suitable form, and that the archduke rendered an account to your Majesty of what resulted from it, and of everything that occurred.

The Council conceives that it would be inexpedient to make any formal declaration, either in favor of the Prince of Wales or the Parliament, until it is known with greater certainty what course things will take; it would be desirable to make the archduke acquainted with these motives, so that he may conform himself to the events which may arise. The same instructions ought to be given to Don Alonzo, approving at the same time, of his having gone into mourning for the King of England; he should equally be told that, for the present, no other charge should be made, and that, if any proposals of negotiation should be made to him, he ought to listen to them with pleasure, and reply that he would render an account of the whole to your Majesty. The Council think, that, for the rest, it is better that things should go on as before, for there is no reason to think that the Parliamentarians desire any change in their relations with Spain, nor that they entertain any doubt about the intentions of Don Alonzo to treat with them, seeing that the Parliament is only at the commencement of its career, and that it would best suit it to strengthen its position by the continued residence of the ambassadors of foreign powers. If the contrary should happen, Don Alonzo will demand time for the opportunity of informing your Majesty. Don Alonzo should likewise be recommended to take very particular care to inform your Majesty daily, and in all ways, of whatever shall take place in England; it will be necessary to write the same thing to the archduke.

The Council being of opinion that it would be desirable for your Majesty to make some manifestation on the occasion of the death of King Charles, thinks that the most suitable mode would be for your Majesty to go into mourning in the same form as on the occasion of the death of the late King Louis of France. .

Your Majesty will command whatever your Majesty pleases.

IV.—DELIBERATION OF THE SPANISH COUNCIL OF STATE ON THE SUBJECT OF SEVERAL LETTERS FROM DON ALONZO DE CARDEÑAS, TREATING OF VARIOUS MATTERS.

Madrid, 6th June, 1649.

[Written by the King's hand: "Let it be done in conformity with the advice of the Council. Executed at mid-day." GERONIMO DE LA TORRE.]

SIRE: The Count of Monterey, the Duke of Medina de la Torres, and the Marquises of Castel Rodrigo, Valparaiso, and Velada, being present in Council, have, agreeably to the commands of your Majesty, taken into consideration the letters of Don Alonzo de Cardeñas, of the dates of the 13th and 27th of April, and the 3d of May, in which, among other things, Don Alonzo gives a detailed account to your Majesty of the state of English affairs at that period, of the conversation which he had held with an agent of the Parliament relative to the desire of the Parliament to maintain friendly relations with your Majesty, and to know if an ambassador sent by the Parliament would be favorably received in Spain. Don Alonzo also informs your Majesty that he has received a letter from Mr. Francis Cottington, dated from the Hague, in which the latter announces to Don Alonzo the resolution taken by his master, the Prince of Wales, of sending him (Cottington) to Spain, accompanied by another person, for the purpose of unfolding to your Majesty the condition of his affairs, and of asking for your assistance; he stated that he had set out in the month of May, and passed through Brussels. Don Alonzo relates also what he had said in reply.

The Council, after having examined this subject with very particular attention, considers it one of the gravest questions which could present themselves, and is of opinion that there is occasion for your Majesty's most prudent reflections, since the arrival of Cottington in Spain cannot fail to lead to great inconvenience; firstly, because it is not yet known what resolutions will be taken in France, with respect to the same proposition which has already been, or is about to be made by a person sent thither by the same prince (the Prince of Wales); and next, on account of the present condition of your Majesty's affairs in the midst of the numerous trials with which it has pleased God to visit you. The circumstance of the English Parliament having likewise proposed to send a person to Spain is attended with equally great inconvenience. It would be undesirable to make any declaration before the Parliament shall have well established itself, and can offer further guarantees of its durability. All these points require mature and profound examination before arriving at any resolution, and it is certain that there is much to be said on both sides. The Council, while in abstaining from expressing one at the present time, and until circumstances require it, represents to your Majesty that it considers it important (after the intelligence received of the departure of F. Cottington and his companion for Spain) to despatch a courier with all haste to the archduke to inform him of the contents of the letters of Don Alonzo de Cardeñas on the subject of these two points, namely, the arrival of Cottington, and the question put relative to the manner in which a person sent by the Parliament would be received in Spain; the archduke should be told that, if Cottington arrives at Brussels, or passes through Flanders, his highness should endeavor, in private, and with all possible address, to converse with him, and learn (as if it were of his highness's own accord) with what object he wished to repair to Spain, and with what mission he is charged. His highness will tell him in conversation that, considering the state of affairs, it would be more correct for him to remain at Brussels, to put himself in communication with his highness before proceeding further, and to acquaint him with the object of his negotiation, to the end that he might inform your Majesty of it, and receive your reply before he (Cottington) had engaged too far in his journey. By circuitous proceedings, and without depriving him of hope, but, on the contrary, testifying the utmost good-will, and assuring him of your Majesty's benevolence, and what he might hope from it, his highness could tell him how serviceable it would be, for the restoration of the Prince of Wales, that peace should be concluded between France and Spain, for that this would be the secret means of obtaining the advantages that are desired and proposed to be obtained. In order to be able to deliberate with greater certainty, the archduke ought to make known to your Majesty the reception events have met with in France, what is there proposed to be done, and what reply has been made there to the Prince of Wales's envoy. His highness should be made to feel of what consequence it is that Cottington and his companion should not persist in their intention of coming to Spain, and, if possible, that they should not come at all; at the same time addressing them in the terms of friendship and good-will; and if, notwithstanding all the efforts of his highness, Cottington absolutely resolves to come, his highness should allow him to do so, informing your Majesty of what has taken place in this respect.

It will be necessary to acknowledge to Don Alonzo the reception of his letters, and to tell him that it would have been better to have been less positively explicit with the agent of the Parliament, who asked him if a person sent by the Parliament would be well received (in Spain); in the event of the question being directly renewed, let him reply that he will communicate with your Majesty; but let him not say that he has already done so, and let him seek, with all possible prudence and address, to avoid this subject; for the rest, Don Alonzo can be told that he is left to his own discretion, and that it is a question that should remain in suspense until it is known how far the Parliament shall have established its affairs and strengthened its power.

In case Cottington should be already on his way, and the courier (hastened from hence) should not arrive in time (to the archduke), it will be necessary to send orders to the authorities at Irun and Saint Sebastian to the effect that, if Cottington should arrive there, he should be detained, that your Majesty should be immediately informed of it, and that Cottington should be made to await the reply. This report ought to be sent by an express, and Cottington, during his detention, should be treated with every politeness.

Your Majesty, however, will command what your Majesty pleases.

V.—DON ALONZO DE CARDEÑAS TO THE COUNT DE PENARANDA.

London, 20th June, 1649.

The despatches forwarded to his Majesty which accompany the present letter, will inform your lordship about the affairs of this country, and the manner in which the (English) Government resolved to declare to me on the 16th instant, that if I did not present new credentials it would treat with me no longer; this resolution was taken, not that any consideration of interest or convenience whatsoever prevented the Parliament from continuing its relations with me, but because natural pride, stimulated by success, fills these men with an arrogance which takes account of nothing.

This circumstance appears to render necessary my departure from hence, supposing that his Majesty has taken the resolution to make no formal declaration either in favor of the Prince of Wales or of the Parliament, for, in this case, it would be impossible to present new credentials. Besides, even when it might be of advantage to do so, the single fact that the Parliamentarians have attempted to compel his Majesty to the adoption of this step, in a manner so opposed to the regard and respect which are due to him, requires that it should be well considered whether it would be suitable to present credentials, at all events so readily. I doubt not, therefore, that his Majesty will give orders for my departure, and in that case I hope permission to return to Spain will be accorded me. My health is much in need of my native air; and this is why I have thought it proper to beg your lordship to say a few words to that effect, if necessary, to procure for me what I so much require, and at the same time to cause payment to be made of the salary due to me, and a sufficient amount for my travelling expenses on the road. May God, &c.

VI.—DON ALONZO DE CARDEÑAS TO THE KING OF SPAIN.

London, 13th August, 1649.

Sire: In my despatch of the 24th of July, I informed your Majesty that the government of this country was proposing to send to its agent, who for two years has resided in Flanders, new credentials, which accredit him to the archduke. I have likewise informed your Majesty of the discontent produced here by the news of the intercourse which Councillor Brun, as your Majesty's ambassador, has held with the Prince of Wales; the copy of the letter which your Majesty wrote to the Prince, expressing your condolences on the occasion of the death of his father, has been published; the title of King of Great Britain, which your Majesty employed, has been brought forward, as well as the manifestations and solemn reception which have been made to the Prince in Flanders. The information which I have now to lay before your Majesty is this, that immediately these news reached here, the Parliament resumed the project of sending agents to Spain, France, and other sovereign courts and republics; but as I have not heard, up to the present time, that credentials have yet been sent to the agent who is at Brussels, and as I have not been informed by advices from Flanders that the agent has presented them, it is to be supposed that the Parliament has changed its opinion or suspended its decision. I am told that ten days ago the question was discussed in the Council of State, whether these persons ought to be sent as simple agents of the Parliament, or as ambassadors; it is added that the first sent ought to be commissioned to Spain, in the hypothesis that he would meet with a better reception there than anywhere else; this is inferred from my sojourn here, for it cannot be admitted that it would be otherwise at the very time that your Majesty has an ambassador here. In the event of the envoy of the Parliament not being received in Spain, I should be made to leave here with the briefest possible delay.

I am assured that it has been thus decided, and that the same thing will be done with respect to the ambassador of Holland, to whom it is complained of bitterly that the States-General (with the exception of the province of Holland) have not been willing to recognize the new Republic, nor to receive as its ambassador a representative of the Parliament, who was then at the Hague, and to whom the Parliament had forwarded credentials, after the death of Dorislaüs, although the ambassador of the States, when he came with Adrien de Pauw to intercede in favor of the late king, was the bearer of credentials from the States-General to the Parliament. It is true, that it was then supposed that he was accredited to the Crown (of England), and that the Parliament had not yet erected itself into a sovereign power, and had not yet changed the monarchical form of government for the republican. The Parliament demands that this ambassador should now present to it new credentials: disagreement on this subject between the Parliament and the States-General begins to make itself apparent, and it is especially increased since the vessels of the Parliament have seized a ship from Amsterdam, which was on her way to Ireland, with a cargo of considerable value, which ship will be considered, it is said, as a fair prize, in spite of the proceedings and threats made by the ambassador of the States-General, in order to obtain its restitution. From this circumstance, the pride of these people may be judged of, and their behavior towards their neighbors, although they may have need of them.

I have begun to take measures, through the medium of certain Members of Parliament who show themselves my friends, to make these people understand, as if it originated from me alone, that it will be of no advantage to them to press their resolution of sending some one to Spain, and that if the envoys of the Prince of Wales do not proceed to Spain (the Parliament people have heard it spoken of as probable that they would proceed thither in consequence of relations which have subsisted between the ministers of Flanders and the resident at Vic), which I have interpreted as an act of neutrality, I should regard it as a prudent resolution on the part of the Parliament not to hasten the despatch of its agents till the question has been maturely considered, and until the Parliament has strengthened its affairs, and firmly established its power. I do not know what will be the result of my proceeding, but whatever it may be, I shall render an account of it to your Majesty. May God preserve your Majesty, &c.

VII.—THE COUNT DE PENARANDA TO DON ALONZO DE CARDEÑAS.

Brussels, 3d July, 1649.

* * * I HAVE read with very particular attention the two copies of your despatches to his Majesty, and my opinion is, that everything that has occurred was very natural and necessary, for from the moment that the Parliament took the resolution to exile the king, and to have done with royalty, what probability was there that it would be willing to treat with a minister accredited to the king? Your Excellency has made it known in good time in Spain; but as your Excellency has received commands from His Majesty (a copy of which has been likewise sent to me) to furnish an account of everything, and to alter his position in nothing, there is no room for discussion or counsel. Yesterday a courier arrived here in great haste from Spain with a despatch for your Excellency; I have not yet seen it, but the Secretary, Navarro, has written me a few words about its contents; the sum of it is, that we should endeavor to prevent Cottington from going down there (to Spain) on behalf of the King of England, and that your Excellency in like manner should prevent an ambassador from the Parliament going thither. It is easy to understand the end proposed by this line of action: it is desired to remain indifferent and neutral with respect to both parties; but there is much probability that it will happen to us, as usually happens in such cases, that is, of letting both parties escape, and quickly; at the same time, I do not see what means exist, for your Excellency or ourselves, of making the Parliament people change their opinion who wish to send ambassadors or ministers to Spain, at least, of declaring that the king does not

wish to receive them, which would be a formal rupture. I will read the despatch, if it please God, and will not fail to tell your Excellency what occurs to my mind. It has come most opportunely, for this poor devil made his entry into Brussels yesterday with a pomp equal to that which it would have been possible to employ for the reception of his father, if he had taken the fancy to come here on his way to Spain. Thereupon, I thought it my duty to make known to your Excellency all that has taken place.

The archduke was with the army in France, near Guise, when the English minister presented himself one day at head-quarters and laid before them two things: first, the necessity in which his master found himself placed of requesting six thousand doubloons in charity, and next, the desire of a friendly interview between his king and the archduke (it is true that he has not spoken to me of either one or the other). The first condition of this interview was that he should come with twenty domestics, without ceremony or reception anywhere; but, little by little, the affair has assumed proportions which have altogether changed its character: the minister has desired that the king should be formally received at Anvers, here, and everywhere, with the strictest ceremony and with as many salutes of artillery as possible. I have known nothing about it, for the orders must have been sent after his highness (the archduke) had taken the field; as, however, it appeared to me that the affair was becoming unreasonably serious, and as I thought the king would not approve that demonstrations, so disagreeable to the Parliament, should be made here, I wrote a few words to the secretary Navarro about it, long before reading the king's despatches; but as the business must have been already fairly in progress, no great attention has been given to what I said. In truth, the English, especially this farce-actor (*picarillo*) of a resident, have slyly insinuated themselves among us; and I begin to perceive that they have two objects in view: first to arouse the jealousy of the Parliament and compel it to mistrust the king our master, and afterwards to hold out a warning to Cardinal Mazarin by pointing out to him that we other Spaniards have done so here without having the same obligations as the French, and without being connected by such intimate ties of relationship. Your Excellency will make whatever use you think suitable of this intelligence, for, indeed, it is unreasonable that, contrary to the intentions of the king, and to our concerns who have so distant a communication with him, these gentlemen should believe us fully engaged in the re-establishment of this poor King of England; having, indeed, so much business on our hands, it would be very remarkable charity in us to excite new enemies. This is all I can say at present on the subject; I reserve saying more about it until I shall have made myself acquainted with his Majesty's despatch.

It is announced to me that the King of England will set out from here in two days to go in quest of his highness; I have just returned from seeing him; his countenance resembles his father's as strongly as possible.

VIII.—THE COUNT DE PENARANDA TO THE SECRETARY AUG. NAVARRO.

Brussels, 5th July, 1646.

I ACKNOWLEDGE to you that these English fatigue me. I perceive that they abuse our courtesy, and that it is intentionally and altogether in opposition with the intentions and interests of the king our master. This is why it appeared to me to be necessary to despatch this courier to apprise his highness and the ministers of what has occurred between them and me, so that they might act, down there, as shall seem most suitable, and attain, if possible, what the king desires.

In the first place, it should be known, as I am assured, that the whole of this intrigue is conducted by the grand equerry of the queen; his name is Mr. Jermyn, an intimate favorite of the Queen of England, who implicitly follows his counsels. This Jermyn belongs to the Cardinal's coterie; and all those machinations which tend to make Ireland accept the protection of France (about which we know, however, from Don Alonzo's despatches) have been conducted on Jermyn's suggestion, and by himself. He is a heretic of the worst description, who does not think so much of the interests of his master as of maintaining himself in the good graces and preserving the favor of the cardinal, who furnishes him with the means of existence and support. I have had two conversations with him: the first was sufficiently impertinent on his part; he exhibited his rancor against us with very little reserve, as well as the notions and principles of the cardinal, with which he is imbued; but the second conversation, which I held with him yesterday evening, was more than impertinent: it was impudent, and even imprudent; for, to speak only of his least fault, every time he mentioned the two kings, he named the King of France first, and afterwards ours, which his master himself would not have done. Cottington and the Resident do not conceal the discontent which this man excites in them, and do not hesitate to let it be understood that the king, the father of the young Prince of Wales, was lost by following the counsels of the court of Paris, and that his son will be the same.

I have already told you what passed yesterday between myself and Cottington; to-day the Resident came to my house, and in the course of conversation, I found a favorable opportunity to speak to him as follows: "Mr. Resident—The king my master has no need of fresh enemies, he has enough already; you know with what courtesy and benevolence the king and his highness have treated you and received you here. I see, and we all see, that this young king goes to the school of France, that he is guided by a mother as French, as you know, and that he follows the counsels of M. de Jermyn, whose intentions and dispositions you well know. I speak to you candidly and sincerely; the king will act very unwisely if he send ambassadors to the king my master, being himself in France, and the ambassadors will do well not to charge themselves with this mission. The kings of Spain have always cultivated friendly relations, fraternity, and a good understanding with the kings of England, as you know; but it is altogether impossible that the King of England, a courtier of France, and the cardinal, should not be suspected by the king my master whilst he is engaged in such a raging war with France; even if that should not be, it would be better for the King of England to establish himself in some spot where he could have a court of his own, and let the French assist him, as they wish to do so; and as the ties of relationship and alliance which unite him to the crown of France oblige them to do; and that he should endeavor to induce this crown, out of regard for him, to conclude an advantageous peace, without wishing that it should be an unjust one. But whilst he does not do so, I repeat to you, he will follow very bad counsel if he sends ambassadors to Spain, and the latter would not find themselves very well off. I speak frankly to you, and entirely of my own accord, for you can plainly see that I have not been able to render any account to the king of what I have observed here, nor to receive yet any commands from his Majesty on this subject."

The reply was to thank me, and to say that I had spoken the most perfect truth, assuring me at the same time that if one of the king's ministers had been present, he would have said the same. Such was our conversation, in which I began to prepare the way for what the king, our master, desires, according to the letter you wrote me; and they cannot suspect that it comes from his Majesty, or that his Majesty or his highness have been already pre-occupied with the subject. I think my words have produced some effect, and that it will be easy to accomplish the king's desire, by following the road into which I have struck. In my conscience, I confess to you that I fear there may be some persons who think we have gone too far in the politeness shown to the prince, and that it ought to be strongly recommended to Don Alonzo not to suffer the Parliament to conceive any resentment on this account. What can be said in reply, when it is seen that the King of France has not yet written a single letter to this poor devil (the Prince of Wales), nor made the slightest manifestatation for six months that his father's head has been struck off, and when at the same time, he (the Prince of Wales) asks and obtains from us all this that the King of France has not done? It is perfectly certain that it is the queen who commands her son what to do, and that she herself receives instructions from this Jermyn, who again receives his orders from the cardinal.

With respect to the peace, he has been very impertinent; he wished to know in detail all that had passed, and discussed all the points with me as if he were some grand mediator, or some personage of great authority in the world. I have communicated to him the copies of the last two letters of the nuncio and the Venetian ambassador, as well as the replies that have been made to them. He listens to what is said to him, but much more to what he says himself; he speaks very slowly. In fine, he is one of the most wearisome personages that I have ever known in my life. The Resident told me that he was going to see his highness on the part of his master; so I was desirous that the courier who is the bearer of the present should arrive there before him.

IX.—THE COUNT DE PENARANDA TO THE KING OF SPAIN (PHILIP IV.).

Brussels, 6th July, 1649.

Sire: Whilst his highness the archduke was with the army in France, near Guise, the English minister arrived at head-quarters; he wished us to regard him as the man most deserving of confidence in those things that relate to your Majesty's service, and he has spoken to his highness of his master's strong desire to come to an understanding with your Majesty, for whom he expresses the greatest respect. He announced that his master proposed repairing to Ireland, but passing through France on his way, as much for the convenience of the journey as to have an interview with his mother; that he would visit the camp *incognito*, accompanied only by twenty persons; not looking to being received with the usual ceremony, or any éclat, and solely with the view of seeing his highness, either at the camp or wherever his highness might be. The minister has further asked for a gift of six thousand doubloons, considered as alms, and given out of commiseration, and to enable his master to prosecute his journey. His highness communicated this proposition to an assembly at which I assisted; and although the embarrassments and inconveniences which might result from it have been represented, especially as your Majesty's intentions touching the interest of the prince were not known, still, considering the form in which the affair presented itself after the propositions of the minister, it was thought that it would be impossible, without incurring much blame, to refuse either the interview or the pecuniary assistance. The minister did not speak to me upon the subject until the matter was resolved upon; but when he did speak to me of it, I told him that this was a grave resolution taken by his master, of going to France, he being so young, and accepting for his guidance the instructions of the minister of a Court whose counsels had brought the late king to the scaffold; and this the minister himself acknowledged. I also gave him to understand that this step taken by the prince could not but give rise to suspicions, on account of all those considerations with which he could not be unacquainted; he confined himself to replying in general terms, having already attained the object of his mission. His highness arrived here after the capture of Ypres; Don Francisco Cottington, and other persons, named as envoys extraordinary from the new king to your Majesty, have also arrived. The reception which his highness ought to give the prince has been discussed, and it was decided that it should take place in the park, and without ceremony of any kind. The king arrived at ——, where his highness should have awaited him; but the enemy having commenced a movement on the line of his highness, he quitted that place to march by the side of the fleet, leaving preparations for the reception of the king according to the conditions agreed upon, namely, that it should take place incognito, and without any ceremony or publicity; but the English entirely changed what had been agreed upon, by declaring to his highness that they wished the king to be publicly received, the citizens to be under arms, salutes of artillery to be fired, and other ceremonies to be observed with great pomp. This was resolved upon whilst his highness was at camp, and it has thus been carried into execution.

The king is accompanied by a certain M. Jermyn, grand equerry and favorite of the queen, sent from Paris, by way of Amiens, to receive and accompany the king. This man is a confidant of Cardinal Mazarin's, and it is not a very bold conjecture to suppose that this change of opinion, touching the reception of the king, was suggested and directed by Cardinal Mazarin. I knew nothing of these public manifestations demanded by the English, but after having reflected upon it I considered the matter deserving of much attention, seeing that we have not yet learned that the French have sent any ambassador to express their condolences to the King of England, although so many months have already elapsed since his father's death, although he is himself so near, and although their obligations are much greater than any your Majesty can have. It is an intrigue which has for its object that your Majesty should be the first sovereign to endeavor to re-establish the King of England on his throne, and that you should thus unseasonably expose yourself to make the English Parliament your enemy. It was under this sad impression that I decided to speak to Cottington yesterday in the terms which your Majesty will be pleased to read in the copy of the letter which I wrote the same day to the Secretary Navarro; and then the minister having called to see me yesterday, I said to him all that is contained in the copy of the second letter that I wrote to the Secretary Navarro. * * *

I have likewise furnished an account of the whole affair to Don Alonzo de Cardeñas, in the form which your Majesty will be pleased to see in the inclosed letter, to the end that he should endeavor to prevent the Parliament from taking offence, and that he should uphold their confidence until it shall please your Majesty to express your will. This is all of which it appears to me necessary to inform your Majesty. May God preserve your Majesty.

X.—THE ARCHDUKE (LEOPOLD) TO THE KING OF SPAIN.

Cambray, 8th July, 1649.

By the courier whom your Majesty sent to me with despatches relative to the affairs of England, I have received your Majesty's letter of the 10th ultimo, in which your Majesty orders me to endeavor to prevent Don Francisco Cottington from repairing to your dominions in the capacity of ambassador of the King of Great Britain, and, in the event of being unable to dissuade him therefrom, to permit him to pursue his journey, reducing matters to the position which has been adopted from the beginning. I think it my duty to remind your Majesty that I refused the title of king to the Prince of Wales before informing your Majesty thereof. Your Majesty replied by commanding me to accord him this title, providing that the letter should be predated, which could not be done here (at Brussels), from whence letters are conveyed in two days to the Hague where the King (of England) was then staying. At the same time, your Majesty wrote to the king to express your condolences on the occasion of his father's death, and you have ordered the Counsellor Brun to offer (by word of mouth) the same condolence; this the counsellor has performed at Breda, and he will render an account of the same to your Majesty.

In order to avoid treating the Prince of Wales as king, as your Majesty has done and ordered me to do, I have sent him the passport he demanded of me to proceed to his possessions in France; from thence, as I am informed by the minister who has been here since the time of King Charles I. his father, he means to repair to Ireland. When I asked him why he did not set out from Holland itself, he replied that it was because he had not sufficient maritime force to cross the English Channel, and also because he desired to see his mother, who is still at Paris. He has sent Don Francisco Cottington to me in the quality of ambassador accredited to your Majesty. I have observed the same etiquette towards him which the Archduke Albert observed towards the other English ambassadors, according to the instructions which I have received on this subject from your Majesty's former ministers in these provinces.

The king has entered Anvers, from whence he has gone to Brussels; I shall see him at Valenciennes the day after to-morrow; from thence he will pass through Cambray to Peronne in your Majesty's dominions. The honors due to the rank of king have been rendered him, which it was impossible to avoid from the moment your Majesty wrote to him, according him that title. By the first opportunity I shall render an account to your Majesty of what he may say to me.

As to Cottington, whom it is sought to detain here, I have nothing to add to what the Count de Penaranda has said in his letters to Augustin Navarro, the copies of which are annexed to the present, unless it is that the English minister, who was here to-day, asked Navarro for a passport for Cottington; I inquired why he wished for one, since his master was about to enter France; I told him that he would need one to send ambassadors to your Majesty if he were out of the territory of France and in one of your Majesty's States, but not when he was on the point of entering France; the minister appeared satisfied with this observation. I shall endeavor to obtain intelligence of the manner in which the King of England will be received in France, and will transmit it to your Majesty.

Don Alonzo de Cardeñas will render an account to your Majesty of the manner in which the English Government has began to act towards him in London. He writes me that it is demanded that I shall take an agent of the Parliament under my protection who happens to be here. Don Alonzo sees no inconvenience in my protecting him; for myself, I hesitate to do so, for fear it should be deemed an act of adhesion to the Parliament; the agent is, however, in sufficiently safe-keeping, for those who assassinated Dr. Dorislaus have assassinated him, not because he was an agent of the Parliament, but because he had been a public accuser of the late King Charles. Moreover, I have not yet resolved upon the reply to be made to Don Alonzo; both parties seek to provoke declarations which shall sanction what each desires, the king his succession to the throne, and the Parliament its government. May God, &c.

XI.—DELIBERATION OF THE SPANISH COUNCIL OF STATE ON THE SUBJECT OF THE TWO PRECEDING DESPATCHES FROM THE COUNT DE PENARANDA AND THE ARCHDUKE LEOPOLD.

Madrid, 2d August, 1649.

SIRE: The Council of State, at which the Duke de Medina de las Torres and the Marquises of Castel-Rodrigo and Valparaiso were present, have, conformably to your Majesty's commands, taken into consideration the two letters inclosed, one from the Archduke Leopold, of the date of the 8th of July, and the other from the Count de Penaranda, of the 6th of the same month, as well as of the documents of which they speak. The two letters are in reply to what your Majesty has deigned to write on the subject of the etiquette which the archduke ought to observe, with respect to the King of England, on the occasions which might present themselves. The course which his highness has thought proper to take has been to follow the etiquette which was adopted by the Archduke Albert. These letters also furnish an account of the resolution taken to conduct the new King of England into your Majesty's dominions, and of his passage to France. The Count de Penaranda speaks of it at length, and sets forth inconveniences which might result therefrom to your Majesty's service; he speaks also of the steps that have been and are still being taken, to prevent Cottington and another person, sent by the new king, proceeding to Spain; he finally gives an account of the conversations he has held on this subject with Cottington and the King of England's minister at Brussels, and of the freedom with which he spoke to them.

The Council, after having long deliberated on these points, and with all possible attention, represents to your Majesty that, in the letter written on the 10th of April to the Archduke, it was recommended to him to make no formal declaration either in favor of the new King of England, or in favor of the Parliament, until it was known with greater certainty what turn affairs should take, to the end that his highness might be able to act in the most suitable manner in the circumstances which should present themselves. It was written to the archduke that he could reply to the King of England's letters, giving him the title of King, Majesty, and all his other titles; but it was added, for the sake of precaution, on this subject towards the Parliament, that is to say, not to give it offence, that the letter was to be predated, so that it could be said that that was done before news were received that the posterity of the defunct king had been excluded from the throne by the Parliament. Since then, Don Alonzo de Cardeñas has announced that Don Francisco Cottington and another person were to come to Spain as envoys of the new King of England, and the Archduke was thereupon written to for the purpose of recommending him first to endeavor, with the greatest address and all possible secrecy, to detain Cottington and learn the nature of his proposals, and afterwards to await the reply after having rendered a full account to your Majesty.

Although your Majesty's command has not been executed in Flanders, and a change has taken place in the aspect of the affair relative to the journey of the King of England in that province, nevertheless the public demonstrations made there in favor of the king cannot be disapproved; for, although your Majesty had resolved, and although the orders sent to Flanders and England had for their object to leave things in abeyance, and to make no declaration either for the king or the Parliament, seeing that it is for your Majesty's interest to be on good terms with the Parliament and not to excite its displeasure; still, if the Parliament testified any discontent at what has been done in the king's favor at Flanders, it will be always possible to say in excuse that the said manifestations were due to this prince in his quality of king, proclaimed, declared, and acknowledged upon oath king of Scotland and Ireland, and that it was impossible to avoid them without neglecting all the rules of urbanity. Besides, if even this prince did not bear those titles, it would have been impossible to avoid doing for him what has been done, seeing that this was a prince passing through your Majesty's dominions, and that it is the etiquette to make such demonstrations in journeys of this kind, in favor of any foreign prince, even where there is not the concourse of circumstances and titles which are combined in the person of the King of England.

The Council is of opinion that immediately the resolution was formed of receiving the Prince of Wales as he has been received, according to the report contained in these letters, it would have been well to have written to Don Alonzo de Cardeñas to explain to him the motives of these proceedings, that he might make use of them with the Parliament in the form which should appear most suitable to him. It might even be written to the Archduke that, in case he had not done so, he might do so now. The same thing should be written from here to Don Alonzo, and it should be recommended to him that, without making any declaration or positive step, he should give the Parliament to understand, as though it came from himself, how much satisfaction its good-will afforded your Majesty.

His Highness the Archduke should likewise be informed that the best thing he can do will be to abide by the orders which have been sent him from hence on this subject; but that, if any other journey or transit should present itself, the matter should be managed without noise and with great prudence. A letter to the same effect should also be written to the Count de Penaranda.

APPENDIX VII.

(Page 198.)

M. DE CROULLÉ TO CARDINAL MAZARIN.

23 Mai, 1650.

* * * J'ENVOIE à V. E. des mémoires des tapisseries et principaux tableaux qui sont en vente à Somerset, avec les prix qu'ils sont estimés, plus haut néanmoins, à ce que j'ai su, de dix schellings par aune de tapisseries. Il a déjà été vendu plusieurs tableaux et entr'autres une grande Vénus de Tissian qui était estimée quinze cents livres sterling, qu'un colonel du Parlement a achetée sept cents livres sterling seulement; c'est elle qui fut donnée par le roi d'Espagne au roi d'Angleterre, lors prince de Galles, en son voyage d'Espagne, que l'on dit être une des plus belles pièces du monde; celui qui l'a achetée dit quelle est trop grande pour sa chambre, et qu'il s'en déferait s'il trouvait quelqu'un qui en fût amoureux; mais je sais que ci qui lui en donne envie est qu'elle paraît éscaillé et qu'il appréhende qu'elle se gâte, à quoi ceux qui s'y connaissent disent qu'il n'y a point de danger pourvu qu'elle soit maniée avec soin, et de plus qu'il est bien aise, en cas de révolution, de n'avoir point de si grandes pièces qui ne sont pas aisément transportées; on l'aurait, sinon pour le prix, pour peu plus qu'elle ne coûte. * * *

Estat de quelques tableaux exposés en vente à la maison de Somerset (*May* 1650.)

209 tableaux estimés en tout: 20,307 schellings,
ou 24,382 liv. 8 s.

Savoir les principaux:—
8 Raphaël;
24 Titien;
9 Corrége;
5 Tintoret;
6 Holbeen;
5 Rubens;
15 Vandyk;
9 Jules Romain, etc.

Sept portraits du feu roi Charles Ier, de sa femme et de ses enfants, par Vandyk, estimes: 150, 60, 200, 25, 60, 30, 420 sch.

Deux satyres écorchés, du Corrége, estimes chacun	1000 sch.
Les douze Césars, du Titien,	1200 sch.
Une petit Notre-Dame, de Raphaël,	800 sch.
Le Voyage d'Emaüs, du Titien,	600 sch.

L'Enterrement du Christ, par le même,	600 sch.
Une Notre-Dame, de Raphaël,	2000 sch.
La maîtresse du Titien, par lui,	100 sch.
Un Mercure qui montre à lire à Cupidon, du Corrége,	800 sch.
Les cartoons de Raphaël des Actes des Apôtres,	300 sch.
Une grande Nativité, par Jules Romain,	500 sch.
Charles V., empereur, et l'impératrice, sa femme, du Titien,	30 sch.
Une Vierge, Christ et Saint Jean, du Corrége,	50 sch.
Vénus et Adonis, du Titien,	80 sch.
Cinq ducs de Venise, du Tintoret,	25 sch.
Le duc de Mantoue, par Rubens,	30 sch.
Vandyk, par lui-même,	15 sch.

Plus 169 pièces de tapisseries, formant diverses séries de tableaux de l'Histoire Sainte, de la Mythologie et de l'Histoire Romaine, estimées en tout . . . . . 49,953 liv. st. 15 sch.

Environ . . 1,248,841 liv. 5 sous.

APPENDIX VIII.

(Page 201.)

M. DE CROULLÉ TO CARDINAL MAZARIN.

Londres, 10 Janvier, 1650.

* * * Aussitôt que les ordres pour le retour de l'ambassadeur d'Espagne ont été divulgués, le lord Ascham a été nommé par le Conseil d'État pour aller résident en Espagne; il fut peu de temps après voir ledit ambassadeur, et lui faire une simple civilité, qui n'ayant, à ce que l'on dit, été reçue que fort froidement avec témoignage qu'il doutait que le roi son maître reçût bien un envoyé de ceux qui persécutent sans relâche ceux de sa religion, le maître des cérémonies y a depuis été, par ordre du Conseil d'État, sur la plainte faite par ledit ambassadeur de ce qu'une compagnie de soldats, sous prétexte du payement de quelques taxes, a été dans sa maison, où elle a fait plusieurs insolences, et lui porta un résultat du Conseil, signé du Parlement, dans lequel il est qualifié ambassadeur, qui désavoue l'action dont il lui promet toute satisfaction, et de plus qu'ayant su les termes sur lesquels il en est de son retour, bien qu'il ne leur ait rendu aucunes lettres de créance, voulant reconnaître les témoignages d'affection qu'il a montrés à cet État, ils désirent, en étant avertis, lui faire toutes les civilités qu'ils pourront et qu'ils savent être dues au ministre d'un si puissant prince. Le général, le jour précédent, sur le même sujet de

sa plainte, lui envoya l'adjudant général de son armée pour lui donner les mêmes témoignages de satisfaction, et le pria d'envoyer quelques-uns des siens à leur conseil de guerre pour en faire entendre le détail; à quoi l'ambassadeur dit que tout consiste à l'insolence que des gens ont eue d'entrer dans sa maison et en violer le respect; et sur ce que l'adjudant se déchargea sur ce qui concerne ceux qui les ont conduits, comme n'étant point sujets à leur juridiction, l'ambassadeur lui dit que c'était un alderman qu'il lui nomma, qui a le département du quartier où est sa maison, et se laissant sans doute emporter à son ressentiment, ajouta que ce gouvernement n'a point de plus passionnés ennemis que cet alderman et autres de la faction presbytérienne.

Cette résolution prise d'envoyer ledit lord Ascham en Espagne, justement au moment de la retraite dudit ambassadeur, qui, ce semble, la devait plutôt empêcher, jointe à ce que ces messieurs-cy ont dit plusieurs fois qu'ils ne hasarderont jamais d'envoyer qui que ce soit sans être assurés de son admission, fait croire qu'ils le sont déjà, ou du moins qu'il y a tant de disposition qu'ils n'en doutent point.

II.—M. SERVIEN TO M. DE CROULLÉ.

28 Janvier, 1650.

MONSIEUR: J'ai reçu votre du 17e du courant. Les avis que j'ai de Madrid ne se trouvent pas fort conformes à ce qui s'est publié à Londres de la réponse que le roi d'Espagne a faite au milord Cottington. Vous marquez que ledit roi a répondu qu'il ne se mêlait point des différends entre les rois et leurs parlements, et que, sur cette présupposition, le maître des cérémonies avait été chez l'ambassadeur Cardeñas lui témoigner, par ordre du Parlement, quelque gratitude de cette réponse. Cependant la vérité de la chose est que Cottington ayant demandé assistance de la part de son maître au roi Catholique, on lui avait répondu que Sa Majesté n'avait pas au monde une plus grande passion que de pouvoir lui témoigner, par des effets solides, combien elle détestait l'exécrable action de la mort violente du roi, son père; que c'était la cause commune de tous les roi; qu'il fallait que tous eussent continuellement dans l'esprit le dessein d'en prendre la vengeance; que pour lui il y contribuerait avec plaisir plus que nul autre; mais que l'état de ses affaires présentement ne lui pouvait permettre de donner les assistances qu'il souhaiterait qu'après la conclusion de la paix avec la France; qu'il avait contribué et continuerait encore de contribuer toutes les facilités que dépendraient de lui pour l'avancement de cette paix; mais qu'il fallait que S. M. B. tournât ses offices du côté de la France, pour la presser de se relâcher sur divers points essentiels du traité, et particulièrement sur la restitution de la Catalogne; et que, s'il obtenait cela de nous, il pouvait être assuré que, quand même la France ne concourrait point à son rétablissement, il lui donnerait de belles assistances d'argent, d'hommes et de vaisseaux, qu'il ne serait pas longtemps sans avoir mis tous ses sujets à la raison, et sans se voir avec autant de puissance et d'autorité que ses prédécesseurs en aient jamais eu.

Voilà la pure vérité des négociations qu'a eues jusques ici le milord Cottington, que je sais d'un lieu à n'en pouvoir doubter. J'ai été bien aise de vous en informer afin que vous vous en prévaliez dès delà pour le service du roi; d'autant plus que je suis averti par la même personne que le roi d'Espagne envoie ordre à Cardeñas de déguiser le fait de toute autre façon, et d'insinuer aux principaux du Parlement que la France s'est relâchée depuis peu de beaucoup de points essentiels de la paix générale, afin d'être bientôt en état de travailler de toutes ses forces au rétablissement du roi de la Grande-Bretagne; que, pour lui, il était résolu de continuer la guerre jusqu'à ce qu'il eût recouvré tout ce qu'il avait perdu, mais qu'il fallait en échange que le Parlement d'Angleterre lui en donnât le moyen en fomentant la sédition de Bordeaux, et lui donnant des assistances sous main, parce qu'autrement il serait contraint de prendre son parti, et d'accepter les conditions avantageuses que la France lui offrait.

Maintenant que vous serez informé de ce que Cardeñas a charge d'insinuer dans les esprits de delà, vous aurez beau champ de faire une contre-batterie en publiant la vérité du fait, qui est tout autre que se qu'il dira, et faisant connaître que cette couronne est résolue de tenir ferme sur les points du traité qui sont encore contentieux, et notamment sur la restitution de la Catalogne; mais que, pour nous fortifier dans cette résolution, il faudrait que le Parlement d'Angleterre nous fournît sous main quelques assistances d'hommes ou d'argent, pour nous donner moyen de nous défendre des grands préparatifs que les Espagnols font pour nous attaquer de tous côtés la campagne prochaine.

Cependant qu'il serait assez difficile dans la disposition où sont les esprits de delà, d'en tirer ces sortes d'assistances, il faut au moins que vous ayez toujours pour but d'empêcher qu'ils n'en donnent aux ennemis, sur les fausses suppositions que Cardeñas leur fera. Je ne m'étendrai pas davantage sur ce sujet, remettant à votre prudence et à votre adresse d'en tirer le fruit qui se pourra, et, comme je dis, en tous cas nous garantir des préjudices que les artifices de Cardeñas nous pourraient faire.

La même personne me marque que le Roi d'Espagne a donné ordre à Cardeñas de se garder bien de donner aucun écrit, ni de traiter tout ceci que, comme il le dit, *extrajudicialmente*, se contentant de parler en secret aux principaux du Parlement, sans faire aucun acte positif; et vous verrez en effet qu'il se conduira de cette sorte, ce qui vous fera juger combien a eu peu de fondement la question de ceux qui vous ont demandé si vous aviez order, aussitôt que l'ambassadeur d'Espagne aurait présenté des lettres de créance et demandé audience, de faire de même. Il ne se peut rien de plus avisé que la réponse que vous avez faite à cette question; cependant leurs MM. désirent que vous vous conduisiez avec la même circonspection que le roi d'Espagne ordonne à son ministre.

On me marque encore que Cardeñas a ordre d'unir, autant qu'il le pourra, le Parlement d'Angleterre avec la province de Hollande en particulier: ce qui vous doit obliger à une conduite contraire, sans pourtant paraître; me remettant, sur ce point, à ce qui vous aura été mandé par le sieur Brasset, en conséquence des dépêches que je lui ai écrites.

APPENDIX IX.

(Page 202.)

I.—M. SERVIEN TO M. DE CROULLÉ.

6 Novembre, 1649.

Monsieur: J'ai reçu vos lettres auxquelles pour réponse je vous dirai qu'il faut que vous insinuiez toujours de delà qu'on ne songe ici qu'à entretenir une bonne correspondance avec l'Angleterre, et à remédier à tout ce qui pourrait avoir apporté de la difficulté au commerce, et causé mauvaise satisfaction. Mais pendant qu'on travaille ici à donner bon ordre à tout, il est juste qu'on fasse de même à Londres, et on verra s'il y a de l'artifice et de la dissimulation en nos paroles lorsqu'elles portent assurance qu'on veut vivre en une parfaite intelligence avec l'Angleterre.

On a renouvelé avec tant de rigueur les ordres pour toute la navigation, et pour réparer les dommages que M. Augier a représenté que divers marchands avaient reçus, que je suis assuré que les plus critiques et mal-affectionnés à cette couronne seront obligés d'avouer qu'on veut entièrement remédier à tout ce qui peut altérer la bonne correspondance qui est entre les deux royaumes.

Si, après l'expédition d'Irlande, M. Cromwell vient en France, étant, comme il est, personne de mérite, il y sera bien reçu, car assurément tout le monde l'ira recevoir au lieu où il débarquera; mais je ne crois pas qu'on lui conseille d'entreprendre un semblable voyage.

On m'assure de Bruxelles que l'ambassadeur d'Espagne, qui est à Londres, sera rappelé sous prétexte que l'archiduc a des affaires à conférer avec lui. Je vous prie de ne perdre aucune conjoncture pour donner au Parlement les dernières défiances des Espagnols, ce que je ne doute pas que vous fassiez fortement et adroitement en toutes sortes de rencontres.

II.—M. DE CROULLÉ TO CARDINAL MAZARIN.

Londres, 15 Novembre, 1649.

. . . . AINSI, monseigneur, j'ai lieu de persévérer dans ma créance que l'on ne traitera d'aucune chose, je ne dis pas sans reconnaissance, mais du moins sans une adresse particulière au parlement d'Angleterre, qui de cette sorte, ayant été ci-devant faite du vivant du défunt roi d'Angleterre, pourrait être prise comme une suite et non pas comme une nouveauté, leur reconnaissance ne pouvant être inférée que de l'admission de leurs ambassadeurs, s'ils en envoyaient, et non pas d'une simple lettre du roi, qui, portant dans cette mauvaise conjoncture de temps les affaires dans l'adoucissement, pourrait être d'un plus grand avantage au roi d'Angleterre même que ne saurait être la mauvaise intelligence avec la France, à laquelle on n'a ici que trop de disposition; la suite qui en pourrait être appréhendée est que bientôt après ils n'envoyassent, et que par là on ne tombât dans l'embarras que l'on veut éviter. . . . .

[The same letter goes on to say:—]

. . . . Ce qui se dit du dessein de Cromwell de passer en France procède de ceux qui le désirent pour de différents intérêts; et pour ce on lui fait dire quantité de choses que j'ai toujours négligé d'écrire comme étant sans certitude et sans apparence, et entre autres que, regardant ses cheveux déjà blanchis, il a dit que, s'il avait dix ans de moins, il n'y a point de roi dans l'Europe qu'il ne fît trembler, et qu'ayant un meilleur motif que le défunt roi de Suède, il se croyait encore capable de faire plus pour le bien des peuples que n'a jamais fait l'autre pour son ambition. . . . .

III.—M. DE CROULLÉ TO CARDINAL MAZARIN.

Londres, 6 Decémbre, 1649.

MONSEIGNEUR: Je reçus samedi au soir la lettre dont il a plu à Votre Eminence de m'honorer du 26 du passé, qui me fut apportée de la poste toute ouverte, où elle avait été reportée au conseil d'Etat, après y avoir demeuér depuis le mercredi au soir. Le respect n'ayant pas été gardé pour ce qui venait de Votre Eminence, je ne dois pas trouver à redire que toutes mes autres lettres aient eu la même destinée; mais bien que, quelques ombrages que ces messieurs ici puissent avoir, ils se soient oubliés jusqu'à en user de telle sorte, après avoir bien examiné en moi-même de quelle sorte je devais me comporter, j'ai jugé que le meilleur était de le passer sous silence, ayant su que le conseil d'Etat n'aurait pas mieux aimé sinon que j'en eusse fait bruit, afin d'avoir prétexte à me demander en vertu de quoi et de quelle autorité je suis ici, et de là prendre occasion de faire querelle, que j'éviterai avec autant de soin que j'apporterais de résolution si j'étais dans un temps où l'on dût témoigner tous ses ressentiments, ou qu'il me fût commandé de la faire. Votre Eminence, monseigneur, jugera bien que c'est leur but de ce qu'ayant proposé moi-même à quelqu'un qu'en cas que mes lettres eussent été ouvertes, on les fît recacheter et que je les prendrais comme sans m'en apercevoir, ils n'ont pas seulement voulu se servir de cet expédient, mais qu'elles m'aient été rendues toutes ouvertes, afin que je ne pusse douter qu'ils l'ont ainsi voulu. . .

. . . . Je passe plus avant que je n'ai fait ci-devant, et dis que non-seulement nous ne pouvons espérer aucune correspondance avec ces messieurs ici, s'il ne leur est rendu une lettre du roi qui antorise de traiter avec eux, mais que sans cela nous ne devons presque pas douter d'une prompte rupture. Les causes qui les y obligent sont assez connues, il me serait superflu d'en faire une déduction; mais, pour les cacher d'un prétexte spécieux, ils ne manqueront pas de se servir de celui de la religion, et pour ce de ne rien omettre pour obliger ceux de la leur de remuer en France, afin de pouvoir aussitôt accourir à leur secours. Pour cet effet, l'on m'assure qu'il y a quantité d'émissaires, plusieurs de Jersey et Guernesey, qui passent pour Normands, et quelques autres encore, entre lesquels on dit être un médecin allemand dont je tâcherai d'apprendre le nom et de quelle façon il est fait, qui ne travaillent qu'à les pousser à se soulever par la promesse d'un grand secours dont ils les assurent. De ce côté ici, outre ce l'on soupçonne fort qu'ils ont reçu des lettres de Bordeaux qui les apellent; et quoqu'il n'en soit venu personne exprès, c'est une chose assez facile à négocier parce qu'il y a ici quantité de marchands de ce pays-là qui sont de la religion, et même des catholiques, par le moyen desquels la chose peut être aussi adroitement et plus secrètement fait que par un envoyé. Un gentilhomme m'a assuré que l'on lui a offert emploi pour ce pays-là, et qu'il y en a plusieurs de sa connaissance qui y sont engagés, et qui avaient été arrêtés par Cromwell, dès auparavant son départ, par la promesse de cet emploi. Autant que ma faible lumière peut me donner de jour, je ne vois pas que l'on puisse éviter en France ou de s'accommoder ou de rompre avec ces gens ici dans fort peu de temps, si ce n'est que l'on leur puisse procurer d'ailleurs tant d'affaires qu'ils n'aient pas le loisir de penser à celles des autres. Cet accommodement, si l'on en prenait la résolution, serait un moyen de divertir l'orage qui se forme, et comme la nécessité l'aurait fait faire dans un temps, la raison dans un autre serait assez forte pour s'en départir. Si cela était, je pourrais peut-être tirer assurance que l'on n'enverrait point si tôt d'ambassadeur en France, ou du moins qu'ils n'en eussent auparavant dépêche un en Espagne, dont la proposition peut-être assez appuyée de l'honnêteté publique qui y répugnerait, la reine de la Grande-Bretagne étant présente et en étant fille. Sur ce que plusieurs leur ont objecté, mais non pas moi, qu'il faut, avant que de pouvoir être reconnus par les princes et Etats, qu'ils leur fassent savoir par des ambassadeurs ce qu'ils sont, deux des plus considérables du conseil d'Etat, avec lesquels j'étais en discours il y a quelques jours, me dirent que ce qu'ils avaient fait étant public, personne ne le pouvait ignorer, et qu'encore qu'ils n'en aient pas averti les princes par des ambassadeurs, ce n'est pas qu'ils ne le voulussent bien, et que pour ce, si l'on les veut assurer qu'ils seront admis, ils en enverront partout avant qu'il soit huit jours, mais que de les hasarder dans l'incertitude, c'est ce qu'ils ne feront jamais; que dès lors qu'ils seront recherchés par la France, ou que l'on y voudra recevoir leurs ambassadeurs, ils seront tout prêts de renouveler tous les traités d'alliance d'entre les nations; mais que de se tenir toujours dans l'incertitude, et d'attendre notre temps pour cependant perdre le leur, c'est ce qu'ils ne feront point, et qu'il leur faut nécessairement être uns ou autres; que pour témoigner que leur intention est telle, aussitôt que les défenses de ce qui concerne le négoce auront été révoquées en France, ils feront le même, dont ils me donnaient leur parole; que leur intérêt, disent-ils, les y porte assez; mais que néanmoins celui de l'observation de leurs résolutions prévaudra à tout autre.

IV.—M. DE CROULLÉ TO CARDINAL MAZARIN.

Londres, 7 Novembre, 1650.

. . . . Ce que m'écrit M. le comte de Brienne m'apprend qu'en cas que ces gens-ci envoient en France, l'on est résolu d'écouter et de recevoir leur envoyé, mais non pas assurément connaître si, pour prévenir l'union que l'on croit toujours qui se conclura bientôt entre eux et l'Espagne, on désirerait qu'ils le fissent; en ce cas, je pense que, si la crainte de n'être pas bien reçus les a jusqu'ici retenus, quand ils seront assurés du contraire, ce qui se pourrait faire adroitement et sans qu'il parût que la recherche en vînt du côté de la France, il serait aisé de les y porter et de faire choisir quelqu'un qui, s'il n'était pas des plus affectionnés, du moins aurait la disposition de le devenir; et lors j'ose presque assurer qu'en leur ôtant cette jalousie qu'ils ont, il serait fort facile d'accommoder tout cela, et qu'ils se contenteraient, pour la satisfaction des demandes qui serviraient de prétextes à leur envoi, de faire compensation pour partie avec les prises qu'ils ont faites, et pour le surplus de prendre des assurances, plutôt pour la forme que pour le retirer, ne faisant point de doute que, bien qu'ils affectent l'indifférence sur la reconnaissance de tous les princes, ils achèteraient pourtant celle de France avec une amitié ferme beaucoup plus que tout cela. . . . .

Ainsi, monseigneur, par la connaissance que V. E. a des intérêts des Etats et la particulière de celui-ci, à laquelle tout ce que je puis lui mander n'ajoute aucune lumière dans la bonne posture où il se trouve, elle jugera, s'il lui plaît, s'il est ou non du bien de la France de s'accommoder avec eux. Leur nouvelle République se fortifie de tous côtés; l'Angleterre est toute paisible, sans qu'il y ait un seul pouce de terre qui ne les reconnaisse, et ne soit bien assuré; l'Irlande est presque toute assujettie, et outre les intelligences qu'ils ont en Ecosse, elle a reçu de si grandes pertes qu'il ne se peut qu'elle n'en soit très-affaiblie. Les Ecossais de plus sont divisés entre eux, et il semble que toutes choses ensemble concourent à l'affermissement de ces gens-ci et à la perte tant du roi de la Grande-Bretagne que de ceux qui se joignent à lui. De plus ils sont puissants par mer et par terre; ils vivent sans ostentation et sans faste, sans émulation etre eux, épargnent pour leur particulier et prodiguent pour leurs affaires publiques auxquelles chacun travaille comme dans les siennes propres; ils ont grande quantité d'argent qu'ils administrent bien, observent une trèssévère discipline, récompensent bien et punissent sévèrement. Je sais bien que, dans le dessein dont ils ne se cachent point de vouloir détruire toutes les monarchies, tous les princes sont intéressés à les perdre, à quoi leurs crimes obligent tout le monde en général de contribuer; mais je pense que, n'étant pas encore en état de le faire, il est meilleur de conniver pour un temps et les retenir, qu'en se tenant trop fermes les porter à faire ce dont les ennemis de la France ne manqueraient de se prévaloir. Pour ajouter à mon sentiment et à celui de beaucoup d'honnêtes gens celui que l'on public, je vous dirai que l'on tient ici la guerre avec la France si infaillible que, si l'on voulait y faire des gageures sur ce sujet, on le pourrait pour de grandes sommes, qu'avant qu'il soit la fin du printemps les Anglais auront une armée de France. . . . . . .

V.—DON ALONZO DE CARDEÑAS TO KING PHILIP IV.

London, August 13, 1649.

Sire: In my despatch of the 24th of July, I informed your Majesty that the government of this country intended to send their agent, who has resided in Flanders for two years, new letters of credence, accrediting him to the archduke. I also informed your Majesty of the discontent occasioned here by the news of the dealings which Councillor Brun, as your Majesty's ambassador, has had with the Prince of Wales; the letter which your Majesty wrote to the prince, to express your condolence with him on the death of his father, has been published; many remarks have been made regarding the title of King of Great Britain, which your Majesty used in addressing him, and regarding the solemn reception which has been given to the prince in Flanders. What I now have to communicate to your Majesty is that, as soon as this news arrived here, the Parliament resumed its plan of sending agents into Spain and France, and to other republics and sovereign courts; but as I have not yet heard it stated that credentials have positively been sent to the agent, who is at Brussels, and as I have not received information from Flanders that the agent has presented them, it is to be supposed that the Parliament has either changed its purpose, or suspended its decision. I am told that for the last ten days, the Council of State has been discussing the question whether they should send these persons as simple agents, or as ambassadors; it is added that the first who is sent will be sent into Spain, on the supposition that he will be better received there than anywhere else, which is inferred from my staying here, for it cannot be admitted to be otherwise, seeing that your Majesty has an ambassador in this place. In case the envoy of the Parliament should not be received in Spain, I should be despatched hence with the least possible delay. I am assured that it has been so decided, and that the same course will be pursued towards the ambassador of Holland, to whom bitter complaints have been made, that the States-General (with the exception of the province of Holland), have refused to recognize the new Commonwealth, or to acknowledge as its ambassador an envoy from the Parliament, who was at the Hague, to whom the Parliament had sent letters of credence, after the death of Dorislaus; although the ambassador of the States, when he came with Adrian Pauw, to intercede on behalf of the late king, was the bearer of credentials from the States-General to the Parliament. It is true that then it was supposed that he was accredited to the Crown [of England], and that the Parliament had not yet erected itself into a sovereign power, and had not yet changed monarchical government into republican. The Parliament demands that this ambassador should now present to it new letters of credence; some discontent on this subject is beginning to manifest itself between the Parliament and the States-General, and it has greatly increased since the ships of the Parliament seized a vessel belonging to Amsterdam, which was on its way to Ireland with a cargo of considerable value; which ship, it is said, will be considered a fair prize, in spite of the endeavors and threats used by the ambassador of the States-General to obtain its restitution. You may judge, by this fact of the pride of these people, and of their proceedings towards their neighbors, though they stand in need of them.

I have begun to take steps, by means of certain members of Parliament, who have proved themselves my friends, to intimate to these people, as if it were my opinion only, that it is of no advantage to them to hasten their resolution to send some one into Spain; and that if the envoys of the Prince of Wales do not go into Spain (the

Parliamentarians had heard it said that it was probable they would do so, in consequence of the relations which the ministers of Flanders have had with the Resident Vic; which I have interpreted as an act of neutrality), I should regard it as a prudent resolution on the part of the Parliament not to hurry the despatch of their agents, until the question is fully matured, and the Parliament has thoroughly established its power, and consolidated its affairs. I do not know what will be the result of my proceeding, but whatever it is, I shall inform your Majesty.

May God keep your Majesty, &c.

VI.—DELIBERATION OF THE SPANISH COUNCIL OF STATE ON THE AFFAIRS OF ENGLAND.

Madrid, October 9, 1649.

[The Council was attended by the Count de Monterey, Don Francisco de Melo, and the Marquis de Valparaiso.]

Sire: In conformity with your Majesty's orders, the Council has taken into consideration the two letters of Don Alonzo de Cardeñas, dated August 13th, in which among other things, he speaks of the resolution which the Parliament of England had adopted, to send residents or ambassadors to Spain, France, and other States. He says also that Cromwell had not yet started for Ireland, and that it was believed that, if he went thither, the presbyterians would take advantage of his absence to recover what they have lost, and would put themselves in communication with Ormonde; he further states that the troops of the Prince of Wales, under the command of Inchiquin, had taken Tredagh by storm, and that Ormonde was encamped before Dublin. The Council, after having examined these various points, gave the following opinion:—

The Count de Monterey thinks that the best thing that can be done for the king's service in relation to England, is not to declare for either the King or the Parliament, until we see what turn affairs are likely to take, and what party will have the upper hand; and that it would even be better for the Parliament party to triumph over the King's party, not only because of the few obligations we are under to his father, but because we might obtain greater advantages from the Parliament. It had already become known that the new King of England was about to send Don Francis Cottington and another ambassador to the Court; and your Majesty had resolved to write to his highness the archduke (as has been already done) to direct him, if those persons passed through Flanders, to endeavor to learn what their instructions are, and to report whatever he might ascertain; that moreover, the archduke should endeavor to detain them until he had received an answer from this place; but that, if they absolutely insisted on continuing their journey, he should allow them to proceed. On the other hand, orders have been sent to the functionaries in Guipuzcoa that, if these persons should come thither, they should detain them by treating them with all sorts of politeness, and that they also are to wait your Majesty's answer. The Count is of opinion that the same course might be pursued towards the persons whom the Parliament may send, by despatching orders to the same effect into Flanders, in case those ambassadors should pass that way, as well as to Don Alonzo de Cardeñas and to the ports of Spain. When it afterwards becomes necessary to adopt a definitive resolution, your Majesty will please to order Don Alonzo de Cardeñas to send exact information of the forces which the Parliament has at its disposal, and of the extent to which its government is established: Don Alonzo will also inform your Majesty of the number of the king's forces, and what he may have in England, Ireland, and Scotland, as well as from his allies.

Don Francisco de Melo is of the same opinion as the Count de Monterey; he adds that he believes that the affairs of England must be treated without any fixed principle, and without any determination on the part of your Majesty. On the question as to whether it would be more suitable to your Majesty to see the king restored or a republican government established in that country, or that the conflict between the two parties should be prolonged; he thinks that it is the moment to derive from that quarter some advantage to counterbalance the revolt of Portugal and the conquests of England; he would desire to know what your Majesty may be pleased to order for the attainment of this object.

The Marquis de Valparaiso concurs in the opinion of the Count de Monterey. Your Majesty will be pleased to ordain what may seem to you most suitable.

[Subscribed in the King's handwriting: "Let the opinion of the Council be followed."]

APPENDIX X.

(Page 213.)

NOTE PRESENTED TO KING PHILIP THE FOURTH BY LORD COTTINGTON AND SIR EDWARD HYDE, AMBASSADORS OF CHARLES THE SECOND.

May, 1650.

SIRE: We are persuaded that your Majesty is well convinced of our entire devotedness to your service, and that since we have had the honor to be received at this Court we have, as doth become faithful servants of your Majesty, combined with zeal for the cause of the king our master the respect and consideration due unto your Majesty, taking care to propose no measures which could be an embarrassment to your Majesty or an advantage to your enemies. We have ever relied upon the firm hope that when God in His great mercy shall have inclined the hearts of your enemies to a just peace, and shall have relieved you of the war which you now have to support, your Majesty will not fail to bestow a friendly consideration on the just cause of the king of Great Britain, and support it with a vigor which will correspond with your Majesty's royal and Christain-like disposition, and that in the meanwhile your Majesty will lend unto the King our master such assistance as the affairs of your kingdom will permit, and that you will encourage him to maintain the confidence which he has displayed in throwing himself into the arms of your Majesty, resolved to contract no other friendship than such as shall accord with the sympathy which he professes for the Catholic religion and your Majesty's interests. This devotedness for the service of your Majesty, which is ever combined in us with zeal and solicitude for the honor and advancement of the king our master, obliges us to convey to you information that has reached us of the landing in Andalusia of a person who has been sent as an agent by the cruel and bloodthirsty rebels in England, and that he is on his way to this Court with letters addressed by these assassins to your Majesty. We have learned that his chiefest purpose is to corrupt such Englishmen as, by virtue of treaties, are resident in this kingdom, and to cause them to renounce the fidelity and allegiance which they owe to their king, as well as by proposing to them certain oaths, the formula of which he brings with him, as by aid of menaces and other devices. It is easy to believe that he will also have received among his instructions the one of endeavoring to infuse into the minds of your Majesty's subjects the same poison, to persuade them to the same contagious doctrine which inculcates the hatred of all government, of all authority, more especially that of kings, and to inculcate them with the levelling and anarchical spirit. This person does not pretend to have been sent by any usurper in arms against his king; he comes in the name of that infamous populace which has deserted the dignity and sacred office of kings to the contempt and cruelty of a rabble, and which has plunged its hands into the blood of its crowned and anointed king with no other pretext, no other reason than that he was king. These men publicly proclaim their enmity to all monarchical government, and in the very statute, or act of parliament as they call it, by which they attempted to overwhelm and annihilate monarchical government in England, they attack all other monarchies, but especially, and with a remarkable malignity and insolence, the sacred person of your Majesty, and comment with an intolerable arrogance upon the just and prudent conduct of your Majesty in your kingdom of Naples; thus attempting to seduce the subjects of your realm. Lest it may happen that your Majesty be not sufficiently informed of the foregoing, we shall forward, at your Majesty's command, a copy of the act of which we speak.

We are too well informed and too firmly persuaded of the horror with which your royal heart is filled against these rebels and regicides to fear that you would consent to grant to this person a reception of such a kind as would be any credit to those who have sent him; and we cannot imagine that your Most Catholic Majesty, being the first and only prince to whom the king our master has offered not only a perpetual friendship, but also all that he has and all that he hopes for, could be the first and only sovereign to bestow, by his favors, a dignity and importance to this new government and the authority of the rebels, who have so odiously murdered the father of their king. It is on this account that we present ourselves humbly before your Majesty, and as devoted servants suggest, that while this individual continues in the realm of your Majesty it is necessary that his conduct, his negotiations, and his intrigues, be vigilantly watched, lest he may exercise a calamitous influence on the peace and tranquillity of this kingdom and of your Majesty. We therefore beseech of your Majesty, on the part of our master and in the name of his dignity, that the person may not enjoy in this Court either access or any such favors as may attract to him the English residing in your Majesty's kingdom, and enable him by their help to corrupt them and seduce them from the fidelity which they owe to their legitimate sovereign; a matter which would speedily come to pass if these Englishmen were to find protection here by any other intervention than that of the king our master.

May God protect and prosper your Most Catholic person as we desire and as the entire world needs.

Cottington.
Hyde.

*** As I have been unable to discover the English original of this document, the above is translated from the Spanish copy in the Archives of Simancas.—Translator.

APPENDIX XI.

(Page 213.)

I.—FIRST DELIBERATION OF THE SPANISH COUNCIL OF STATE ON THE DEMANDS OF THE AMBASSADORS OF CHARLES THE SECOND.

Madrid, 10th May, 1650.

[The Council of State, at which Don Francisco de Melo, and the Marquis de Valparaiso were present, give the following opinion on the contents of the document presented by the envoys of the King of England.]

SIRE: In conformity with the orders of your Majesty, dated the 24th of April last, at a Council at which were present Don Francisco de Melo and the Marquis de Valparaiso, we have taken into consideration the document presented to your Majesty by the envoys of the King of Great Britain. They therein express their firm hope that your Majesty will support cordially the cause of their master. They go on to say, that actuated by a sincere zeal for your Majesty's service, they feel bound, on having been informed of the arrival of an envoy sent to this Court by the Parliament, to announce to your Majesty that this envoy has received instructions to excite the English who are in your Majesty's service, into renouncing the obedience due to their king; they infer, likewise, that he will endeavor to communicate to the minds of your Majesty's subjects a hatred and aversion for monarchical government, to which the members of the Parliament have declared their mortal enmity; they notice further the proceedings of the Parliament of England against your Majesty, in the Act or Statute which contains an expression of disapprobation of your Majesty's conduct at Naples, and an endeavor to excite the people of this country against your Majesty. They promise, upon your Majesty's orders, to lay before you a copy of this Act, and entreat of your Majesty to cause the envoy of the Parliament to be watched, lest by his intrigues he should endanger your Majesty's interests; and, moreover, that he should not have granted to him too ready an access or too much favor at this Court—circumstances which might cause the English residing in the states of your Majesty, to fail in fidelity to their King.

The Council of State proposes to your Majesty, that the following answer might be given to these envoys, if your Majesty so ordains. That, as they know themselves, it is impossible to refuse a hearing even to the greatest criminals. That, in other respects, your Majesty thanks them for the information which they have given: that advantage shall be taken of it in due time and place: that they may continue to furnish any further intelligence which may reach them: That they are requested to transmit the copy of the Act of Parliament of which they speak, and accounts of everything which may affect the interests of your Majesty, especially as regards the kingdom of Naples. Your Majesty will be pleased to order what you think fit.

[In the margin is written in the King's hand, "The advice of the Council shall be adopted."]

II.—SECOND DELIBERATION OF THE COUNCIL OF STATE ON THE SAME SUBJECT.

Madrid, 22d October, 1650.

[The Council of State, at which were present Don Francisco de Melo and the Count de Penaranda, give the following opinion on the contents of the document presented by the envoys of the King of England, in which they demand that the ships of their master may be well received equally in the ports of Flanders as in those of Spain.]

SIRE: By an Ordinance of the 14th of this month, your Majesty directed the Council to take into consideration (as was accordingly done), a document proceeding from the envoys of the King of England, in which they represent that certain of their ships of war having entered the port of Ostend for repairs and the purchase of provisions, did not obtain a reception conformable to the orders which your Majesty has been pleased to give on the subject, and were subjected to embargoes, taxes, and other impositions. They intreat your Majesty to cause a communication to be made to his highness the archduke, to the end that all the vessels of their King may be well received in the port of Ostend, as in all the others at which they may put in; and that it may be permitted them to execute their manœuvres and procure such provisions as they may require, in conformity with the articles of the treaty. They pray that the same orders may be given to all the corregidors and magistrates of all the other ports, in order that the said ships may enter these ports and depart from them freely and without obstacle. The envoys acknowledge the great obligation which their master will have contracted towards your Majesty, if his ships are allowed in the ports of Flanders and the other States of your Majesty, the same privileges which they enjoy in those of France.

The Council, at which were present Don Francisco de Melo and the Count de Peñaranda, is of opinion, that your Majesty might cause a communication to be made to his highness the archduke, recommending him to grant a favorable reception to the ships of the King of England, in the ports of his States, and to observe in their regard the stipulations of treaty of peace as has hitherto been done. With regard to the envoys of the King of England, they might be informed of the orders which have been sent to the archduke, with an intimation, at the same time, that orders of the same kind would not be sent to the other ports before it had been ascertained that they had failed to regard the ordinances already made on this subject, and that, on the occurrence of any such extent the proper directions would be transmitted without delay.

Your Majesty will be pleased to order what seems fit.

[Written in the King's hand: "Very good."]

APPENDIX XII.

(Page 214.)

I.—DON ALONZO DE CARDEÑAS TO KING PHILIP IV.

London, 14th December, 1649.

SIRE: I have learned that admission to the ports of Portugal, has been granted to the prizes, which the vessels of the new King of England and the Irish frigates combined, have made of the ships and merchandise of this kingdom for the benefit of Prince Palatine Rupert, and that these prizes have been there recognized as lawful and sold. I suspected that this concession had been made, because the new King of England, immediately after his father's death, had recognized the tyrant of Portugal, and admitted to his Court as ambassadors, certain persons, who, in this same capacity, have appeared at the Hague and Paris, where the new king has resided, since he succeeded his father. Having considered it proper to obtain certain information upon this matter, I wrote on the subject to the Count of Peñaranda, who communicated with the Chevalier Brun, that he also might make inquiries; this the latter has done, as he informs me in a letter of the 29th November, a copy of which I forward herewith for your Majesty's inspection. At the same time, I made inquiries in France through a safe channel and with the help of an agent, trustworthy, though English, and obtained the information which I enclose. Your Majesty will thereby see how very little the new King of England has profited of the tragical fate of the king, his father, who was overwhelmed in misfortunes by his own faults and from his own mistaken principles. These his son adheres to, as if success had given them authority, and as if he were not himself suffering from their sad consequences. As long as the queen-mother continues to exercise her influence on the resolutions of the king, and as long as the councillors who surround him, and direct all his actions, remain in submission to the queen, this prince will undoubtedly imitate the conduct and example of his father; and if, notwithstanding that he has lost the crown of England, and runs the risk of losing the kingdoms of Ireland and Scotland, if notwithstanding that he so much needs the succor of your Majesty to recover the one and preserve the other, he fails in his duty to your Majesty, and in the requirements of justice and loyalty (inasmuch as your Majesty has recognized him as King of Great Britain, and caused to be conferred upon him in Flanders every homage and every courtesy which he could have desired, had he been in tranquil possession of his crown), if, notwithstanding this be his conduct, what reason have we to hope that the prince will change his opinion, when he finds himself restored to his rights, and no longer in need of assistance. I have thought it necessary to render a particular account of all that has passed, and of all that I have learned. Such information will be useful in case it should be considered advisable to complain of the conduct of this prince. These causes of complaint, coupled with those which have been already afforded by the conduct of his father, will justify in the eyes of the world what is now recommended by expediency and good policy with regard to this government (the republic of England), namely, either to recognize it and receive its ambassadors, or to enter into alliance with it if circumstances and the interests of your Majesty should make it expedient.

II.—CHEVALIER ANTONIO BRUN TO DON ALONZO DE CARDEÑAS.

The Hague, November 29, 1649.

JUDGING by the turn which affairs are taking here, it may be said that the poor king [of England] is hastening to his ruin in every possible way, unless God should work some miracle in his favor. I have ascertained beyond doubt that he has received the envoy of the tyrant of Portugal in the capacity of an ambassador, and his Resident has been unable to deny it, but he excuses it by saying, that as the Portuguese bears that title in reference to the States-General here, his master was unable to treat him otherwise, for had he not done so, he would have lost the support of his brother-in-law, the Prince of Orange. I replied that his deceased father had already done the same thing in London; to which the Resident answered, that at that period the late king was under the control of the Parliament to such a degree that he was obliged to sign the sentence of death which had been passed against his great friend, the Viceroy of Ireland. This being the case, if we had some strong alliance with the leaders of the Parliament of England against France, we might do what they desire; but that we should be the first gratuitously to do such an act, and only in the hope of a possible result, appears to me to be very hard.

III.—REPORT SENT FROM PARIS BY THE PERSON APPOINTED TO ASCERTAIN WHETHER THE ENVOY OF PORTUGAL, WHO IS AT THAT COURT IN THE QUALITY OF AN AMBASSADOR, HAS HAD AN INTERVIEW WITH THE KING OF ENGLAND, AND WHETHER HE HAS TREATED OF ANY AFFAIRS WITH HIM.

THE ambassador of Portugal has been with the King of Scots on several occasions, as well as with the Queen of England; he has had several conferences and secret interviews with both mother and son. The ambassador, on leaving France, left in Paris a Resident named Suarez, a creature of Calatrava; this Suarez has been frequently to see the King of Scots; his Majesty received him, and has treated of various affairs with him, and has written several letters to Portugal since his return from Flanders into France; these letters were all addressed—"To the King of Portugal," and in them he was termed, "my brother." The Queen of England, in writing to the Queen of Portugal, has made use of this form: "To my dear sister, the Queen of Portugal." In this correspondence, the Portuguese has promised to assist the King of Scots, and to receive into the ports of his dominions the king's ships, any prizes they may take from the ships of the Parliament of England; which is now done.

APPENDIX XIII.

(Page 218.)

I.—M. DE CROULLÉ TO CARDINAL MAZARIN.

Londres, 16 Mai, 1650.

. . . LEDIT ambassadeur (d'Espagne) a plusieurs fois envoyé des écrits signés de lui au conseil d'Etat, qui y ont été reçus et considérés, sinon comme venant d'un ambassadeur, du moins d'une personne qui appartient à un prince avec lequel on se veut bien entretenir.

II.—M. DE CROULLÉ TO CARDINAL MAZARIN.

Londres, 4 Juillet, 1650.

. . . . IL se dit aujourd'hui que le général Fairfax, sur le point de partir pour Ecosse, a remis sa commission. J'eus l'honneur de mander à V. E., il y a quelque temps, que le Parlement avait ordonné que tant lui que le lieutenant général remittraient leurs anciennes pour en prendre de nouvelles, et que je croyais que c'était une chose déjà faite. C'est, dit-on, sur l'instance de satisfaire à cet ordre qu'il a mieux aimé remettre; à quoi il a encore été porté par la méfiance qu'il connaît que l'on a de lui, et par le déplaisir de ce qu'il ne lui restait que le nom de cette charge dont Cromwell a toute l'autorité. Possible que, quand il ne s'y serait pas porté, l'on eût trouvé quelque autre prétexte de la lui demander, parce qu'il se dit tout haut que les presbytériens, au parti desquels sa femme le pousse toujours, n'attendent que de voir l'armée engagée avec les Ecossais pour les seconder par des soulèvements de deçà, et que, pour cet effet, ils ont intelligence avec une partie de l'armée qui se déclarerait aussitôt, quoique la chose soit assez difficile par le bon ordre que l'on y a mis en établissant la milice des provinces en des mains assurées, et laissant outre cela quelques troupes trés-affidées en chacune. Elle n'est pourtant pas impossible, ni que Cromwell n'entretienne lui-même ce dessein pour donner jour à ses ennemis de se déclarer et avoir sujet de les perdre ainsi qu'il a fait plusieurs fois par de semblables voies. . .

. . . . L'on m'a fait donner avis que Cromwell a reçu des lettres de messieurs de Bouillon et de Turenne; mais je pense qu'on ne l'a dit en confidence à ceux dont je le tiens qu'afin qu'ils me le rapportassent et que je l'écrive, ce que, tout faux qu'il peut être et que je le crois, j'ai jugé devoir faire, puisqu'il pourrait être que, sur la moindre recherche, jointe à ce que l'on mande que les brouilleries de Bordeaux se renouvellent, ces gens-ci se porteraient à les assister d'une partie de leur flotte qui est à Lisbonne.

III.—M. DE CROULLÉ TO CARDINAL MAZARIN.

Londres, 12 Septembre, 1650.

. . . . Un homme de ma connaissance m'a dit avoir reçu lettres d'Allemagne d'un de ses correspondants, qui est homme intelligent, qui lui mande que, s'étonnant de voir au lieu où il est tant de monnaie d'Angleterre entre les mains des officiers et soldats, il avait eu la curiosité de savoir d'où elle pouvait venir, et qu'ayant fait étroite amitié avec le gouverneur de la place, il a su qu'il a été envoyé d'ici 100,000 livres sterling suivant le traité fait entre l'Espagne et ces gens-ci, par lequel l'Espagne s'engage de continuer la guerre avec la France et de ne faire jamais la paix sans les y comprendre en qualité d'alliés, moyennant quoi ceux-ci doivent fournir tous les mois à Bruxelles une somme considérable. L'on ne m'a jamais voulu dire le nom de la place, mais seulement que le gouverneur y a été mis, ou a appartenu à M. le maréchal de Turenne.

APPENDIX XIV.

(Page 221.)

I.—VISCOUNT SALOMON DE VIRELADE TO CARDINAL MAZARIN.

1650.

Il est si difficile de réussir aux affaires qui sont entreprises avec témérité et sans avoir pris les précautions nécessaires, qu'on ne saurait blâmer ceux qui usent de circonspection avant les commencer, surtout les négociations si délicates que celles d'Angleterre où j'ai demandé passe-port, bien qu'il n'y ait point de guerre entre les deux nations, parce que n'agissant que pour les marchands ils pouvaient me rendre responsable, parlant au nom des communautés, de ce que tous les jours ils demandent aux particuliers et prennent sur eux à main armée par droit de représailles. Comme particulier, je n'aurais pas craint ces violences qui eussent été honteuses à notre nation si elles eussent été exercées sur moi comme personne publique.

J'avais aussi deux fins en écrivant, ou d'engager le régime d'Angleterre à traiter en me faisant réponse, ou en me donnant sauf-conduit, à se contenter de la reconnaissance des marchands sans en exiger une plus formelle de la part du roi que sa permission; ou en me refusant le passe-port que je demandais, j'éviterais l'affront qui m'eût été très-sensible parce qu'il eût intéressé toute la France, si on m'eût chassé comme on a fait l'ambassadeur de Hollande de le sieur de Croullé, et estime qu'il vaut mieux avoir cette déclaration par écrit, avant avoir mis le pied en leur pays, que de la recevoir plus injurieusement de leur bouche.

J'avais encore une autre considération; c'est que les Anglais, étant extrêmement fiers et glorieux, ont néanmoins complaisance et se laissent gagner par civilités, qui est la raison qui les porte à aimer sur toutes les nations les Italiens qui ont l'avantage de l'adresse et courtoisie sur tous les autres peuples de l'Europe; et par cette raison j'ai estimé que, leur écrivant avec grand respect et compliment, ils se porteraient à avoir ma négociation plus agréable. J'ai réussi en ce point de les obliger à me faire réponse, ce qu'ils n'avaient fait, ni directement ni indirectement, aupavavant à toutes les lettres qui leur ont été écrites et aux témoignages plus exprès et plus formels des intentions qu'on avait de les satisfaire, desquelles ma lettre, qui n'était qu'un simple compliment, ne faisait aucune mention. Il est vrai que cette réponse est conçue en terms un peu aigres, mais qu'on dit être fort familiers à cette nation impérieuse, et desquels pourtant j'infère qu'ils affectent quelque forme de justice en leur procédé; mais quand ils prennent un prétexte faux qui est le déni de justice de la part de la France, ils nous donnent lieu de nous servir d'une défense véritable fondée en l'injustice qu'ils ont faite aux vaisseaux Français; et ainsi ils se convainquent eux-mêmes du reproche qu'ils nous imputent, et s'ôtent le moyen de nous rien demander des prises faites sur eux parce que les pertes de nos marchands excèdent beaucoup si on venait à compensation. Pour la liberté du commerce, ils offrent de la rendre pour toutes nos denrées, soudain qu'en France on le leur permittrait de même; mais tout ce que nous pouvions désirer d'eux ils le mettent à un prix qui est ou bien haut, ou bien considérable, suivant les diverses réflexions politiques qu'on fera sur cette matière; c'est la reconnaissance de leur Etat nouveau de la part du roi, dont ils prétendent aussi bien qu'il n'est pas le juge au fond.

II.—SUMMARY OF THE INSTRUCTIONS NECESSARY TO VISCOUNT SALOMON FOR CONDUCTING THE NEGOTIATION WITH ENGLAND.

Premièrement demande très-humblement résolution à savoir si, représentant les intérêts des marchands et qu'un comité soit appointé pour l'ouïr, ou qu'il soit même admis au conseil d'Etat ou au Parlement, dans ses requêtes ou autres actes il doit qualifier le régime d'Angleterre d'Etat de République, ou autres tels titres et qualités que les Anglais désireront:

2º S'il ne pourra pas renouveler les offres faites au sieur Augier, agent des affaires d'Angleterre dès l'an 1647, et acceptées dès lors par ledit Parlement d'Angleterre, pour les prises faites jusques audit temps, à condition que ledit régime d'Angleterre fasse la même justice aux marchands Français; ou si ayant représenté les diligences faites en France par l'autorité du roi et de ses ministres pour donner aux Anglais satisfaction en justice, il ne doit point protester du déni de justice en Angleterre aux marchands Français:

3º Demande si venant à demeurer d'accord de l'amnistie réciproque et générale pour toutes les prises faites sur mer respectivement entre les deux nations, et que pour parvenir à ladite amnistie, il y eût quelque membre du Parlement ou personnes puissantes dans ledit Etat intéressés auxdites prises, il ne peut pas leur en promettre dédommagement pour les attirer et les mettre dans les intérêts ou dépendances de la France, par forme de pension qui les engage au service de S. M.; et pour cet effet il supplie S. M. de faire un fonds que les marchands ès villes maritimes du royaume souffriront volontiers être pris par augmentation dans les bureaux des entrées et douanes établis dans les ports, pour gagner les plus puissants d'Angleterre qui se trouveront disposés, moyennant telles gratifications, à se porter au service de la France et à favoriser la liberté du commerce:

4º Demande que, pour le rétablissement et sûreté du commerce à l'avenir, il lui soit permis, en continuant les offres faites par M. le comte de Brienne, de promettre aux Anglais que dorénavant il n'y aura plus de représailles accordées, et que les commissions données, s'il y en a seront révoquées, pourvu qu'il sen usent de même, fassent cesser toutes hostilités et déprédations sur mer et révoquent toutes leurs lettres de représailles:

5º Demande que les ordonnances des 10 Juillet 1643 et 20 Mai 1647 soient renouvelées et que copies de semblables ordonnances lui soient délivrées, portant itératives défenses aux sujets du roi de prendre ou acheter aucuns effets sur lesdits Anglais et de les molester en façon quelconque; laquelle ordonnance on puisse faire publier au même temps que les Anglais en accorderont une semblable en faveur des sujets du roi:

6° Demande si les Anglais, venant à un traité, désirent que les vaisseaux marchands de leur nation ne soient point visités sous prétexte de robe d'ennemis cachée quand ils seront rencontrés par des vaisseaux de guerre du roi, et prétendent qu'ils ne sont tenus que de baisser les voiles et faire honneur à la bannière et pavillon de France, ledit privilége de n'être point visité ne leur peut pas être permis, un semblable etant accordé par eux aux vaisseaux Français qui trafiqueront en Ecosse ou autres lieux qui seront en guerre déclarée avec lesdits Anglais, l'inconvénient n'étant point plus grand que les Espagnols reçoivent leurs marchandises par des vaisseaux Anglais que par les vaisseaux Français qui les leur portent tous les jours :

7° Demande s'il ne doit pas faire instance pour obtenir une décharge des droits et impositions qu'on exige en Angleterre des Français, auxquelles impositions les naturels du pays ni les autres étrangers ne sont point sujets, et si, obtenant ledit privilége et décharge, il ne peut pas promettre quelque gratification à ceux qui la moyenneront :

8° Demande qu'il plaise à S. M. promettre lever les défenses de l'entrée des draperies et autres manufactures de soie et laine, à condition que les Anglais permettent l'entrée des vins et manufactures de France en Angleterre, et révoquent l'acte de ladite prohibition du 28 Août (7 Septembre) 1649 :

9° Demande qu'il puisse promettre, suivant les offres de M. le comte de Brienne, par ordre de monseigneur le cardinal, que le traité qui sera projeté et concerté entre lesdits Anglais et lui, suivant les ordres qu'il recevra tous les jours, sera confirmé, approuvé et autorisé de S. M., si, après l'avoir communiqué à son Conseil, elle le trouve agréable :

10° Demande que, ne pouvant obtenir le rétablissement entier du commerce, il lui soit permis pour le moins de tâcher à la remettre en quelque partie et dans quelque province s'il ne se peut pour tout le royaume ; comme, si la Normandie s'oppose à l'entrée des draperies, qu'au moins elles puissent être reçues en Guyenne, la Rochelle et Bretagne, pourvu que les Anglais permottent l'entrée des vins desdites provinces :

11° Demande de quelle sorte se doit traiter avec le général Cromwell, et s'il ne doit pas lui faire concevoir, par l'exemple du prince d'Orange, de Mansfeld, du duc de Weimar et autres, que c'est avantage, honneur et sûreté, aux hommes de sa valeur et de son poids, d'avoir l'amitié et protection de France dont les inclinations nobles et belliqueuses se portent toujours à estimer et favoriser les personnes de courage et mérite extraordinaire :

12° Demande que le sieur Croullé, qui a les cachets du roi en Angleterre, ne puisse agir sans sa participation et consentement, bien que ledit Sieur Salomon ne prétende point engager le nom ni l'autorité du roi en sa négociation.

III.—WALTER FROST TO M. SALOMON, VISCOUNT DE VIRELADE.

Whitehall, December 11–21, 1650.

SIR: I have received your letter from Paris, of the 10th of December (new style), which, as I am bound by the duties of my office, I have laid before the Council of State, to whom I must produce all that I receive from abroad, and at whose last meeting, several letters were read by others, written to various members of the Council, and one written to a merchant; of none of which the Council can take cognizance, they being letters of private persons regarding a public affair. But that the very civil letter you have written to me may not remain altogether unanswered, I give you the trouble to read these few lines, to let you know that you cannot be more sensible than I am of the great benefit it would be to our two nations, if traffic and commerce between them were free and uninterrupted. I am well assured that you are not ignorant on which side the first breach took place, as it is impossible for you not to have heard of the great injuries which the people of this Commonwealth have suffered from the State of France, by reason of the piracies of the French upon our ships in the seas of the Levant, not to mention other wrongs done to the Commonwealth, of which we are not insensible; and although remonstrances have long since been made to that State to obtain justice, we have never been able to obtain it, either for the said piracies, or for other injuries, too numerous to be here stated at length, wherefore I will not trouble you with them. For this reason we have, according to the law of nations, given letters of reprisals to those who have suffered losses, that they might have the means of doing themselves justice; it being, in fact, a matter of very common observation, that clear and prompt justice is not ordinarily practised on the other side of the Channel. As to the interdiction of French wines, in which we know that the towns of Bordeaux and Nantes are most interested, we only resorted to it after the French had prohibited our manufactures of wool and silk; and I am persuaded that, if they can do without our manufactures, we can also easily dispense with the wines of France, and that we shall have the means of making them know that trade should be reciprocal. Time may also teach us that we can likewise do without other things manufactured in France. But as your mission from abroad, with powers to act for Bordeaux, Nantes, and other communities, might be with the approbation of your king, I cannot help you in it, as there is no one here who can treat with you about these affairs, except the sovereign power or its delegates; and that power will receive addresses from none but the sovereign power of

France, which alone can give the necessary credentials to treat of such affairs. I cannot, therefore, procure you a safe-conduct to come in the capacity, and with the credentials you indicate: and if you were here, none of our merchants could treat with you concerning such matters, as they are affairs of State, and not of the nature of their private affairs. But if the State of France is willing to consider the injuries and denials of justice which it has committed, and will save us the trouble of righting ourselves, and will, by you, make overtures of a public address from it to this Commonwealth, respecting these affairs, and in the form usual between sovereign States, I do not doubt that this State will be glad to receive any honest and just propositions which may be made to terminate differences, and restore liberty of trade for the common good. And, as I hope that, by the presence of God with us, the force and strength of this Commonwealth will never be used to injure others, so the state in which it is at present, by the same Divine presence and blessing, is such that we can do justice to our people against those who refuse it. Nevertheless, we should be desirous to live peaceably with all, and should prefer to receive those who have done us injury to do us justice voluntarily, rather than extort it from them by force, at the cost of present sufferings to those who may be personally innocent, and whose misfortune it is, and not their fault, that they depend on a State which had rather expose its innocent subjects to reprisals, than do justice to the just demands which are made upon it. I will only add that I hope for a happy accommodation of affairs, and that, in order to attain thereto by just and honorable means, I will contribute all that lies in the power of your affectionate servant,

WALTER FROST.

APPENDIX XV.

(Page 222.)

COLBERT'S REPORT REGARDING TRADE WITH ENGLAND.

1650.

BIEN que l'abondance dont il a plu à Dieu de douer la plupart des provinces de ce royaume semble le pouvoir mettre en état de se pouvoir suffire à lui même, néanmoins la Providence a posé la France en telle situation que sa propre fertilité lui serait inutile et souvent à charge et incommode sans le bénéfice du commerce qui porte d'une province à l'autre et chez les étrangers ce dont les uns et les autres peuvent avoir besoin pour en attirer à soi toute l'utilité.

Nous avons laissé perdre l'usage et le bien du commerce, soit par la nonchalance avec laquelle nos peuples s'appliquent à cet honnête exercice, soit aussi par l'interruption que les étrangers y causent.

Le remède du premier mal, qui vient de nous-mêmes, des humeurs et inclinations turbulentes contraires à un légitime trafic, est plus difficile à trouver après les troubles qui ont agité la France et qui ont ôté aux marchands la liberté et sûreté de transporter leurs denrées; et la confiance nécessaire au négoce ne pouvant s'établir dans la confusion et la violence des factions dont chacun veut mettre à couvert ses effets, la crainte survenue du péril qui procède des hostilités étrangères a achevé notre ruine, ôtant le courage aux marchands d'envoyer ou demander rien aux étrangers pour ne pas exposer à une visible perte tout ce qu'ils risqueraient.

Tant que nous n'avons eu affaire qu'à l'Espagne nous nous en sommes garantis assez heureusement; mais depuis que, par un surcroît de malheurs, les Anglais nous ont déclaré une, guerre qui n'est pas moins fâcheuse qu'imprévue, cette surprise en l'état où nous nous trouvons, sans armée navale pour résister aux leurs très-puissantes, et dans l'abattement des peuples des villes frontières, et le peu de secours que reçoivent les finances du roi depuis la cessation du commerce, et les troubles qui empêchent de faire un fonds suffisant pour armer une flotte telle qu'elle serait nécessaire, il est difficile que le commerce puisse se rétablir tant que ce désordre continuera et qu'on souffrira les représailles que les Anglais donnent, fondées sur diverses prises faites par des vaisseaux Français ou vendues dans les ports de France.

Pour obvier aux suites de cet inconvénient qui nous pourtait enfin causer une guerre fâcheuse, il semble qu'il n'y a que deux moyens qui se réduisent enfin à un, c'est de traiter avec eux; ou par un traité particulier, avec les intéressés qui demandent, disent-ils, justice et restitution des choses prises et confisquées sur eux, ce qui se réduit à un long examen ou discussion où il faut apporter beaucoup de considération et faire comparaison des prises faites par less Anglais sur nos marchands avec plus d'injustice; ou il faut venir à un traité général avec le régime présent d'Angleterre qui, ayant renversé la forme de l'Etat ancien, nous oblige par cette mutation à prendre nos sûretés avec eux par de nouvelles conventions, ou au moins à renouveler et confirmer les anciens traités entre la France et l'Angleterre, avec cette différence néanmoins que les prétentions des rois d'Angleterre (qui n'ont point été transmises à leur peuple et dont la République ne peut avoir succédé) ayant rendu nos rois moins exacts à demander diverses conditions pour le commerce avec lesdits Anglais, dont les autres nations, et particulièrement les Espagnols, se sont prévalus, nous pouvons à présent tirer divers avantages en ce changement pour l'égalité du commerce sur lequel ils nous traitaient très-iniquement tant par les impositions sur les marchandises que nos marchands en tiraient ou y transportaient, qu'ils appellent d'esdavache, de cajade, du survoyeur et du coquet, qui étaient des impôts que les rois augmentaient tous les jours aussi par des licences particulières et privilèges à des compagnies, exclusivement à tous autres, du transport de diverses marchandises, par le choix qu'en avait le pourvoyeur du roi Angleterre qui décriait et mettait à vil prix le résidu de nos denrées où il n'aurait pas mis sa marque, comme aussi par l'inégalité des poids et mesures, si fort condamnée dans l'Ecriture et par laquelle néanmoins ils ne donnent qu'au poids particulier et ne reçoivent aucune marchandise que dans des balances publiques beaucoup plus fortes.

Pour remettre le commerce, il y a deux choses nécessaires, la sûreté et la liberté. La sûreté dépend d'une mutuelle correspondance à empêcher les pirates et courses des particuliers qui, au lieu de s'appliquer en leur navigation à l'honnête exercice du commerce, rompent avec violence le lien de la société civile par lequel les nations se secourent les unes les autres en leurs nécessités. Cette sûreté ne se peut établir que par des défenses respectives dans les deux Etats de faire des prises sur les marchands des deux nations; et parce que le prétexte du commerce que nos alliés font avec nos ennemis portant leurs effets dans nos vaisseaux, à donné occasion à des vaisseaux Français l'attaquer les Anglais, et que les confiscations ont éte fondées sur cette raison par une explication qu'on a donnée à l'ordonnance de François Ier en l'an 1543 sur le fait de l'amirauté, art. 43, néanmoins il semble qu'il vaut mieux consentir que les Espagnols et autres nos ennemis tirent cette commodité par le moyen de nos alliés, pourvu que les Anglais s'obligent à obtenir le même privilége pour nos marchands quand ils passeront, devant les armées d'Espagne, leurs effets dans des vaisseaux Anglais, pour ne pas, pour causer un dommage de peu de conséquence aux Espagnols, donner occasion à la continuation d'une piraterie qui ruine le commerce, étant certain que jamais des vaisseaux de guerre ne visitent des marchandises sans laisser des marques de la rapine des soldats qui n'ont pas la modestie de se retenir, trouvant facilité à prendre; l'inconvénient qu'on peut trouver que, sous la couverture de nos alliés, les sujets de nos ennemis fassent quelque profit, se pouvant remarquer tous les jours encore plus grand par la facilité que les propres sujets du roi y prêtent sans qu'on les en puisse empêcher.

Cette déclaration réciproque aux vaisseaux de guerre des deux nations interdirait d'arrêter, sous quelque prétexte que ce soit, les vaisseaux marchands, et défendrait aussi l'entrée des ports aux forbans et corsaires pour vendre leurs marchandises, avec injonction d'un sévère châtiment à ceux qui en achéteraient. A quoi les gouverneurs des places et des ports, capitaines et officiers de la marine seront obligés de tenir la maine, car on ne doute point que la cessation des hostilités ne remette en peu de temps le commerce et par conséquent l'abondance publique et la richesse des particuliers, et notablement les droits du roi par la réception des marchandises étrangères qui ne viennent point et la sortie des denrées du pays qu'on n'ose exposer à la mer.

Pour ce qui est du passé et prises faites sur des marchands Anglais, elles sont de deux natures et conditions: ou bien elles sont faites sur les commissions roi du d'Angleterre dont nous ne saurions répondre, ni avoir empêché que les sujets du roi, et même commandant ses vaisseaux, n'aient pris commission d'un autre prince cousin du roi et dont la reine sa mère est présente et si considérée en France qu'au milieu de la guerre civile le parlement de Paris la gratifia d'une pension notable, puisqu'on voit tous les jours que divers Français et même des chefs des troupes du roi suivent le maréchal de Turenne et servent l'archiduc et les ennemis de la France. Mais tout ce que pouvait faire le roi avec son conseil était de faire défense à tous les ports de recevoir les prises faites par les vaisseaux et au nom du roi d'Angleterre, qui n'ont point de ports si commodes qu'en France pour retirer leurs prises, au lieu que ledit Parlement et République possède tous les ports d'Angleterre qui leur servent de retraite. Ou bien les prises ont été faites par des vaisseaux du roi avec sa commission et bannière de France. Il se trouvera que les vaisseaux Anglais étaient chargés de robe d'ennemi, ou qu'ils n'ont pas voulu amener et obéir aux lois de la mer; au contraire ont tiré sur les vaisseaux Français; que s'il se trouve quelques abus commis par les capitaines des vaisseaux du roi, on en peut demander la justice qui ne sera jamais déniée, au lieu de représailles sur de pauvres marchands qui n'ont point participé auxdites prises, en quoi l'injustice est évidente.

Et d'autant que les pertes faites par nos marchands, qui ne se plaindraient pas peut-être s'ils avaient été pris de la même sorte que les Anglais, excèdent ou pour le moins égalent les leurs, il y a de l'apparence qu'il faudra venir à consentir que chacun gardera ce qu'il a pris, vu l'impossibilité de la restitution que les Anglais même ne demanderaient pas après une guerre ouvert, ainsi qu'il a été pratiqué en tous les traités faits avec leur nation. Il nous serait désavantageux d'avoir été leurs amis et alliés s'ils nous traitaient si rudement et avec des conditions onéreuses, après avoir observé si religieusement une ponctuelle et exacte neutralité pendant les guerres civiles où le roi Angleterre même s'est plaint diverses fois que la France favorisait ouvertement le Parlement.

Pour la liberté du commerce, il y a deux choses à désirer: l'une la décharge des impositions et de celles que les Anglais lèvent sur les marchands Français et où les Espagnols même ne sont sujets en vertu de leurs traités; nous avons raison de demander pour le moins des conditions égales, le commerce de la France ayant été toujours plus utile à l'Angleterre, et l'entrée de ceux de notre nation n'y étant point si dangereuse que celle de ce peuple méridional, avare et ambitieux : l'autre, qui regarde particulièrement la province de Guyenne, la Rochelle et Nantes, est qu'ils laissent entrer les vins de France en Angleterre, en leur permettant l'entrée de leurs draps directement suivant les traités faits avec leurs rois pour le commerce, au lieu que nous recevons tous les jours leurs draps par les Hollandais qui leur portent aussi nos vins transvasés dans d'autres futailles. L'intérêt des fermes du roi est visible en cette permission réciproque, les douanes ne pouvant subsister si toutes les marchandises n'y sont reçues indifféremment avec liberté et n'en sortent de même.

Le point où les Anglais s'attachent le plus et pour lequel ils veulent relâcher et condescendre à tout ce qu'on leur peut demander est la reconnaissance de leur République, en quoi les Espagnols nous ont précédés et obtenu en conséquence l'adjonction de la flotte Anglaise pour attaquer celle des Portugais qui vient du Brésil. On a à craindre une plus étroite union des négociations de l'ambassadeur d'Espagne en Angleterre. C'est à nosseigneurs les ministres à prescrire la forme de cette reconnaissance, jusqu'où elle doit aller, en quoi la France sera excusable devant Dieu et les hommes si elle est contrainte de venir à la reconnaissance de cette République pour prévenir les ligues et mauvais desseins des Espagnols, qui font toutes les injustices et se soumettent à toutes les bassesses imaginables pour nous nire. Il semble que cette affaire, bien que délicate, se peut traiter de telle sorte que cette nation orgueilleuse s'en peut contenter, sans préjudice au roi d'Angleterre, ou favoriser le mauvais exemple de la dégradation de la royauté, après ce que la France a fait en faveur des Hollandais qui ne se contentaient pas, comme les Anglais, d'un compliment, et ont fait voir enfin que la foi Germanique, ou plutôt Batavique, n'était pas plus solide que l'Anglaise.

APPENDIX XVI.

(Page 224.)

STATEMENT PRESENTED TO QUEEN ANNE OF AUSTRIA AND HER COUNCIL, BY CARDINAL MAZARIN, REGARDING THE COMMONWEALTH OF ENGLAND.

Janvier, 1651.

SUR la question proposée, il semble d'abord que si on se règle par les lois de l'honneur ou de la justice, l'on ne doit point reconnaître la République d'Angleterre, puisque le roi ne saurait rien faire de plus préjudiciable à sa réputation que cette reconnaissance par laquelle non-seulement il abandonne l'intérêt du roi légitime, son proche parent, voisin et allié, mais lui fait une offense publique, et qu'Elle ne saurait rien faire de plus injuste que de reconnaître des usurpateurs qui ont souillé leurs mains du sang de leur souverain, et qui se sont violemment attribué le droit de le condamner à mort par une entreprise barbare, de dangereux exemple dans toutes les monarchies, et qui fait horreur à tous les gens de bien. Le roi d'Angleterre en fera des plaintes et en témoignera sans doute des ressentiments qui feront de la (peine). La raison d'Etat obligerait plutôt de secourir le roi sons fils en Ecosse et en Irlande, étant extrêmement à craindre que, si les remuements de ces deux royaumes sont une fois apaisés, la République d'Angleterre ne devienne plus orgueilleuse par ces heureux succès, voyant son autorité ètablie au dedans, ne fasse des entreprises au dehors, et n'emploie la grande force qu'elle a sur pied plutôt contre la France que contre les autres Etats, à cause de l'animosité naturelle et grande jalousie qui a été de tout temps entre les deux nations, et qui se trouve anjourd'hui extrêmement augmentée par les hostilités qui ont été excitées depuis peu sur la mer entre les sujets des deux royaumes.

Mais comme les lois de l'honneur et de la justice ne doivent jamais rien faire faire qui soit contraire à celles de la prudence, il faut considérer que toutes les démonstrations que l'on pourrait faire présentement en faveur du roi d'Angleterre n'amèneraient pas son rétablissement; qu'un plus long refus de reconnaître la République, qui est en possession de l'autorité souveraine, ne servira de rien pour augmenter ou confirmer les droits du roi; que ce que nous pourrions faire maintenant pour lui ne servirait qu'à nous rendre incapables de l'assister un jour plus utilement dans une conjoncture plus favorable; que l'état des affaires de France ne permet pas de lui donner aucune sorte d'assistance pour lui aider à rétablir ses affaires; ou même que les Anglais étant les maîtres de la mer, ôtent tous les moyens de lui en envoyer, et que la part que l'on prendrait maintenant dans sa querelle, ou les ressentiments qu'on voudrait témoigner (de nouveau?) pour les Anglais ne serviraient qu'à leur acquérir de nouveaux avantages; que la France, à cause de la grande guerre dont elle se trouve chargée au dehors, et des diverses factions dont elle est agitée au dedans, qui la jetteraient dans un péril extrême si les Anglais venaient à se déclarer en faveur d'une des factions, et qu'ils pussent y engager, comme il serait à craindre avec le temps, les religionnaires de ce royaume; surtout ce que la nécessité du temps et des affaires obligera de faire en faveur de la République, n'empêchera pas que ci-après on ne puisse se prévaloir des conjonctures favorables qui se présenteront quand on sera en meilleur état pour faire quelque grande entreprise, et qu'il y aura plus d'apparence d'y pouvoir réussir heureusement; et que d'ailleurs il y a sujet de craindre que, si les Espagnols sont une fois plus étroitement liés avec les Anglais, comme ils y travaillent avec chaleur, ils ne les empêchent de s'accommoder avec nous, et ne les engagent sinon à nous faire une guerre ouverte, du moins à leur donner de puissantes assistances contre nous; il ne reste pas lieu de douter que l'on ne doive sans délai entrer en négociation avec la République d'Angleterre, et lui donner le titre qu'elle désire.

Il y a néanmoins une condition absolument nécessaire, et sans laquelle il serait inutile de s'engager à faire cette reconnaissance, qui est d'être assuré auparavant qu'on en retirera quelque utilité capable d'emporter à la balance le préjudice qu'on pourra recevoir en la réputation; car présupposé qu'on puisse avec quelque certitude se promettre quelque avantage de ce qu'on fera, je n'estimerai pas qu'il se fallût beaucoup arrêter aux formalités; mais il serait doublement préjudiciable de faire une bassesse si, après l'avoir faite, les Anglais demeuraient dans l'indifférence et la froideur, et si ces avances ne servaient qu'à les rendre plus orgueilleux et plus difficiles dans les conditions du traité qui devra être fait avec eux pour accommoder les différends que nous avons ensemble.

La voie la plus honorable pour entrer en négociation avec eux serait qu'ils envoyassent ici un ambassadeur qui sera reçu et honoré comme ministre d'une république libre. Le roi de Portugal en a usé de cette sorte après sa proclamation, ayant envoyé, vers tous les princes qui n'étaient point obéissants d'Espagne, des ambassadeurs pour en donner part et pour se mettre en possession de sa nouvelle souveraineté par la réception qui leur serait faite.

Si les Anglais ont une véritable disposition à s'accommoder avec nous, ils recevront favorablement cet expédient et ne feront pas difficulté de renouveler la communication qui a été interrompue depuis le changement arrivé en Angleterre, puisque'elle doit produire d'abord un effet qui leur est avantageux et qu'ils souhaitent si fort, que l'exemple de ce qui aura été fait par le roi, qui tient le premier rang parmi les rois de l'Europe, servira comme de règle à tous les autres, et qu'ils ne peuvent pas refuser avec raison de faire pour nous ce qu'ils ont voulu faire pour l'Espagne où leur envoyé a été tué. On pourrait même leur faire valoir qu'ayant commencé leur compliment par le lieu qu'ils ne devaient pas, ils nous ont donné sujet de plainte qu'on veut oublier pour le bien des deux nations.

Ce qu'il y aurait de plus à craindre et qu'il faut soigneusement éviter est que les Anglais, qui visiblement penchent plus du côté d'Espagne que de France, n'aient l'intention de nous engager en leur faveur afin de s'en servir comme d'un éperon pour hâter les Espagnols à les reconnaître ouvertement et à s'unir avec eux.

La précaution dont on pourrait user serait d'exiger d'eux, s'il est possible, de ne point traiter avec l'Espagne pendant quelque temps, jusqu'à ce que la négociation que nous conduirons avec eux soit terminée ou rompue, ou bien d'ébaucher ou arrêter tellement les conditions de l'accommodement avant que de venir à aucune reconnaissance, qu'il n'y ait pas lieu d'appréhender que l'accommodement se puisse rompre après que la reconnaissance aura été faite.

En un mot, comme les Anglais ne voudront peut-être pas acheter notre reconnaissance par les conditions d'un traité éventuel, nous devons aussi éviter de reconnaître la République sans être déjà assurés que l'accommodement entre les deux nations s'en ensuivra, car autrement on s'exposerait à une honte publique sans aucun profit.

APPENDIX XVII.

(Page 225.)

DRAFT OF INSTRUCTIONS TO M. DE GENTILLOT ON HIS MISSION TO ENGLAND.

Janvier—Février, 1651.

Le roi est entiérement persuadé que les différends et hostilités, arrivés depuis quelque temps sur la mer entre les Français et les Anglais, procèdent plutôt de quelque désordre et malentendu entre ceux qui ont commandé jusqu'ici les vaisseaux de guerre que d'aucun dessein qui ait été formé de part ni d'autre d'entrer en rupture, ni même d'interrompre la bonne intelligence qui avait été entretenue jusqu'aux dernières années entre les deux nations, et dont la confirmation semble également nécessaire pour le bien et commodité de l'un et de l'autre.

Sur cette présupposition, Sa Majesté a trouvé bon que le sieur de Gentillot s'en allant en Angleterre travaille adroitement et sans éclat, par le moyen des amis et habitudes qu'il a en ce pays-là, à se bien informer s'il y a une véritable disposition à faire cesser par un bon accommodement les différends qui sont entre les deux nations et à rétablir entre elles une bonne correspondance.

Le sieur de Gentillot, pour agir utilement dans l'exécution de ce dessein, doit être assuré avant tautes choses que le Parlement d'Angleterre n'a point fait de traité particulier avec les Espagnols contre la France, et qu'il n'est point tellement engagé avec eux qu'il ne puisse faire tous les accommodements et confédérations qui seront jugés utiles pour les deux royaumes. . . . .

L'exemple de ce qui est pratiqué envers l'ambassadeur de Portugal oblige doublement d'user de cette circonspection avant qu'entrer en aucun traité avec le Parlement, puisque, pour favoriser les Espagnols, on a longtemps maltraité ledit ambassadeur, et que sous prétexte d'examiner son pouvoir ou par des démarches inusitées, on a différé l'audience qui lui doit être donnée, quoiqu'il n'ait été envoyé que pour faire honneur audit parlement et pour terminer amiablement les différends que le Portugal peut avoir avec l'Angleterre, ce qui a donné lieu de soupçonner que le traitement qu'il recevait était une condition secrète au traité fait avec les Espagnols.

D'ailleurs, nous avons sujet de nous plaindre que les discours obligeants qui ont été faits ici au sieur Morrell et les bennes dispositions qu'on lui a témoignées n'aient encore rien profité pour faire cesser les hostilités que les vaisseaux Anglais exercent contre les sujets du roi, et que l'on s'en soit seulement servi en Angleterre pour avancer les affaires des Espagnols. Au moins ce procédé, joint au traitement que reçoit l'ambassadeur de Portugal, nous doit donner sujet de craindre qu'aprés que nous aurons fait ce que ledit Parlement désire de nous, il ne devienne dés le lendemain plus difficile dans les intérêts que nous avons à démêler avec lui, lesquels demeurant indécis, et causant la continuation des hostilités qui s'exercent sur la mer, donneraient lieu aux Espagnols de se prévaloir de notre peu de prévoyance et de triompher de notre facilité qui ne nous aurait servi de rien.

Il est donc absolument nécessaire, pour ne rien faire qui puisse exposer la réputation d'un grand royaume, de s'assurer avant toutes choses, non-seulement que le Parlement d'Angleterre est en pleine liberté de traiter avec nous et n'a point d'engagement avec les Espagnols qui les en empêche ou qui nous soit préjudiciable, mais que l'on convienne présentement et en termes généraux des moyens d'accommoder tous les différends qui pourraient faire durer ou renouveller ci-apres quelque sorte de mauvaise intelligence entre les sujets des deux royaumes.

Les Anglais ne manqueront pas de demander que le roi reconnaisse apparement leur République par des lettres et autres démonstrations publiques. Sur quoi le sieur de Gentillot représentera qu'il n'y aura point de difficulté sur cet article, que Sa Majesté est disposée de faire ce qu'on désire d'elle sur ce sujet, et que c'est un point que le Parlement peut se tenir pour accordé selon son désir; mais que, pour les considérations touchées ci-dessus, il nous importe d'être assurés qu'après la reconnaissance faite nous ne rentrions pas en rupture ou en mauvaise intelligence pour les différends qui sont aujourd'hui entre les deux nations, et que les hostilités cesseront entièrement.

L'assurance ne peut être autre que de convenir en même temps d'un projet d'accomodement pour les différends qui sont entre les deux nations et qui semblent avoir procédé principalement de deux causes : la première, de la prohibition des marchandises d'Angleterre fait à l'instance du Parlement de Paris ; la seconde, de la prise de quelques vaisseaux Anglais faite par ceux du roi équipés en guerre contre l'Espagne. . . .

Touchant la première cause, l'on n'ignore pas en Angleterre que S. M., pour la pacification des troubles de son royaume, été obligée d'accorder cette défense aux instantes supplications qui lui en ont été faites par son Parlement de Paris en faveur de ladite ville, et que S. M. qui a toujours fait traiter favorablement les étrangers dans son royaume, et particulièrement les marchands Anglais, ne s'est portée qu'avec déplaisir à ce qui a été désiré d'Elle en cette rencontre par quelques-uns de ses sujets, en même temps qu'il y en a d'autres qui en reçoivent du préjudice. Or Sa Majesté est même résolue de faire tout ce qui dépendra d'elle pour mettre les choses dans l'état qu'elles étaient avant cette défense.

Si on veut examiner sans passion la seconde cause des différends, il se trouvera que tout le sujet de plainte est de notre côté: quoique S. M. n'ait jamais donné commission ni à ses sujets, ni à aucun autre pour agir contre l'Angleterre, qu'elle ait fait observer par tous ses Etats une si exacte neutralité entre les deux partis d'Angleterre que même elle a refusé la retraite dans ses ports aux vaisseaux du Roi de la Grande-Bretagne, qu'elle a défendu l'entrée et vente dans son royaume de toutes le prises qu'ils auraient faites et pourraient faire ci-après sur les marchands et autres tenant le parti du Parlement, qu'elle a depuis fait publier des défenses très-rigoureuses à ses sujets d'armer ou qu'on recoive la commission de quelque pouvoir étranger que ce soit, et qu'elle a toujours offert de faire prononcer, selon la justice et les lois observées de tout temps entre les deux nations, sur toutes les plaintes qui lui ont été portées des prises faites par ses vaisseaux où les Anglais se sont trouvés intéressés; nonobstant toutes ces favorables déclarations et procédures le Parlement d'Angleterre n'a pas laissé d'interdire le commerce avec la France et d'accorder des lettres de marque ou de représailles contre les sujets du roi, et ensuite ne faire pas seulement attaquer et prendre tous les vaisseaux marchands qu'ils ont rencontrés sans aucune raison ni prétexte, mais même de faire attaquer les vaisseaux de guerre de S. M. par les siens, témoin le combat contre l'escadre de Turenne qui venait dans la rivière de Bordeaux servir Sa Majesté et où la frégate *la Charité* fut prise, l'attaque que les Anglais firent aussi sur quatre vaisseaux du roi aux côtes du Portugal, où celui du chevalier de Fonteny fut pris et lui tué réellement après la prise, et témoin enfin la prise du vaisseau *le Jules* qu'ils n'ont pas laissé de prendre quoiqu'il ait baissé le pavillon et n'ait rendu aucun combat, ce qui est commencer une espèce de guerre sans l'avoir dénoncée auparavant et sans en avoir aucun sujet légitime.

Il serait bien à propos que le sieur de Gentillot, ayant représenté ce que dessus à ceux du Parlement avec lesquels il a quelque habitude, qu'il reconnaîtra mieux disposés à la réconciliation des deux nations et capables de la procurer, essayât de les engager à faire quelque ouverture d'accommodement pour découvrir en quels termes ils estiment qu'il se puisse faire promptement, en donnant assurance que de ce côté-ci on est entièrement disposé à toutes les choses raisonnables qui pourraient être faites avec honneur. Cependant on a déjà donné charge à une personne de qualité de se tenir prête pour aller à Londres de la part du roi pour la reconnaissance ci-dessus, et puis ajuster les autres choses pour le rétablissement de la bonne intelligence entre les deux nations aussitôt qu'on aura eu des nouvelles dudit Gentillot.

Il semblerait surtout nécessaire, l'accommodement étant résolu et projeté, que la République envoyât en cette cour quelqu'un de sa part pour donner avis du changement qu'elle a fait en la forme du gouvernement d'Angleterre, comme elle a fait en Espagne, aux Pays-Bas, à Hambourg et autres endroits où on a voulu recevoir ses ministres. Néanmoins, comme ils pourront dire d'avoir déjà envoyé le sieur Augier qui n'est pas encore venu, s'ils apportent trop de difficultés a consentir à cet envoi, le sieur de Gentillot pourra ne pas s'y arrêter.

Le projet dudit traité pourrait être aux termes suivants :

Qu'il y aura à l'avenir bonne correspondance et amitié entre le roi Très-Chrétien de France et de Navarre, ses pays et sujets d'une part, et la République d'Angleterre, ses pays et sujets d'autre part.

Que les traités ci-devant faits entre les rois de France et d'Angleterre pour régler la façon de vivre et la forme du commerce entre les deux nations demeureront en leur force et vertu, et seront inviolablement observés entre S. M. et ladite République.

En conséquence de quoi les hostilités cesseront, dés le jour du traité, entre les sujets des deux Etats, et toutes lettres de marque et de représailles seront révoquées dès ledit jour, et sera le commerce rétabli en la même liberté et aux mêmes conditions qu'il était fait avant le changement arrivé en Angleterre, moyennant que les défenses qui ont été faites de part et d'autre seront aussi révoquées, Sa Majesté et ladite République se réservant chacun le pouvoir qui leur appartient d'établir, dans les lieux de leur obéissance, tels droits, péages et impositions qu'elles jugeront à propos sur les marchandises et denrées venant de l'un ou l'autre pays.

Toutes actions et demandes des vaisseux et autres choses prises de part et d'autre sur la mer avant le jour du traité, demeureront éteintes et abolies pour ôter tout sujet de nouveau trouble à l'avenir entre les deux nations, et néanmoins *le Jules* et autres vaisseaux de guerre qui se trouveront avoir été pris appartenant immédiatement à Sa Majesté ou à ladite République, seront restitués de bonne foi en l'état qu'ils étaient lorsque la prise a été faite.

Les vaisseaux de guerre de Sa Majesté seront reçus dans les ports d'Angleterre et ceux de ladite République dans les ports de France, aux conditions et précautions tenues aux traités précédents, et l'entrée desdits ports sera interdite aux vaisseaux de guerre des ennemis de Sa Majesté en Angleterre, et à ceux des ennemis de la République dans les ports de France.

Le Roi et ladite République me pourront donner à l'avenir aucune sorte d'assistance aux ennemis l'un de l'autre.

S'il reste quelque sujet de différend entre les deux Etats ou leurs sujets, il sera terminé amiablement et selon la justice, sans que pour raison de ce l'amitié et bonne intelligence de Sa Majesté et de ladite République puisse être altérée.

Toutes ces conditions sont si raisonnables et si avantageuses pour l'Angleterre qu'il n'y a pas lieu de croire que ledit Parlement y fasse difficulté, vu même que le droit de faire les traités et confédérations est une plus solide marque de souveraineté, et que celui qui sera fait présentement sera un acte plus authentique que celle dont ladite République est en possession, que toutes les lettres et compliments qui peuvent être faits pour la reconnaître, lesquels sont plus sujets à être révoqués ou changés qu'un traité signé de part et d'autre qui doit servir de loi aux deux nations pour leur négoce et forme de vivre ensemble; ce que le sieur de Gentillot saura trés-bien faire valoir afin d'augmenter la disposition que les Anglais peuvent avoir déjà de traiter avec nous.

Il pourra même laisser entendre que si ladite République désire quelque engagement plus étroit avec la France, principalement contre l'Espagne, l'on y est entièrement disposé de ce côté-ci. Il lui sera très-facile de faire connaître l'avantage que les Anglais y trouveraient, et les moyens que nous pourrions leur fournir de se prévaloir, soit du côté des Indes ou ailleurs, de l'état où se trouve à présent réduite la monarchie d'Espagne à laquelle ils ont grand intérêt de ne pas laisser reprendre les avantages qu'elle a eus ci-devant lorsqu'elle a formé des entreprises sur l'Angleterre. Et en cas que ledit sieur de Gentillot y trouve disposition du côté des Anglais, sur les avis qu'il en donnera, l'ambassadeur qui passera en Angleterre sera chargé et aura pouvoir suffisant d'en traiter.

Le sieur de Gentillot pourra sur ce sujet les faire adroitement souvenir de la maxime qui a toujours été tenue par les plus sages ministres de leur nation, qu'il est plus avantageux à l'Angleterre d'être en guerre ouverte avec l'Espagne que d'avoir la paix avec elle, et qu'au contraire en ce qui regarde la France, soit par le voisinage, soit par la puissance de notre gouvernement, et par l'avantage que l'Angleterre tire de notre commerce, l'amitié lui en doit être très-considérable; d'autant plus que quelque mal et quelque incommodité que nous peut apporter la rupture, la France est toujours le royaume dont l'Angleterre a le plus à espérer ou à craindre; et même dans le trafic, la prise que nous faisons d'un seul vaisseau Anglais nous fait le plus souvent dédommagés de la perte que nous aurions de trois des nôtres, pour la valeur des marchandises dont ils sont ordinairement chargés. . . .

On remet au sieur de Gentillot de s'adresser, pour le bon succès de sa négociation, aux personnes qu'il croira les mieux intentionnées et les plus capables de la faire réussir.

Le sieur Augier a témoigné que la France se portant à la reconnaissance ci-dessus, ill ferait favoriser le plus possible cette couronne en contribuant avec chaleur ce qui peut dépendre de lui pour la bonne intelligence des deux nations. Le sieur Gentillot le verra et lui dira confiance que leurs Majestés ont en sa parole, et qu'elles lui en demandent maintenant les effets.

Il verra aussi le sieur Fleming, et lui rendra la lettre de M. de Bellièvre. C'est une personne qui en tout temps a témoigné affection pour cette couronne et a rendu tous les services qu'il a pu aux ministres de S. M., et on ne doute point qu'il ne continue à le faire en cette conjoncture qui a tant d'importance au bien et au repos des deux nations.

Sur toutes choses, il est absolument nécessaire que ledit sieur de Gentillot tienne le secret de son voyage bien secret, de crainte que, s'il était découvert par les Anglais, il ne rencontrât des obstacles à entrer en négociation avec eux, pareils à ceux qui se sont formés quand l'on a su que le sieur Salomon y allait être envoyé.

APPENDIX XVIII.

(Page 242.)

INSTRUCTIONS TO THE COUNT D'ESTRADES ON HIS MISSION TO ENGLAND.

Montereau, 23 Avril, 1652.

M. d'Estrades, pour traiter avec les Anglais et disposer les choses à un bon accommodement avec eux, doit être informé que nous avons présentement trois différends principaux avec la République d'Angleterre.

Le premier est sur la forme de traiter avec elle, puisqu'elle ne veut entrer en aucune sorte de négociation ni de conférence que le roi ne la reconnaisse pour République libre et souveraine, et ne lui écrive aux mêmes termes que lui ont écrit les autres souveraines qui ont déjà fait cette reconnaissance.

Le second est touchant les prises faites sur la mer de part et d'autre par représailles ou autrement, touchant les moyens de rétablir le commerce entre les deux nations, touchant la forme de vivre et de se saluer quand les vaisseaux de guerre ou autres des deux Etats se rencontreront à la mer, et touchant l'observation des anciennes alliances et précédents traités.

Le troisième est touchant les hostilités ou représailles qui s'exercent présentement de part et d'autre.

Pour le premier, nous demeurons d'accord qu'il précède les autres dans la négociation et dans l'exécution. Pour cet effet, le sieur d'Estrades peut promettre, à ceux qui ont charge de traiter ou conférer avec lui, que le roi est prêt de reconnaître la République et de lui écrire une lettre avec les mêmes titres qui lui ont été donnés jusqu'ici par les autres rois, de faire rendre cette lettre par un gentilhomme qui sera envoyé exprès en Angleterre, et de la faire suivre, si on le désire, par une ambassade solennelle.

Mais cet article ne peut être accordé ni exécuté que l'on ne soit en même temps d'accord du troisième avec les Anglais, car il ne serait ni honorable pour le roi, ni juste pour les Anglais, que Sa Majesté leur envoyât faire un compliment en la forme qu'ils désirent, si elle n'est assurée que la lettre ayant été rendue et la reconnaissance faite, les hostilités et les représailles cesseront de part et d'autre. Sans cela, il semblerait que les Anglais voudraient ajouter le mépris à l'offense, si en même temps que nous leur faisons des civilités, ils continuaient d'attaquer les vaisseaux des sujets du roi sur la mer.

Pour le second article, comme il contient la matière de tous les traités précédent, il faudra nécessairement le renvoyer par-devant des commissaires qui seront nommés de part et d'autre, parce qu'ils auront besoin d'un plus long délai pour examiner et résoudre les différends qui sont entre les deux nations pour raison des prises, du commerce, de la forme de vivre en se recontrant sur la mer et de l'observation des anciennes alliances, qu'il n'en faudra pour les deux autres articles qui peuvent être accordés et conclus en un moment. Lesdits commissaires auront pouvoir d'arrêter ce qui se trouvera raisonnable de part et d'autre, et d'en assurer le payement, selon ce que ledit sieur d'Estrades a témoigné par ses lettres que c'était l'intention des Anglais.

L'on ne doit pas craindre que ce second article soit capable d'empêcher l'accommodement, puisque dès à présent l'on est prêt, de la part du roi, de rétablir les choses au même état qu'elles étaient avant l'interruption du commerce entre les deux nations si les Anglais le désirent; ou s'ils souhaitent d'introduire quelque nouveau règlement, l'on est prêt d'en convenir pourvu qu'il soit égal pour les uns et pour les autres.

Quant aux premier et troisième articles, les Anglais ne pouvant pas refuser de les traiter conjointement, il sera nécessaire que ledit sieur d'Estrades les ajuste en même temps, c'est-à-dire qu'il ne s'engage point à l'envoi d'un gentilhomme chargé d'une lettre du roi pour reconnaître la République d'Angleterre, qu'il n'ait parol et ne soit assuré que, dès le jour même ou le lendemain de l'arrivée dudit gentilhomme, quelqu'un du corps du Parlement d'Angleterre aura pouvoir de signer une convention avec lui par laquelle il sera porté que toutes les hostilités et représailles cesseront de ce jour-là, et que dans deux mois, ou plus tôt si faire se peut, on enverra de part et d'autre des commissaires, avec pouvoir suffisant, au lieu dont il sera convenu pour traiter et s'accorder ensemble de tous les autres différends.

Si les Anglais font difficulté de révoquer ou faire cesser les hostilités et représailles pour toujours, à quoi portant on ne voit aucune apparence, il faudra ménager que la cessation dure pour deux ou trois ans tout au moins.

Le roi, désirant d'avancer cette négociation autant qu'il se pourra, a envoyé au sieur d'Estrades la lettre que Sa Majesté écrit au Parlement de la République d'Angleterre, et au cas qu'il y ait quelque difficulté sur les termes, il n'aura qu'à la renvoyer à Sa Majesté et faire savoir ce qu'on désire afin qu'elle y fasse pourvoir promptement.

Le sieur d'Estrades choisira, parmi les officiers qui sont près de lui ou ailleurs, telle autre personne qu'il reconnaîtra plus propre pour être chargée de cet emploi, lui délivrera ladite lettre et la commission du roi qui lui donne pouvoir de traiter, et le fera partir sans délai pour se rendre à Londres en diligence, après néanmoins avoir tiré assurance de ce qui est porté ci-dessus.

Sa Majesté a déjà commandé qu'on envoyât au sieur d'Estrades toutes les expéditions nécessaires, à quoi M. le comte de Brienne n'a pas manqué de satisfaire; de sorte que ledit sieur d'Estrades les ayant reçues, il ne reste qu'à lui recommander que, si en avançant cette négociation, comme on le désire par deçà, il engage Sa Majesté à quelque chose, il n'oublie pas de prendre garde que ceux qui traiteront avec lui soient suffisamment autorisés pour faire tenir en Angleterre les choses qu'ils lui aurant promises. Il n'oubliera pas aussi de remercier de ma part M. Cromwell des offres obligeantes qu'il me fait faire, dont je me sens extrêmement son redevable, et de lui faire sur ce sujet toutes les civilités qu'il jugera à propos.

II.—CARDINAL MAZARIN TO THE COUNT D'ESTRADES.

Montereau, 23 Avril, 1652.

MONSIEUR: Vous apprendrez de nouveau les intentions du roi touchant ce que l'on peut faire avec les Anglais par la lettre que M. de Brienne vous écrit. Celle-ci ne sera qu'un abrégé des principaux points que l'autre contient qui vous servira peut-être à la mieux comprendre.

L'attaque de Gravelines nous met dans une pressante nécessité de savoir les intentions des Anglais, parce que la place ne pouvant être secourue que par mer, la chose peut être enterprise avec espérance du succès, pourvu que les Anglais ne s'en mêlent point; mais étant comme impossible s'ils sont joints à l'Espagne et obligés de favoriser ses desseins contre nous, il est de la dernière importance de découvrir promptement leurs résolutions en traitant avec eux du différend que nous avons ensemble.

Si le traité que nous devons faire avec eux peut être conclu bientôt, ce sera le meilleur et il réglera tout. Vous savez en ce cas que nous sommes prêts; en premier lieu, de reconnaître la République d'Angleterre et de lui écrire aux termes qu'elle peut raisonnablement désirer; en second lieu, de nommer présentement des commissaires pour examiner, avec ceux que la République nommera, les prises qui ont été faites de part et d'autre sur la mer, et pourvoir avec sûreté à la satisfaction de ceux à qui elle se trouvera due, à la charge néanmoins que d'abord, en rendant la lettre du roi avec la suscription que la République a désirée, on conviendra de surseoir toutes hostilités et représailles de part et d'autre.

Si cet article est accordé nous serons assurés pour les secours que nous entreprendrons d'envoyer à Gravelines; et toutefois pour plus de précaution, il sera bon d'en toucher un mot à M. Cromwell pour avoir sa parole s'il est possible, ce qu'on pourra faire en demandant quelque chose de plus, comme par exemple la liberté, pour les vaisseaux du roi destinés pour ce secours, de relâcher en sûreté dans les ports d'Angleterre si le vent contraire ou quelque autre considération les y oblige.

Pour obliger les Anglais à désirer davantage de se réunir avec nous, il ne sera pas mal à propos d'entrer avec eux en traité de la cession de Dunkerque; et en effet le roi leur remettra volontiers cette importante place pourvu, en premier lieu, qu'ils se joignent avec nous contre l'Espagne et qu'ils y demeurent unis tant que la guerre durera, avec obligation de nous assister de leurs forces de mer pour la défense de nos places maritimes; en second lieu, qu'ils nous donnent une somme d'argent considérable, comme pourrait être un million d'or ou huit cent mille écus; en troisième lieu, qu'ils commencent leur assistance présentement pour le secours de Gravelines, pour lequel ils nous prêtent de leurs vaisseaux; en quatrième lieu, qu'ils s'obligent de laisser la religion catholique en l'état où elle est à présent dans Dunkerque, et s'il est possible, de ne mettre dans la place qu'une garnison catholique.

S'ils faisaient difficulté de se déclarer ouvertement contre l'Espagne par le secours de Gravelines, en nous fournissant un bon nombre de vaisseaux pour transporter en France (lorsqu'on leur remettra Dunkerque) la garnison qui est maintenant dans la place, ils pourraient donner ordre secrètement, à ceux qui auraient soin de votre conduite, de faire ce que vous leur ordonnerez, et vous les pourriez engager à vous mettre dans Gravelines avec toute votre garnison.

Dans l'état présent des affaires, nous aurons sujet de nous consoler de la perte de Dunkerque si elle produit la conservation de Gravelines et la jonction des Anglais avec nous contre l'Espagne aux conditions marquées ci-dessus.

Si toutefois toutes lesdites conditions étaient trop malaisées à obtenir, le roi vous permet de partir par degrés de quelquesunes des moins importantes, estimant plus utile, dans la conjoncture présente, de conclure promptement un traité de'alliance avec les Anglais qui sauve Gravelines, que de le différer pour l'espérance d'obtenir quelque condition plus avantageuse pour laquelle il faudra renvoyer par deçà et employer plus de temps, à cause que, pendant cette longeur, Gravelines se pourrait perdre.

Enfin tout est remis à votre prudence et à l'affection que vouz avez pour le service du roi. Je vous dirai seulement qu'il importe merveilleusement que vous envoyiez en diligence à M. Cromwell une personne intelligente qui puisse, étant sur les lieux, s'éclairer des desseins qu'il peut avoir. Car s'il est vrai, comme les nouvelles publiques de Londres le portent, que la République d'Angleterre soit en termes de s'accommoder avec Messieurs les Etats, et que votre accommodement avec elle soit incertain ou tiré de longueur, il y aurait sujet de croire que les propositions d'accommodement dont M. Cromwell vous a fait parler n'ont été faites que pour nous amuser; et il serait à craindre que ladite République, pour profiter de la dépense qu'elle a faite en composant une si puissante flotte, ne se portât à faire quelque entreprise contre cet Etat, dont nous savons qu'elle est extrêmement sollicitée par les envoyés de M. le prince.

En ce cas, il faudrait promptement en donner avis â M. Brasset,[1] et agir de concert avec lui pour voir s'il n'y aurait pas moyen d'engager Messieurs les Etats, qui ont de puissantes force sur la mer, à nous donner quelque assistance, leur intérêt les obligeant à empêcher les Anglais de prendre des avantages sur nous qui leur donneraient moyen, étant les plus forts sur la mer, de se rendre enfin les maîtres du commerce de France; mais il ne faudra faire cette tentative qu'après avoir perdu toute espérance de notre accommodement avec les Anglais et avoir reconnu qu'ils ont résolu de nous attaquer.

[1] The French ambassador at the Hague.

APPENDIX XIX.

DON ALONZO DE CARDEÑAS TO DON GERONIMO DE LA TORRE.

London, 19th July, 1652.

THE Parliament has resolved to publish a manifesto against the Dutch, which will contain a statement of the complaints of the Commonwealth. It is reported that the manifesto will appear within two days, and that it will be followed by hostilities. Within the last few days a squadron of ships belonging to the Parliament inflicted a severe defeat on the vessels of the Dutch, which came from the west, to the number of forty sail. The English captured seven of them, burned four, and drove twenty of them on shore near Calais; the loss was as great as if they had struck on a shoal, for the French on the coast completely pillaged them. The cargo of one of the burned ships was worth 400,000 ducats, according to the report of those who were on board.

Great insults have been offered here to Gentillot, the envoy of the King of France. Before he entered London, he wrote to the Master of Ceremonies to announce that he came on the part of his Most Christian Majesty to the Parliament, with credentials which authorized him to acknowledge the English Commonwealth, in case it would revoke the letters of marque which had been granted against France. An offer to this effect had been made to the King of France on the part of England by William Villiers, brother of the Duke of Buckingham, upon which he had orders to communicate with the Parliament. The Master of Ceremonies carried this letter to the Council of State, where, after a deliberation, it was decided that Villiers should be summoned; the letter of Gentillot was shown him, and he was interrogated concerning it. It would have gone hard with him, if he had not denied everything, and even demanded permission of the Parliament to challenge Gentillot to a duel. The Council contented itself with ordering him to make a declaration in writing, in which he should disavow the offer made, it is said, by him to the Court of France. The Master of Ceremonies sent an exceedingly rude reply to Gentillot, informing him that it was plain, from the declaration of Villiers, which he communicated to him, that his statements were an imposture. Immediately after this, the Frenchman came to London; the Council summoned him before it, and causing him to stand erect and uncovered, interrogated him upon divers matters, beginning by asking him who he was, from what country he came, what his name was, why he came, and who sent him. He replied that he was a Frenchman, that his name was Gentillot, that he came as envoy from the King of France, and that he found they did not treat him according to his character of envoy. He was asked if he brought letters of credence, to which he answered—Yes; he was then asked why he had them not with him to present them; to which he replied by giving every sort of excuse, founded on the orders which he said he had received. He was then directed to leave the chamber, and wait; at the end of a quarter of an hour he was summoned again, and ordered to present his letters of credence in three days, and to attend to report upon them, with a threat of being ordered out of London, and the country, at a short notice, in case he did not do so.

APPENDIX XX.

(Page 245.)

I.—M. DE GENTILLOT TO M. SERVIEN.

Calais, 17 Septembre, 1652.

VOICI des nouvelles non moins fâcheuses que véritables. Les Anglais ont pris les vaisseaux que l'on avait préparés pour le secours de Dunkerque, après les avoir guettés plus de dix jours, à ce que rapporte le capitaine d'un vaisseau brûlot.

M. le commandeur de Boismorand, qui commandait un vaisseau nommé *le Berger*, dit que M. de Vendôme ayant commandé sept vaisseaux et autant de brûlots pour aller à Calais charger les vivres, gens et munitions que l'on devait jeter dans Dunkerque, l'amiral ayant retenu seulement six ou sept brûlots avec *l'Anna* et un autre grand vaisseau, cette petite escadre prit la route vers Calais où elle arriva sur le soir et mouilla l'ancre. Ce qu'à peine elle avait fait quand cinquante-quatre voiles Anglaises lui fondirent sus à pleines voiles. Dans le commencement elle crut que les Anglais la prenaient pour Anglaise, si bien que pour les désabuser elle arbora ses pavillons. Les Français, voyant que les parlementaires ne laissaient pas de les joindre, appareillèrent dans le dessein de gagner la Hollande, et pour cet effet levèrent l'ancre; mais ils ne firent pas grand chemin sans être enveloppés par les Anglais qui les ont tous pris, á la réserve du commandeur de Boismorand qui, à la faveur de la nuit et du feu des ennemis, trouva moyen d'éviter leur rencontre et de se sauver. Ce fut Samedi au soir. Il est arrivé ici environ les six ou sept heures de ce matin.

Le capitaine du brûlot, qui est arrivé un peu après l'autre, dit qu'ayant été pris et reconnu par le général Blake qu'il avait servi autrefois et ledit général ayant cru que son vaisseau n'était que frété et n'appartenait pas au roi par ce que ledit capitaine lui en dit, le lui avait rendu, et qu'ayant éte parmi les ennemis il avait vu quelque chose du mauvais traitement que messieurs les chevaliers avaient reçu par les Anglais avec menace d'un plus rigoureux, en haine des prises que les autres chevaliers ont faites sur eux en Provence. Ils sont venus, je dis les Anglais, jusques auprès de nous chercher notre amiral *l'Anna* et les autres vaisseaux qu'ils ont grand regret de n'avoir pas pu surprendre. Ils disent qu'ils les saisiront en quelque part qu'ils aillent; mais tout le monde croit que le vent a été si favorable à leur retraite à Brest, que ces perfides perdront leur temps et leur peine à les chercher.

II.—THE DUKE DE VENDOME TO ADMIRAL BLAKE.

Dieppe, 23 Septembre, 1652.

J'ai été extrêment surpris d'une nouvelle que je viens d'apprendre. Quelques matelots qui étaient sur les vaisseaux du roi, mon maître, m'ont rapporté qu'une escadre de son armée, que j'avais envoyée pour le secours de Dunkerque, a été attaquée et presque toute prise vers la rade de Calais par la flotte de la République d'Angleterre que vous commandez. J'envoie ce gentilhomme vers vous pour en savoir la vérité, et ne puis croire, n'y ayant point de guerre déclarée entre les deux nations, ni aucun juste sujet d'exercer des hostilités entre l'une et l'autre, que ce qui a été entrepris contre les vaisseaux de Sa Majesté ait été fait par l'ordre de la République. Vous aurez pu voir par ceux que j'avais donnés au sieur de Menillet, qui commandait l'escadre, qu'il était expressément chargé de ne se point mêler des différends d'entre l'Angleterre et les Provinces-Unies, et d'entretenir toute sorte de bonne correspondance avec les sujets de votre Etat. Cela me fait espérer que la République, étant informée de ce qui s'est passé donnera les ordres nécessaires pour la restitution des vaisseaux qui ont été menés en Angleterre et que vous ne refuserez pas d'y contribuer ce qui dépendra de vous. J'attendrai votre réponse avant qu'en écrire à Sa Majesté; ne doutant point qu'elle ne soit conforme à la raison et telle qui j'ai sujet de la désirer, je demeurerai, monsieur, votre très-affectionné, etc.

III.—THE DUKE DE VENDOME TO THE COMMONWEALTH OF ENGLAND.

Dieppe, 23 Septembre, 1652.

TRES-ILLUSTRES SEIGNEURS: Envoyant ce gentilhomme à M. l'amiral Blake, qui commande votre flotte, pour lui demander la restitution de quelques vaisseaux du roi, mon maître, que j'avais envoyés au secours de Dunkerque, avec ordre exprès à celui qui les commandait d'entretenir toute sorte de bonne correspondance avec vos sujets, je l'ai voulu charger de cette lettre pour supplier bien humblement vos Seigneuries d'ordonner ladite restitution, puisqu'il n'y a point eu jusqu'a présent de guerre déclarée entre les deux nations, et que Sa Majesté n'a point cru qu'il y eût aucun juste sujet d'exercer des hostilités entre elles. Je me promets cet effet de la bonne justice de vos Seigneuries, et sur cette assurance elles me feront la faveur de me croire.

Très-illustres seigneurs, de vos Seigneuries,
Le très-humble serviteur.

IV.—M. DE GENTILLOT TO M. SERVIEN.

Calais, 24 Septembre, 1652.

Depuis mes précédentes il n'est rien arrivé, sinon que le Parlement d'Angleterre a envoyé Vendredi un commissaire à Douvres pour faire donner du pain et passage aux matelots des navires du roi, et déclarer aux officers que l'ordre et l'intention du Parlement, étaient qu'ils fussent traités civilement. Cependant ils ont pris, sans rien restituer aux uns et autres, leurs nippes. Ils ont retenu Menillet et quelques autres officers, jusques au retour des vaisseaux qui les ont portés. Ils en ont envoyé à Dieppe. Quelques-uns ont pris parti parmi eux. Ils disent que ce n'est que par représailles. Ils ont fort examiné s'il n'y avait pas de ces chevaliers qui ont pris de leurs navires sur la mer Méditerranée.

L'on me mande de Londres qu'ils ont fait un grand bruit de réjouissance, parmi les Communes, de la prise de ces navires, et que les plus sensés et tous les marchands et citoyens ont été très, fâchés, les uns croyant que cela excédait l'ordre des représailles et laisserait un sujet aux Anglais de méfiance plus forte qu'auparavant de notre amitié, que pourrait faire passer les choses trop avant; les marchands de peur qu'on ne saisît leurs effets en France et que tout espoir de bonne intelligence ne fût ôte, à laquelle on avait espéré de bons tempéraments.

L'on me mande que les agents de M. le Prince et de M. du Doignon n'ont pas plus d'audience qu'auparavant, c'est-à-dire rien, et que leurs instructions ou affaires n'ont d'organe que l'ambassadeur d'Espagne; mais si votre ressentiment pour cette dernière insulte paraît trop, que le Parlement prendra de plus confidentes mesures avec eux.

V.—THE COUNCIL OF STATE OF ENGLAND TO THE DUKE DE VENDOME.

12 December, 1652.

My Lord: The Parliament of the Republic of England, having received on the 20th of October last, a letter from your highness, dated Dieppe, the 8th of September, 1652, demanding the restoration of certain vessels, belonging to the king of France, which have been captured a short time since by Colonel Robert Blake, General of their

Fleet, have commanded us, to whom they have confided and entrusted the affairs of the Admiralty, to return an answer to the same.

The Council of State, is perfectly assured of the inclination of the Parliament of the Republic of England, to maintain friendliness and correspondence, as well with the king your master, as with their other neighbors. But finding, that during some years, the persons, goods, and vessels of English merchants, trading in the Mediterranean, have been plundered and captured, not only by the subjects of the King of France, but also by his own ships, and that no satisfaction can be obtained by any representation which has been made to the Court of France, the Council has authorized the said general, to try and obtain reparation for these injuries upon the ships and goods of the French nation; and as soon as restitution shall have been obtained, and satisfaction given for the said wrongs and grievances, the Council will be prepared, in the name of the Parliament, to comply with the wishes of your highness as expressed in your letter,

THURLOE, *Clerk of the Council.*

Whitehall, 2d December, 1652 (O. S.)

Signed in the name, and by the order of the Council of State established by authority of Parliament.

B. WHITELOCKE, *President.*

APPENDIX XXI.

(Page 246.)

I.—THE ARCHDUKE LEOPOLD TO KING PHILIP IV.

Brussels, February 6, 1652.

DON ALONZO DE CARDENAS being provided with no other authority given from your Majesty than the letters which were his first credentials with the Parliament of England, and foreseeing that his present negotiations may involve the English in a war with France and Portugal, has requested me to give him instructions as to the next course for him to pursue, while he is waiting for such commands as your Majesty may give with regard to the matters contained in his despatches. Don Alonzo thinks it advisable for the future to seek for an opportunity of leading the English to break faith with France. He says that the possibility of capturing Calais is the idea that would most readily lead to this result, this being the conquest that most immediately suggests itself. He adds that, as the war with Portugal depends on the recovery of Catalonia, the conclusion of this second treaty may be deferred till afterwards.

At first sight, considering how advantageous it would be to your Majesty that France should sustain such a loss in her own territory as to be deprived of Calais, a town so important, one moreover from which she has gained so many naval victories in these provinces—and considering, moreover, how advantageous it would be, on your Majesty's account to bring France into collision with an enemy that, since its last victories, has shown itself so powerful and haughty, I confess to your Majesty, that I should almost be induced to think that Don Alonzo should seek to urge on the English to the conquest of Calais, were I not deterred by the following considerations:—

The English are constitutionally inconsistent in their friendship with foreigners, and if at any time they should become the enemies of your Majesty while Calais is in their hands, they would, with Dover, have the two gates of the English Channel, by means of which they could close the sea to all, and by their powerful ships of war, could intercept all communication between Spain and their provinces, to the imminent danger of the loss of them on our part.

Although the French are divided into different parties, no one of them would consent to lose the least particle of French soil. The dissensions that exist there now, at least those which are exposed to the public eye, arise only from a desire to satisfy individual passions; but if the French were to see so important a place occupied by the English, who might from this spot extend their conquests as they did in former times; they would probably cease to regard aught but their danger, and they would unite in the pursuit of one common interest. The advantages which we now reap from their discords would then cease immediately.

It is equally probable that the Hollanders, who are already on no very good terms with the Parliament of England, seeing such conquest made by England, would league themselves with France; for they would not be less concerned than ourselves at seeing their ships, in the passage of the Channel, delivered to the mercy of English politeness. In this case it is to be feared that the Hollanders would eagerly seek to buy over our maritime places which are at present in the occupation of the French, which would oblige us again to declare war; for it is in order to hinder them from accepting the purchase of these places, which was offered to them by the French, that they have been given to understand that your Majesty is determined to recover these places, into whatever hands they may fall.

This then is the answer that I have made to Don Alonzo de Cardeñas, recommending him to continue his parleys on two points, rupture with France and rupture with Portugal, until he has received a reply to the despatches which he has addressed to your Majesty. I have also told him that if the English are determined to break faith with

France, it is better that the cause of rupture should have reference to Britany or Normandy. May God, &c.

II.—DON ALONZO DE CARDEÑAS TO PHILIP IV.

SIRE: Since the battle of Worcester, affairs have taken such a turn that no movement can be observed at all likely to affect the public peace and tranquillity, especially as those in government are intent upon ameliorating the condition of the republic, and are, moreover, so inflated with pride that they affect not to concern themselves about the influx of ambassadors and foreign ministers, who, they say, are seeking on all sides to procure the recognition of the republic, and to conciliate its friendship. For instance, the Ambassadors Extraordinary from Holland, came here on the 29th of December last, expressing their deep regret that they had not done this when the republic sent a special ambassador to Holland, to solicit an alliance. Immediately on their arrival they took prompt and active measures to procure an audience with the Parliament which was granted to them on the 29th of the same month. On that occasion, M. Catz, who held the highest rank among the three who were sent, and who directed them in the negotiations which they were desirous of concluding, made a Latin speech, of which he had caused a written copy to be made; I inclose a copy to your Majesty. One of them, I have moreover sent to Flanders, to the Archduke, and to the Hague, to Councillor Brun, in order that both of these may be informed of the hostile feelings which are beginning to be shown by these people with regard to Spain, evidenced by many indications contained in this document. This is no new thing to me, for I had observed the hostile feelings of one of these named Schaep, when he came to London two years ago, as commissary sent by his province, Holland, to make the proposals which he did in fact address to the English Government.

Having considered how disadvantageous it would be to your Majesty that the interests of these two republics should be united, I had begun, before the arrival of these envoys, to consider the best means of bringing about an agreement between them and your Majesty, if it should be impossible to hinder the arrangements alluded to, so as to provide that no stipulation or convention should be entered into that might prove prejudicial to your Majesty's interests. Accordingly, having conferred on this matter with our friends in the Parliament by the only medium that remained, through which communication was possible, I had resolved to introduce the proposal of some treaty. I have found, however, that there are difficulties in doing this; the resentment that is felt here on account of the impunity enjoyed by the assassins of the Resident has been an obstacle, and at present this resentment is fomented by the presbyterians, who are partisans of Holland. Another obstacle exists in the resolution taken by the Parliament to send no ambassador to Spain, and to conclude no treaty with any minister of your Majesty until they have obtained the satisfaction which they profess is rightly due to them. To this must be added our desire that some proposals should first emanate from those connected with the Parliament; but I have been unable so to influence them as to accomplish this, although I have sought to do so in different covert ways, and although I did myself make overtures to an individual belonging to the Government before members of the Government were prohibited paying visits to, or receiving visits from ministers of foreign powers; and even after this prohibition, I attempted to do so by the intervention of a confidential agent. One of the members of the Government, having learned that I hesitated to bring any proposals of alliance before the Parliament, fearing lest they should be discarded, on account of the affair of the assassins of the Resident Ascham, told my confidential agent that it appeared to him, that if I ever had this intention, there was no opportunity more favorable than the present, while the Parliament is but ill satisfied with the Hollanders, the French, and the Portuguese, and that he believed it is for us to make the first advances with reference to an alliance with the republic of England against France and Portugal, with whom your Majesty is in open war, just as it would be proper for the Parliament to make the first overtures, if the alliance referred to was that of your Majesty, in order to assist the Parliament to conquer Scotland, or Ireland, or to recover any other provinces. I have found it impossible to derive more than this from them. Seeing the advantages that would accrue to your Majesty from any treaty whatsoever with these people, and finding a favorable opportunity to form it in the absence of Henry Vane, who has just set out as commissioner to Scotland, and who is a man of great influence, and moreover very hostile to Spain, I have determined to request an audience from the Council of State, before the arrival of the envoys from Holland, in order that I may give them no reason to suspect that I have any wish to neutralize the effects of their negotiation by seeking an audience after their arrival. The Council of State waited for two or three days before fixing the day of audience, whilst the Master of the Ceremonies was absent from London, which city he had left, in order that he might prepare accommodation for the Holland envoys at Gravesend and Greenwich; it had been intimated that they were only awaiting a favorable wind in order to embark on the 26th of December—the day was fixed for the 29th. The Hollanders had audience with the Parliament on the morning of that day, while I obtained an interview with the Council of State in the evening. It appeared to me advisable to begin with the affair of the assassins of Ascham, and I spoke of the rights of the church to immunity with more force than I had done before. As it was necessary to tell them something of the state of that matter, although I had received no intelligence about it, I sought to encourage their hope that satisfaction will be given to them. I then spoke of the necessity of rendering the friendship between the two States more distinct, and I concluded my interview by urging that justice should be rendered to the Spaniards who had had property in the ship *La Santa Clara.* The President of the Council of State replied briefly by assuring me that the Council would take into consideration what I had been saying, and would send me an answer on the following day. I have since learned that after my departure the four statements which I had left, were read, and that a day was taken in order to discuss them. On that day they were read again, and although the first statement appeared to them reasonable (that, namely, which referred to the affair of those charged with the assassination of the Resident), the President and four or five other members insisted with some warmth that I should be told that a definite reply would be sent to me when satisfaction had been rendered; but the other members were of an opposite opinion, urging that my note explained the procedure followed in Spain in this matter, that it gave hope that punishment would be inflicted on the guilty parties, and that it expressed the feelings of your Majesty, and your Majesty's desire to give satisfaction, which was in itself the first step in giving satisfaction. As a result of this deliberation, it was resolved to render to Parliament an account of the contents of all my notes. The Council recognized the necessity of their being specially authorized by the Parliament to conclude a treaty with me, and reported to me accordingly. Agreeably to the report of the Council, the Parliament returned to it the notes which treated of the letters of proof, and of the vessel *La Santa Clara,* and recommended that a resolution should be formed touching this matter. As to the statement relating to the affair of the assassins of Ascham, this was referred to a Parliamentary Committee, with directions to insist in their reply on the necessity of punishing these men. The third statement, referring to a treaty to be concluded with the republic, was the subject of protracted discussion; the Presbyterians used all their efforts to persuade the rest that no treaty of alliance ought to be concluded with me before satisfaction had been received for the affair of the assassination; but the Independents had a majority, and decided that negotiations should be commenced. Thereupon a Presbyterian, finding that no other means of injury remained, said that it would be right for the Council, before giving me a reply, to demand of me the production of the full authority granted by your Majesty to treat with the republic. A resolution having been passed to this effect, the Master of the Ceremonies came to me, on the 19th day of this month, and placed in my hands a copy of the order of Parliament, as well as of the order that the Council of State had given him to convey it to me. I replied that your Majesty would send me a reply when you had seen these two statements. Our friends here could not believe that I was acting without the full authority of your Majesty, and they insisted on my producing these credentials. I assured them that I had none, but that they would be sent in a short time; they then sought to induce the Parliament to content itself with my official character, and with the authority conferred upon me by my letters of credence, and to commence negotiations in virtue of these letters. It has appeared to me necessary to give your Majesty an account of all this, before even an answer is remitted to me, in order that, if this course should appear suitable to your Majesty, full and general powers may be transmitted to me, authorizing me to carry on any negotiation that may be necessary with the Parliament of this republic, and to conclude it; or rather, that full powers may be given to any one who may take my position here, if there is occasion. The instructions should be very minute, in order that it may be known what is to be demanded. I shall suspend negotiations till the arrival of orders from your Majesty, and your Majesty's reply to the present despatch. I beg that your Majesty will as speedily as possible cause to be drawn up and sent by different ways complete and detailed instructions, that I may know the basis of the negotiations I am to make in case any questions regarding them may arise, which is very probable.

I think I ought also to inform your Majesty of what I have heard, namely, that the Presbyterians and other members of Parliament who are not favorably disposed towards us, say in their private conversation that at the present day no treaty of peace exists between Spain and England, since there is no obligation to consider the treaty concluded with Charles I. still valid; that consequently no violation would be done to it were the republic of England to take any resolution they may choose, and as soon as it suits them. This deserves mature consideration, and I should regard it as a great evil if the assassins of the Resident were not ultimately punished, and the government of this country should cease to send ambassadors to your Majesty. The ancient treaty of peace will therefore be very precarious till it has been formally renewed between your Majesty and this republic.

III. PART OF A LETTER FROM DON ALONZO DE CARDEÑAS TO PHILIP IV.

February 15, 1652.

In a letter dated Feb. 13, 1652, Don Alonzo develops still further what he had said, in his letter of Jan. 23, relative to the projected coalition between Spain and the Parliament of England, to which he proposed a common expedition against Calais, on condition that the English should aid Spain against Gravelines, Dunkirk, and Mardyke. He gives the reasons which have induced him to delay any parley on this subject, and earnestly solicits a reply to his despatch of Jan. 23, with full powers and commands relative to his official character, in case any opportunity might offer of concluding any arrangement against the French as well as against the Portuguese.

IV. DON ALONZO DE CARDEÑAS TO DON GERONIMO DE LA TORRE.

London, February 25, 1652.

DEAR SIR,

ABOUT four days ago I sent a despatch, addressed to his Majesty, by way of Flanders; in case the ordinary courier to Spain should not reach his destination, as sometimes happens, I have thought it necessary to send a duplicate of this despatch by a vessel bound for Bilboa. I therefore send them herewith; I send also the despatch referring to the Calais question, with an extract from a letter of Dr. Augustus Navarro, dated Feb. 3, in which mention is made of the reasons which have operated in Flanders to delay the proposal until orders have been received from his Majesty. It has appeared to me appropriate to add also the answer which I sent, thinking that it may arrive in time, before any resolution is made on the subject. To this I have nothing to add, except to assure you of my respect, and of my desire that you may be preserved for many years.

V. AUG. NAVARRO BRIENNE TO DON ALONZO DE CARDEÑAS.

Brussels, February 3, 1652.

I have laid before his highness (the archduke) what you have written to me, desiring to know his opinion as to the most suitable terms in which to address the English commissioners, when they exhibit their projects, as you suppose, with reference to two points, namely, the rupture between England and France in case assistance is granted to England in the capture of Calais, and the war with Portugal which would be more advantageous to the Parliament. You have concluded, as we have also here, that the advantages to his Majesty, attendant upon a war between the English Government and France, would be incalculable. The question with regard to Portugal, which should precede the recovery of Catalonia, admits of more delay.

On such delicate questions as these, the wish here is that you should receive directions from his Majesty. Now, it is not easy to despatch to his Majesty a courier praying that his will on this subject may be communicated, that will depend much on the time that will be taken by the ordinary courier who leaves this city on the sixth of this month; the packet that you address to Madrid shall be remitted to him.

I wrote to you last week relative to the inconveniences that are to be apprehended from the occupation of Calais by the English; for being in possession of Dover, and consequently of the two sides of the Channel, on the day that any rupture shall occur between his Majesty and them, the Channel will be closed to our vessels, and communication between his Majesty and the other states will be rendered impossible.

It has been thought also that the Hollanders might perhaps be induced to form some new alliance with France on the same account; and there is reason to fear lest they would seek to buy the maritime places, which the French would use as a means of engaging them against us.

If the English Government wishes to break with France, and any expedition is made into Brittany or Normandy, a useful diversion would be gained in France; but perhaps also that would oblige the two parties in France to unite when they found foreigners' taking advantage of their dissensions. This it is that his highness wished me to say to you, adding that you might seek skilfully to bring about a rupture between France and England, or to suspend the two negotiations—that namely of which I have just spoken, as well as that relating to Portugal, till orders arrive from his Majesty.

VI.—DON ALONZO DE CARDEÑAS TO AUG. NAVARRO BRIENNE.

London, February 9, 1652.

I have read what you have been pleased to tell me relative to the two points about which I consulted his highness the archduke, as well as your thoughts as to the inconvenience that would result from the occupation of Calais by the English. They are certainly prudent in the highest degree; but one consideration that causes me to hesitate admitting them is, that the evil which is supposed to be imminent was nevertheless never realized during the period of two hundred years in which the English occupied this town (a period in which is included the reign of the Emperor Charles V. and his son), up to the time that it was lost in the reign of Queen Mary. On the other hand, we must take into account the advantages that would result from this to his Majesty, and the injury which would be sustained by our enemies, with whom we are in undisguised conflict. It seems to me that we ought to prefer a great advantage which is certain and apparent, to problematical chances, and leave something to be disposed of by fate and the future. Moreover, the town being once in the hands of the English, it would be a fruitful source of discord between France and England, and the national hatred that has always existed between these two countries would be perpetually inflamed. As to the danger of losing our Flemish provinces, that would only be possible in the event of Spain being at war with England, and in that case France, in order to recover her town of Calais, would unite with Spain, which would make it an easy matter to drive the English to any extremities we please.

With regard to any conquests that Parliament might make in Brittany and Normandy, this is not a plan which can be at all entertained as practicable, for the English could not hope to obtain, in such a land contest, the assistance of our armies, and they are not prepared by themselves to break with France. And as to the threatened coalition between Holland and France, this would equally occur whether the republic of England should unite with us in the capture of Calais, or of other towns in Brittany or Normandy. As far as regards the purchase of our maritime places by the United Provinces, it is not thought here that they would do this, for this Government is opposed to such a measure, and it would be so the more reasonably inasmuch as the conduct which would determine such a resolution on the part of the Hollanders would be its own.

However, I will not press any negotiation on this matter, and I will confine myself to holding conferences on this subject as well as on that of Portugal until I receive from his Majesty such orders as his Majesty may think advisable to send. Only I fear lest the spring, which is the best time for agitating the question, may pass; at that time the English will have their fleet ready. It is, indeed, already in preparation, and is said to number a hundred and fifty vessels, of which a hundred and twenty belong to the State, besides thirty merchant vessels freighted for the use of the State.

VII.—DON ALONZO DE CARDEÑAS TO PHILIP IV.

London, September 20, 1652.

SIRE: In various despatches I have already informed your Majesty of the proposition which I laid before the commissioners of Parliament for the renewal of the treaty of peace between your Majesty and the republic of England, agreeably to your Majesty's instructions; I have also spoken to your Majesty of the contents of a note which I sent to them, a copy of which I have sent to your Majesty. Lastly, I have related in detail the steps which I took in order to obtain a reply, and of the reply that was finally given me on the 22d of August; copies of all these I have also sent to your Majesty. In this reply I am told that the Council of State waited till I should present formally before them the articles which I had to propose; I have therefore signed and presented to these same commissioners, on the 12th of this month, the articles contained in the document which I hereby enclose. They are extracted from the last treaty which was concluded with the late king, excepting that such changes have been made as were demanded by the altered condition of affairs. The clause which your Majesty particularly recommended is inserted in Article III.; it provides that neither of the parties contracting should give any aid or assistance, direct or indirect, to rebels or enemies of the other party. The last article was added by me on account of the prohibition which has been made here of importing into England any kind of merchandise in ships not belonging to England, or not belonging to the nation from whom the products are sent, or to the country from which these products are derived. It appeared to me right and appropriate that all subjects whatsoever of your Majesty should be able to transport, from the different States belonging to your Majesty, all products and merchandise, although they might not themselves belong to the countries from which the said products were originally derived. I have learned that these articles were read in the Council on the same day, September 12, as well as the note accompanying them, a copy of which I append to this communication. Moreover, I add hereunto a copy of the note in which I made answer respecting those charged with the murder of Ascham, who are still in prison, for I learned that the Council would have been displeased if I had neglected to do this; all this has been sent to the commissioners of foreign affairs. I will send to your Majesty any reply that may be made to it.

VIII. NOTE AND PROPOSITIONS PRESENTED TO THE COUNCIL OF STATE IN ENGLAND, ON THE 12TH OF SEPTEMBER, 1652, BY DON ALONZO DE CARDEÑAS.

Don Alonzo de Cardenas, of the Council of his Catholic Majesty, and his ambassador to the Parliament of the Republic of England, states, that after having seen the reply which the honorable Council of State has at length made on the 12th (22d) of August, to his notes of the 6th of June (May 27th) and of the 6th (16th) of August, in which document it is first of all stated that the Parliament abides by its resolution to continue and maintain friendship and friendly relations with the king his master, as had been already expressed on other occasions and in preceding notes, especially in that of the 10th (20th) of April, and, moreover, that the Council of State is waiting until the said ambassador shall present to it certain articles for the renewal of the treaty of peace as has been proposed by it, it has seemed proper to the said ambassador to draw up the articles which he has the honor hereby to present, in order that the Council may give them its consideration, and, if they are judged to be equitable and calculated to promote the interests of the two States, may order them to be carried out. The said ambassador reserves for himself the permission to add, change, or suppress, before the definite conclusion of the treaty, anything that may appear to him to be demanded by circumstances that may arise during the course of the discussion.

ARTICLES PROPOSED BY DON ALONZO DE CARDEÑAS OF THE COUNCIL OF HIS CATHOLIC MAJESTY, AND HIS AMBASSADOR TO THE PARLIAMENT AND REPUBLIC OF ENGLAND, FOR THE RENEWAL OF THE TREATY OF PEACE, ALLIANCE, AND FRIENDSHIP, BETWEEN THE KING, HIS MASTER, AND THE PARLIAMENT OF THE SAID REPUBLIC.

I.

IN the first place, there shall be from this day a good, general, sincere, true, constant, and perfect amity, alliance, and peace of perpetual duration, and reciprocally inviolable, as well on land as on the sea and all rivers, between his Most Serene Majesty the King of Spain, his heirs and successors, and the republic of England, and between all kingdoms, states, territories, countries, and subjects whatsoever of the two powers, as well for the present as for the future, of what rank and dignity soever they may be, so that the aforesaid subjects and peoples shall mutually aid and second one another, and maintain relations and communications of good-will.

II.

Neither his Most Serene Majesty the King of Spain, nor his heirs and successors, nor the Parliament of the said republic shall do or undertake, either of themselves or by means of others, anything that may be prejudicial to the interests of the other contracting party, or of any of its kingdoms, possessions, or territories in whatsoever part it may be situated, on land or sea, ports or rivers, under any pretext and occasion whatsoever; and neither of the two parties shall give, support, or consent to any war or design that may or can be prejudicial to the interests of either.

III.

Neither of the two parties shall consent, that, by any one of its subjects, vassals, peoples, or inhabitants respectively, there should be lent any aid, or assistance, or favor, or counsel, directly or indirectly, by land or sea or rivers, to the enemies or rebels of the other party, of what kind soever they may be; nor that, by the said subjects or vassals, there should be furnished, to those who would attack or who have attacked the possessions, territories, and states of the said king and the said republic, or to those who might alienate or cause to be alienated, from the obedience and authority of either of the two parties, any soldiers, provisions, money, arms, horses, instruments of war, ammunition, or any other aid tending to excite or maintain war.

IV.

Moreover, his Most Serene Majesty the King of Spain and the Parliament of the said republic renounce, as they do in fact renounce by the present treaty, all leagues, confederations, alliances, capitulations, and agreements, concluded, in any manner whatsoever, to the prejudice of the other party, and contrary or such as may become contrary to this treaty of peace and to the good understanding of the two parties, or to anything that may be contained in this treaty. The two parties shall declare to be null and void the said leagues, and promise that none such shall be constituted.

V.

His Most Serene Majesty the King of Spain and the Parliament of the republic of England shall bind themselves so to act that their respective subjects shall, for the future, inflict no injury upon each other; and they shall revoke all kinds of letters of reprisal or marque, as well as all other commissions which imply any permission to make any kind of prize, that may be prejudicial to the interests of the said king or the said republic, or of their respective subjects, and which may have been given to their own subjects or to foreigners; the two parties shall declare them null, as they in fact do declare them by the present treaty; and those who contravene them shall be punished; and besides the punishment inflicted, they shall be compelled to restore all damage caused to those who may have been injured and who may demand indemnification.

Letters of reprisal or marque shall not for the future be delivered by either of the two parties to their subjects or respective inhabitants, nor to strangers, unless the grievances have been previously represented, and a copy of the demands forwarded to the ambassador of his Most Serene Majesty or of the republic, who may reside at the Court of the State against the subjects of which the said letters of reprisal or marque may be demanded, and unless they are cognizant of the proceeding, excepting in cases permitted by the law of nations relative to reprisals and according to the rules prescribed by the law.

VI.

Between the aforesaid Most Serene Majesty the King of Spain, and the aforesaid Republic, as also between their subjects and the inhabitants of their respective states, on land as well as on the sea, and on all rivers, and in all the kingdoms, states, domains, towns, ports, villages and localities of the said king and the said republic, there shall be and continue to be free commerce, as it existed before the war between king Philip II., King of the Spaniards, and Elizabeth, Queen of England, agreeably to the treaty of peace of the year 1604, article IX., and conformably to usages consecrated by the ancient alliances and treaties concluded before the said period; in such sort that, without any pass or other permit, general or special, as well by land as by sea and all rivers, the subjects of the said King of Spain, and those of the said republic of England, may mutually come to, enter, navigate, and visit all towns, localities, ports, rivers, gulfs, and settle in any port whatsoever where, before the above-mentioned period, there was reciprocal commerce, according to the usages consecrated by ancient alliances and treaties; that they may convey their merchandise in carts, on horses, in sacks, on vessels laden or to be laden; that they may buy and sell all things which they may desire, and to provide themselves with all things necessary to living and travelling at moderate prices; that they may attend to their money affairs, and to the repair of their vessels or conveyances belonging to themselves, or hired or borrowed, and that they may quit the said ports with their goods, merchandise, and all other things whatsoever, after having complied with only the laws and dues that are applicable according to the local regulations; and lastly, that they may depart and return freely to their own country, or into foreign countries without any hindrance, and according to their pleasure.

VII.

It shall be permitted to arrive, and sojourn at, and to return to the ports of the said Most Serene Majesty the king of Spain, and the said republic of England respectively with the same liberty; not only with merchant ships intended for the transport of merchandise, but also with other private vessels armed and provided for resistance to enemies; whether these vessels enter into the said ports in consequence of unfavorable weather, or of free will for the purpose of obtaining stores; it being always understood that, if these vessels arrive through determinate purpose, and not because they have been driven by storms, their number shall not exceed six or eight, and that they shall not reside in the ports or in the neighborhood any longer time than may be necessary, in order to repair their losses, or to provide themselves with necessary stores, so that there may be no obstacle to the passage and the free commerce of other friendly nations. In cases, however, which may arise relative to a larger number of ships of war, it shall not be permitted to them to enter, without having beforehand apprised the said King, or the said Republic, nor without their respective permissions; and further it shall be provided that no hostile act, or act that may be prejudicial to the interests of the said King or said Republic, be committed in the ports of the said King and the said Republic, but that the said vessels shall remain quiet and peaceable as friends and allies, taking care that, under pretext of commerce, there be not furnished by the subjects, vassals or inhabitants of the said kingdoms, or of the said republic respectively, any aid, or assistance, in provisions, arms, or instruments of war, or any other military favor or support, to the profit of rebels or enemies of either of the said parties, and that every individual who may seek to do this may be punished with the most severe penalties that are inflicted on seditious persons and disturbers of public peace, and the faith of treaties. The respective subjects of both States shall not be treated on the territories of the other more rigorously than those belonging to the nation, as regards commercial sales and transactions, as well in reference to price as in every other relation; under all these relations the position of the foreigners shall be equal to that of the natives, no laws or customs whatsoever being allowed to produce a contrary effect.

VIII.

Immediately after the signing of the articles of the present treaty, the Parliament of the republic of England shall command, and shall publish by an edict the command, that no subject, inhabitant or vassal of the said republic shall carry or transport in any manner, direct or indirect, in his own name, or in the name of any one else, with any ship or vessel, nor give or lend his name to another, that he may transport any ships or bottoms, any merchandise, manufactured products or any other objects whatsoever, of Portugal or of its conquered possessions, into Spain or into other kingdoms and possessions of his Most Serene Majesty the King of Spain, nor to carry on their ships into the said countries any Portuguese merchant or trader, under pain of incurring the anger of the Parliament, and other penalties inflicted on those who despise the commands of their rulers. For this purpose, and in order more effectually to provide against any species of fraud that may result from the resemblance of merchandise from England, Scotland and Ireland, it is provided, by the present article, that all merchandise which is to be transported into the kingdoms and states of the said King of Spain should be provided with the register and seal of the town from which they have been taken, and, thus registered and marked, they shall be regarded as English, Scotch or Irish without any difficulties or disputes; and they shall be regarded as legitimate, unless any fraud shall be proved, but without causing at the same time any obstacle to the passage of this merchandise. Those goods which are neither registered, nor provided with seals, shall be confiscated and regarded as forfeited. All Portuguese who may be found on the said vessels shall be arrested and imprisoned.

IX.

Goods belonging to England, Scotland, or Ireland may come freely from the states of the republic of England into Spain, and into the states of his Most Serene Majesty the King of Spain, as has been above stipulated, on paying all customary rights and rents.

X.

With regard to goods that may be purchased in Spain, or any other kingdoms or states of his Most Serene Highness the King of Spain, by English, Scotch, or Irish merchants, and which they may convey in vessels, either belonging to themselves, or borrowed or hired for this purpose, always excepting, as has been before said, Portuguese vessels, no rights or rents shall be increased, provided that the said goods be conducted and carried into the states of the republic of England, or into the ports of provinces friendly to the King of Spain, and not into Portugal or into any of the states or territories of Portugal. And in order that there may be no fraud in this respect, and that the said goods be not carried into other places or kingdoms, or transported into Portugal or into any of its dependencies, it is provided that the said merchants, at the time when they may load their vessels, either in Spain, or in other kingdoms or states of said Most Serene Majesty the King of Spain, shall declare before the judicial authority of the place where they intend to take the said goods, that in case they may be carried into other countries than those that have been specified, they may pay to his Most Serene Majesty the King of Spain a duty of thirty per cent. If afterwards, within the space of one year, they produce a certificate given to them by the magistrates of the place, proving that they have delivered the said goods to the states or territories of the Republic of England, or the ports of countries belonging to the King of Spain or to friendly countries, and taxes which they have paid shall be restored to them.

XI.

As soon as the present treaty shall have been signed by the Parliament of the republic of England, the said republic shall forbid all persons whatsoever from conveying goods from Spain, or from other kingdoms or states of his Most Serene Majesty the King of Spain, into any other countries than those belonging to the republic of England, or to the dependencies of Spain, under penalty of the confiscation of all their goods to the treasury of the Parliament of the said republic of England; half of the goods, or their value, being given to the party denouncing the fraud, after having first paid a duty of thirty per cent. to the delegates of his Most Serene Majesty the King of Spain. In this case confidence will be placed in the proofs received in Spain, and which will be sent to England duly authenticated. At the same time it is to be understood that this prohibition to convey goods from Spain into other states than the states and territories of the republic of England and its other provinces, shall not in any sense apply to the kingdoms or states which hold free commercial relations with Spain, for it shall be permitted to the subjects of the republic of England to convey goods from the states of Spain to such places, always observing the conditions and precautions above mentioned. The penalties declared against offenders in the preceding articles remain in full force.

XII.

No magistrate or functionary of the towns and cities of the states and territories of the republic of England, appointed to deliver certificates of discharge and to inspect the registration of goods, shall allow or permit the least fraud in this respect, under penalty of incurring the anger of the Parliament of the republic of England, the loss of his office, and other penalties which the Parliament may think proper to inflict.

XIII.

As the said King and the Parliament promise solemnly at no time to lend any military aid to rebels or to the enemies of either party, so also it is forbidden to their respective subjects, and to the inhabitants of their kingdoms and states, whatever may be their nation, quality, or rank, to furnish, under pretext of commerce, or under any other pretext, or by any motive, any aids to the rebels or enemies of the said king and of the said republic; it is forbidden to furnish them with money, subsistence, arms, horses, weapons of war, ammunition, artillery or other instruments of war, or any other warlike implements whatsoever. Those who disobey this order shall be punished with the most severe penalties inflicted against the seditious and those who disturb public peace and faith.

XIV.

In order that abundant advantages may result from this treaty of peace to the subjects and populations of his Most Serene Majesty the King of Spain in his provinces and states, as well as to the subjects and populations of the republic of England in its provinces and states, the two contracting parties, both conjointly and separately, shall see that the communication and passage between the ports of their respective states shall not be closed, as has been already mentioned, in order that each may arrive freely with their ships, goods, or conveyances, only providing that ordinary rents and dues are paid, and may leave with the same liberty, carrying with them other goods, whenever it shall please them.

XV.

As to divers ancient treaties and conventions relating to commerce concluded between the ancient Kings of England, Scotland, and Ireland, and the states of the Dukes of Burgundy and of the Princes of Belgium, treaties and conventions which have been so often interrupted, and so often evaded in different ways during past disturbances, it is agreed by the present treaty that they shall resume their ancient authority and validity, and that the two contracting parties shall act in the same manner as was ordinarily observed before the war between Queen Elizabeth of England and King Philip II. of Spain, in conformity to the stipulations on this matter of the treaty of peace in the year 1604, Art. 22.

And in case either of the two contracting parties shall have to complain of any infraction on the part of the other, or if their respective subjects complain that the treaty is not observed, or that they are charged with burdens not sanctioned by usage, then the two parties shall nominate delegates who shall investigate this subject, and shall summon before them, if it be necessary, experienced and skilful merchants, in order to treat of it in as conciliatory and faithful a mode as possible, and make reparation for wrongs done, and re-establish anything that has been changed by the lapse of time, or by abuses which they may discover.

XVI.

And in order that the commercial relations which may result from this treaty of peace may not remain inoperative, which will be the case if the subjects of the republic of England in the travels which they may make with the kingdoms and states of his Most Serene Majesty the King of Spain, or during their residence in these states for commercial or other purposes, are molested on account of their religion, the aforesaid, his Most Serene Majesty, wishing to guarantee security to commerce by land and by sea, shall provide that the said subjects be not in any way molested or disturbed, contrary to the commercial right of people, on account of their religion, so long as they shall occasion no offence to others.

And the said Parliament shall provide on its own part that, in none of the states of the said republic shall the subjects of his Most Serene Majesty the King of Spain be molested or disturbed on account of their religion, contrary the commercial right of people, so long as they shall occasion no offence to others, and this, notwithstanding the law, statutes, or usages that may be in force with the two contracting parties that may be contrary to this.

XVII.

If in any case the subjects of either party transport goods prohibited from or to the respective kingdoms, states, or territories of the said Most Serene Majesty the King of Spain and of the said republic of England, in this case the offending persons shall alone incur penalties, and only the prohibited goods shall be liable to be confiscated.

XVIII.

If subjects of either of the contracting parties die during their stay in the states of the other, their goods shall be preserved for their heirs and successors, duties and fees having been deducted.

XIX.

Concessions and privileges granted by the kings of Spain and of England to merchants of the two contracting parties who may visit their respective states, if they have ceased from any reason whatsoever to be granted, shall be renewed, and resume their entire force and validity.

XX.

If at any time, which may God forbid, any misunderstanding shall arise between his Most Serene Majesty the King of Spain and the republic of England, of such a character as to suspend commercial relations, then, the respective subjects of the two parties shall have, counting from the day when they are first warned of this state of things, an interval of six months in order to remove their goods, and during this period they shall not be allowed to suffer any arrest, interruption, or damage either in their persons or in their businesses.

XXI.

Neither the King of Spain nor the Parliament of England shall retain any ships belonging to the respective subjects of their states in their ports or rivers, nor shall cause them to be retained either for military service, or for any other service, to the prejudice of their allies; unless the said king or the Parliament of the said republic give notice previously to the other party, according as the vessels may belong to the subjects of one or the other, and obtain its consent.

XXII.

In case any enterprise shall be undertaken, during the continuance of this peace and friendship, contrary to its validity or to its operation on land, sea, or rivers, by the subjects, vassals, or populations of the said King of Spain, his heirs and successors, or by the subjects of the said Parliament of the republic of England, or by allies included in this treaty, or their heirs or successors, or by the subjects of these allies, the present treaty of peace and amity shall not the less continue in force, and only the guilty parties, and not others, shall be punished for every attempt of this kind.

XXIII.

If there shall arise in the states of the said King of Spain, or of the said republic of England, any claim on the part of any one not a subject of the said king, or of the said republic, on account of capture or loss, the case shall be brought before the proper judge in the states of the king or of the republic, according as the prosecution may be brought against a subject or subjects of the king or of the republic.

XXIV.

The subjects of the said King of Spain shall be allowed, when it may seem good to them, to convey, with all freedom and security, into the ports or states of the republic of England, all kinds of goods, produced or manufactured, in any part whatsoever of the states, kingdoms, and territories of the King of Spain, or any vessels whatever belonging to the subjects of the said king, in whatever part of his states they may reside.

Vessels belonging to the kingdoms, islands, provinces, towns, or to the subjects of the said king, inhabiting any part of his states, shall be allowed to convey freely all goods, property, or products, natural or manufactured, into any other place than that to which they themselves belong, but which is in allegiance to the King of Spain.

If any goods or property are conveyed into Spain from any part whatsoever of states belonging to his Crown, it shall be permitted to any subject of the said king to convey these same goods or articles of the territory of Spain into any province whatsoever belonging to the republic of England, in any vessel whatsoever belonging to a subject of the king, in any of his provinces; and no laws, statutes, or usages shall be allowed to infringe upon this right.

APPENDIX XXII.

(Page 246.)

I.—INSTRUCTION AU SIEUR DE BORDEAUX S'EN ALLANT EN ANGLETERRE.

2 Décembre, 1652.

Bien que le sieur de Bordeaux soit en sorte instruit de l'état des choses et ait une si particulière connaissance de ce que Sa Majesté désire de son service qu'il est assez inutile de dresser un mémoire de ce qu'il aura à faire, néanmoins afin qu'il s'y porte avec plus de fermeté, Sa Majesté est résolue delui donner celui-ci.

Il sait bien que les Anglais ont non seulement décerné des lettres de marque contre les sujets de Sa Majesté, mais même qu'ils ont procédé avec une telle arrogance qu'ils ont fait attaquer ceux de la couronne, et comme ennemis déclarés fait servir leurs forces à procurer aux Espagnols divers avantages que sans leur aide ils n'eussent osé se promettre de remporter.

Il n'ignore pas aussi que Sa Majesté a fait passer en Angleterre par diverses fois le sieur Gentillot pour reconnaître le nouveau régine, mais avec ordre de ne le point faire que premièrement ceux de Parlement n'eussent engagé leur foi à surseoir l'exécution des lettres de représailles et ensuite de députer des Commissaires pour avec aux de Sa Majesté prendre connaissance des dommages soufferts par les sujets des deux états, en intention de chercher les moyens de les soulager en leurs pertes. Mais ceux du régime n'ayant pas approuvé qu'on leur fit acheter la reconnaissance qu'on en faisait comme d'une république fondée et qui avait une entière et légitime autorité dans l'Angleterre, firent entendre au sieur Gentillot qu'il eut à sorter de leurs états.

Cela avait été exécuté devant que les vaisseaux de la nouveau régime eussent attaqué ceux de Sa Majesté et qu'il eut déclaré que les lettres de marque ne faisaient point de rupture entre les alliés, soutenant son dire par une raison tirée des traités qui les permittent, mais avec cette restriction et précaution de ne pouvoir être délivrées qu' après un deni de justice à l'intéressé, et cela pourrait être excusé si cette république était demeurée ès termes accoutumés d'accorder la permission à un complaignant de prendre, saisir et arrêter les effets et navires de la nation dont il se plaint, mais il est inouî et c'est une chose qui répugne aux droits des gens que sans avoir déclaré la guerre à un roi ou attaque ses vaisseaux.

Néanmoins comme Sa Majesté demeure persuadée que l'équité, la raison et le respect qui lui est dû, ne sont point entièrement effacés de l'esprit de ceux qui exercent présentement l'autorité de gouvernement en Angleterre, espérant même que la reconnaissance qu'elle fera de leur république les satisfera, en sorte que ne sa laissant plus emporter à leurs passions, se soumettront à la droite raison et feront pour condescendre aux choses justes qui leur seront demandées, Sa Majesté s'est résolue d'envoyer vers eux.

Aussitôt que le sieur de Bordeaux sera arrivé à Londres, il en fera avertir le Maitre des Cérémonies et après lui avoir déclaré qu'il n'est pas ambassadeur, lui fera entendre qu'il est chargé de lettres pour le Parlement de la république et la priera de le dire à celui qui préside à cette assemblée et de lui faire avoir audience. Y étant admis, il représentera à ceux du dit Parlement l'avantage que la bonne intelligence qui sera entre les nations leur apportera, et que c'est l'intention de Sa Majesté de la garder entière, et sincère et avec autant de soin et d'exactitude qu'elle faisait avec les rois d'Angleterre, que ressouvenant bien que les traités étaient de nation à nation, comme de roi à roi, et ayant exalté l'honneur qui leur est rendu par Sa Majesté d'envoyer vers eux, leur fera entendre le vrai sujet de son voyage, appuyant les demandes qu'il est chargé de leur faire de toutes les raisons que lui pourra fournir son expérience et sa capacité, en sorte s'il est possible qu'il obtienne d'eux la restitution des vaisseaux de Sa Majesté, de leurs canons et apparaux comme des munitions de guerre et debouche dont ils étaient chargés.

Qui mésurerait les choses par la droiture et qui serait assuré que ceux du dit régime l'eusse en telle considération qu'ils fassent incapables de rien faire qui y fut opposé, on ne mettrait point en doute que le sieur de Bordeaux n'obtint de leur équité et de leur prudence ce qu'il leur demandera.

Mais soit l'emportement qu'ils ont fait paraître en diverses rencontres, soit que bien souvent les hommes préoccupés de leurs passions s'y laissent en sorte entrainer qu'ils ne voient que ce qu'elles leur présentent, il est à craindre qu'il aura un refus et qu'il lui sera parlé en des termes dont un nouvel état se derrait abstenir traitant avec le ministre d'un grand roi.

Si cela leur arrive, Sa Majesté désire que le sieur de Bordeaux leur réponde ensorte qu'ils s'aperçoivent que la France n'ignore pas ce qui lui peut-être dû par une république naissante, mais évitera de rien dire qui fasse rupture ni qui les offense pour ne leur donner aucun prétexte de se déclarer ennemis de cette Couronne, paraissant à Sa Majesté qu'il vaut mieux pour un temps qu'ils couvent les mers et exercent la piraterie qu'ils reprochent aux autres, que s'ils entreprenaient quelque chose de pris, ce serait dejoindre leurs forces aux Espagnols et prendre en protection les rebelles.

Que si la fortune de cet état était telle que mieux conseillés qu'ose le promettre ils accordent la restitution des dits navires et de l'équipage, lors le dit sieur de Bordeaux ou ne une seconde audience, cela étant remis à sa prudence, leur proposera de députer des commissaires pour aviser à ce qui sera à faire pour les particuliers intéressés ès prises qui ont été faites de part et d'autre et leur déclarera que Sa Majesté y est disposée, afin que sans y apporter aucun difficulté ni longueur, ils fassent choix et nomination de députés.

Ce qu'il évitera de mettre en avant si ceux du Parlement d'Angleterre fesaient difficulté de consentir à l'entière et prompte restitution des navires du roi, de crainte qu'ils ne publiassent que son envoi n'avait point en d'autre fin que determiner les differends des particuliers, étant de l'avantage de Sa Majesté qu'elle a depêché vers eux pour demander le sien et que la reconnaissance qu'il aura faite de leur état ne lui puisse être imputé à bassesse comme l'on a fait à plusieurs autres princes qui sont allés au devant des désirs des Anglais, et nouvellement le Roi Catholique sous espérance d'en étre assisté en la guerre qu'il fait durer à la ruine de la Chrétienté et qu'il aurait souvent pu finir s'il y eut été aussi disposé que ceux qui le servent l'ont osé publier.

Et n'ayant le dit sieur de Bordeaux rien sa obtenir d'eux repassera en ce royaume sans attendre aucun ordre, si ce n'est qu'il jugent que leur faisant honte de leur dureté et de leur injustice et que ménageant avec addresse quelques uns des plus accrédités parmi eux il peut conduire à bon port l'affaire dont il est chargé.

Que si au contraire ils se rendent à la raison et qu'ils se disposassent à faire choix de plusieurs pour ariser aux moyens de régler les affaires de mer, ajouter ou diminuer aux précédents traités ce qui peut bonifier le commerce, pour en suite faire que les nations l'exercent avec profit et repos, en ce cas le dit sieur de Bordeaux dépêchera vers Sa Majesté pour recevoir ses commandements et les pouvoirs et instructions nécessaires pour travailler à une affaire si importante.

Fait à Paris. le 2 Décembre, 1652.

II.—LOUIS XIV. TO THE PARLIAMENT OF ENGLAND.

2 Decembre, 1652.

Très chers et grands Amis—Nous envoyons vers vous le sieur de Bordeaux l'un des conseillers en notre Conseil d'Etat, maître des requêtes ordinaire de notre hôtel et president en notre grand conseil que nous avons destiné notre ambassadeur en Savoye, pour vous faire entendre la bonne volonté que nous vous portons, et le désir que nous avons de continuer avec votre république la bonne correspondance qui a de tout temps été observée entre les deux nations. Nous l'avons aussi chargé de vous dire que comme nous n'avons rien entrepis que vous ait pu faire croire que nous n'etions pas en cette disposition ni qui ait pu causer du préjudice à votre état, nous avons été surpris dervoir nos vaisseaux attaqués pat les votres. Car bien que vous ayez fait expédier à aucuns de vos marchands des lettres de marque, si est-ce qu'il est inouï qu'on les ait exécutées contre les vaisseaux du prince et ce n'est point une chose extraordinaire et qui ne sait pas prévue par les traités d'accorder ces sortes de lettres. Au contraire bien loin d'être défendues, elles sont permises, mais c'est après un deni formel de justice qui ne nous peut-être reproché, et qui aura connaissance de tous les soins que nous avons apportés pour être bien informés des pertes souffertes par nos sujets et des prises qu'aucuns d'eux pouvaient avoir faites sur les votres qui étaient obligés de les satisfaire, jugerait et avouerait sans doute que notre intention n'a j'amais été autre que de faire observer les traités qui ont été passés entre les nations pour la sureté et commodité de leur commerce et le faire fleurir au commun avantage des deux Etats. Le dit sieur de Bordeaux selon la charge que nous lui en avons donnée vous fera plus particulièrement connaitre les résolutions que nous avons prises de vivre en étroite union avec vous, espérant que vous ajouterez entière créancs à tout ce qu'il vous dira de notre part, ainsi que nous vous en conjurons, nous prierons Dieu qu'il vois ait, très chers et grands amis, en sa sainte et digue garde. Ecrit à Paris, le deuxième jour de Décembre, 1652.

Votre bon amis et confedéré,
LOUIS.

APPENDIX XXIII.

(Page 317.)

M. DE BORDEAUX TO M. SERVIEN.

Londres, 3 Mai, 1653.

AVANT hier, qui était Mardi dernier, le Général Cromwell alla au Parlement après en avoit été absent trois semaines, et s'assit au plus bas bout du Parlement, et ne dit jamais mot tout le temps que le Parlement se tint. Hier, il vint de même au Parlement ; et comme, environ midi, ou y débattait touchant un nouveau Parlement, et quand celui ci prendrait fin, et qu'il serait bon de lui donner pour fin le 5 de Novembre prochain, le dit Général Cromwell se leva tête nue, et fît une petite harangue en ces termes:—

"Messieurs, vous n'avez que faire de vous mettre tant en peine, touchant les affaires qui sont maintenant sur le tapis; car ayant mûrement considéré que le gouvernement de tant de personnes était méchant, tyrannique et plein d'oppression, et voyant qu'on y avait employé des sommes immenses sans que jamais ou en ait donné aucune compte, c'est pourquoi j'ai résolu de mettre le gouvernement de cette nation entre les mains de peu de gens, mais gens de bien; et, partout, dès à présent je déclare qu'il n'y a plus de Parlement, et n'en reconnais plus."

Ayant achevé son petit discours, il se couvrit et se promena deux en trois tours dans la chambre du Parlement; et voyant que le Parlement ne bougeait, le dit général commanda au Major Harrison de faire entrer les soldats qui étaient en garde; ils entrèrent sans dire aucun mot, et pour lors le dit Major, le chapeau à la main, avec tant respect, s'en alla à la chaire du speaker, et, baisant la main, le prit par la sienne, et le conduisit hors du Parlement, comme un gentilhomme fait une demoiselle, et tout le Parlement le suivit. Le Général Cromwell prit la masse, et la donna aux soldats.

Hier, après diner, on devoit choisir un nouveau Président au Conseil d'Etat; mais le dit Général Cromwell y étant venu leur déclara qu'ils ne se missent plus en peine de s'assembler en ce lieu, et que leur pouvoir était expiré.

Ensuite de cela, le conseil de guerre s'y tint, et en y appela le maire de Londres, qui présenta son égrée, marque de justice, au général qui la lui rendit, et lui dit qu'il devait exercer la justice de même, comme si rien n'était advenu.

Hier-au-soir, les soldats allèrent prendre les scéaux au logis de ceux qui les gardaient; et au matin, ce jourd'hui, on a envoyé deux barques remplies de soldats, pour garde une partie de l'argent Espagnol qui est encore dans ses vaisseaux, le reste étant dans la tour. L'armée fait une déclaration pour justifier ses actions.

Avant hier, arriva un messager d'Hollande apportant réponse des Etats au Parlement; le messager a donné la lettre au Chevalier Guillaume Strickland, et lui l'a mise en mains propres du Général Cromwell.

Tout le peuple universellement se réjouit, et pareillement la noblesse, de la généreuse action du Général Cromwell, et de la chûte du Parlement qui est fort vilipendé en la bouche d'un chacun. On a écrit sur la maison du Parlement:—

This House is now to be let, unfurnished,

Et on chante des chansons partout contre eux. Il s'en vendait une publiquement que le Général Cromwell, par sa grande modération, a commandé de nôtre plus chantée, et en a fait supprimer quarante mille exemplaires qui ont été près chez l'imprimeur. On ne laisse pas d'en vendre sans mains.

Le dit Général Cromwell a changé tous les principaux officiers de l'armée navale. T'en envoie les noms comme ils sont imprimés.

END OF VOL. I.

CATALOGUE
OF
BLANCHARD & LEA'S PUBLICATIONS.

CAMPBELL'S LORD CHANCELLORS. New Edition—(Just Issued.)

LIVES OF THE LORD CHANCELLORS
AND
KEEPERS OF THE GREAT SEAL OF ENGLAND.
FROM THE EARLIEST TIMES TO THE REIGN OF KING GEORGE IV.

BY LORD CHIEF-JUSTICE CAMPBELL, A. M., F. R. S. E.

Second American, from the Third London Edition.

Complete in seven handsome crown 8vo. volumes, extra cloth, or half morocco.

This has been reprinted from the author's most recent edition, and embraces his extensive modifications and additions. It will therefore be found eminently worthy a continuance of the great favor with which it has hitherto been received.

Of the solid merit of the work our judgment may be gathered from what has already been said. We will add, that from its infinite fund of anecdote, and happy variety of style, the book addresses itself with equal claims to the mere general reader, as to the legal or historical inquirer; and while we avoid the stereotyped commonplace of affirming that no library can be complete without it, we feel constrained to afford it a higher tribute by pronouncing it entitled to a distinguished place on the shelves of every scholar who is fortunate enough to possess it.—*Frazer's Magazine.*

A work which will take its place in our libraries as one of the most brilliant and valuable contributions to the literature of the present day.—*Athenæum.*

The brilliant success of this work in England is by no means greater than its merits. It is certainly the most brilliant contribution to English history made within our recollection; it has the charm and freedom of Biography combined with the elaborate and careful comprehensiveness of History.—*N. Y. Tribune.*

BY THE SAME AUTHOR—TO MATCH—(Now Ready.)

LIVES OF THE
CHIEF-JUSTICES OF ENGLAND,
From the Norman Conquest to the Death of Lord Mansfield.

SECOND EDITION.

In two very neat vols., crown 8vo., extra cloth, or half morocco.

To match the "Lives of the Chancellors" of the same author.

In this work the author has displayed the same patient investigation of historical facts, depth of research, and quick appreciation of character which have rendered his previous volumes so deservedly popular. Though the "Lives of the Chancellors" embrace a long line of illustrious personages intimately connected with the history of England, they leave something still to be filled up to complete the picture, and it is this that the author has attempted in the present work. The vast amount of curious personal details concerning the eminent men whose biographies it contains, the lively sketches of interesting periods of history, and the graphic and vivid style of the author, render it a work of great attraction for the student of history and the general reader.

Although the period of history embraced by these volumes had been previously traversed by the recent work of the noble and learned author, and a great portion of its most exciting incidents, especially those of a constitutional nature, there narrated, yet in "The Lives of the Chief-Justices" there is a fund both of interesting information and valuable matter, which renders the book well worthy of perusal by every one who desires to obtain an acquaintance with the constitutional history of his country, or aspires to the rank of either a statesman or a lawyer. Few lawyers of Lord Campbell's eminence could have produced such a work as he has put forth. None but lawyers of his experience and acquirements could have compiled a work combining the same interest as a narration, to the public generally, with the same amount of practical information for professional aspirants more particularly.—*Britannia.*

NIEBUHR'S ANCIENT HISTORY—(A new work, now ready.)

LECTURES ON ANCIENT HISTORY,

FROM THE EARLIEST TIMES TO THE TAKING OF ALEXANDRIA BY OCTAVIANUS, CONTAINING

The History of the Asiatic Nations, the Egyptians, Greeks, Macedonians, and Carthaginians.

BY B. G. NIEBUHR.

TRANSLATED FROM THE GERMAN EDITION OF DR. MARCUS NIEBUHR, BY DR. LEONHARD SCHMITZ, F. R S. E.,

With Additions and Corrections from his own MSS. notes.

In three very handsome volumes, crown octavo, extra cloth, containing about fifteen hundred pages.

From the Translator's Preface.

"The Lectures on Ancient History here presented to the English public, embrace the history of the ancient world, with the exception of that of Rome, down to the time when all the other nations and states of classical antiquity were absorbed by the empire of Rome, and when its history became, in point of fact, the history of the world. Hence the present course of Lectures, together with that on the History of Rome, form a complete course, embracing the whole of ancient history. * * * * We here catch a glimpse, as it were, of the working of the great mind of the Historian, which imparts to his narrative a degree of freshness and suggestiveness that richly compensate for a more calm and sober exposition. The extraordinary familiarity of Niebuhr with the literatures of all nations, his profound knowledge of all political and human affairs, derived not only from books, but from practical life, and his brilliant powers of combination, present to us in these Lectures, as in those on Roman history, such an abundance of new ideas, startling conceptions and opinions, as are rarely to be met with in any other work. They are of the highest importance and interest to all who are engaged in the study, not only of antiquity, but of any period in the history of man."

The value of this work as a book of reference is greatly increased by a very extensive Index of about fifty closely printed pages, prepared by John Robson, B. A., and containing nearly ten thousand references; in addition to which each volume has a very complete Table of Contents.

MEMOIRS OF THE LIFE OF WILLIAM WIRT.

BY JOHN P. KENNEDY.

SECOND EDITION, REVISED.

In two handsome 12mo. volumes, with a Portrait and fac-simile of a letter from John Adams. Also,

A HANDSOME LIBRARY EDITION, IN TWO BEAUTIFULLY PRINTED OCTAVO VOLUMES.

In its present neat and convenient form, the work is eminently fitted to assume the position which it merits as a book for every parlor-table and for every fireside where there is an appreciation of the kindliness and manliness, the intellect and the affection, the wit and liveliness which rendered William Wirt at once so eminent in the world, so brilliant in society, and so loving and loved in the retirement of his domestic circle. Uniting all these attractions, it cannot fail to find a place in every private and public library, and in all collections of books for the use of schools and colleges; for the young can have before them no brighter example of what can be accomplished by industry and resolution, than the life of William Wirt, as unconsciously related by himself in these volumes.

HISTORY OF THE PROTESTANT REFORMATION IN FRANCE.

BY MRS. MARSH,

Author of "Two Old Men's Tales," "Emilia Wyndham," &c.

In two handsome volumes, royal 12mo., extra cloth.

NEW AND IMPROVED EDITION.

LIVES OF THE QUEENS OF ENGLAND,

FROM THE NORMAN CONQUEST.

WITH ANECDOTES OF THEIR COURTS.

Now first published from Official Records, and other Authentic Documents, Private as well as Public.

NEW EDITION, WITH ADDITIONS AND CORRECTIONS.

BY AGNES STRICKLAND.

In six volumes, crown octavo, extra crimson cloth, or half morocco, printed on fine paper and large type.

Copies of the Duodecimo Edition, in twelve volumes, may still be had.

A valuable contribution to historical knowledge, to young persons especially. It contains a mass of every kind of historical matter of interest, which industry and resource could collect. We have derived much entertainment and instruction from the work.—*Athenæum.*

The execution of this work is equal to the conception. Great pains have been taken to make it both interesting and valuable.—*Literary Gazette.*

A charming work—full of interest, at once serious and pleasing.—*Monsieur Guizot.*

LIVES OF THE QUEENS OF HENRY VIII.

AND OF HIS MOTHER, ELIZABETH OF YORK.

BY MISS STRICKLAND.

Complete in one handsome crown octavo volume, extra cloth. (*Just Issued.*)

MEMOIRS OF ELIZABETH,

SECOND QUEEN REGNANT OF ENGLAND AND IRELAND.

BY MISS STRICKLAND.

Complete in one handsome crown octavo volume, extra cloth. (*Just Issued.*)

(NOW READY.)

MEMORIALS AND CORRESPONDENCE OF CHARLES JAMES FOX.

EDITED BY LORD JOHN RUSSELL.

In two very handsome volumes, royal 12mo., extra cloth.

THE GARDENER'S DICTIONARY.

A DICTIONARY OF MODERN GARDENING. By G. W. Johnson, Esq. With numerous additions, by David Landreth. With one hundred and eighty wood-cuts. In one very large royal 12mo. volume, of about 650 double-columned pages.

This work is now offered at a very low price.

(NOW READY.)

WISE SAWS AND MODERN INSTANCES.

BY THE AUTHOR OF SAM SLICK.

In one royal 12mo. volume.

THE ENCYCLOPÆDIA AMERICANA;

A POPULAR DICTIONARY OF ARTS, SCIENCES, LITERATURE, HISTORY, POLITICS, AND BIOGRAPHY.

In fourteen large octavo volumes of over 600 double-columned pages each.

For sale very low, in various styles of binding.

Some years having elapsed since the original thirteen volumes of the ENCYCLOPÆDIA AMERICANA were published, to bring it up to the present day, with the history of that period, at the request of numerous subscribers, the publishers have issued a

SUPPLEMENTARY VOLUME (THE FOURTEENTH),

BRINGING THE WORK THOROUGHLY UP.

Edited by HENRY VETHAKE, LL. D.

In one large octavo volume, of over 650 double-columned pages, which may be had separately, to complete sets.

MURRAY'S ENCYCLOPÆDIA OF GEOGRAPHY.

THE ENCYCLOPÆDIA OF GEOGRAPHY, comprising a Complete Description of the Earth, Physical, Statistical, Civil, and Political; exhibiting its Relation to the Heavenly Bodies, its Physical Structure, The Natural History of each Country, and the Industry, Commerce, Political Institutions, and Civil and Social State of all Nations. By HUGH MURRAY, F. R. S. E., &c. Assisted in Botany, by Professor Hooker—Zoology, &c., by W. W. Swainson—Astronomy, &c., by Professor Wallace—Geology, &c., by Professor Jameson. Revised, with Additions, by THOMAS G. BRADFORD. The whole brought up, by a Supplement, to 1843. In three large octavo volumes various styles of binding.

This great work, furnished at a remarkably cheap rate, contains about NINETEEN HUNDRED LARGE IMPERIAL PAGES, and is illustrated by EIGHTY-TWO SMALL MAPS, and a colored MAP OF THE UNITED STATES, after Tanner's, together with about ELEVEN HUNDRED WOOD-CUTS executed in the best style.

YOUATT AND SKINNER ON THE HORSE.

THE HORSE.

BY WILLIAM YOUATT.

A new edition, with numerous Illustrations.

TOGETHER WITH A GENERAL HISTORY OF THE HORSE; A DISSERTATION ON THE AMERICAN TROTTING HORSE; HOW TRAINED AND JOCKEYED; AN ACCOUNT OF HIS REMARKABLE PERFORMANCES; AND AN ESSAY ON THE ASS AND THE MULE.

BY J. S. SKINNER,

Assistant Postmaster-General, and Editor of the Turf Register.

This edition of Youatt's well-known and standard work on the Management, Diseases, and Treatment of the Horse, embodying the valuable additions of Mr. Skinner, has already obtained such a wide circulation throughout the country, that the Publishers need say nothing to attract to it the attention and confidence of all who keep Horses or are interested in their improvement.

YOUATT AND LEWIS ON THE DOG.

THE DOG. By William Youatt. Edited by E. J. Lewis, M. D. With numerous and beautiful illustrations. In one very handsome volume, crown 8vo., crimson cloth, gilt.

LIBRARY OF ILLUSTRATED SCIENTIFIC WORKS.

A series of beautifully printed volumes on various branches of science, by the most eminent men in their respective departments. The whole printed in the handsomest style, and profusely embellished in the most efficient manner.

☞ No expense has been or will be spared to render this series worthy of the support of the scientific public, while at the same time it is one of the handsomest specimens of typographical and artistic execution which have appeared in this country.

DE LA BECHE'S GEOLOGY—(Just Issued.)

THE GEOLOGICAL OBSERVER.

BY SIR HENRY T. DE LA BECHE, C. B., F. R. S.,

Director-General of the Geological Survey of Great Britain, &c.

In one very large and handsome octavo volume.

WITH OVER THREE HUNDRED WOOD-CUTS.

We have here presented to us, by one admirably qualified for the task, the most complete compendium of the science of geology ever produced, in which the different facts which fall under the cognizance of this branch of natural science are arranged under the different causes by which they are produced. From the style in which the subject is treated, the work is calculated not only for the use of the professional geologist but for that of the uninitiated reader, who will find in it much curious and interesting information on the changes which the surface of our globe has undergone, and the history of the various striking appearances which it presents Voluminous as the work is, it is not rendered unreadable from its bulk, owing to the judicious subdivision of its contents, and the copious index which is appended.—*John Bull.*

Having had such abundant opportunities, no one could be found so capable of directing the labors of the young geologist, or to aid by his own experience the studies of those who may not have been able to range so extensively over the earth's surface. We strongly recommend Sir Henry De la Beche's book to those who desire to know what has been done, and to learn something of the wide examination which yet lies waiting for the industrious observer.—*The Athenæum.*

KNAPP'S CHEMICAL TECHNOLOGY.

TECHNOLOGY; or, CHEMISTRY APPLIED TO THE ARTS AND TO MANUFACTURES. By DR. F. KNAPP, Professor at the University of Giessen. Edited, with numerous Notes and Additions, by DR. EDMUND RONALDS, and DR. THOMAS RICHARDSON. First American Edition, with Notes and Additions by Prof. WALTER R. JOHNSON. In two handsome octavo volumes, printed and illustrated in the highest style of art, with about 500 wood-engravings.

The style of excellence in which the first volume was got up is fully preserved in this. The treatises themselves are admirable, and the editing, both by the English and American editors, judicious; so that the work maintains itself as the best of the series to which it belongs, and worthy the attention of all interested in the arts of which it treats.—*Franklin Institute Journal.*

WEISBACH'S MECHANICS.

PRINCIPLES OF THE MECHANICS OF MACHINERY AND ENGINEERING. By PROFESSOR JULIUS WEISBACH. Translated and Edited by PROF. GORDON, of Glasgow. First American Edition, with Additions by PROF. WALTER R. JOHNSON. In two octavo volumes, beautifully printed, with 900 illustrations on wood.

The most valuable contribution to practical science that has yet appeared in this country.—*Athenæum.*

Unequalled by anything of the kind yet produced in this country—the most standard book on mechanics, machinery, and engineering now extant.—*N. Y. Commercial.*

In every way worthy of being recommended to our readers.—*Franklin Institute Journal.*

ILLUSTRATED SCIENTIFIC LIBRARY—(***Continued.***)

CARPENTER'S COMPARATIVE PHYSIOLOGY—(**Just Issued.**)

PRINCIPLES OF GENERAL AND COMPARATIVE PHYSIOLOGY; intended as an Introduction to the Study of Human Physiology, and as a Guide to the Philosophical Pursuit of Natural History. By WILLIAM B. CARPENTER, M. D., F. R. S., author of "Human Physiology," "Vegetable Physiology," &c. &c. Third improved and enlarged edition. In one very large and handsome octavo volume, with several hundred beautiful illustrations.

MULLER'S PHYSICS.

PRINCIPLES OF PHYSICS AND METEOROLOGY. By PROFESSOR J. MULLER, M. D. Edited, with Additions, by R. EGLESFELD GRIFFITH, M. D. In one large and handsome octavo volume, with 550 wood-cuts and two colored plates.

The style in which the volume is published is in the highest degree creditable to the enterprise of the publishers. It contains nearly four hundred engravings executed in a style of extraordinary elegance. We commend the book to general favor. It is the best of its kind we have ever seen.—*N. Y. Courier and Enquirer.*

MOHR, REDWOOD, AND PROCTER'S PHARMACY.

PRACTICAL PHARMACY: Comprising the Arrangements, Apparatus, and Manipulations of the Pharmaceutical Shop and Laboratory. By FRANCIS MOHR, Ph. D., Assessor Pharmaciæ of the Royal Prussian College of Medicine, Coblentz; and THEOPHILUS REDWOOD, Professor of Pharmacy in the Pharmaceutical Society of Great Britain. Edited, with extensive Additions, by PROF. WILLIAM PROCTER, of the Philadelphia College of Pharmacy. In one handsomely printed octavo volume, of 570 pages, with over 500 engravings on wood.

THE MILLWRIGHT'S GUIDE.

THE MILLWRIGHT'S AND MILLER'S GUIDE. By OLIVER EVANS. Eleventh Edition. With Additions and Corrections by the Professor of Mechanics in the Franklin Institute, and a description of an improved Merchant Flour Mill. By C. and O. Evans. In one octavo volume, with numerous engravings.

HUMAN HEALTH; or, the Influence of Atmosphere and Locality, Change of Air and Climate, Seasons, Food, Clothing, Bathing, Mineral Springs, Exercise, Sleep, Corporeal and Mental Pursuits, &c. &c., on Healthy Man, constituting Elements of Hygiene. By Robley Dunglison, M. D. In one octavo volume.

ACTON'S COOKERY.

MODERN COOKERY IN ALL ITS BRANCHES, reduced to a System of Easy Practice, for the Use of Private Families; in a Series of Practical Receipts, all of which are given with the most minute exactness. By Eliza Acton. With numerous woodcut illustrations; to which is added a Table of Weights and Measures. The whole revised, and prepared for American housekeepers, by Mrs. Sarah J. Hale. From the Second London Edition. In one large 12mo. volume.

THE DOMESTIC MANAGEMENT OF THE SICK-ROOM, necessary, in aid of medical treatment for the cure of diseases. By A. T. Thomson, M. D. Edited by R. E. Griffith, M. D. In one volume royal 12mo., extra cloth.

LANGUAGE OF FLOWERS, with illustrative poetry. Eighth edition. In one beautiful volume, royal 18mo., crimson cloth, gilt, with colored plates.

AMERICAN ORNITHOLOGY. By Charles Bonaparte, Prince of Canino. In four folio volumes, half bound, with numerous magnificent colored plates.

LECTURES ON THE PHYSICAL PHENOMENA OF LIVING BEINGS. By Carlo Matteucci. Edited by Jonathan Pereira, M. D. In one royal 12mo. volume, extra cloth, with illustrations.

GRAHAM'S CHEMISTRY, NEW EDITION. Part I.—(Now Ready.)

ELEMENTS OF CHEMISTRY;

INCLUDING THE APPLICATIONS OF THE SCIENCE IN THE ARTS.

BY THOMAS GRAHAM, F. R. S., &c.,

Professor of Chemistry in University College, London, &c.

Second American, from an entirely Revised and greatly Enlarged English Edition.

WITH NUMEROUS WOOD-ENGRAVINGS.

EDITED, WITH NOTES, BY ROBERT BRIDGES, M. D.,
Professor of Chemistry in the Philadelphia College of Pharmacy, &c.

To be completed in Two Parts, forming one very large octavo volume.

PART I, now ready, of 430 large pages, with 185 engravings.
PART II, preparing for early publication.

From the Editor's Preface.

The "Elements of Chemistry," of which a second edition is now presented, attained, on its first appearance, an immediate and deserved reputation. The copious selection of facts from all reliable sources, and their judicious arrangement, render it a safe guide for the beginner, while the clear exposition of theoretical points, and frequent references to special treatises, make it a valuable assistant for the more advanced student.

From this high character the present edition will in no way detract. The great changes which the science of Chemistry has undergone during the interval have rendered necessary a complete revision of the work, and this has been most thoroughly accomplished by the author. Many portions will therefore be found essentially altered, thereby increasing greatly the size of the work, while the series of illustrations has been entirely changed in style, and nearly doubled in number.

Under these circumstances but little has been left for the editor. Owing, however, to the appearance of the London edition in parts, some years have elapsed since the first portions were published, and he has therefore found occasion to introduce the more recent investigations and discoveries in some subjects, as well as to correct such inaccuracies or misprints as had escaped the author's attention, and to make a few additional references.

INTRODUCTION TO PRACTICAL CHEMISTRY, including Analysis. By John E. Bowman, M. D. In one neat royal 12mo. volume, extra cloth, with numerous illustrations.

DANA ON CORALS.

ZOOPHYTES AND CORALS. By James D. Dana. In one volume imperial quarto, extra cloth, with wood-cuts.

Also, an Atlas to the above, one volume imperial folio, with sixty-one magnificent plates, colored after nature. Bound in half morocco.

These splendid volumes form a portion of the publications of the United States Exploring Expedition. As but very few copies have been prepared for sale, and as these are nearly exhausted, all who are desirous of enriching their libraries with this, the most creditable specimen of American Art and Science as yet issued, will do well to procure copies at once.

THE ETHNOGRAPHY AND PHILOLOGY OF THE UNITED STATES EXPLORING EXPEDITION. By Horatio Hale. In one large imperial quarto volume, beautifully printed, and strongly bound in extra cloth.

BARON HUMBOLDT'S LAST WORK.

ASPECTS OF NATURE IN DIFFERENT LANDS AND DIFFERENT CLIMATES. With Scientific Elucidations. By Alexander Von Humboldt. Translated by Mrs. Sabine. Second American edition. In one handsome volume, large royal 12mo., extra cloth.

CHEMISTRY OF THE FOUR SEASONS, SPRING, SUMMER, AUTUMN, AND WINTER. By Thomas Griffith. In one handsome volume, royal 12mo., extra cloth, with numerous illustrations.

NEW AND IMPROVED EDITION.—(Now Ready.)

OUTLINES OF ASTRONOMY.

BY SIR JOHN F. W. HERSCHEL, F. R. S., &c.

A NEW AMERICAN FROM THE FOURTH LONDON EDITION.

In one very neat crown octavo volume, extra cloth, with six plates and numerous wood-cuts.

This edition will be found thoroughly brought up to the present state of astronomical science, with the most recent investigations and discoveries fully discussed and explained.

We now take leave of this remarkable work, which we hold to be, beyond a doubt, the greatest and most remarkable of the works in which the laws of astronomy and the appearance of the heavens are described to those who are not mathematicians nor observers, and recalled to those who are. It is the reward of men who can descend from the advancement of knowledge to care for its diffusion, that their works are essential to all, that they become the manuals of the proficient as well as the text-books of the learner.—*Athenæum.*

There is perhaps no book in the English language on the subject, which, whilst it contains so many of the facts of Astronomy (which it attempts to explain with as little technical language as possible), is so attractive in its style, and so clear and forcible in its illustrations.—*Evangelical Review.*

Probably no book ever written upon any science, embraces within so small a compass an entire epitome of everything known within all its various departments, practical, theoretical, and physical.—*Examiner.*

A TREATISE ON ASTRONOMY.

BY SIR JOHN F. W. HERSCHEL. Edited by S. C. Walker. In one 12mo. volume, half bound, with plates and wood-cuts.

A TREATISE ON OPTICS.

BY SIR DAVID BREWSTER, LL. D., F. R. S., &c.

A NEW EDITION.

WITH AN APPENDIX, CONTAINING AN ELEMENTARY VIEW OF THE APPLICATION OF ANALYSIS TO REFLECTION AND REFRACTION.

BY A. D. BACHE, Superintendent U. S. Coast Survey, &c.

In one neat duodecimo volume, half bound, with about 200 illustrations.

BOLMAR'S FRENCH SERIES.

New editions of the following works, by A. Bolmar, forming, in connection with "Bolmar's Levizac," a complete series for the acquisition of the French language:—

A SELECTION OF ONE HUNDRED PERRIN'S FABLES, accompanied by a Key, containing the text, a literal and free translation, arranged in such a manner as to point out the difference between the French and English idiom, &c. In one vol. 12mo.

A COLLECTION OF COLLOQUIAL PHRASES, on every topic necessary to maintain conversation. Arranged under different heads, with numerous remarks on the peculiar pronunciation and uses of various words; the whole so disposed as considerably to facilitate the acquisition of a correct pronunciation of the French. In one vol. 18mo.

LES AVENTURES DE TELEMAQUE, PAR FENELON, in one vol. 12mo., accompanied by a Key to the first eight books. In one vol. 12mo., containing, like the Fables, the Text, a literal and free translation, intended as a sequel to the Fables. Either volume sold separately.

ALL THE FRENCH VERBS, both regular and irregular, in a small volume.

ELEMENTS OF NATURAL PHILOSOPHY;

BEING

AN EXPERIMENTAL INTRODUCTION TO THE PHYSICAL SCIENCES.

Illustrated with over Three Hundred Wood-cuts.

BY GOLDING BIRD, M.D.,
Assistant Physician to Guy's Hospital.

From the Third London edition. In one neat volume, royal 12mo.

We are astonished to find that there is room in so small a book for even the bare recital of so many subjects. Where everything is treated succinctly, great judgment and much time are needed in making a selection and winnowing the wheat from the chaff. Dr. Bird has no need to plead the peculiarity of his position as a shield against criticism, so long as his book continues to be the best epitome in the English language of this wide range of physical subjects.—*North American Review*, April 1, 1851.

From Prof. John Johnston, Wesleyan Univ., Middletown, Ct.

For those desiring as extensive a work, I think it decidedly superior to anything of the kind with which I am acquainted.

From Prof. R. O. Currey, East Tennessee University.

I am much gratified in perusing a work which so well, so fully, and so clearly sets forth this branch of the Natural Sciences. For some time I have been desirous of obtaining a substitute for the one now used—one which should embrace the recent discoveries in the sciences, and I can truly say that such a one is afforded in this work of Dr. Bird's.

From Prof. W. F. Hopkins, Masonic University, Tenn.

It is just the sort of book I think needed in most colleges, being far above the rank of a mere popular work, and yet not beyond the comprehension of all but the most accomplished mathematicians.

ELEMENTARY CHEMISTRY;

THEORETICAL AND PRACTICAL.

BY GEORGE FOWNES, PH. D.,
Chemical Lecturer in the Middlesex Hospital Medical School, &c. &c.
WITH NUMEROUS ILLUSTRATIONS.
Third American, from a late London edition. Edited, with Additions,

BY ROBERT BRIDGES, M. D.,
Professor of General and Pharmaceutical Chemistry in the Philadelphia College of Pharmacy, &c. &c.

In one large royal 12mo. volume, of over five hundred pages, with about 180 wood-cuts, sheep or extra cloth.

The work of Dr. Fownes has long been before the public, and its merits have been fully appreciated as the best text-book on Chemistry now in existence. We do not, of course, place it in a rank superior to the works of Brande, Graham, Turner, Gregory, or Gmelin, but we say that, as a work for students, it is preferable to any of them.—*London Journal of Medicine.*

We know of no treatise so well calculated to aid the student in becoming familiar with the numerous facts in the science on which it treats, or one better calculated as a text-book for those attending Chemical Lectures. * * * * The best text-book on Chemistry that has issued from our press.—*American Med. Journal.*

We know of none within the same limits, which has higher claims to our confidence as a college class-book, both for accuracy of detail and scientific arrangement.—*Augusta Med. Journal.*

ELEMENTS OF PHYSICS.

OR, NATURAL PHILOSOPHY, GENERAL AND MEDICAL. Written for universal use, in plain, or non-technical language. By NEILL ARNOTT, M. D. In one octavo volume, with about two hundred illustrations.

NEW AND IMPROVED EDITION.—(Now Ready.)

PHYSICAL GEOGRAPHY.

BY MARY SOMERVILLE.

A NEW AMERICAN FROM THE LAST AND REVISED LONDON EDITION.
WITH AMERICAN NOTES, GLOSSARY, ETC.

BY W. S. W. RUSCHENBERGER, M.D., U.S.N.

In one neat royal 12mo. volume, extra cloth, of over five hundred and fifty pages.

The great success of this work, and its introduction into many of our higher schools and academies, have induced the publishers to prepare a new and much improved edition. In addition to the corrections and improvements of the author bestowed on the work in its passage through the press a second time in London, notes have been introduced to adapt it more fully to the physical geography of this country; and a comprehensive glossary has been added, rendering the volume more particularly suited to educational purposes.

Our praise comes lagging in the rear, and is wellnigh superfluous. But we are anxious to recommend to our youth the enlarged method of studying geography which her present work demonstrates to be as captivating as it is instructive. We hold such presents as Mrs. Somerville has bestowed upon the public, to be of incalculable value, disseminating more sound information than all the literary and scientific institutions will accomplish in a whole cycle of their existence.—*Blackwood's Magazine.*

From Lieutenant Maury, U. S. N.

National Observatory, Washington, *June* 26, 1853.

I thank you for the "Physical Geography;" it is capital. I have been reading it, and like it so much that I have made it a school-book for my children, whom I am teaching. There is, in my opinion, no work upon that interesting subject on which it treats—Physical Geography—that would make a better text-book in our schools and colleges. I hope it will be adopted as such generally, for you have Americanized it and improved it in other respects.

Yours, truly,
M. F. MAURY.

Dr. W. S. W. Ruschenberger, U. S. N.,
Philadelphia.

From Thomas Sherwin, High School, Boston.

I hold it in the highest estimation, and am confident that it will prove a very efficient aid in the education of the young, and a source of much interest and instruction to the adult reader.

From Erastus Everett, High School, New Orleans.

I have examined it with a good deal of care, and am glad to find that it supplies an important desideratum. The whole work is a masterpiece. Whether we examine the importance of the subjects treated, or the elegant and attractive style in which they are presented, this work leaves nothing to desire. I have introduced it into my school for the use of an advanced class in geography, and they are greatly interested in it. I have no doubt that it will be used in most of our higher seminaries.

JOHNSTON'S PHYSICAL ATLAS.

THE PHYSICAL ATLAS

OF NATURAL PHENOMENA.

FOR THE USE OF COLLEGES, ACADEMIES, AND FAMILIES.

BY ALEXANDER KEITH JOHNSTON, F. R. G. S., F. G. S.

In one large volume, imperial quarto, handsomely and strongly bound. With twenty-six plates, engraved and colored in the best style. Together with one hundred and twelve pages of Descriptive Letter-press, and a very copious Index.

A work which should be in every family and every school-room, for consultation and reference. By the ingenious arrangement adopted by the author, it makes clear to the eye every fact and observation relative to the present condition of the earth, arranged under the departments of Geology, Hydrography, Meteorology, and Natural History. The letter-press illustrates this with a body of important information, nowhere else to be found condensed into the same space, while a very full Index renders the whole easy of reference.

SCHMITZ AND ZUMPT'S CLASSICAL SERIES.

Under this title BLANCHARD & LEA are publishing a series of Latin School-Books, edited by those distinguished scholars and critics, Leonhard Schmitz and C. G. Zumpt. The object of the series is to present a course of accurate texts, revised in accordance with the latest investigations and MSS., and the most approved principles of modern criticism, as well as the necessary elementary books, arranged on the best system of modern instruction. The former are accompanied with notes and illustrations introduced sparingly, avoiding on the one hand the error of overburdening the work with commentary, and on the other that of leaving the student entirely to his own resources. The main object has been to awaken the scholar's mind to a sense of the beauties and peculiarities of his author, to assist him where assistance is necessary, and to lead him to think and to investigate for himself. For this purpose maps and other engravings are given wherever useful, and each author is accompanied with a biographical and critical sketch. The form in which the volumes are printed is neat and convenient, while it admits of their being sold at prices unprecedentedly low, thus placing them within the reach of many to whom the cost of classical works has hitherto proved a bar to this department of education; while the whole series being arranged on one definite and uniform plan, enables the teacher to carry forward his student from the rudiments of the language without the annoyance and interruption caused by the necessity of using text-books founded on varying and conflicting systems of study.

CLASSICAL TEXTS PUBLISHED IN THIS SERIES.

I. CÆSARIS DE BELLO GALLICO LIBRI IV., 1 vol. royal 18mo., extra cloth, 232 pages, with a Map, price 50 cents.

II. C. C. SALLUSTII CATILINA ET JUGURTHA, 1 vol. royal 18mo., extra cloth, 168 pages, with a Map, price 50 cents.

III. P. OVIDII NASONIS CARMINA SELECTA, 1 vol. royal 18mo., extra cloth, 246 pages, price 60 cents.

IV. P. VIRGILII MARONIS CARMINA, 1 vol. royal 18mo., extra cloth, 438 pages, price 75 cents.

V. Q. HORATII FLACCI CARMINA EXCERPTA, 1 vol. royal 18mo., extra cloth, 312 pages, price 60 cents.

VI. Q. CURTII RUFI DE ALEXANDRI MAGNI QUÆ SUPERSUNT, 1 vol. royal 18mo., extra cloth, 326 pages, with a Map, price 70 cents.

VII. T. LIVII PATAVINI HISTORIARUM LIBRI I., II., XXI., XXII., 1 vol. royal 18mo., ex. cloth, 350 pages, with two colored Maps, price 70 cents.

VIII. M. T. CICERONIS ORATIONES SELECTÆ XII., 1 vol. royal 18mo., extra cloth, 300 pages, price 60 cents.

IX. CORNELIUS NEPOS, 1 vol. royal 18mo., price 50 cents.

ELEMENTARY WORKS PUBLISHED IN THIS SERIES.

I.

A SCHOOL DICTIONARY OF THE LATIN LANGUAGE. By DR. J. H. KALTSCHMIDT. In two parts, Latin-English and English-Latin.

Part I., Latin-English, of nearly 500 pages, strongly bound, price 90 cents.
Part II., English-Latin, of about 400 pages, price 75 cents.
Or the whole complete in one very thick royal 18mo. volume, of nearly 900 closely printed double-columned pages, strongly bound in leather, price only $1 25.

II.

GRAMMAR OF THE LATIN LANGUAGE. BY LEONHARD SCHMITZ, Ph. D., F. R. S. E., Rector of the High School, Edinburgh, &c. In one handsome volume, royal 18mo., of 318 pages, neatly half bound, price 60 cents.

SCHMITZ AND ZUMPT'S CLASSICAL SERIES—Continued.

III.

ELEMENTARY GRAMMAR AND EXERCISES. BY DR. LEONHARD SCHMITZ, F. R. S. E., Rector of the High School, Edinburgh, &c. In one handsome royal 18mo. volume of 246 pages, extra cloth, price 50 cents. (Just Issued.)

PREPARING FOR SPEEDY PUBLICATION.

LATIN READING AND EXERCISE BOOK, 1 vol., royal 18mo.

A SCHOOL CLASSICAL DICTIONARY, 1 vol., royal 18mo.

It will thus be seen that this series is now very nearly complete, embracing eight prominent Latin authors, and requiring but two more elementary works to render it sufficient in itself for a thorough course of study, and these latter are now preparing for early publication. During the successive appearance of the volumes, the plan and execution of the whole have been received with marked approbation, and the fact that it supplies a want not hitherto provided for, is evinced by the adoption of these works in a very large number of the best academies and seminaries throughout the country.

But we cannot forbear commending especially both to instructors and pupils the whole of the series, edited by those accomplished scholars, Drs. Schmitz and Zumpt. Here will be found a set of text-books that combine the excellencies so long desired in this class of works. They will not cost the student, by one half at least, that which he must expend for some other editions. And who will not say that this is a consideration worthy of attention? For the cheaper our school-books can be made, the more widely will they be circulated and used. Here you will find, too, no useless display of notes and of learning, but in foot-notes on each page you have everything necessary to the understanding of the text. The difficult points are sometimes elucidated, and often is the student referred to the places where he can find light, but not without some effort of his own. We think that the punctuation in these books might be improved; but taken as a whole, they come nearer to the wants of the times than any within our knowledge.—*Southern College Review.*

Uniform with SCHMITZ AND ZUMPT'S CLASSICAL SERIES—(Now Ready.)

THE CLASSICAL MANUAL;

AN EPITOME OF ANCIENT GEOGRAPHY, GREEK AND ROMAN MYTHOLOGY, ANTIQUITIES, AND CHRONOLOGY.

CHIEFLY INTENDED FOR THE USE OF SCHOOLS.

BY JAMES S. S. BAIRD, T. C. D.,

Assistant Classical Master, King's School, Gloucester.

In one neat volume, royal 18mo., extra cloth, price Fifty cents.

This little volume has been prepared to meet the recognized want of an Epitome which, within the compass of a single small volume, should contain the information requisite to elucidate the Greek and Roman authors most commonly read in our schools. The aim of the author has been to embody in it such details as are important or necessary for the junior student, in a form and space capable of rendering them easily mastered and retained, and he has consequently not incumbered it with a mass of learning which, though highly valuable to the advanced student, is merely perplexing to the beginner. In the amount of information presented, and the manner in which it is conveyed, as well as its convenient size and exceedingly low price, it is therefore admirably adapted for the younger classes of our numerous classical schools.

SCRIPTURE GEOGRAPHY AND HISTORY.—(Just Ready.)

OUTLINES OF

SCRIPTURE GEOGRAPHY AND HISTORY.

Illustrating the Historical Portions of the Old and New Testaments.

DESIGNED FOR THE

USE OF SCHOOLS AND PRIVATE READING.

BY EDWARD HUGHES, F. R. A. S., F. G. S., &c. &c.

In one neat volume, royal 12mo., extra cloth, of about four hundred pages, with twelve colored Maps.

The intimate connection of Sacred History with the geography and physical features of the various lands occupied by the Israelites renders a work like the present an almost necessary companion to all who desire to read the Scriptures understandingly. To the young especially, a clear and connected narrative of the events recorded in the Bible, is exceedingly desirable, particularly when illustrated, as in the present volume, with succinct but copious accounts of the neighboring nations and of the topography and political divisions of the countries mentioned, coupled with the results of the latest investigations, by which Messrs. Layard, Lynch, Olin, Durbin, Wilson, Stephens, and others have succeeded in throwing light on so many obscure portions of the Scriptures, verifying their accuracy in minute particulars. Few more interesting class-books could therefore be found for schools where the Bible forms a part of education, and none, perhaps, more likely to prove of permanent benefit to the scholar. The influence which the physical geography, climate, and productions of Palestine had upon the Jewish people will be found fully set forth, while the numerous maps present the various regions connected with the subject at their most prominent periods.

HISTORY OF CLASSICAL LITERATURE.—(Now Ready.)

HISTORY OF ROMAN CLASSICAL LITERATURE.

BY R. W. BROWNE, M. A.,

Professor of Classical Literature in King's College, London.

In one handsome crown octavo volume, extra cloth.

ALSO,

Lately Issued, by the same author, to match.

A HISTORY OF GREEK CLASSICAL LITERATURE.

In one very neat volume, crown 8vo., extra cloth.

From Prof. J. A. Spencer, New York, March 19, 1852.

It is an admirable volume, sufficiently full and copious in detail, clear and precise in style, very scholar-like in its execution, genial in its criticism, and altogether displaying a mind well stored with the learning, genius, wisdom, and exquisite taste of the ancient Greeks. It is in advance of everything we have, and it may be considered indispensable to the classical scholar and student.

From Prof. N. H. Griffin, Williams College, Mass., March 22, 1852.

A valuable compend, embracing in a small compass matter which the student would have to go over much ground to gather for himself.

GEOGRAPHIA CLASSICA:

OR, THE APPLICATION OF ANCIENT GEOGRAPHY TO THE CLASSICS. By SAMUEL BUTLER, D. D., late Lord Bishop of Litchfield. Revised by his Son. Sixth American, from the last London Edition, with Questions on the Maps, by JOHN FROST, LL. D. In one neat volume, royal 12mo., half bound.

AN ATLAS OF ANCIENT GEOGRAPHY.

By SAMUEL BUTLER, D. D., late Lord Bishop of Litchfield. In one octavo volume, half bound, containing twenty-one quarto colored Maps, and an accentuated Index.

www.ingramcontent.com/pod-product-compliance
Lightning Source LLC
LaVergne TN
LVHW011148110826
845150LV00006B/1188

* 9 7 8 1 4 2 5 5 4 6 6 5 6 *